# PRICE MANAGEMENT

# PRICE MANAGEMENT

*by*

## HERMANN SIMON

*Johannes Gutenberg-Universität, Mainz, West Germany*

1989

AMSTERDAM · NEW YORK · OXFORD · TOKYO

ISBN North-Holland 0 444 87327 9


*Publishers*
ELSEVIER SCIENCE PUBLISHERS B.V.
P.O. Box 1991
1000 BZ Amsterdam
The Netherlands

*Sole distributors for the U.S.A. and Canada*
ELSEVIER SCIENCE PUBLISHING COMPANY, INC.
655 Avenue of the Americas
New York, N.Y. 10010
U.S.A.

*HF*
*5416*
*.5*
*.S56*
*1989*

**Library of Congress Cataloging-in-Publication Data**

```
Simon, Hermann.
    Price management / by Hermann Simon.
      p.    cm.
    ISBN 0-444-87327-9
    1. Pricing.   I. Title.
  HF5416.5.S56  1989
  658.8'16--dc20
```

89-7830
CIP

PRINTED IN THE NETHERLANDS

# *Contents*

# *Foreword*

In many modern markets the importance of price is continuously increasing. Price is a mirror of the value which products and services offer. Price differentiation reflects differences in perceived qualities, positioning strategies, and service benefits.

With increasing market saturation, product standardization, and globalization, companies are forced to use price more actively as a competitive weapon. Recent surveys show that managers feel strong pressures with regard to pricing.

At the same time, there is a huge discrepancy between the theory and the practice of pricing. Price theory is one of the most highly developed fields in economics and marketing science. Practical price decisions, on the other hand, are largely made on the basis of very simple cost-plus methods or other rules of thumb. The gap between theory and practice is mainly due to the negligence of the information, measurement and implementation problems in theoretical pricing models.

The present book attempts to bridge this gap. We do not confine ourselves to theoretical structures but apply the tools and the methods which theory provides. We put particular emphasis on the application problems and give detailed recommendations about when and how certain techniques should - and should not - be used.

The book is targetted at both academics and practitioners. Managers in marketing and controlling who are in charge of pricing analysis and decisions will benefit most. Many of the hundreds of managers in the German language area who participated in our pricing seminars and worked with a German language version of the book were able to implement many of the procedures.

The book consists of 12 chapters. Chapter 1 structures the pricing problem and presents the elements of a price decision. The following three chapters look at pricing analysis and decisions under a short-term or static perspective. Pricing in oligopoly, under inflationary conditions, and the impact of taxes on prices are major issues being discussed. In chapters 5 and 6 we address strategic and long-term aspects of pricing such as diffusion, product life cycle and experience curve. Pricing of innovations, preemptive strategies, and international market entry pricing are some of the problems in these chapters.

The remaining chapters address problems like market segmentation, nonlinear pricing, the role of psychology and perception for price setting, the impact of the trade on prices, pricing for industrial products and price negotiations. There is a common thread running through all chapters: to provide the reader with insights and tools which allow him to exploit the profit potential of his products or services more fully.

Many friends and colleagues have been helpful in making this book possible. First and foremost I would like to thank Pil H. Yoo who is now a professor at Sung Kyun Kwan University in Seoul, South Korea. While he was a research fellow in Germany he made extremely valuable contributions to the book; the chapters on dynamic pricing and market segmentation have particularly profited from his thoughts. Professor Gert Assmus of the Amos Tuck School in Hanover, New Hampshire, helped to translate and to adopt substantial parts. The bulk of practical insights originated from the cooperation with Dr. Eckhard Kucher and Dr. Karl-Heinz Sebastian, both directors of UNIC, a consulting institute in Bonn, West Germany. Together with them I worked on more than fifty pricing projects in various countries comprising an annual sales value of many billion US-Dollars. To Professor Robert J. Dolan of the Harvard Business School I am grateful for critical and helpful comments. Dr. Klaus Hilleke-Daniel, Dr. Georg Tacke, Artus Hanslik, Martin Möhrle, Carsten Wiese, and Michelle Lafond assisted in the technical work. Gabriele Kauffmann typed numerous drafts. I would like to thank them all for their contributions.

Last, but not least my thanks go to Cecilia, Jeannine, and Patrick who paid their share of the book in time - the most precious of all currencies and one which I can never repay.

Boston, January 1989                                              Hermann Simon

Chapter 1

# *Elements of Price Management*

## 1.1 The Strategic Role of Price

The price of a product or service is the number of monetary units a customer has to pay to receive one unit of that product or service. In order to understand the strategic role of price we should consider price in a broader price-value-context as illustrated in Fig. 1.1.

A customer will buy a product or service if its perceived value (measured in monetary units) is greater than the price. If the customer can select between several competitive products, he will most likely prefer the one which offers the highest net value, i.e., the greatest differential between perceived value and price.

Therefore, price is an extremely important competitive weapon. This is illustrated in terms of the "strategic triangle" (Ohmae 1982) in Fig. 1.2.

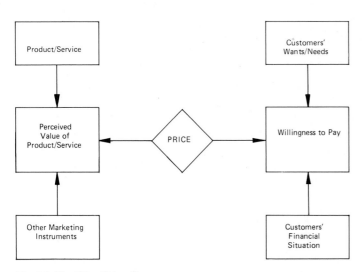

Fig. 1.1. The Price-Value-Context

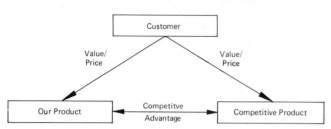

Fig. 1.2. The Role of Price in the Strategic Triangle

Despite its increasingly crucial role in competitive strategy price should never be viewed and judged in isolation. Frequently managers complain about "price problems" and "price pressures". Managers should be aware that those problems are never mere "price problems" but have their real causes in weaknesses related to the product, image, communication, etc. In the same vein it is self-deceiving to explain the successes of price-aggressive competitors, e.g., Japanese, Koreans, generic companies through low prices alone. Most of these new price-aggressive competitors have been consistently providing reasonable or even good product quality.

## 1.2 Price and the Marketing Mix

Price is one element of the marketing mix. Its relationship to other marketing mix variables concerns first the question of relative importance and second the interaction between different elements. The marketing literature agrees that the elements in the mix fulfill complementary tasks (Kotler 1984). Nevertheless the product (that is, its value, benefit, or utility) and the price play particularly significant roles. By that we do not mean to diminish the importance of other marketing variables. But often they constitute necessary (e.g., distribution: securing availability; advertising: providing information, awakening interest) rather than sufficient conditions for the success of a product. Price alone determines the amount the customer must sacrifice to acquire a product.

The following facts shed some light on the relative importance of price: An analysis in the UK identified product weaknesses and insufficient price-value relations as the main causes for failure (Kraushar 1970). Davidson (1976), in an analysis of fifty successes and fifty failures, concluded that only products that provide superior benefits at equal prices or equal benefits at lower prices have probabilities of success greater than 50 percent. High prices turned out to be the second most important factor of failure in a Canadian study (Cooper 1979).

Besides its fundamental role as determinant of the price-value relation, price is extremely important for the following reasons:

1. For a large number of products empirical research shows that price elasticity is about twenty times greater than advertising elasticity (Lambin 1976). That is, a

1%-price change has a sales effect twenty times as big as a 1%-change in the advertising budget.

2. The sales effect of a price change shows up relatively quickly (Ehrenberg and England 1987), while variations of other variables may take longer to affect sales, e.g., there are significant time lags of advertising effects, while this is rarely the case for price.

3. In contrast to almost all other marketing measures, pricing actions can be taken without much preparatory work. A price change can be implemented immediately. Changes in product and advertising strategy take much more time. This time aspect applies also to competitive price reactions.

4. Empirical reaction elasticities of competitors are almost twice as high for a price change as for an advertising change (Lambin et al. 1975, Lambin 1976). This result is consistent with the second and third point above. At the same time, it allows for the reverse conclusion that competitors expect especially strong effects from a price change.

5. Price is the only marketing instrument whose use does not require an initially negative cash flow. An optimal value usually can be realized even in a tight financial situation (e.g., start-up companies, new products). Often this is not possible in the case of advertising or sales force activities, which initially incur only expenses.

6. Price is the only marketing device – besides the product program – that plays a major role in strategic planning concepts, especially in connection with the experience curve (Abell and Hammond 1979; Henderson 1974, 1979).

A variety of developments suggest that the significance of price has increased in recent years:

– The inflation rates of the decade 1975–84 have led to a higher price consciousness, this level is likely to be retained over an extended period of time even with lower inflation.

– Stagnating real incomes in the late seventies and early eighties have induced consumers to switch to cheaper products.

– The increased competitive pressure has enhanced the role of price in industrial purchasing.

– Market saturation and overcapacities, i.e., a change from seller's market to buyer's market, are leading to shake-out processes which are fought out by aggressive pricing.

– New competitors (e.g., Japanese, Koreans, or generic companies) fight for market entry with aggressive pricing strategies. They have shaken up rigid market and price systems (e.g., automobiles, pharmaceuticals, consumer electronics, cigarettes), thereby forcing many traditional suppliers into price wars.

– Consumerism and the efforts of various consumer organizations as well as new information technologies are leading to increased market and price transparency. People compare quality and price more frequently and systematically. In a study

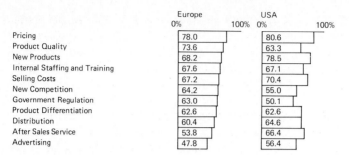

Fig. 1.3. "Pressure" in Various Marketing Areas as Perceived by Managers (Source: USA, Marketing News, June 11, 1986, p. 1; Europe, Author's study 1986)

we did in Germany only 5.7% of the respondents considered a price comparison for major household appliances as "too difficult and bothersome".
– Elimination of resale price maintenance (in many countries and for most product categories) produced more intensive price competition at the retail level.

Two recent studies confirm the increased significance of price. Managers in the United States and in Europe were asked to rate their perceived "pressure" with respect to various marketing areas. The results are reproduced in Fig. 1.3. In a similar study done about 20 years ago price was ranked in the sixth place (Udell 1964).

The increased importance of price will be retained in the future. Overcapacities, market saturation, homogenization of quality, emergence of new competitors, etc. will continue to create a competitive environment where price plays a crucial role. This pressure makes it indispensable to exploit profit potentials more systematically and professionally through better pricing.

Summary: The price-value relationship has a dominant influence on the buying decision. Price is distinguished from other marketing devices by the force and speed of the sales effect, the shortness of time it takes to change it, the elasticity of competitive reactions, and cash flow implications. A number of developments suggest that price has increased in marketing significance over recent years and will continue to increase in the future.

## 1.3 Variety and Complexity of Price Formation

We defined the price of a product or service as the number of monetary units a buyer has to pay for one unit of the product or service. This definition is simple and clear. The practical determination of price can be equally simple, as in the following cases:
– price of an item sold in a supermarket,
– price of a liter of gasoline at the gas station,
– price of a standard industrial product sold at list price.

However, these "standard" prices belie the variety and complexity of price situations which we encounter in the real world. The subsequent examples illustrate this variety and complexity:

– besides the basic unit price, discounts, rebates, and bonuses have to be determined,
– prices for different package sizes or forms of a product are required,
– the pricing for one product may require simultaneous price decisions for substitute or complementary products, e.g., for automobiles the base car price and prices for various options as well as spare parts are determined at the same time,
– if several products are sold together (e.g., hardware and software) management has to decide whether to set a single price for the whole system or prices for each component (so-called unbundling of prices),
– prices in different time periods/the temporal pricing pattern may have to be considered, e.g., an early subscription price and a "normal" price; a special introductory price; prices for different seasons, days of the week, or time of the day,
– some prices are fixed for a given period of time (e.g., prices in mail order catalogues, prices in contracts), whereas other prices can be changed any time (e.g., gasoline price),
– some prices are determined in advance of the sale (e.g., new automobile models), whereas other prices are determined on the spot (e.g., negotiated prices), or even after the sale (e.g., a doctor's fee),
– if prices can be differentiated, prices for individual customers, customer groups/market segments, or sales regions/countries have to be determined,
– frequently a price consists of several components, e.g., a fixed plus a usage-related charge as in the case of utilities, telephone services, etc.,
– some prices are negotiated, in these cases guidelines, delegation of pricing authority, etc. have to be determined,
– in some cases suppliers have to quote a specific and fixed price in advance (as in competitive bidding), whereas in other cases the prices quoted by suppliers serve only as a basis for negotiation.

### What is "Price"?

In view of this complexity determining actual prices can be extremely difficult both for the seller and the buyer due to the following reasons:

### Divergence of "Official" and Actual Prices

Official list prices are often pure "myths". Actual prices lie frequently far below list prices. It can be extremely difficult to obtain information on the actual competitive prices. In the European truck industry, discounts in the range of 25 to 60% from the list prices were not unusual in the mid 80's. Personal computers are often sold at 30–40% below the list price. In many regions of the world, hotel list prices have little to do with prices actually paid.

## Type of Price Formation

If price consists of a fixed and a usage component, the actual unit price varies with consumption. Frequently the usage and payment occur at different points in time, so individual unit prices are difficult to ascertain or to measure for the user.

## Non-linear Pricing

Quantity-dependent or so-called "non-linear" prices have become a popular pricing strategy. Non-linear pricing is frequently implemented as a "3 for the price of 2"-type or a loyalty bonus. An example of the latter are frequent flyer programs.

## Complexity of Terms of Payment

All kinds of rebates, discounts, customer loyalty bonuses, allowances for terms of payment, financing methods, and installment payment conditions need to be listed here. These conditions determine how much the buyer actually pays.

## Kind and Complexity of the Product or Service

Insurance agencies and banks offer their services at highly differentiated and complex terms. Comparisons are difficult and sometimes impossible. In many markets prices include extra services such as guarantee, service, training, or technical counseling to varying degrees.

Pharmaceuticals are, for instance, often offered in different galenic forms, package sizes and doses. Table 1.1 shows a comparison of competing pharmaceutical brands.

This example, which covers only about one fifth of all packages available, illustrates the complexity of price comparisons. Comparisons may be even more complicated because some regimens require taking complementary medications, while others do not; size of a daily dose may vary depending on the diagnosis, and so on.

## Base of Price Comparison

The choice between competitive products can be influenced by the base of price comparison. The buyer of an automobile, for example, can use the purchase or the

Table 1.1
Product Forms and Prices in a Pharmaceutical Market

| Brand | Galenic Form | Package | Daily Dose | Price in Pharmacy | Price per Daily Dose |
|-------|--------------|---------|------------|-------------------|----------------------|
| A | Capsules | 50 | 3 | 17.00 | 1.02 |
| B | Film-pills | 50 | 2 | 19.18 | 0.77 |
| C | Lozenges 40 mg | 50 | 5 | 5.95 | 0.595 |
|   | Lozenges 80 mg | 100 | 2.5 | 19.21 | 0.48 |
| D | Film-lozenges | 100 | 3 | 21.53 | 0.65 |
| E | Pills | 30 | 2 | 8.59 | 0.57 |

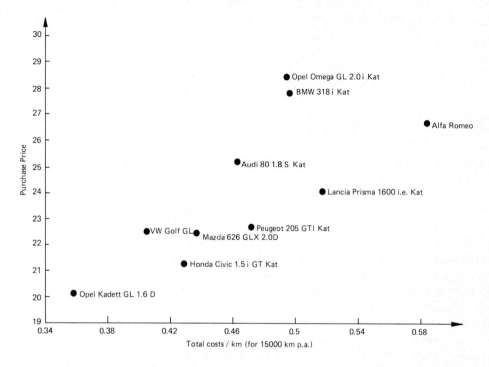

Fig. 1.4. Positioning of Automobile Models with Respect to Alternative Bases of Price Comparison (Purchase Price, Costs/km in DM, Source: Capital 3/1987)

costs per kilometer as criterion of comparison. Fig. 1.4 shows the resulting positioning of 10 mid-sized cars. The correlation between these two criteria is not high (correlation coefficient of 0.56). Thus, it is of utmost importance for the manager to know which base of price comparison his buyers use.

*Aggregation Problems with Respect to Time and Space*

While it is simple to determine the price of a product at a certain day in a certain store, determining representative prices for the aggregate market is difficult. This can be achieved only after considerable timelags. A product manager in the consumer goods sector usually does not know the average price the product is selling for in the current week or month; nor has he this information for competitive products. Nielsen data are available only after a time lag of several weeks and may contain possible distortions due to the aggregation over time and the survey method. Check-out scanner data will radically change this situation. Price and sales data can be made available almost instantaneously and standardized data are reported in weekly intervals. This improves the basis for timely price decisions considerably.

## 1.4 Price Management and Pricing Research

The aim of price management is to determine the optimal price or pricing strategy appropriate to the firm's objectives and to implement that strategy.

Price is central to various sub-disciplines of economics and management. Macro-economic price theory is dominated by issues such as the determination of prices by supply and demand, economic efficiency of the price system, and problems of market equilibrium. Research results in this field have not been very useful for practical pricing decisions.

Microeconomic price theory has a long history of research in price formation. Cournot's famous work dates back to 1838, and milestones such as the contributions by Launhardt (1885), Hotelling (1929), Chamberlin (1933), Robinson (1933), or von Stackelberg (1934) are not recent. Krelle's monograph (1976) provides the most comprehensive overview.

Microeconomic models are distinguished by logical consistency, very precise assumptions, and normative statements. From management's perspective, however, most microeconomic models are of little practical relevance. The empirical applica-tion of theoretical concepts, crucial for managers, is often lacking. Problems of acquiring information and implementation remain largely unaddressed. It is therefore not surprising that this research field has had very little impact on price decisions in practice. Alfred (1972) summarizes the contribution as follows: "Company pricing policy is an area where the academic world has long since retreated in despair of ascribing consistency of principles or rationality of practice."

Only recently price has attracted increased attention from marketing scientists. A qualitative/descriptive and a quantitative/methodology-based direction can be iden-tified. The first is represented by works of Shapiro (1972), Oxenfeldt (1975) and Monroe (1979). Their research is characterized by numerous important insights but also by many quite general statements. Mainly "directional recommendations" can be derived by the qualitative approach.

The first quantitative empirical approaches to pricing originated from econometric analyses – often primarily directed at advertising (e.g., Telser 1962, Lambin 1976). In recent years the focus has shifted to measurement issues. The development of the conjoint measurement technique marks a major breakthrough in the scientific foun-dation of price decisions. Moreover, efforts have been made to integrate economic price theory and marketing (Rao 1984, Nagle 1987). But there remains a lack of theory. The 1984/85 research program of the Marketing Science Institute states that "pricing research is at an early stage of development in the academic marketing literature". Bonoma, Crittenden, and Dolan (1986) still say that managers "find little help in the marketing literature which they perceive as not addressing their key concerns."

It is necessary to integrate phenomena like customers' response to price, competi-tive reaction, product life cycle, experience curve, segmentation, etc. into price

Table 1.2
Pricing Research in Economics and Marketing

|  | Economics | Marketing | |
|---|---|---|---|
|  |  | qualitative | quantitative |
| Study of price | very intensive |  | less intensive |
| Managerial relevance of issues | rather low | high | medium/high |
| Precision of normative recommendations | high | low | high |
| Practical implementability | low | high | medium |

decision models. While advances have been made in some of these areas, we have still a very long way to go to arrive at satisfactory price decision support systems. A similar opinion is expressed by Monroe and Marundar (1988). Table 1.2 summarizes the state of the art in the various areas.

## 1.5 Pricing Determinants

Pricing is dependent on external and internal determinants. External determinants are beyond the firm's control (e.g., consumer characteristics, market structure, competitors, legal conditions). These factors determine together with the non-price marketing activities (e.g., distribution, advertising) the number of product units which can be sold at alternative prices. The relationship between alternative prices and the resulting sales quantity is called the price response function

$$q = f(p), \tag{1.1}$$

where $q$ and $p$ represent unit sales and price, respectively. The price response function can also be represented in the form of a table or a graph. It measures the sales effect of price and represents the first determinant of price formation. We discuss various price response functions in Chapter 2.

The second determinant of price is the cost function. This function assigns to each production quantity $q$ a cost figure $C$, i.e.,

$$C = g(q). \tag{1.2}$$

The cost function is a pricing determinant because costs are a function of the quantity $q$, which in turn depends on price $p$ (quantities produced and sold are assumed to be equal). We analyze cost functions in Chapters 3 and 5.

Knowledge of the price response and cost function alone is not enough to determine an optimal price. We need a criterion to evaluate the consequences of alternative prices. This third pricing determinant is called the objective function.

Profit maximization is the most important objective function both in theory and practice. The theoretical justification is that this objective function – unlike revenue-, sales-, or market share-oriented objectives – explicitly includes both revenue and cost consequences of alternative prices. Some researchers dispute the practical relevance of the profit maximizing principle. Yet we think these objections arise because no clear distinction is made between short- and long-term profit orientation. Nobody would seriously claim that a firm should take maximum advantage of each profit opportunity appearing in the short run, to soak buyers in a boom and to pressure suppliers in a recession, or to neglect product or market development in favor of a higher cash flow in the short run. Such behavior might maximize short-term profit, but it certainly leads to sub-optimal results in the long run. One of the main purposes of this book is to work out differences between short- and long-term orientation in pricing. As a survey of about 300 firms undertaken by Wied-Nebbeling (1985) shows, long-term profit objectives play a predominant role.

In practice, several objectives are often pursued simultaneously. Frequently these objectives are not compatible, e.g., profit- and market share-objectives. The inconsistencies are rarely made explicit. According to the author's experience, capacity utilization has a particularly strong effect on price decisions. Underutilized capacity puts a strong pressure on managers to accept relatively low prices. The effect of capacity utilization can be partially captured by opportunity costs, i.e., in the shortage situation the actual costs should be replaced by the opportunity costs which are determined by the profits from alternative orders. But in addition to this economic effect capacity utilization has a strong psychological impact on managerial pricing decisions.

Other determinants include product line considerations, competitive behavior, strategic goals, etc. It is not practical to incorporate all these objectives and restrictions into a comprehensive pricing model. It is more useful to use simple models for price optimization and to consider more complex aspects by means of subjective judgments.

Summary: Pricing determinants are the price response, the cost, and the objective functions. The price response function is determined by market and competitive factors as well as non-price marketing activities of the firm. The cost function relates costs to production volume. Long-term profit maximization is the most important objective function.

## 1.6 Price Management and Market Structure

The economic setting where goods and services are exchanged is denoted as the market. Actual markets involve a confusing multitude of forms and behaviors of

Table 1.3
Morphologic Market Scheme

| Buyers | Suppliers One | Few | Many |
|---|---|---|---|
| One | bilateral monopoly | limited monopoly of demand | monopoly of demand (monopsony) |
| Few | limited monopoly of supply | bilateral oligopoly | oligopoly of demand (oligopsony) |
| Many | monopoly of supply | oligopoly of supply | polypoly |

participants. But the variety of patterns can be reduced to a few basic types without unduly restricting its diversity. It is advisable to base the pricing analysis on these market types.

In order to categorize market structures it is useful to look separately at the supply and the demand side. If we categorize both sides according to the number of participants, we obtain the so-called morphologic market scheme; it is represented in Table 1.3.

Alternative market definitions are based not on market structure but on intensity of competition (see Krelle 1976). In this definition a firm has a monopoly status if it is not affected by competition. An oligopoly exists when a firm is subject to competition from any single other firm. A firm that is not affected by the action of individual competitors but by the collective behavior of all competitors operates in a polypoly.

A different market classification suggested by Frisch (1933) and Schneider (1972) is related to actual observable behavior of firms. Under this scheme, monopolistic behavior exists when a firm makes decisions assuming that sales depend only on its own price and on the behavior of its customers but not on competitors' prices. If, in contrast, the firm assumes that behavior of competitors does affect sales, it is in a competitive situation. One case of special interest is when the firm expects competitive reactions prompted by its own actions; such a behavior pattern is called oligopolistic.

Competition can be either perfect or imperfect. Perfect competition is only realized at stock markets and commodity exchanges (again, only within approximately homogenous classifications). Perfectly competitive markets are less interesting from the perspective of price management because price is not a parameter set by the firm but is determined by the market; the "law of one price" prevails.

Many real markets are imperfect and have "many customers". This situation applies to most consumer goods markets. In Wied-Nebbeling (1985, p. 135) 84.3 % of

*H. Simon*

Table 1.4
Cumulative Market Shares of Leading Suppliers in Selected Markets (Source: Adams 1982, Oberender 1984)

| Market | Country | Year | No. of Competitors Included | Cumulative Market Share % | Total Number of Competitors |
|---|---|---|---|---|---|
| Passenger Cars | Germany | 1986 | 4 | 64.7 | > 20 |
| Passenger Cars | USA | 1980 | 3 | 70.0 | > 20 |
| Trucks | Europe | 80's | 5 | > 90.0 | > 10 |
| Beer | USA | 1980 | 5 | 75.0 | > 10 |
| Beer | Germany | 1979 | 4 | 34.3 | > 1000 |
| Computers (size class 6 and 7) | USA | 1979 | 4 | 73.2 | < 10 |
| Gasoline | USA | 1979 | 4 | 28.8 | > 20 |
| Gasoline | Germany | – | 5 | 65.8 | > 20 |
| Cigarettes | Germany | 1960 | 2 | 81.0 | < 10 |
| | | 1982 | 2 | 55.5 | < 10 |
| Ready to eat cereals | USA | 1977 | 4 | 85.0 | > 10 |

the firms surveyed said they had more than 50 buyers. Markets in which only "one buyer" or "few buyers" appear on the demand side are limited mainly to the industrial sector (e.g., automobile supply firms).

On the supply side the prevailing market structure is partial oligopoly. The bulk of the market is controlled by a few large firms in a partial oligopoly, usually with numerous smaller firms sharing the balance of the market. Table 1.4 gives several examples.

Wied-Nebbeling (1985) found that more than 50% of the respondents expected competitive reactions to their own price reductions (in a recession even 75%). Therefore, markets with many buyers on the demand side and oligopolistic interdependency on the supply side deserve a particular attention.

On the other hand, we see many fragmented markets, particularly for specialties, where the largest firms have only a small share of the total (see Porter 1980 for examples). Whether the traditional oligopoly will be less prevalent in the future than today remains to be seen. We observe many new markets with a so-called "mob competition", e.g., at the Hanover (West Germany) electronics fair in 1987 more than 350 suppliers exhibited personal computers. In a typical national market today more than 500 auto models are sold (e.g., in West Germany 503 models at the end of 1988). Price management has to take these new developments into account.

Summary: Markets can be classified according to structural, economic, or behavior-related criteria. Real markets are almost always imperfect. Their structures are often characterized by "many buyers" on the demand side and "a few suppliers" on the supply side.

Chapter 2

# *The Static Price Response Function*

## 2.1 Systems Context

We begin this chapter with a discussion of the systems context in which the static price decision is made. We show that the knowledge of the price response function is essential for rational pricing decisions. Then we present the concept and theory of the price response function. Finally we discuss the calibration and application of price response functions.

Managers should understand the systems context and the information requirements of pricing. Fig. 2.1 shows a simplified representation of the systems context for the static case. In static analysis we do not include the time dimension, i.e., we typically consider one period. If data from several periods are used, it is assumed that market conditions do not change over time and that dynamic relations do not exist.

The objective is to determine the price which maximizes the profit. Fig. 2.1 shows that there is no direct, simple relationship between price and profit. Price affects profit through several intermediate variables. Both our own price and competitive prices influence sales and market share. The price response function captures this relationship. Multiplying price and sales yields revenue. Revenue minus cost is profit.

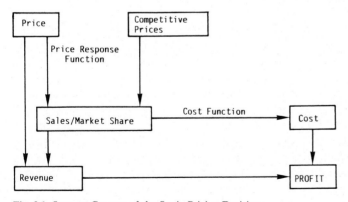

Fig. 2.1. Systems Context of the Static Pricing Decision

There are two critical relations in Fig. 2.1: The price response function and the cost function. While the cost function can be determined on the basis of internal cost data, the calibration of the price response function poses a difficult problem.

Fig. 2.1 suggests that the knowledge of this relationship is critical for a rational pricing decision. Any pricing method (e.g., cost-plus pricing) which does not explicitly consider the price response function may lead to sub-optimal results. There is simply no way one can determine the optimal price without understanding how the price affects sales and market share. In addition to the relations shown in Fig. 2.1, there may be interrelations between competitive prices. This so-called "competitive reaction" is discussed in Chapter 4.

*Classification of Price Response Functions*

Static price response functions can be classified according to the following criteria:
- market situation: monopolistic vs. competitive,
- level of aggregation: individual (micro) vs. aggregate (macro),
- form of representation: table, graphical, mathematical equation,
- source of data/measurement: customer survey, expert judgment, price experiments, actual market data.

This chapter discusses both the monopolistic and the competitive case.

In a typical mass market the manager is interested in the macro rather than micro price response function. However, if the price is determined or negotiated on an individual base, the micro function is important. This is also the case if a market is segmented.

## 2.2 Concept and Theory of the Price Response Function

### 2.2.1 Theoretical Foundation

In order to explain the concept of the price response function, it is useful to start at the individual level.

*Individual Price Response Function*

Depending on the product category a customer faces one of the two following decision situations:

– He buys either one unit or does not buy the product at all. The decision depends on the price and we refer to this case as "yes:no-case". Examples are consumer durables, e.g., video recorders, personal computers, etc.

– He buys less or more units of the product depending on the price. We call this situation the "variable quantity-case". Many non-durables belong to this category, e.g., chocolates, soft drinks, services such as the telephone usage, etc.

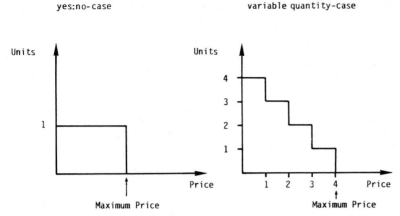

Fig. 2.2. Individual Price Response Functions for Two Different Purchase Situations

Fig. 2.2 illustrates the individual price response functions for both cases.

In the "yes:no-case" the customer buys the product if the price is less than the product's perceived value or utility. The maximum or "reservation price" a customer is willing to pay for the product is equal to its utility to him. In the "variable quantity-case" such comparisons of price and utility are made for each unit of the product. As we see from Fig. 2.2 the customer is willing to pay 4 monetary units for the first product unit, but only 3 for the second unit. This is so because the marginal utility of an additional product unit decreases (first Law of Gossen). The higher the price is, the fewer units the customer buys in the "variable quantity-case".

If the price is set on an individual base, both cases have different managerial implications. In the "yes:no-case" the manager has to find the individual buyer's maximum price and should charge this price. This is the core problem in any price negotiation. If a uniform price has to be set for all potential buyers, then the manager is interested in the aggregate price response function to optimize the uniform price.

### Aggregate Price Response Function

The aggregate price response function is obtained by adding the quantities which each customer buys at a given price. Customers can be homogeneous or heterogeneous in this regard. In reality they are almost always heterogeneous. In Fig. 2.3 we demonstrate the aggregation process for three heterogeneous customers and contrast the "yes:no-case" and the "variable quantity-case".

In both cases the aggregate price response function has a negative slope and can be approximated by a continuous curve if we consider a large number of customers. It is nevertheless important to keep the differences in the individual response functions in mind. These differences are particularly important for market segmentation (see Chapter 8).

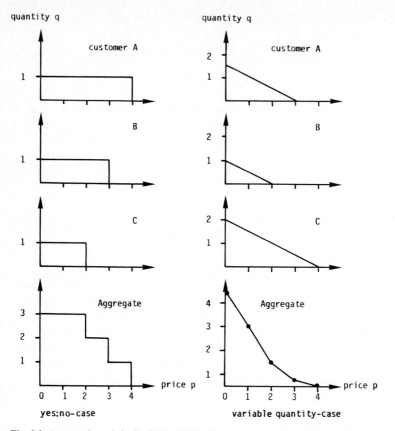

Fig. 2.3. Aggregation of the Individual Price Response Functions of Three Heterogeneous Customers

*Price Elasticity*

The most popular measure of the impact of price on sales is price elasticity. In general, elasticity refers to the relation of a relative change of one variable to the relative change of another variable caused by the first. The price elasticity of sales is given as

$$\varepsilon = \frac{\text{(relative) percentage change in sales volume}}{\text{(relative) percentage change in price}}. \tag{2.1}$$

Hence, if a price reduction of 10% causes an increase of the sales volume of 20%, the price elasticity is $20/-10 = -2$, i.e., the relative volume change is twice as large as the relative price change. The negative sign is due to the fact that price and sales change are inversely related.

In the case of an infinitely small price change the price elasticity is defined as

$$\varepsilon = \frac{\delta q}{\delta p}\frac{p}{q}, \tag{2.2}$$

where $\delta q/\delta p$ is the derivative of the price response function with respect to price.

Sales of a product often depend not only on its own price but also on the prices of other products. The degree of this dependency is measured by the cross-price elasticity, which is defined as

$$\varepsilon_{AB} = \frac{\delta q^A}{\delta p^B}\frac{p^B}{q^A}. \tag{2.3}$$

The cross-price elasticity gives the percentage change in unit sales $q^A$ of product A caused by a 1%-change in product B's price $p^B$. If A and B are substitutes, i.e., products competing against each other, the cross-price elasticity is positive. If, in contrast, they are complements (e.g., cameras and film), then it is negative.

Summary: Managers should know the price response function to make rational pricing decisions. The function can be determined at the individual or at the aggregate level. At the individual level we distinguish between the "yes:no-case" and the "variable quantity-case". In both cases the relationship between the price and the perceived value is critical for the customer's decision. The aggregate price response function is negatively sloped and can be approximated by a continuous curve. The most popular measure of price response is price elasticity.

## 2.2.2 Mathematical Price Response Functions

*Monopoly*

The most systematic way to represent a price response function is by means of a mathematical equation. We consider the monopoly case first. By definition, the sales quantity is the dependent and the price the independent variable.

*Linear Price Response Function in Monopoly*

The simplest hypothesis is to assume a linear relationship between price $p$ and sales $q$:

$$q = a - bp. \tag{2.4}$$

Fig. 2.4 illustrates the linear function.

The parameter $a$ denotes the highest possible sales (at $p = 0$) and $b$ represents the absolute change in sales resulting from a change in price by one unit. A higher value of $b$ implies a more price sensitive demand. Since no sale is made if the price equals $a/b$, we call this ratio the "maximum price".

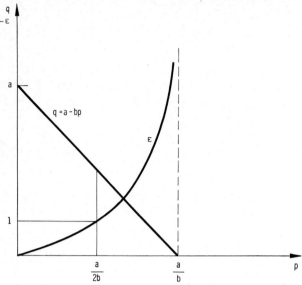

Fig. 2.4. The Linear Price Response Function in Monopoly

The price elasticity of the linear function can be written as

$$\varepsilon = \frac{\delta q}{\delta p} \frac{p}{q} = \frac{-bp}{a - bp}.$$  (2.5)

The price elasticity is shown in Fig. 2.4, it increases with price.

Simplicity is the main advantage of the linear function. Only two parameters need to be calibrated. But this function is not based on a well-founded theory. The following statement is still valid: "it may be just as correct to draw a straight line as to use any other form" (Fog 1960, p. 49). In spite of its simplicity the linear function often yields a satisfactory fit to empirical data.

*Multiplicative Price Response Function in Monopoly*

A multiplicative price response model represents the sales $q$ as a non-linear function of price $p$.

$$q = ap^b \quad a > 0, \, b < 0.$$  (2.6)

It is illustrated in Fig. 2.5. The absolute sales effect of a change in price depends

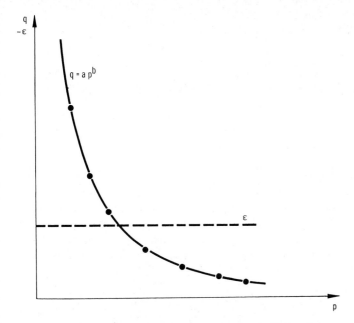

Fig. 2.5. The Multiplicative Price Response Function in Monopoly

on the price level. The lower the price, the greater the sales effect of a price change. The multiplicative function has a constant price elasticity.

$$\varepsilon = \frac{\delta q}{\delta p} \frac{p}{q} = b. \tag{2.7}$$

This "isoelasticity" is an advantage of this function. The model is simple and only two parameters need to be calibrated. Its theoretical foundation is little better than that of the linear model, though.

Another price response function occasionally suggested in the literature is similar in form to the multiplicative function but makes price elasticity proportional to price (e.g., Robinson and Lakhani 1975, Landau 1976, Thompson and Teng 1984):

$$q = ae^{bp} \quad \text{with } b < 0, \tag{2.8}$$

where $e$ is the base of natural logarithms.
    Price elasticity is a linear function of $p$:

$$\varepsilon = bp. \tag{2.9}$$

*Competitive Case*

*The Dependent Variable*

In the competitive case, either sales $q_i$ or market share $m_i$ of brand $i$ can be used as the dependent variable. The two variables are closely related.

$$\text{or} \quad \begin{aligned} m_i &= q_i/Q, \\ q_i &= m_i Q, \end{aligned} \tag{2.10}$$

where $Q$ denotes the total demand.

If the total demand $Q$ is independent of price, these two variables can be used interchangeably as the dependent variable. If $Q$ depends on price, i.e., if the price elasticity of the total demand is not zero, we need two models; one that represents the effect of price on market share $m_i$, and another that captures the impact of price on $Q$. The price elasticity of sales $q_i$ is obtained as the sum of the two corresponding price elasticities:

price elasticity of $q_i$ = price elasticity of $Q$ + price elasticity of $m_i$.

The two submodels can be either treated separately or integrated into one model which directly measures the impact of price $p_i$ on sales $q_i$.

*The Independent Variables*

As for the independent variables in the competitive case, we can consider several alternative ways to incorporate the price of the brand in question, $p_i$, and the competitive prices. Table 2.1 shows several alternatives.

Alternative 1 is usually too cumbersome and often entails multicollinearity problems, i.e., the effects of individual competitive prices on sales $q_i$ cannot be separated. Alternative 2 can be viable if we have well-defined subgroups of competitive products, e.g., branded products vs. generics.

Table 2.1
Alternative Definitions of Independent Variables in a Competitive Price Response Function

| Dependent Variable | No | Independent Variable |
|---|---|---|
| $q_i$ or $m_i$ | 1 | $p_i$ and all individual competitive prices $p_j$ |
| | 2 | $p_i$ and the average competitive prices $p_j$ of subgroups |
| | 3 | $p_i$ and the overall average competitive price $p$ |
| | 4 | absolute differential between $p_i$ and $p$ |
| | 5 | relative price $p_i/p$ |

In most cases it is advisable to use the overall average competitive price as in alternatives 3, 4, or 5. Then we have to define the (overall) average competitive price. The average can be either unweighted or weighted by market share (here the weights can be either time-constant or time-varying). In addition, $p_i$ can be either included or excluded when the average is calculated.

Kucher (1985) investigated these various options and arrived at the following conclusions:
- the way the independent variables are defined makes a great difference in the estimation results of the (competitive) price response functions,
- market share-weighted average prices yielded better results than unweighted averages (in terms of goodness of fit, significance, economic plausibility),
- constant market share-weights produced better results than time-varying weights,
- $p_i$ should not be included in the calculation of the average competitive price.

It is obvious that there is no single best way to define the independent variables. Therefore, we should be very careful in these definitions.

## Competitive Price Response Functions

We discuss four types of competitive price response functions:
- the linear model,
- the multiplicative model,
- the attraction/multinomial logit model,
- the Gutenberg model.

Table 2.2 shows the mathematical form of each model.

Fig. 2.6 illustrates the four models. The solid lines represent the sales $q_i$ and the broken lines the price elasticity at alternative values of $p_i$. The average competitive price is held constant at $\bar{p} = 2$ in all four cases.

The figure shows that within a certain price interval (indicated by the squares) all functions are very similar. If prices vary only within such a narrow interval, it is next to impossible to distinguish empirically between the four models. Several attempts

Table 2.2
Competitive Price Response Models

| Model | Dependent Variable | The Most Common Form of the Right Hand Side |
|---|---|---|
| Linear | $q_i$ or $m_i$ | $a - bp_i + c\bar{p}$ |
| Multiplicative | $q_i$ or $m_i$ | $a(p_i/\bar{p})^b$ |
| Attraction | $m_i$ | $a_0 + a_i p_i^{bi} / \sum_j a_j p_j^{bj}$ |
| Gutenberg | $q_i$ or $m_i$ | $a - bp_i - c_1 \sinh(c_2(p_i - \bar{p}))$ |

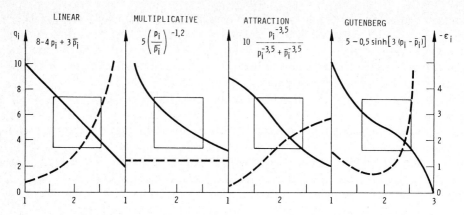

Fig. 2.6. Competitive Price Response Functions

have been made to evaluate these models empirically. In Table 2.3 the results of two such studies are reproduced.

The results are inconclusive. No model is inherently superior. In a similar study, Ghosh et al. (1984, p. 208) reach the following conclusion: "If we consider both parameter validity and forecast accuracy, linear and multiplicative models perform at least as well as the attraction model." Since these models have different advantages and disadvantages we discuss each of them in more detail.

*Linear Model*

The biggest advantage of this model is simplicity. Only three parameters need to be determined. The assumption of constant absolute sales responses to changes in

Table 2.3
Empirical Comparisons of Competitive Price Response Models

| Study | Criterion | Linear | Multi-plicative | Attraction | Guten-berg |
|-------|-----------|--------|----------------|------------|------------|
| Simon (1982c) | average $R^2$ | 0.6379 | 0.6746 | – | 0.6320 |
| 24 non-dura-bles | % of cases with the highest $R^2$ | 25% | 50% | – | 25% |
| Kucher (1985) | average $R^2$ | 0.2754 | 0.2592 | 0.2800 | 0.3308 |
| 13 non-dura-bles | % of cases with the highest $R^2$ | 0% | 17% | 17% | 66% |

both prices ($p_i$ and $p$) is somewhat unrealistic particularly for large price differentials.

## Multiplicative Model

This function is also relatively simple. The price elasticity is equal to the exponent *b*. The model is asymmetric, i.e., the slope is greater at low relative prices. Preston (1963) argues that this asymmetry is reasonable for products with a market share of less than 50% because a price increase affects only the purchases by previous buyers (a minority) while a price cut may affect the rest of the market (a majority).

## Attraction Model

The hypothesis that underlies this model is that the "attraction" (or utility/value/preference) of brand *i* relative to the "attraction" of all brands determines *i*'s market share:

$$m_i = \frac{\text{attraction of brand } i}{\text{sum of attraction of all brands}}.$$

Price is one attribute that determines the "attraction" which can be operationalized in several ways:
- multiplicatively $a_i\, p_i^{bi}$,
- additively $a_i + bp_i$,
- as a form of the part worth model $f(p_i)$,
- as a form of the multinomial logit model $e^{vi}$,

with $v_i = \sum\limits_k z_k x_{ki}$,                                                  (2.11)

where $v_i$ is attractiveness of brand *i*, $z_k$ weight of attribute *k*, $x_{ki}$ level of attribute *k* at product *i*.

Price is one of the attributes in (2.11) and has a negative weight.

All alternatives yield a curve similar to the one shown in Fig. 2.6. For further details the reader is referred to McFadden (1973), Gensch and Recker (1979), and Guadagni and Little (1983). Attraction type models are "logically consistent" in the sense that the market share of each brand lies always between 0 and 1 and the market shares add up to 1. These models are most useful when price and other product attributes are simultaneously considered.

## Gutenberg Model

Gutenberg hypothesized that small price differentials have underproportional and large differentials have overproportional effects on market share and sales (Guten-

*H. Simon*

Market Share $m_i$ or Sales $q_i$

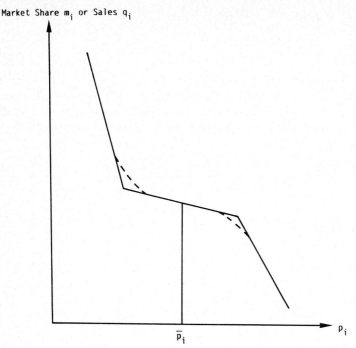

Fig. 2.7. Gutenberg Price Response Function

berg 1976). The hypothesis was originally expressed as a doubly-kinked price response curve as in Fig. 2.7.

Gutenberg called the area between the two kinks "monopolistic interval" because he assumed that customers do not switch suppliers if the price lies within this interval. This reluctance to switch is due to the switching cost as well as the preference for the current supplier.

There is a lot of anecdotal/empirical evidence that supports the Gutenberg hypothesis:

– "The persons often held the view that the changes in price must be of a certain magnitude before any effects will be noticeable." (Fog 1960, p. 43),

– a manufacturer of shoe polish: "There is a definite price interval. If the price rises above this interval, sales decrease. If the price drops below the interval, sales increase." (ibid.),

– a can manufacturer: "By virtue of our reputation we shall be able to charge prices which are 5 to 10 percent higher than other prices, but definitely not more than that." (ibid.),

– a textile company: "The price will have to be reduced by at least 25 Kronen before it would have any effect on sales at all." (ibid.),

– "Cereal makers must have considered their demand functions to become quite elastic at prices exceeding those of the nearest substitutes by more than four cents per pack." (Scherer 1978, p. 34),

– "While consumers seem to be willing to pay up to 6 cents more per package, a substantial number of customers are lost when the price differential exceeds this figure." (Peckham 1973, p. 15).

According to our own experience managers typically think of price response functions in terms of the Gutenberg model. When price response curves are subjectively estimated they are frequently of this type. The hypothesis is less often supported by actual market data. We attribute that to the fact that prices outside the "monopolistic interval" are rarely observed (see also Telser 1962).

Albach (1973) suggested the following mathematical form with sales as the dependent variable

$$q_i = a - bp_i - c_1 \sinh(c_2(p_i - \bar{p})), \tag{2.12}$$

where $a$, $b$, $c_1$, and $c_2$ are parameters to be estimated.

The graph of this function has no kinks but is a smooth curve (see the dashed line in Fig. 2.7). It is symmetric with respect to the overall average competitive price $\bar{p}$.

Summary: We discussed four alternative price response models: linear, multiplicative, attraction (logit), and Gutenberg. The linear and the multiplicative models are simple but lack theoretical foundation. Models of the attraction type are particularly useful when price is considered together with other product attributes. The Gutenberg model postulates over-proportional sales responses to big price differentials and is relevant when a relatively wide price interval is considered.


## 2.3 Calibration of the Price Response Function

*Data Collection Methods*

In order to calibrate the price response function we need data on prices, sales/market shares, and possibly other variables. These data can be collected using the following methods:
– expert judgment,
– customer survey,
– price experiment,
– collection of actual market data.

Table 2.4 provides an evaluation of these methods on various criteria.

*Expert Judgment*

In his landmark article on "decision calculus", Little (1970) suggested to utilize expert judgments to calibrate the advertising response function. This method has

Table 2.4
Comparison of the Methods of Collecting Price Response Data

| Criterion | Method Expert Judgment | Customer Surveys | | Price Experiments | Actual Market Data |
|---|---|---|---|---|---|
| | | Direct | Conjoint Measurement | | |
| Validity | medium | very low | medium-high | medium-low | high |
| Reliability | medium-high | un-certain | uncertain | high | low |
| Costs | very low | low-medium | medium | medium-high | depends on availability and accessibility |
| Applicability to New Products | yes | ques-tion-able | yes | yes | no |
| Applicability to Established Products | yes | yes | yes | yes | yes |
| Overall Evaluation | useful for new products, new situations | question-able | very useful | useful | useful for es-tablished products |

proved useful also for the calibration of the price response function. If the product in question is a genuine innovation, this may be the only way to calibrate the price response function.

The questions the experts are supposed to answer should be tailored to each specific case. Our experience from numerous applications suggests the following:

1. If possible, five to ten experts should be interviewed.
2. Large divergencies in the estimates are not unusual. If more judgments are collected, the validity is likely to increase.
3. Experts should be diverse in terms of background and position in the hierarchy.
4. The interviews should be done by a neutral outsider.
5. The results should be discussed in a meeting where all respondents are present and a consensus should be reached. This leads to better results than simply calculating the average of the individual estimates.
6. A Delphi approach can be applied but is usually too time-consuming and adds little incremental value.

The following two examples demonstrate the use of this method. The first example concerns a new consumer nondurable to be introduced in three European countries. Competitive prices were of minor relevance. The marketing managers in these three countries were asked to provide the following estimates:
- the lowest realistic price and the sales expected at this price in the first year,
- the highest realistic price and the associated sales,
- the expected sales at the medium price.

Fig. 2.8 shows the result. Since a uniform price was to be set in all countries, the sales response estimates were aggregated. The aggregated price response function is shown in the lower part of the figure.

In the second example the entry of a new major competitor was expected. The company wanted to know how the product should be priced if the entry occurred. We ignore here the dynamic effects and competitive reactions. Eight managers were asked to provide their sales estimates with and without competitive entry at five alternative prices. Fig. 2.9 shows the mean estimates. The negative numbers are price elasticities (the reference price is 100).

This method is simple to apply and cost effective. It can also be used together with other procedures in order to cross-validate the results.

## Customer Surveys

Customer surveys on price response are of two different types.
- One can either directly ask customers how they would react to certain price levels, price changes, or price differentials,
- or one can ask customers about their preferences and infer from these data the information on price response.

## Direct Price Response Surveys

In a direct response survey the respondent is asked questions of the following type:
- Would you buy the product at this price?
- At which price would you buy the product?
- At which price differential would you switch from brand $x$ to brand $y$?

On the basis of this information price response functions can be easily derived. This direct method was very popular in the 60's (Gabor and Granger 1964, 1966; Abrams 1964, Adam 1969).

The direct method is simple and cheap to use. The validity and reliability of the results obtained by this method are, however, questionable for the following reasons.
1. There is a discrepancy between the stated intentions to buy and the actual purchases.
2. The price-related questions may induce an unrealistically high price-consciousness.
3. The price is viewed in isolation. In reality, customers weigh the price against other product attributes, i.e., make a trade-off. The conjoint method addresses this issue of trade-off in a systematic way.

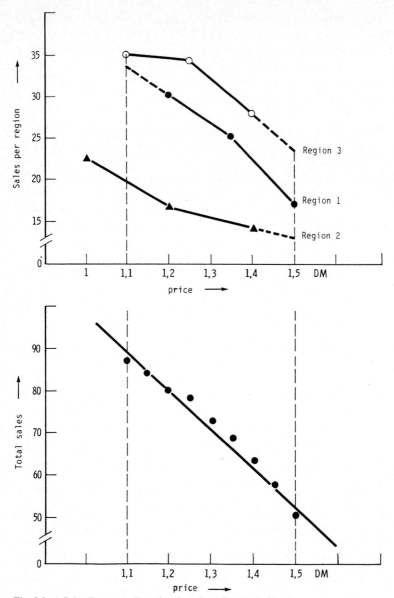

Fig. 2.8. A Price Response Function Based on Expert Judgments

## Conjoint Measurement

In conjoint measurement the respondent is not directly asked about his behavior in various price situations but presented with several product attributes or full product

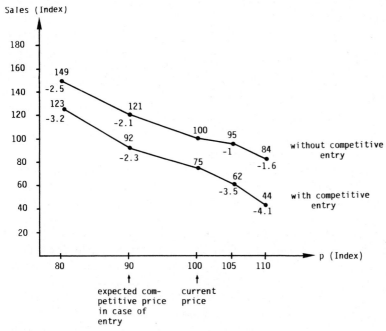

Fig. 2.9. Price Response Estimates for Alternative Competitive Situations

profiles (including price). He simply indicates his preference for each product profile. From these data the effect of price is inferred by means of a preference model.

To calibrate a price response function via the conjoint measurement technique, one should proceed as follows:
1. determine the relevant product attributes,
2. determine the attribute levels,
3. design the questionnaire,
4. calculate the preference functions,
5. calibrate the price response function.

We discuss two applications, one from the automobile market, and the other from the pharmaceutical market. In the automobile case the attributes and their levels were:

| Attribute | Level |
|---|---|
| Brand: | 1, 2, 3 |
| Maximum Speed | 200, 220, 240 km/h |
| Gasoline Consumption | 12, 14, 16 liters per 100 km |
| Price | 50,000; 60,000; 70,000 DM |

Table 2.5
Example of a Paired Comparison

| Attribute | Auto A | Auto B |
|---|---|---|
| Brand | 1 | 2 |
| Max. Speed | 200 | 240 |
| Gasoline Consumption | 12 | 16 |
| Price | 50,000 | 70,000 |

Thus we have $3 \times 3 \times 3 \times 3 = 81$ possible combinations of the four attributes each of which has three levels. Via fractional design (Addelman 1962, Green and Srinivasan 1978) this number can be reduced to 9. Paired comparisons of full product profiles were made to measure the preferences. Table 2.5 shows one such paired comparison.

Each respondent is asked to indicate whether he prefers A or B. In this study 32 such paired comparisons were required. From these preference data part worths (= contributions to overall preference) can be calculated for each attribute and for each level. Standardized software is available for such calculations (e.g., MONANOVA, UNICON, TRADE OFF, LINMAP). Fig. 2.10 shows the part worths associated with each level of each of the four attributes.

The utility (preference) of a specific profile is obtained by adding the part worths associated with the attribute levels which the profile has. This summation is done in Table 2.6 for three profiles and for one respondent.

Auto A has the highest utility for this respondent. In order to transform the part worths into individual price response functions we assume that each respondent selects the model with the highest utility (single choice model). Based on this assumption, we can construct a price response function of the type shown in the left part of Fig. 2.2, i.e., the "yes:no-case". By adding up the individual functions we get the aggregate price response function for a specific auto model shown in Fig. 2.11.

The negative numbers are price elasticities (the reference price is DM 60,000).

The second example is from the pharmaceutical industry and uses a different choice model. The attributes considered were
– efficacy    (3 levels),
– dosing      (3 levels),
– safety      (3 levels),
– price       (5 levels: DM 0.70, 0.90, 1.10, 1.30, 1.50 per daily dose).

Instead of the full-profile approach we used trade-off matrices of the type shown in Table 2.7.

Each interviewed doctor was asked to rank order the 15 combinations according to his preference of prescription. Altogether six matrices of this kind were required.

The part worths of the attribute levels were calculated from these matrices. In order to transform the part worths into a price response function we used an

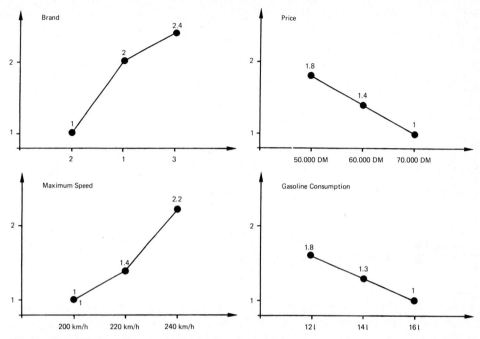

Fig. 2.10. Part Worths of Four Attributes for One Respondent

attraction type model where market share $m_i$ is expressed as

$$m_i = \frac{\text{utility of brand } i}{\text{sum of utilities of all brands}}.$$

Market shares at five alternative prices were calculated for each individual doctor. In Table 2.8 such a calculation is reproduced.

Table 2.6
Utilities of Three Profiles for One Respondent

| Auto A | | Auto B | | Auto C | |
|---|---|---|---|---|---|
| Attribute | Part Worth | Attribute | Part Worth | Attribute | Part Worth |
| Brand 1 | 2.0 | Brand 2 | 1.0 | Brand 3 | 2.4 |
| 50,000 DM | 1.8 | 60,000 DM | 1.4 | 70,000 DM | 1.0 |
| 200 km/h | 1.0 | 220 km/h | 1.4 | 220 km/h | 1.4 |
| 12 1/100km | 1.6 | 14 1/100km | 1.3 | 16 1/100km | 1.0 |
| Utility: | 6.4 | | 5.1 | | 5.8 |

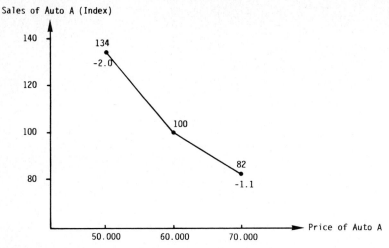

Fig. 2.11. Aggregate Price Response Function for an Auto Model Calibrated by the Conjoint Measurement Technique

The market shares (associated with each price level) for each doctor were weighted by each doctor's patient share and then added up across doctors to yield the aggregate price response function reproduced in Fig. 2.12.

The negative numbers are price elasticities (with $p = 1.10$ as reference price). Their magnitude is typical for a pharmaceutical product.

Alternatively we can derive the price response function by first calculating average part worths across respondents. We can then use these average part worths to simulate directly the aggregate price response function. This method is computationally simpler because we simulate the response function only once rather than for each respondent. However, it yields less accurate results because differences in the part worths between respondents may not be correctly reflected in the average. Many alternative preference models are used in conjunction with conjoint measurement. For further details the readers are referred to Green and Srinivasan (1978), Cattin and Wittink (1982), and Corstjens and Gautschi (1983).

Table 2.7
Trade-Off Matrix

| Efficacy | Price | | | | |
|---|---|---|---|---|---|
| | 0.70 | 0.90 | 1.10 | 1.30 | 1.50 |
| low | | | | | |
| medium | | | | | |
| high | | | | | |

Table 2.8
Price Response Function of a Pharmaceutical Brand for an Individual Doctor Based on Part Worth Model

| | | | | | |
|---|---|---|---|---|---|
| 1 Price per Daily Dose | 0.70 | 0.90 | 1.10 | 1.30 | 1.50 |
| 2 Part Worth of Price | 1.4 | 1.3 | 1.1 | 0.7 | 0.1 |
| 3 Sum of Part Worths of Non-Price Attributes | 3.2 | 3.2 | 3.2 | 3.2 | 3.2 |
| 4 Utility of Brand $i$ at Price $p_i$ $(3+4)$ | 4.6 | 4.5 | 4.3 | 3.9 | 3.3 |
| 5 Sum of Utilities of All Brands | 20.3 | 20.2 | 20.0 | 19.6 | 18.9 |
| 6 Market Share of Brand $i$ $(4:5)$ | 22.6% | 22.3% | 21.5% | 19.8% | 15.8% |

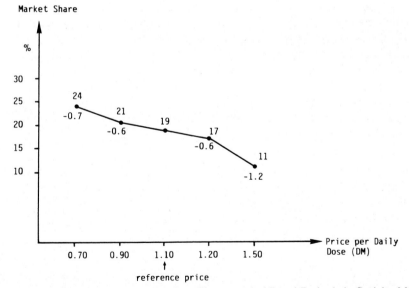

Fig. 2.12. Price Response Function for a Pharmaceutical Brand Derived via Conjoint Measurement

Summary: Consumer survey is an important method to calibrate price response functions. Since the method of direct questioning yields results of low validity, conjoint measurement is a very useful alternative. The respondents have to make the trade-offs between prices and the other product attributes. On the basis of the data on these trade-offs price response functions can be calibrated. The conjoint measurement technique is applicable to both consumer and industrial goods as well as to new and established products.

*Price Experiments*

Price experiments are conducted either in a laboratory setting (simulated shopping) or under real world conditions (e.g., store tests). Prices are systematically varied and the purchasing behavior of the consumers is observed. The big advantage of experiments over surveys is that the data are based on actual behavior rather than verbal statements. The variables can be controlled so that the internal validity is high. The external validity is somewhere between what we can expect from the survey method and the observation of the actual market behavior.

In laboratory experiments consumers are given a certain amount of money and asked to buy a brand from the product category under investigation. It is not clear whether the receipt of free money affects the consumers' behavior. Tests of this type were conducted by Pessemier (1963), Stout (1969), and Nevin (1974). Their results varied in terms of predictive validity. This method is not widely used because it is costly and the results are of low validity.

In real world experiments prices are varied over time or across regions and/or stores. Fig. 2.13 gives the result of such a price experiment for Florida oranges (Green and Tull 1978). In a Latin square design 7 prices were tested in 7 stores over 7 weeks. The figure shows the aggregate price response function.

A linear model explains 85.45% of the variance. A better goodness of fit ($R^2 = 0.8993$) is obtained with the following Gutenberg model:

$$q = 8.79 - 0.542 \sinh(20(p-1)). \tag{2.13}$$

The graphs of both the linear and the Gutenberg model are shown in the figure.

While the manual recording of the sales during a price experiment is bothersome, check-out scanners ease this task considerably. Fig. 2.14 shows the result of a large scale price experiment in a supermarket chain. Prices were varied in 58 stores over 24 weeks so that we have $58 \times 24 = 1,392$ data points.

A linear market share model with the relative price as the independent variable yields

$$m_i = 0.205 - 0.169\, p_i/\bar{p}. \tag{2.14}$$

(34.26) (−28.78)

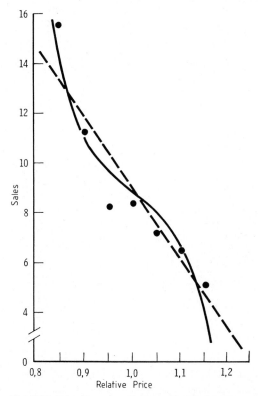

Fig. 2.13. Price Response Function for Florida Oranges Based on a Price Experiment with Latin Square Design

This model explains 37% of the variance. The *t*-statistic indicates an extremely high significance of the price effect. At the relative price of 1 we obtain a price elasticity of $-4.69$. Scanners represent an ideal and cost effective tool to conduct price experiments. We expect an extensive use of this tool in the future.

Summary: Price experiments are a useful way to calibrate price response functions. If possible, an experiment should be conducted in a real world setting rather than under artificial laboratory conditions. The scanner technology reduces the costs of price experiments and enhances the validity of the results obtained by this method.

*Actual Market Data*

In many markets data on actual sales and prices are readily available. In the consumer goods sector, for example, such data are provided by Nielsen, SAMI, and other market research companies. The data are either time-series or cross-sectional.

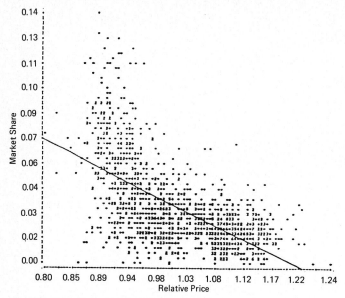

Fig. 2.14. Price Response Function Derived through a Scanner-Based Price Experiment

Regression is the most popular method to calibrate the price response function using actual market data. In the literature numerous calibrations for various models have been reported. Table 2.9 contains a selection of such studies.

Table 2.9
Econometrically Calibrated Price Response Functions Based on Actual Market Data

| Linear | Multiplicative | Attraction/ Multinomial Logit | Gutenberg |
|---|---|---|---|
| Telser (1962) | Massy-Frank (1965) | Urban (1969) | Albach (1973) |
| Weiss (1968) | Lambin (1969) | Weiss (1969) | Simon (1979c) |
| Hilse (1970) | Houston-Weiss (1974) | Bultez (1975a,b) | Simon (1982c) |
| Peles (1971) | Wildt (1974) | Jones- | Kucher (1985) |
| Houston- | Lambin et al (1975) | Zufryden (1979) | |
| Weiss (1974) | Moriarty (1975) | Guadagni-Little | |
| Prasad-Ring | Lambin (1976) | (1983) | |
| (1976) | Wittink (1977) | | |
| | Picconi-Olson (1978) | | |
| | Yon-Mount (1978) | | |

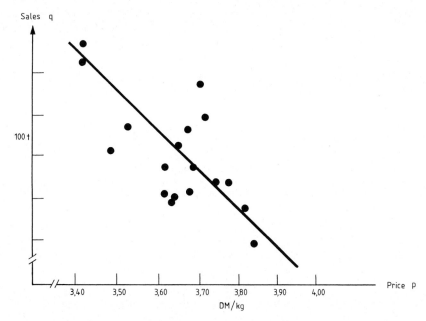

Fig. 2.15. Price Response Function for a Detergent Brand Based on Nielsen-Data

In evaluating the econometric models it is absolutely crucial to apply the "economic plausibility" test as well as the statistical criteria and to examine alternative models. There is not one unique specification or model applicable to all situations. Adjusting for specific markets and competitive conditions is imperative.

We illustrate two applications. Fig. 2.15 shows a simple linear price response function for a detergent brand based on 18 bimonthly observations (Nielsen-data). The figure demonstrates that the absolute prices show considerable variation. Therefore, the absolute price p contributes a lot to the explanation of the variance.

The linear price response function is

$$q = 3595 - 685.6p. \tag{2.15}$$

$$(4.46) \ (-3.11)$$

Price alone explains 37.72% of the variance and the coefficient of the price variable is significant at the 1%-level. At $p = 3.60$ we get a price elasticity of $-2.19$.

It is advisable to use as many explanatory variables as possible in such a model. Confining oneself to the price variable could be misleading. This is demonstrated in

*H. Simon*

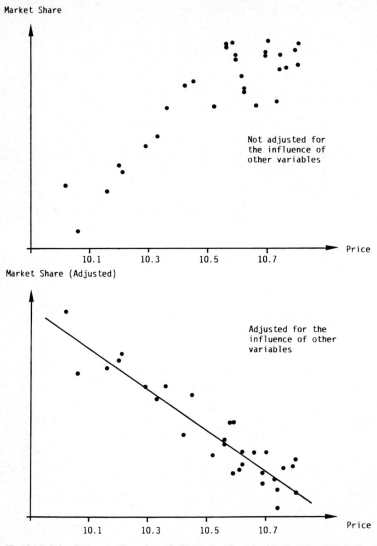

Fig. 2.16. Price Response Functions Calibrated with and without Other Marketing Mix Variables

the next example which concerns a household brand. In the upper part of Fig. 2.16 the brand's price is plotted against its market share (30 bimonthly observations).

We observe a positive correlation between price and market share, which is not intuitively appealing. If we include, however, other marketing mix variables, we obtain the following function:

$$m_i = 0.355 \tag{2.16}$$
$$(1.09)$$
$$-0.147\ p_i$$
$$(-4.04)$$
$$-0.034\ \bar{p}$$
$$(4.08)$$
$$+0.011 \quad \ln \text{ sales force}$$
$$(3.49)$$
$$+0.0002 \quad \ln \text{ advertising,}$$
$$(1.96)$$

$$R^2 = 0.9851.$$

If we adjust for the influence of the other variables, the scatterplot of price $p_i$ vs. market share $m_i$ in the lower part of Fig. 2.16 is obtained. Now the result makes sense. At a price of 10.50 the price elasticity is $-1.01$, the cross-price elasticity is 0.23. The demand for this brand is rather price inelastic. This example demonstrates that it is sometimes important to include other marketing mix variables when calibrating a price response function.

Scanners will greatly enhance the value of actual market data for price response measurements. This is mainly because a scanner can collect the data more reliably and in a more timely manner. Weekly data will more and more replace the traditional monthly or bi-monthly data. With the traditional data intervals many short-term price movements and effects remained undetected.

Fig. 2.17 demonstrates that the use of weekly and monthly data can lead to highly contradictory results on short-term price response and adjustment processes (a dynamic phenomenon).

Weekly scanner data will enable us to measure the price response much more accurately with respect to both its magnitude and its temporal pattern. This will lead to major improvements in pricing practice.

The availability of actual price and sales data varies across industries. In many industries time series data are not available. An alternative approach is to use cross-sectional data, i.e., prices and market shares of the same brand in different regions (e.g., states, sales areas, etc.). Time-series and cross-sectional data can also be combined in a so-called pooled regression.

The price analyst has to be creative in procuring actual data to measure the price response. Fig. 2.18 shows a somewhat unusual application. In this case only data on market shares and prices of nine brands in the market were available for one year.

*H. Simon*

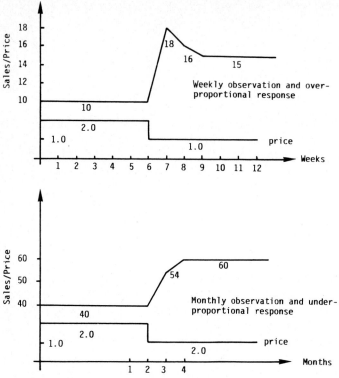

Fig. 2.17. Data Interval and Price Response Structure (Source: Kucher 1985)

The scatterplot reveals a rather strong negative correlation between the two variables (across brands).

We obtain the following multiplicative price response function (across brands):

$$\begin{array}{c}(-1.18)\\(-4.40)\\ \text{market share} = 17.16 \text{ price}\\(12.60)\end{array} \tag{2.17}$$

This function explains 74% of the variance in market shares. The *t*-coefficient indicates that price has a highly significant effect on market share. The data base is extremely limited in this case. Therefore we do not interpret −1.18 as a fully reliable estimate of the price elasticity. We can infer, however, that price is likely to play a major role in this market. The example is supposed to show that even very limited data may contain useful information on the price response.

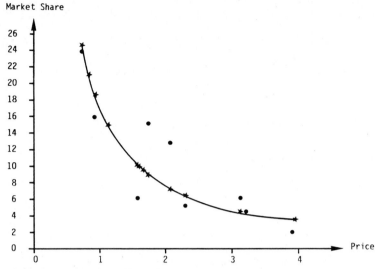

Fig. 2.18. A Calibration of Price Response across Nine Brands

We conclude this section with several guidelines for the econometric calibration of price response functions:
1. Economic plausibility is as important as statistical criteria.
2. One should start with a visual inspection of the data.
3. Alternative specifications of the variables should be tested, e.g., sales vs. market share, different definitions of the competitive price.
4. Alternative models should be tested. If the results are not too different, the simplest model should be adopted.
5. The researcher should be creative in using different kinds of data to extract price response information (time series, cross-sectional, or combinations).

Econometric calibration is a time-consuming process. In some cases this method may not lead to valid results because the data show too little variation or important variables are missing. We warn against using this method in a naive way or applying a standard model without considering the specific conditions in each case.

Summary: Actual market data are very useful in calibrating the price response function. Usually time series data are used for this purpose. But cross-sectional or pooled time series-cross sectional data can also be applied. The calibration is best done by econometric methods. It is imperative to proceed with great care and to test alternative specifications of the variables and different models. Economic plausibility and statistical criteria are equally important for the evaluation of a model. If possible, several methods should be used to cross-validate the price response functions.

Chapter 3

# Price Management under Monopolistic Conditions

## 3.1 Systems Context

In this chapter we discuss how prices should be set under monopolistic conditions. These conditions include the classical monopoly as well as the heterogeneous po-lypoly (so-called "monopolistic competition", Chamberlin 1933). In both cases the manager confines his attention to the behavior of consumers and to their response to price.

The decision maker does not need to be concerned about reactions of competitors. In monopoly, there are no competitors and thus no competitive reactions. In heterogeneous polypoly ("monopolistic competition") competitors are not percept-ibly affected by a single firm's pricing activities and therefore do not react. The absence of competitive reactions simplifies the pricing decision considerably.

In oligopoly, on the other hand, competitors are perceptibly affected by a single company's pricing. Therefore, they are likely to react and competitive reactions have to be taken into account by each company. The inclusion of competitive behavior makes the pricing decision much more complex. We discuss this case in Chapter 4.

The systems context of pricing under monopolistic conditions was illustrated in Figure 2.1. The core of the system consists of two behavioral equations, namely, the price response function and the cost function. These relations determine how price influences profit:

Price → Sales → Revenue → Profit
Price → Sales → Costs → Profit

From these relations we can see that revenue-, sales-, or market share-oriented objectives do not incorporate the full impact of price. If we want to consider all effects of a pricing action, both the revenue and the cost side must be included in the objective function. The above relations also show that the cost function and the price response function are equally relevant for pricing. Since we have already analyzed the price response function in Chapter 2, we now briefly discuss the static cost function.

## 3.2 The Static Cost Function

The cost function expresses cost $C$ as a dependent variable of the production or sales quantity $q$ (both quantities are assumed to be equal). Cost $C(q)$ is the sum of the prices times the quantities of the factors put into the production of the product,

$$C(q) = \sum_i z_i h_i(q) q, \tag{3.1}$$

where $z_i$ represents the price of one unit of factor $i$ and $h_i$ is the production coefficient of factor $i$, i.e., the number of units of factor $i$ required to manufacture one unit of the end product. Formula (3.1) shows that the causal relationship underlying the cost function is the production function as represented by $h_i(q)$. In comparison to the price response function, the cost function is relatively easier to calibrate because (1) we can rely on internal data and (2) the functional relationships are of a technical rather than a behavioral nature.

Marginal analysis plays a central role in pricing and cost accounting because optimality conditions are best expressed via marginal concepts. Changes in cost resulting from a change in production volume are denoted as marginal cost $C'$. Mathematically marginal cost $C'$ is defined as the derivative of the cost function $C(q)$ with respect to $q$

$$C' = \frac{\delta C}{\delta q}. \tag{3.2}$$

Cost functions can best be classified according to the behavior of their marginal cost $C'$. Four types of cost functions are of practical relevance:
- type A: constant marginal cost,
- type B: diminishing marginal cost,
- type C: increasing marginal cost,
- type D: first diminishing and then increasing marginal cost.

Table 3.1 contains mathematical expressions for these four cost functions. $C_{fix}$ denotes fixed cost, $k_i$ and $x_j$ are parameters.

Table 3.1
Major Types of Cost Functions

| Type | Cost Function |
|------|---------------|
| A | $C = C_{fix} + kq$ |
| B | $C = C_{fix} + kq^x, \quad 0 < x < 1$ |
| C | $C = C_{fix} + kq^x, \quad x > 1$ |
| D | $C = C_{fix} + k_1 q^{x_1} + k_2 q^{x_2}, \quad \text{where } 0 < x_1 < 1, \, x_2 > 1$ |

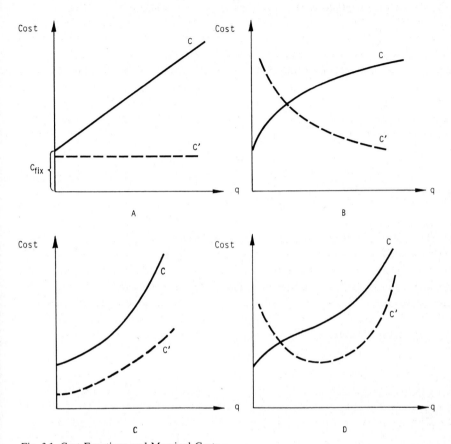

Fig. 3.1. Cost Functions and Marginal Costs

Table 3.2
Relationship between Marginal Cost, Average Variable Cost, and Average Total Cost

| Type | Marginal Cost $C'$ | Avg. Variable Cost Var. Cost/$q$ | Avg. Total Cost $C/q$ |
|------|--------------------|----------------------------------|-----------------------|
| A | constant | constant, $= C'$ | diminishing, $> C'$ |
| B | diminishing | diminishing, $> C'$ | diminishing, $> C'$ |
| C | increasing | increasing, $< C'$ | first diminishing, $> C'$ then increasing, $< C'$ |
| D | first diminishing, and then increasing | first diminishing, $> C'$ then increasing, $< C'$ | first diminishing, $> C'$ then increasing, $< C'$ |

For illustrative purposes, total costs and marginal costs are shown in Fig. 3.1.

Besides total cost $C$ and marginal cost $C'$, the concepts of average variable cost (variable cost$/q$) and average total cost $C/q$ are relevant for price management. Table 3.2 summarizes the relationships between these three.

A survey by Wied-Nebbeling (1975, p. 261) gives some idea of the practical relevance of the four functional types: 37.4% of 343 respondents chose type A and 52.4% type B as the functional type that best represents their firm's cost functions. Thus these two types account for nearly 90% of the empirically relevant cases. Types C and D are relatively unimportant.

## 3.3 Price Floors under Static Conditions

A basic problem in pricing concerns the determination of price floors. A price floor is the lowest price at which a product should be supplied or an order should be accepted. Price floors can be determined on the basis of cost alone. An unequivocal price floor can only be determined for the case of the one-product firm under static conditions. As soon as dynamic relations and/or interdependencies between products are introduced, a clear-cut price floor no longer exists. Even a price of zero does not necessarily represent the bottom line under these circumstances.

*Short-Term and Long-Term Price Floors*

In determining the price floor, it is crucial to distinguish between the long- and short-term view. In the long run, a product has to cover its full cost, i.e., variable plus fixed cost. The long-term price floor, therefore, is determined by the minimum of the average total cost. In the long run, a product should be retained only if its price is higher than its average total cost.

The situation is different in the short-term case. By definition, fixed costs are constant in the short run and must be covered to the largest extent possible. In the case of a uniform price each price higher than average variable cost covers to some extent the fixed costs. The short-term price floor, therefore, lies at the minimum of the average variable cost. The difference between price and average variable cost is called the unit contribution or the contribution margin. A product should be supplied in the short run only if it generates a positive unit contribution.

If price discrimination is possible across individual product units (as when products are made to order), the price floor is not determined by average variable cost but by marginal cost. In this case an additional order will be accepted or an additional unit will be sold as long as its price is higher than marginal cost. If – due to capacity limits – an additional order can be accepted only at the expense of the production of other products, the price floor is equal to the opportunity cost.

We can summarize our discussion of price floors in the static case as follows:
- long-term price floor:                    average total cost;
- short-term price floor:
  · with uniform price:              average variable cost,
  · with price discrimination:       marginal cost,
  · with limited capacity:           opportunity cost.

*Practical Problems of Price Floors*

While the theoretic definition of price floors is rather simple and straightforward, it can be difficult to establish price floors in practice. Problems arise, for example, when the prices of additional orders or marginal business affect the regular business. In these cases the opportunity cost may be difficult to assess.

Consider the example of an airline company. The marginal cost of a vacant seat on a regular flight is close to zero, and therefore, the short-term price floor is near zero. Since any positive price generates a positive contribution margin, this may suggest that all unoccupied seats be offered at a bargain rate, say a standby price. The problem is that some of the passengers who, without the standby option, would have paid the regular price may switch to the lower fare. The company might end up being worse off by introducing the standby tickets (or any other kind of discount).

A second practical problem concerning the price floor arises from the confusion of marginal cost with price floor and contribution margin with profit. For example, the salespeople may accept orders at too low prices. It is therefore very important that the various price floor concepts and the difference between long-term and short-term price floor be well understood by everybody involved in price decisions and price negotiations. If salespeople have pricing authority, it may make sense to withhold the information on the true price floors from them and specify a certain price level which must not be undercut.

## 3.4 Static Price Management with Rules of Thumb

"Rules of thumb" consider the systems context of static price management only partially or implicitly. They are easy to apply, and widely used in the real world. We distinguish between cost-oriented and sales-oriented rules of thumb. Various versions of cost-plus pricing belong to the former and the latter include several pricing procedures based on contribution margins or target returns.

### 3.4.1 Cost-Plus Pricing

In cost-plus pricing, price is determined by adding a markup to the average cost:

$$p = (1 + \text{markup rate}) \cdot \text{average cost}. \tag{3.3}$$

The average cost can be either average total cost or average variable cost. A quotation from a magazine for electrical engineers expresses the concept of cost-plus pricing in a straightforward way: "products must be sold for about two and a half times what they cost to make" (Nimer 1971, p. 48).

Empirical evidence indicates that cost-plus pricing is widely practiced in reality. Nagtegaal (1974, p. 5) confirms "a definite cost-orientation in pricing in Germany". As for England, Johnson (1969, p. 327) talks about a traditional "cost-plus mentality", and Alpert (1971, p. 25) states for the United States that "many firms set prices largely, and sometimes exclusively, on the basis of costs". Wied-Nebbeling's survey (1975) shows that 71.6% of 307 respondent firms use cost-plus pricing at least as a guideline.

*Arguments for Cost-Plus Pricing*

If cost-plus pricing enjoys such popularity, there must be a number of "sound" reasons for it. These include:
- it is very easy to use,
- it is based on "hard" cost data, which helps reduce the manager's feeling of uncertainty,
- a cost-plus price is easily accepted by top management or by controllers,
- in many cases, such as pricing in a supermarket where the manager must set thousands of prices, a simple pricing rule is a practical necessity,
- under competitive conditions, cost-plus pricing can be interpreted as a form of tacit collusion, particularly if the competitors apply conventional industry markup rates.

*Theoretical Evaluation*

The logical weakness of cost-plus pricing is that price is considered a function of cost, whereas the true causal relationship is just the reverse. Cost is determined by production or sales which, in turn, depend on price (see Figure 2.1). This logical fallacy of cost-plus pricing can lead to an irrational pricing policy. If the price is based on total average cost and the cost function is either type A (constant marginal cost) or type B (diminishing marginal cost), the firm might increase the price when sales decrease. We can demonstrate this easily. Suppose the markup rate is $s$, then price is

$$p = (1 + s)C(q)/q. \tag{3.4}$$

The derivative of $p$ with respect to $q$ is negative.

$$\frac{\delta p}{\delta q} = (1 + s)\frac{qC'(q) - C(q)}{q^2}. \tag{3.5}$$

The lower the sales quantity, the higher the fixed cost allocated to a single unit, and the higher the price.

As we will see in subsequent sections, price increase at a time of sales decrease is the opposite of an optimal pricing policy. When the cost function is linear, the average variable cost is independent of sales quantity. Thus if the markup is based on average variable cost in this case, price is not affected by changes in sales quantity.

Under some special conditions cost-plus pricing can lead to optimal prices. Two conditions must be met when the pricing is based on average total cost:

1. The average total cost must be independent of $q$. The cost function then is of the form

$$C = kq \tag{3.6}$$

so that $C/q = k = C'$.

2. The price response function must have the same price elasticity throughout, i.e., it must have the multiplicative form (see Chapter 2). This condition is necessary because the optimal markup is a function of price elasticity $\varepsilon$ and the optimal price is

$$p^* = \frac{\varepsilon}{1 + \varepsilon} C' = \frac{\varepsilon}{1 + \varepsilon} k. \tag{3.7}$$

We will discuss this relationship, which is called the Amoroso-Robinson Relation, in Section 3.5.

If both conditions are met and the markup is optimal, cost-plus pricing leads to the optimal price. When cost-plus pricing is based on average variable cost, condition 1 can be relaxed so that the cost function has only to be linear. In that case, average variable cost $k$ equals marginal cost $C'$ and equation (3.7) remains unchanged. These conditions are more likely to be met in retailing companies than in manufacturing.

In evaluating cost-plus calculations, we should not underestimate the significance of experience (or "tradition"). Conventional markups certainly could be the result of an "adaptive" optimization or a trial-and-error process.

*Target Return Pricing*

A pricing form widely discussed in the American literature (Deakin 1975, Edson 1959, Finerty 1971, Monroe 1979) is target return pricing. Here the markup is determined in such a way that the price yields the target rate of return $r$ on the invested capital $I$, i.e.,

$$p = C/q + rI/q. \tag{3.8}$$

We can see that this form is similar to cost-plus pricing based on total cost in all relevant aspects. It has the same weaknesses as cost-plus pricing because the price response is ignored and irrational pricing behavior may result.

Target rate pricing is widely spread in the United States (Lanzilotti 1958, Weston 1972). One reason is probably the strong ROI-orientation of many large US-corporations. The United States automobile industry reportedly practices a strict target return pricing. Detroit reacted to a 25 percent decrease in sales during the 1974–75 recession with an average price increase of $1,000 per car (Monroe 1979, p. 216).

Summary: Cost-plus pricing is theoretically acceptable only under certain conditions with regard to price elasticity and cost function. Cost-plus pricing does not explicitly consider the effect of price on sales. When sales change, this policy can lead to irrational price decisions. In the worst case it can bring disastrous results. From a practical point of view, the use of this method may sometimes be an organizational necessity, particularly for retail companies. We should at least try to differentiate markup factors in such a way that they approximately reflect the underlying price elasticities.

### 3.4.2 Pricing Based on Contribution Margins

Since the fixed cost by definition does not change over the (short) planning period, it should not influence the pricing decision. Consequently, the analysis should focus on the contribution margin. Here the criterion can be either the break-even quantity or the total contribution.

*Break-Even Analysis*
Break-even analysis proceeds as follows:
1. Set a price $p$.
2. Assume a linear cost function and compute the contribution margin per unit $d$ by subtracting average variable cost $k$ ($=$ marginal cost) from the price $p$

$$d = p - k. \tag{3.9}$$

3. Compute the break-even quantity B-E-Q by dividing fixed cost $C_{fix}$ by the unit contribution margin $d$.

$$\text{B-E-Q} = C_{fix}/d. \tag{3.10}$$

At this quantity fixed cost equals total contribution and profit is zero. To the fixed cost in (3.10) we can add a target return on the invested capital (as in the target return approach). We then get the sales quantity needed to achieve the target rate of return.
4. Evaluate (usually subjectively) whether B-E-Q is achievable or not at the given price, or if so, with what (subjective) probability.

In step 4, the price response function comes into play implicitly because management has to evaluate if $q(p) \geqslant$ B-E-Q or $q(p) <$ B-E-Q.

Table 3.3
Break-Even Quantities for Alternative Prices

| Price [$] | Contribution Margin per unit | Break-Even Quantity [Units] |
| --- | --- | --- |
| 6 | 1 | 100,000 |
| 7 | 2 | 50,000 |
| 8 | 3 | 33,333 |
| 9 | 4 | 25,000 |
| 10 | 5 | 20,000 |

If the above analysis is done for just one price, it can be used only for a yes:no-decision, e.g., whether a new product is to be introduced or not. It becomes more useful if we consider several alternative prices. In step 4, we can judge at which price the B-E-Q is most likely to be reached.

We illustrate this procedure with a simple example. The average variable cost is $5 and fixed cost amounts to $100,000. Table 3.3 shows the break-even quantities for five alternative prices.

Fig. 3.2 shows this relationship graphically.

The break-even quantity decreases exponentially with higher prices which imply higher unit contribution margins. Lower break-even quantities are not necessarily more easily achievable because they are associated with higher prices. The main weakness of break-even analysis is that it does not consider what comes after the break-even point.

Break-even analysis is a practical decision-aid for yes:no-decisions (introduction, keeping, elimination of a product, etc.). It is not very helpful for making pricing decisions because it only partially considers the price response function.

*Maximization of the Contribution Margin*

An economic criterion that makes more sense for pricing decisions than break-even analysis relates a given price to the expected total contribution. Since fixed cost is a constant, the price that maximizes the contribution also maximizes the profit. In order to determine contribution margins, we have to estimate sales quantities for alternative prices. Thus the price response function – even if only for a few discrete points – is explicitly considered. Fig. 3.3 illustrates this procedure.

From the user's point of view, contribution maximization has the advantage of being simple. We have only to calculate and compare contributions for a few alternative prices. Yet this approach has a major disadvantage. Since we consider only a few alternative prices, we cannot identity the optimal price. The optimum may not be among the alternatives considered or lie even outside the price range being considered.

We demonstrate the use of this technique with an example of a new product whose

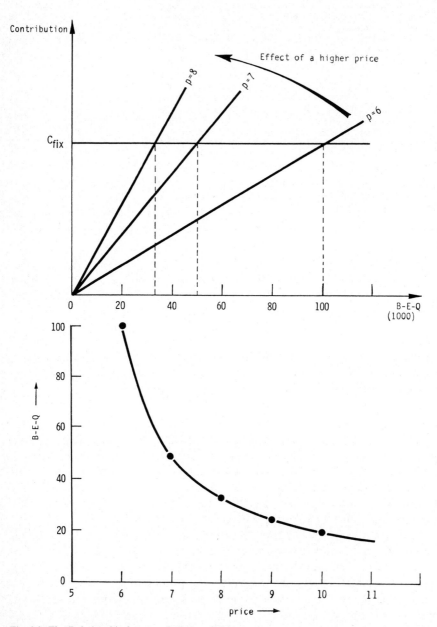

Fig. 3.2. The Relationship between B-E-Q and Price

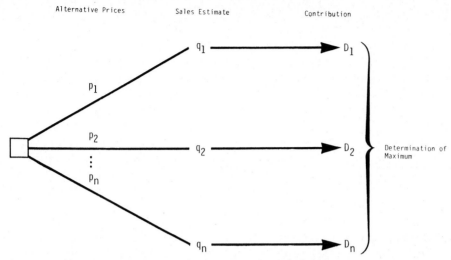

Fig. 3.3. Maximization of the Contribution by Means of a Decision-Tree

price response function was estimated subjectively by the managers. The average variable cost of this product is $0.55 and assumed to be constant. The managers considered the relevant price range to be between $1.10 and $1.50. Fig. 3.4 shows the contribution margins associated with each price level in this range. The maximum

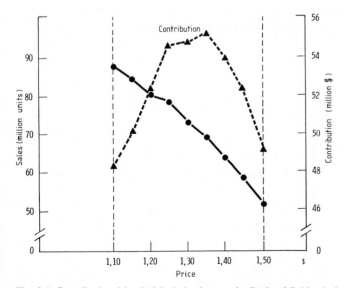

Fig. 3.4. Contribution Margin Maximization on the Basis of Subjectively Estimated Price Response Data

contribution is attained at \$1.35. The contributions at prices of \$1.30 and \$1.25 deviate so little from the maximum that we can reasonably conclude that the optimal price lies in the range of \$1.25–1.35.

According to our experience this simple method is usually well received by practitioners. The presence of the contribution margin curve as in Fig. 3.4 makes the discussion of pricing problems highly focused and less time-consuming. Divergent opinions have to be supported by hard data rather than by mere qualitative arguments.

The procedure of contribution maximization as illustrated in this example produces already close to optimal prices. The only further steps required are to explicitly specify the price response function and then to optimize the profit function.

Summary: Contribution maximization is a simple but logically correct procedure to determine the optimal price. Because of its simplicity, it is highly practical. It can be a big help just to compute and graphically illustrate contributions associated with alternative prices. However, the issue of how price affects sales is not systematically addressed. Therefore, we can't gain any insight into the general relationship between optimal price, response function/price elasticity, and cost. Such insights can be gained only with the help of analytic methods.

## 3.5 Static Price Management with Analytic Methods

### 3.5.1 General Optimality Condition

We first derive the optimality condition for a general price response function $q(p)$. Revenue $U$ is defined as price $p$ times sales $q$ so that the following revenue function is obtained

$$U = pq(p). \tag{3.11}$$

Profit is equal to revenue $U$ minus cost $C$ so that the profit function is

$$G = U - C = pq(p) - C[q(p)]. \tag{3.12}$$

Optimality conditions are best defined via the concepts of marginal revenue and marginal cost. Therefore, we derive the profit function with respect to the price $p$.

$$\frac{\delta G}{\delta p} = \frac{\delta U}{\delta p} - \frac{\delta C}{\delta p} = q(p) + p\frac{\delta q}{\delta p} - \frac{\delta C}{\delta q}\frac{\delta q}{\delta p}. \tag{3.13}$$

At the optimal price $p^*$ (3.13) equals zero, i.e.,

$$\frac{\delta U}{\delta p} = \frac{\delta C}{\delta p} \quad \text{or} \quad q(p^*) + p^*\frac{\delta q}{\delta p} = \frac{\delta C}{\delta q}\frac{\delta q}{\delta p}. \tag{3.14}$$

The left hand side of (3.14) is marginal revenue and the right hand side is marginal cost (both with respect to price). Equation (3.14) simply states that at the optimal price $p^*$ marginal revenue equals marginal cost, i.e., the positive effect of a price increase on unit contribution is exactly cancelled out by the negative effect of the price increase on sales (et vice versa).

One should note that no fixed cost term appears in equation (3.14). This proves that fixed cost should not influence the optimal price. This is an extremely important result since – according to our experience – many practitioners think that fixed cost influences the optimal price.

We can simplify (3.14) by using the price elasticity term

$$\varepsilon = \frac{\delta q}{\delta p} \frac{p}{q}.$$ (3.15)

Multiplying (3.14) by $p^*/q$, substituting $\varepsilon$ for the price elasticity term, and solving for $p^*$, we get

$$p^* = \frac{\varepsilon}{1 + \varepsilon} C',$$ (3.16)

where $C' = \delta C/\delta q$ represents the marginal cost with respect to quantity.

Equation (3.16) is called the Amoroso-Robinson Relation. Note that (3.16) generally does not represent a solution for $p^*$ but is just a transformation of the necessary optimality condition (3.14) because both $\varepsilon$ and $C'$ may depend on $p^*$. From the Amoroso-Robinson Relation we can see that $p^*$ has to be in the range where $\varepsilon < -1$. The optimal price is thus greater than the revenue-maximizing price at which $\varepsilon = -1$.

### 3.5.2 Linear Price Response Function

In the simplest case the price response function is linear, i.e.,

$$q = a - bp.$$ (3.17)

If the cost function is also linear, i.e.,

$$C = C_{\text{fix}} + kq = C_{\text{fix}} + k(a - bp),$$ (3.18)

then profit is

$$G = (a - bp)p - C_{\text{fix}} - k(a - bp).$$

Setting "marginal revenue" equal to "marginal cost", we get

$$a - 2bp^* = -kb. \tag{3.19}$$

Solving (3.19) for $p^*$, we obtain

$$p^* = \frac{1}{2}\left(\frac{a}{b} + k\right). \tag{3.20}$$

The quotient $a/b$ is the maximum price at which sales are zero (see Chapter 2). Thus in the case where both price response function and cost function are linear, the decision rule is very simple: the optimal price $p^*$ lies exactly halfway between marginal cost $k$ (equal to average variable cost) and maximum price $a/b$. When average variable cost $k$ changes, the optimal price changes only by half of the change in $k$, i.e., in this case a cost increase (decrease) should not be passed on to the customers in full.

Using the example of the detergent brand we presented in Figure 2.15, we illustrate the determination of the optimal price in the simple linear case.

The price response function was

$$q = 3595 - 685.6p. \tag{3.21}$$

The maximum price is $p^{\text{max}} = 3595/685.6 = 5.24$ DM.

Average variable ( = marginal) cost is 1.80 DM/kg. The optimum price is then

$$p^* = \tfrac{1}{2}(5.24 + 1.80) = 3.52. \tag{3.22}$$

At this price, $q = 3595 - 685.6 \times 3.52 = 1181.69$ tons are sold in a two-month period. Revenue amounts to DM 4,159,000 and variable cost is DM 2,127,000, making the gross margin DM 2,032,000. At fixed cost of DM 1,000,000 the profit is DM 1,032,000.

Price elasticity at the optimal price is $-2.04$. We can confirm the optimality by applying the Amoroso-Robinson Relation $p^* = (2.04/1.04) \times 1.80 = 3.53 \approx 3.52$.

Fig. 3.5 illustrates these relationships graphically. Price is shown on the horizontal axis. Cost is expressed as a function of price, and thus negatively sloped. Constant marginal cost with respect to price is DM $-1,204,000$; when the price decreases by DM 1, the marginal cost increases by this amount. We have to find the price where the distance between revenue and cost is maximum. It is where revenue and cost curve have the same slope, or where marginal revenue equals marginal cost.

The figure shows also why the revenue-maximizing price $p^u$ is half of the maximum price $p^{\text{max}}$. The revenue parabola is symmetric and has its maximum precisely in the middle. From (3.20) we can see that $p^u$ is attained when $k = 0$. If the

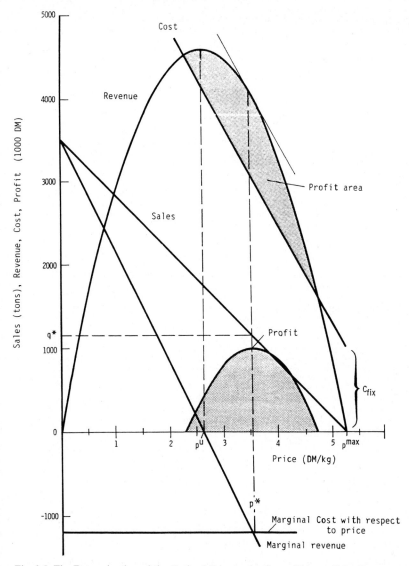

Fig. 3.5. The Determination of the Optimal Price in the Case of Linear Price Response and Cost Function

marginal cost is zero (which may be the case for software, know-how, and services), $p^u$ becomes the profit maximizing price $p^*$.

If the cost function is non-linear, the optimality condition (marginal revenue = marginal cost) still holds. However, in this case it is often difficult to find analytic solutions for the optimal price.

### 3.5.3 Multiplicative Price Response Function

The multiplicative price response function

$$q = ap^b \tag{3.23}$$

has the same price elasticity of $b$ at every point.

If the cost function is linear, i.e., marginal cost is constant and equals $k$, the Amoroso-Robinson Relation (3.16) becomes the solution for $p^*$ because the expression on the right hand side does not depend on $p$.

$$p^* = \frac{\varepsilon}{1+\varepsilon} C' = \frac{b}{1+b} k. \tag{3.24}$$

Under these conditions, cost-plus pricing on the basis of average variable cost $k$ leads to the optimal price. Fig. 3.6 shows the markup as a function of price elasticity.

### 3.5.4 Attraction Price Response Function

The optimal price which meets the Amoroso-Robinson Relation can be determined only by means of a search procedure in this case. We demonstrate the determination

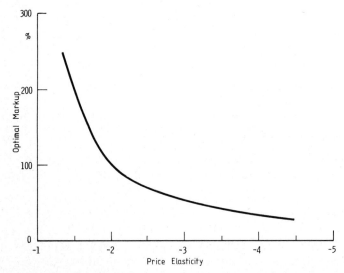

Fig. 3.6. Optimal Markup on Marginal Cost as a Function of Price Elasticity

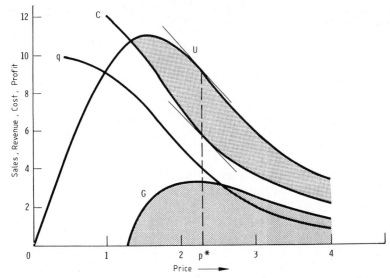

Fig. 3.7. The Determination of the Optimal Price for a Response Function of the Attraction Type

of the optimal price with the example shown in Fig. 2.6:

$$q_i = 10 \frac{p_i^{-3.5}}{p_i^{-3.5} + \bar{p}_i^{-3.5}}, \tag{3.25}$$

where the competitive price $\bar{p}$ is 2. The cost function is assumed to be linear.

$$C = 1 + 1.2 q_i. \tag{3.26}$$

By substituting (3.25) for $q_i$ in (3.26), we can make cost a function of price. Sales, revenue, cost, and profit are shown in Fig. 3.7.

Fig. 3.7 shows that the optimal price (DM 2.26) is slightly higher than the competitive price. This relation, however, cannot be generalized. The optimal market share is 39.1%. Price elasticity equals $b(1 - q_i)$ in the attraction model and is $-2.13$ at this point. We can confirm the optimality of the price via Amoroso-Robinson Relation $p^* = 2.13/1.13 \cdot 1.2 = 2.26$.

### 3.5.5 Gutenberg Price Response Function

For this function the relationship between price and profit is very complex. The profit curve can have either one global maximum or two local maxima and one minimum depending on the shape of the price response function. At all of these

Table 3.4
Parameter Values for Three Cases of the Gutenberg Model

| Parameter | Case 1 | Case 2 | Case 3 |
|---|---|---|---|
| $c_1$ | $-3$ | $-0.2$ | $-0.4$ |
| $c_2$ | 1 | 5 | 4 |
| $k$ | 1.20 | 0.65 | 0.25 |

points the general "marginal revenue = marginal cost"-condition is met. Thus it is not enough to find just one price at which marginal revenue equals marginal cost. In addition, we have to examine wether this price leads to the global profit maximum.

We illustrate three possible cases with a numerical example. We assume the following Gutenberg response function:

$$q = a - c_1 \sinh[c_2(p - \bar{p})], \qquad (3.27)$$

where $\bar{p}$ denotes the competitive price. In all examples we set $a = 10$ and $\bar{p} = 2$. We assume a linear cost function with marginal cost of $k$. The parameter values for the three cases are shown in Table 3.4.

Fig. 3.8 shows the results relevant for the pricing decision in these three cases.

The upper part of the figure shows the profit functions. In the lower part revenues $U$ and marginal revenues $U'$ are shown as solid lines, and costs $C$ and marginal costs $C'$ as broken lines. Thin vertical lines identify the profit functions' maxima and minima. They always run through the intersection of marginal revenue- and marginal cost-curves. Case 1 has one global profit maximum, while Case 2 and Case 3 have two local profit maxima. Table 3.5 summarizes the important numerical results of the three cases.

In Case 1 the price response function is only slightly curved, i.e., similar to a linear function. Therefore, only one optimum exists. In Cases 2 and 3 demand is considerably more sensitive to a big change in price than to a small change. The response function is highly curved, and this is the prerequisite for the existence of a second profit maximum at a low price.

Table 3.5
Profit Maxima of the Three Cases

| Result | Case 1 | Case 2 | Case 3 |
|---|---|---|---|
| global opt. price $p^*$ | 2.87 | 2.46 | 0.54 |
| global profit max. | 11.77 | 16.31 | 22.84 |
| local opt. price | – | 0.96 | 2.40 |
| local opt. profit max. | – | 8.72 | 19.46 |

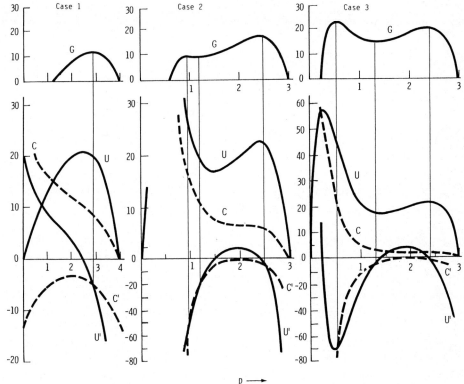

Fig. 3.8. The Three Cases of the Gutenberg Model

The cost function has also an impact on the global optimal price. If marginal cost is constant (linear cost function) at a low level or degressive (Type B from Table 3.1), the global optimal profit is more likely to be attained in the lower price range. Table 3.6 summarizes our discussion.

*Application*
    The product in question is a branded household cleanser whose sales were growing at a far lower rate than the market. Within one year its market share decreased from 13.8% to 9.5%. The price response function, estimated on the basis of Nielsen data, had the following form.

$$q = 2863 - 1045.6 \sinh[6.58(p - \bar{p})/p].$$

The market share-weighted average competitive price was DM 1.62, and the price of

Table 3.6
Qualitative Pricing Recommendations at Different Combinations of Gutenberg Price Response Functions and Marginal Costs

| Marginal cost | Price response function | |
|---|---|---|
| | slightly curved | highly curved |
| constant at high level or progressive | optimal price is high | optimal price tends to be high |
| constant at low level or degressive | optimal price tends to be high | optimal price is low |

this brand was DM 1.79. The average variable cost was DM 0.85. Fig. 3.9 shows revenue-, cost-, and profit-curves. This example corresponds to case 1, the profit function has only one maximum.

The optimal price is DM 1.56; the price-elasticity at this point is $-2.19$. We can confirm the optimality of this price by means of the Amoroso-Robinson Relation $(-2.19 / -1.19) \cdot 0.85 = 1.56$.

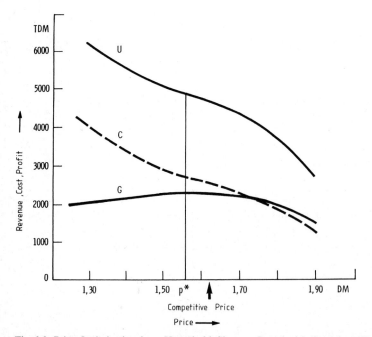

Fig. 3.9. Price Optimization for a Household Cleanser Brand with Gutenberg Function

The firm actually lowered the price by 14.5% to DM 1.53. Market share increased from 9.56% to 11.66% in the period of price reduction, and then to 16.45% in the following two months.

The calibration and optimization of the Gutenberg Model is more complex than those of the simpler functional forms. We advise to test this function under the following conditions

- if a wide price interval is considered as relevant,
- if the price response function is highly curved,
- if marginal cost is constant at a low level or degressive. Under these circumstances it is likely that a second profit optimum exists at a low price. The Gutenberg Model can help identify this profit opportunity.

Summary: In the case of a Gutenberg price response function, two local profit maxima may exist. Then the following recommendations should be observed:

1. The analysis and measurement of the price response must cover a wide interval to ensure that the lower maximum point is included.
2. In addition to the marginal revenue = marginal cost-condition we should check which of the two profit maxima is the global one.

## 3.6 Special Problems in Static Price Management

This section discusses two special topics:
- use of price to control capacity utilization,
- influence of taxes on the optimal price.

### 3.6.1 Use of Price to Control Capacity Utilization

Firms sometimes face a discrepancy between production capacity and demand. Capacity bottlenecks (demand > supply) often result from the successful introduction of new products and/or seasonal demand fluctuations.

The manufacturer has three options in this situation:
- he can let customers wait (delayed delivery),
- he can ration the supply, or
- he can set the price at a level that balances demand and capacity.

Price is the most efficient and the least costly instrument to control the claim on the capacity. If the maximum capacity $q^{max}$ and the price response function $q = f(p)$ are known, the solution to this problem is simple. First, we compute the optimal price $p^*$ and the optimal sales $q^*$. If $q^* > q_{max}$, we plug $q^{max}$ into the price response function and solve for $p$.

In this case we get additional information if we apply the Lagrange-multiplier method. We maximize the objective function under the capacity constraint

$$q^{max} - q(p) = 0. \tag{3.28}$$

The constrained objective function is

$$L = p \cdot q(p) - C[q(p)] - \mathcal{L}[q(p) - q^{max}], \tag{3.29}$$

where $\mathcal{L}$ denotes the Lagrangian multiplier, which measures how profit would change if capacity is expanded by one unit. Deriving (3.29) with respect to $p$ and $\mathcal{L}$, we get

$$\frac{\delta L}{\delta p} = \frac{\delta q}{\delta p} p + q - C' \frac{\delta q}{\delta p} - \mathcal{L} \frac{\delta q}{\delta p} = 0, \tag{3.30}$$

$$\frac{\delta L}{\delta \mathcal{L}} = q(p) - q^{max} = 0. \tag{3.31}$$

From these two equations, we can calculate $p^*$ and $\mathcal{L}$. A simple example illustrates this procedure:

Price response function:     $q = 100 - 10p$
Constant marginal cost:      $k = 4$
Maximum capacity:            $q^{max} = 25$
Unconstrained optimum:       $p^* = 7 \Rightarrow q^* = 30 > 25 = q^{max}$, Profit = 90
Constrained optimum:
   Lagrangian method:    $\delta / \delta p = -20p + 140 + 10\mathcal{L} = 0$
                      $\delta L/\delta \mathcal{L} = 25 - 100 + 10p = 0$
Result:                      $p^* = 7.5$, $q^* = 25$, Profit = 87.50, $\mathcal{L} = 1$.

The Lagrangian multiplier has a value of $\mathcal{L} = 1$, which indicates that an increase in capacity by one unit would increase the profit by one unit.

We do think that controlling the balance between demand and capacity by means of price is generally a more effective method than the other two procedures described above. Some customers may, however, resent this pricing policy because they think that the supplier takes undue advantage of his position.

If capacity is not fully utilized, the manufacturer can differentiate prices for those products that cannot be sold at "normal prices" (e.g., standby tickets of the airlines). We have discussed the possible effects of such a practice on normal business in connection with the price floor problem (Section 3.3).

### 3.6.2 Price Management and Taxes

Taxes influence the optimal pricing on the demand as well as on the supply side.

*Tax Effects on the Demand Side*
The impact of tax on the price response function has rarely been discussed in the

literature. We present a simple model. We assume that the price response function is linear.

$$q = a - b\tilde{p},\qquad(3.32)$$

where $\tilde{p}$ denotes the final "price" after deduction of the tax savings.

The following cases are practically relevant:

a. The purchase price $p$ is fully borne by consumers. In this case, $\tilde{p} = p$ and

$$q = a - bp.\qquad(3.33)$$

b. The purchase price is fully tax-deductible for consumers. If each consumer faces the same tax rate $\tau$, $\tilde{p}$ equals $(1 - \tau)p$ and (3.32) becomes

$$q = a - b(1 - \tau)p.\qquad(3.34)$$

Compared with (3.33) the slope of the response function decreases to $b(1 - \tau)$, and the maximum price increases from $a/b$ to $a/b(1 - \tau)$.

The consumer bears only part $(1 - \tau)$ of the price charged by the supplier. He, therefore, is less sensitive to higher prices or to price increases.

c. Tax deductibility is applicable up to $\bar{p}$. The amount beyond that, $(p - \bar{p})$, is totally borne by consumers. The price response function in this case is

$$q = \begin{cases} a - b(1 - \tau)p, & \text{for } p \leqslant \bar{p} \\ a + b\tau\bar{p} - bp, & \text{for } p \geqslant \bar{p} \end{cases}.\qquad(3.35)$$

d. The purchase price is not tax-deductible if it exceeds a certain level $\bar{p}$. In this case

$$q = \begin{cases} a - b(1 - \tau)p, & \text{for } p \leqslant \bar{p} \\ a - bp, & \text{for } p > \bar{p} \end{cases}.\qquad(3.36)$$

We illustrate the effects of different regulations with a numerical example.

The price response function (3.32) with respect to the final "price" $p$ to the consumer is

$$q = 1000 - 10p.\qquad(3.37)$$

The marginal tax rate of 50% is assumed to be the same for all consumers. The maximum amount for cases c or d is DM 80.

Table 3.7 shows the price response functions and the maximum prices of the four cases. The maximum prices show a wide variation between the cases. The four price response functions are presented graphically in Fig. 3.10.

In case c the price response function has a kink at $p = 80$, while in case d the sales plunge from 600 to 200 units if the price surpasses this level.

Table 3.7
Price Response Functions and Maximum Prices under Different Regulations of Tax Deductions

| Case | Tax-Deductibility | Price Response Function | Maximum Price (DM) |
|------|-------------------|-------------------------|--------------------|
| a | no | $q = 1000 - 10p$ | 100 |
| b | yes, full | $q = 1000 - 5p$ | 200 |
| c | only up to DM 80 | $q = \begin{cases} 1000 - 5p & \text{for } p \leqslant 80 \\ 1400 - 10p & \text{for } p > 80 \end{cases}$ | 140 |
| d | only if $p \leqslant 80$ | $q = \begin{cases} 1000 - 5p & \text{for } p \leqslant 80 \\ 1000 - 10p & \text{for } p > 80 \end{cases}$ | 100 |

To demonstrate the effects of different rules of tax deductions on optimal prices, we base our analysis on a linear cost function with (constant) marginal cost of $k$ so that we can apply the decision rule $p^* = \frac{1}{2}(p^{\max} + k)$.

Fig. 3.11 shows the optimal prices for the four cases as a function of marginal costs. Decision rules for cases c and d are particularly interesting. If marginal cost is sufficiently low, price is set at the tax-price limit. This price is no longer optimal if the optimal price $p^*$ for the function in the range where $p > \bar{p}$ is greater than the tax-price limit. To the right of this point, the decision rule $p^* = \frac{1}{2}(p^{\max} + k)$ holds.

If the optimal price for the functions in the range where $p \leqslant \bar{p}$ is lower than $p$,

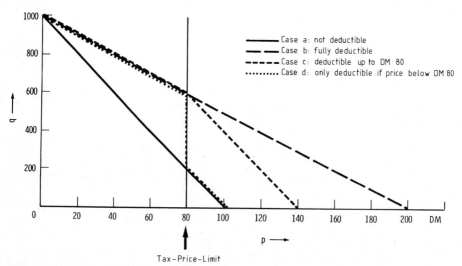

Fig. 3.10. Price Response Functions at Different Rules of Tax Deductions

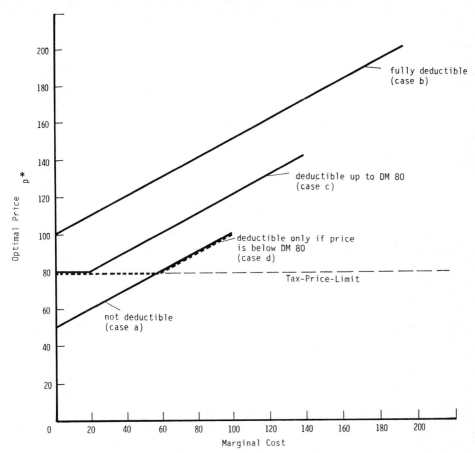

Fig. 3.11. Dependence of Optimal Prices on Marginal Cost at Different Rules of Tax Deductions (Tax Rate of 50%)

then the optimal price path has two kinks. We demonstrate this with the above example but with a lower tax rate of 20%. All other parameters remain the same. We are interested here only in cases c and d.

The price response functions are:

$$\text{case c: } q = \begin{cases} 1000 - 8p & \text{for } p \leqslant 80 \\ 1160 - 10p & \text{for } p > 80 \end{cases},$$

$$\text{case d: } q = \begin{cases} 1000 - 8p & \text{for } p \leqslant 80 \\ 1000 - 10p & \text{for } p > 80 \end{cases}.$$

Fig. 3.12 shows the optimal price paths for these cases.

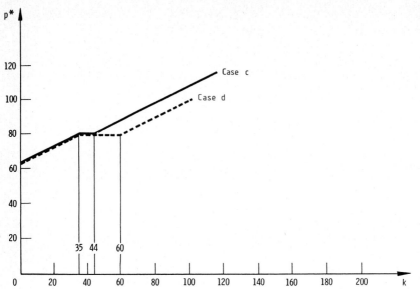

Fig. 3.12. Dependence of Optimal Prices on Marginal Cost in Cases c and d (Tax Rate of 20%)

The optimal price path is kinked at marginal costs of 35 and 44 (case c), or 35 and 60 (case d). If marginal cost is between these values, the changes in marginal cost do not lead to changes in optimal price.

Table 3.8 summarizes the generalized decision rules, where $p_1^{max}$ and $p_2^{max}$ denote the maximum prices of the price response functions below and above the tax-price limit $p$, respectively.

### Tax Effects on the Supply Side

For a manufacturer, the tax he pays is a kind of cost. The issue for him is how to incorporate the tax effects into his pricing decisions.

Taxes which are related to profit or income generally do not influence the optimal price. Taxes related to unit sales are equivalent to unit costs and simply increase the cost figure.

Table 3.8
Optimal Pricing Rules with Limited Tax-Deductibility

| Marginal Cost Interval | Optimal Price |
|---|---|
| $0$ to $2\bar{p} - p_1^{max}$ | $(p_1^{max} + k)/2$ |
| $2\bar{p} - p_1^{max}$ to $2\bar{p} - p_2^{max}$ | $\bar{p}$ |
| $2\bar{p} - p_2^{max}$ to $p_2^{max}$ | $(p_2^{max} + k)/2$ |

Taxes related to revenue have more complex effects. A sales revenue tax (in the form of a value-added tax) changes the profit function as follows:

$$G = p \cdot q(p) - C[q(p)] - \frac{\alpha}{1 + \alpha} p \cdot q(p), \tag{3.38}$$

where $\alpha$ is the rate of value-added tax.

The last term denotes the revenue tax for the total revenue. The decision rule in this case is similar to the Amoroso-Robinson Relation.

$$p^* = \frac{\varepsilon}{1 + \varepsilon} (1 + \alpha) C'. \tag{3.39}$$

The only difference of (3.39) from the original version of the Amoroso-Robinson Relation is that the marginal cost increases by $\alpha C'$.

Summary: Taxes influence the optimal pricing on the demand as well as on the supply side. In the first case they affect the price response function, and in the second case the cost function. Since the taxes have a significant impact on optimal prices, managers should consider them carefully in their pricing decisions.

## 3.7 Price Management and Inflation

In many countries inflation is a chronic phenomenon. This raises a number of issues relevant for pricing decisions. Although price increases are by definition dynamic phenomena, some of these issues can be addressed within the framework of (comparative) static analysis. In this section we discuss the following questions:
1. If the price of a production factor has increased, which cost is relevant for pricing, procurement or current cost?
2. If the inflation rate is different on the purchasing side and on the sales side, what are the implications for pricing?
3. What kind of pricing tactics are available to cope with inflation?

### 3.7.1 Procurement vs. Current Prices of the Production Factors

Factors of production often are not purchased in the same period in which they are used. Suppose a factor to be used in the current period was purchased in an earlier period and the price of this factor has increased in the meantime. Then the question arises which of these two prices represents the relevant cost for pricing, the procurement or the current? We examine this question with a simple model. We do not consider interest rates nor inventory costs because they do not affect the basic structure of the problem.

## Alternative Bases of Calculation

Suppose the factor whose price has increased was purchased in period 0 at price $v_0$. At the beginning of period 1 the remaining inventory is $R$, which is greater than what is needed in period 1. The price has increased to $v_1$. We assume constant production coefficients, and thus a linear cost function of the following type.

$$C_1 = C_{fix} + kq_1 + vhq_1,\tag{3.40}$$

where $h$ the production coefficient of the factor in question, $k$ average variable cost of the final product with respect to the other factors.

In order to determine the nominal profit, we set $v = v_0$ in (3.40). Without loss of generality, we assume a linear price response function

$$q_1 = a - p_1.$$

The optimal price on the basis of $v_0$ is then

$$p_1^P = \frac{1}{2}\left(\frac{a}{b} + k + v_0 h\right).\tag{3.41}$$

In contrast, the optimal price on the basis of $v_1 = v_0 + d$ ($d$ is the amount of the increase of the factor price) is

$$p_1^C = \frac{1}{2}\left(\frac{a}{b} + k + v_1 h\right) = p_1^P + \tfrac{1}{2}dh.\tag{3.42}$$

A simple example illustrates the differences. The assumed parameter values are:

$$a = 100,\ b = 10,\ C^{fix} = 0,\ k = 0,\ h = 1,\ v_0 = 4,\ v_1 = 5,\ R = 50.$$

Table 3.9 shows the optimal values.

The table shows that pricing on the basis of procurement price is optimal. This statement holds not only for linear but for other types of functions as well. Our discussion, however, is incomplete because it does not consider the differences in the remaining inventory of the factor though this is a direct consequence of the pricing

Table 3.9
Effects of Different Bases of Calculation

| Case | Basis of Calculation | Optimal Price $p_1$ | Sales $q_1$ | Profit (nominal) |
|---|---|---|---|---|
| P | procurement price $v_0$ | 7.00 | 30 | 90 |
| C | current price $v_1$ | 7.50 | 25 | 87.50 |

decision. In case P the remaining inventory is $50 - 30 = 20$ units, while in case C it amounts to $50 - 25 = 25$ units. This difference in inventories is important if the remaining inventory has to be evaluated at opportunity costs which are different from the procurement cost $v_0 = 4$.

Suppose, for example, the units not used in period 1 are sold at the current price $v_1 = 5$. Then the profit function is

$$G_1 = (p - k - v_0 h)(a - bp) + (v_1 - v_0)[R - h(a - bp)].  \tag{3.43}$$

This function is maximized at $P_1^C$ according to equation (3.42) and profits are:
– calculated on the basis of procurement cost $v_0$

$$G_1^P = 90 + 20 = 110,$$

– calculated on the basis of current cost $v_1$

$$G_1^C = 87.5 + 25 = 112.5.$$

Thus, pricing on the basis of current factor price is optimal. The current prices of the production factors are the right calculation basis if they represent the opportunity costs, i.e., the proceeds the company can get from the alternative use of the factors.

Summary: For factors whose prices have risen since they were purchased, their current prices are the right basis for pricing if they correspond to the opportunity costs.

### 3.7.2 Cost Inflation and Price Response Function

*Varying Inflation Rates and Net Market Position*
Inflation can affect individual industries and companies in diverse ways. Some industries (companies) are hit hard, while others are affected little. In such situations, it is of interest to a company how its purchase prices and sale prices develop over time. We call the difference in the inflation rate between a company's purchase prices and its sale prices "net market position". It represents the degree to which a company can pass on the cost increases and to which it should absorb them.

The following analysis assumes that the company has no influence on its purchase prices. Then, how the company's net market position develops would solely depend upon the change in the price response function.

*Development Inflation-Neutral*
We assume that both cost and price response functions are linear. The company purchases and uses the factors in the same period. Average variable cost increases

from $k_0$ in period 0 to $k_1 = (1+r)k_0$ in period 1. The price response function in period 0 is

$$q_0 = a - bp_0. \tag{3.44}$$

It changes in period 1 to

$$q_1 = a - b/(1+w)p_1, \tag{3.45}$$

where $w$ represents the rate of change of the maximum price, which is a measure of the customers' willingness to pay so that

$$p_1^{max} = (1+w)p_0^{max}.$$

We call the change in the price response function inflation-neutral, if $w$ is equal to $r$, the inflation rate of cost. That is, if the maximum price and, thus, the optimal price increase at the same rate as the cost, the sales quantity does not change. If $w = r$, the nominal profit also increases at this rate. The "real" profit $G_1^{real} = G_1/(1+r)$, however, remains unchanged.

### Development not Inflation-Neutral

If $w$ is not equal to $r$, the developments of cost and sales are not inflation-neutral. If $r > w$, i.e., average variable cost increases more than the maximum price, then
- optimal price increases proportionately less than cost,
- nominal profit can increase less, as much as, or more than cost,
- real profit decreases.

If $r < w$, i.e., the net market position improves, the implications are just the reverse. In this situation a company can reap windfall profits (e.g., chemical companies in the mid eighties after the decline of oil prices). But this situation is generally of a temporary nature, either customers learn about the lower procurement prices or competition takes care of the distortions.

We illustrate these relations with a numerical example. The parameter values are:

$$k_0 = 4, \quad a = 100, \quad b = 10.$$

Table 3.10 shows the optimal prices as well as the nominal and real profits.

The most important general conclusion we can draw from this table is that it is dangerous to mechanically pass on cost increases to customers.

Another aspect of price management in the inflationary situation deserves to be mentioned. When the increase in costs affects all suppliers, there is a high probability that everybody will increase prices. Under these circumstances it could well be optimal to pass on the increase in costs in full.

Table 3.10

Effects of Different Increase Rates of Cost and Maximum Price on Optimal Prices and Profits (upper figure: optimal price; figure in the middle: nominal profit; lower figure: real profit)

| Increase Rate of Maximum Price $w$ (in%) | Increase Rate of Cost $r$ (in%) | | | |
|---|---|---|---|---|
| | 0 | 10 | 15 | 20 |
| 0 | $p_1^* = 7.00$ | 7.20 | 7.30 | 7.40 |
| | $G_1 = 90$ | 78.40 | 72.90 | 67.60 |
| | $G_1^{real} = 90$ | 71.30 | 63.39 | 56.50 |
| 10 | 7.50 | 7.70 | 7.80 | 7.90 |
| | 111.40 | 99.00 | 93.09 | 87.36 |
| | 111.40 | 90.00 | 80.95 | 72.80 |
| 15 | 7.75 | 7.95 | 8.05 | 8.15 |
| | 122.28 | 109.58 | 103.50 | 97.58 |
| | 122.28 | 99.62 | 90.00 | 81.32 |
| 20 | 8.00 | 8.20 | 8.20 | 8.40 |
| | 133.30 | 120.33 | 120.33 | 108.00 |
| | 133.30 | 109.30 | 109.33 | 90.00 |

Another issue which is important in the context of pricing under inflationary conditions is how inflation affects price awareness and price response. In general, inflation will lead to higher price awareness since it becomes more rewarding for buyers to compare prices. An increasing price awareness was certainly present in the Western countries during the late seventies when inflation rates were relatively high (Gabor 1977, Ruppe and Bochtler 1977, see Chapter 7 for a discussion of price awareness).

If, however, inflation rates reach "exorbitant" levels, this relationship may no longer hold. In a study which we did in the Brazilian market where the annual inflation rates were well above 200% during the period under investigation, we found an amazingly low price sensitivity. We believe that due to the very frequent and substantial price adjustments consumers were not able to make reliable price comparisons. The normal price mechanism seems to be seriously distorted under such circumstances. In the case we investigated, the company raised its prices at a rate far lower than the inflation rate in the hope of achieving a major increase in market share. As it turned out, this strategy was a big mistake.

Summary: In inflationary times managers should carefully consider the inflation rates on the sales as well as on the cost side. Only if costs and consumers' willingness to pay rise at the same rate will the optimal price rise at this rate. Real profit then remains unchanged. In all other cases, the optimal price doesn't increase at the same rate as the cost, but either more or less than the cost.

"Normal" inflation is likely to increase price awareness and price sensitivity. Therefore, price increases should be implemented with caution. Excessive inflation may hamper consumers' price comparisons and, thus, lead to reduced price sensitivity.

### 3.7.3 Inflation and Pricing Tactics

It is advisable to employ special pricing tactics to cope with an inflationary situation.

*Contract Forms and Price Risk*

In the case of a long-term contract, arrangements have to be made between the supplier and the buyer to divide the inflation risk that might arise in the period covered by the contract. Table 3.11 lists some of such risk-sharing arrangements (Dolan 1981).

Which contract forms are preferable depends on the risk-bearing capability of both transaction parties. A general statement is not possible.

Since the other contract forms are self-explanatory, we discuss here only the clause of price indexation. Here the supplier and the buyer agree upon a base price effective at the time of the contract conclusion (or at another time). This price is adjusted according to a specified formula based on indexation. Such an adjustment may take the following form:

$$p_t = p_0(\alpha_1 m_{1t} + \alpha_2 m_{2t} + \alpha_3),$$

where $p_0$ the base price; $\alpha_1$, $\alpha_2$ proportion of the material- and labor-cost in the price; $\alpha_3$ profit proportion in the price; $m_{1t}$ index for material cost at time $t$; $m_{2t}$ index for labor cost at time $t$.

The following example illustrates the method:

$p_0 = 20,$
$\alpha_1 = 0.4, \ \alpha_2 = 0.5, \ \alpha_3 = 0.1,$
$m_{1t} = 1.06, \ m_{2t} = 1.08,$
$p_t = 20(0.4 \cdot 1.06 + 0.5 \cdot 1.08 + 0.1) = 21.28.$

Note that in this version the profit proportion is not indexed. Thus nominal profit

Table 3.11
Contract Forms and Division of Risk

| Division of Risk | Contract Forms |
| --- | --- |
| Supplier bears the total risk | – fixed price |
| ↑ | – new price negotiations when prespecified situations arise |
| | – clause of price indexation |
| ↓ | – actual price at the time of delivery |
| Buyer bears the total risk | – cost-plus contract |

Table 3.12
Actual Use of Contract Forms

| Contract Form | % of buyers who have concluded one of these contract forms with at least one supplier |
| --- | --- |
| Fixed price | 90% |
| Clause of price indexation | 39% |
| New price negotiation when pre-specified situations arise | 50% |
| Actual price at the time of delivery | 65% |
| Cost-plus contract | 20% |

remains constant but real profit decreases with higher inflation. The supplier is generally interested in indexing the profit proportion. But this often meets with the buyer's resistance (Dolan 1981).

Contracts which include a clause of price indexation should specify:
- cost items covered by indexation,
- indices to be used (they should be from reliable and neutral sources),
- the frequency of price adjustment (weekly, monthly, yearly).

Whether a clause of price indexation reduces the risk for the supplier depends on how strongly the indices and the actual costs correlate with each other. Lastly, we should mention a special problem in cost-plus contracts. Here the supplier has no incentive to minimize the costs. If his profit is proportional to the costs, he may even be motivated to maximize the costs.

Table 3.12 gives an idea of the extent to which each contract form is used (source: Long and Varble 1978, see also Allen et al. 1976).

*Other Tactics of Price Adjustment*

In inflationary times, the manufacturer may have to change the price often. This entails costs and influences sales. He should think about whether to increase the price more frequently by small amounts or less frequently by large amounts (see Chapter 6). The more often price adjustments are made, the more important it becomes to keep the adjustment cost low. Important tactics include:
- separate the information on price and the product itself (e.g., product catalogue with separate price list),
- attach price tags on the shelf rather than on the product itself (with scanners this is anyway the usual method),
- maintain a better and less costly price information system between headquarters and sales force and/or the members of the distribution channel.

The manufacturer can adjust the price indirectly by changing package size or the quantity of each product unit. He can also combine price- and quantity-modifications. Such measures may be inevitable when products are sold through vending machines which accept only a certain sum of money. Occasionally, manufacturers choose such measures in order not to surpass a certain "critical" price threshold (see Chapter 7). When the inflation is chronic, however, such tactics can be no more than a short-term stopgap because such price thresholds will be overrun anyway sooner or later.

In recent years computer and software companies have used the "unbundling" technique to implement price changes. Tactically this is similar to changing the package. Instead of charging a single price for the main product or the system and supplying other components and services free, each component is charged separately. The price of the main product is far lower than before, but the price of the whole system is higher than before.

Summary: When a contract covers a long period of time, some arrangements should be made to divide the financial risk between the supplier and the buyer. The optimal division of the risk depends upon the risk-bearing capability of both parties.

In inflationary times, managers should employ pricing tactics that ensure flexibility and low price-adjustment cost and reduce the negative effects of unavoidable price increases.

Chapter 4

# Price Management
# under Oligopolistic Conditions

## 4.1 Systems Context

We defined oligopoly as a market form where competition between individual firms is "perceptible". One firm's pricing actions affect the sales or market shares of all other firms in the market to a substantial degree.

Thus each firm's pricing moves are closely observed by all other firms, which will react with their own pricing moves – or other measures – if necessary. Since these competitive reactions in turn affect the sales and profit of the firm which initiated the pricing action, this firm should consider the impact of the competitive reaction in its pricing decisions. This interdependency constitutes the main difference between price management under monopolistic conditions (as discussed in Chapter 3) and pricing in oligopoly. The competitive reaction is of central significance for price management in an oligopolistic situation.

Fig. 4.1 illustrates the systems context. Broken arrows represent definitional equations, and solid arrows behavioral functions. The oligopolistic firm must consider three behavioral functions when it makes a pricing decision:
- the price response function whose independent variables include the firm's own price as well as competitive prices,
- the cost function,
- the competitive reaction function.

Table 4.1 illustrates the importance of competitive reactions in practice. The table tells us, for example, that 81% of the large firms surveyed think that in recessionary times their competitors will react to their own price reductions with price moves. It also shows that the reaction patterns are different depending on the directions of price change, market conditions, and the size of the firm making the price change.

Another significant finding of Wied-Nebbeling's survey (1985) is the fact that 63.6% of the respondent firms believed that within certain intervals they can change prices without provoking competitive reactions. 72% of these firms stated that such an interval is between 2 and 6%.

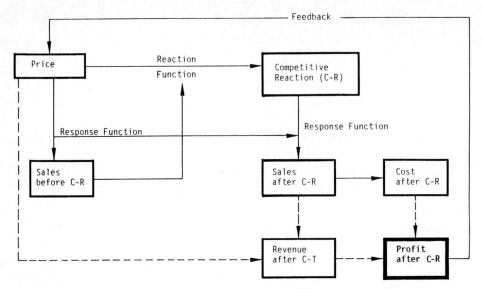

Fig. 4.1. Systems Context for the Static Pricing Decision under Oligopolistic Conditions

We first discuss various "rules of thumb" for pricing in an oligopolistic market. Then we present pricing decision rules for general response and reaction functions. In the last section, we analyze the implications of alternative reaction hypotheses.


## 4.2 Rules of Thumb

*Cost-Plus Pricing*

The procedure of cost-plus pricing can be employed in oligopoly as well as in monopoly. The weaknesses of this procedure we discussed in Chapter 3 also apply


Table 4.1

Expected Competitive Reaction to Price Changes According to Firm Size and Market Conditions (Source: Wied-Nebbeling 1985, p. 176)

| Firm Size | Price Reduction | | | Price Increase | | |
|---|---|---|---|---|---|---|
| | normal market | boom | recession | normal market | boom | recession |
| small | 42.1% | 24.1% | 69.2% | 32.3% | 51.1% | 11.3% |
| medium | 57.6 | 29.5 | 78.8 | 29.5 | 52.3 | 12.1 |
| large | 71.4 | 47.6 | 81.0 | 61.9 | 66.7 | 19.0 |

Table 4.2
Price-Leadership in the U.S. Cigarette Industry 1917–50

| Firm | Price-Leadership | | | |
|---|---|---|---|---|
| | successful | | unsuccessful | |
| | price increase | price decrease | price increase | price decrease |
| Reynolds | 8 | 3 | 0 | 0 |
| American | 2 | 3 | 2 | 0 |
| Liggett and Myers | 1 | 0 | 2 | 0 |
| Total | 11 | 6 | 4 | 0 |

here. An additional criticism in oligopoly is that this procedure doesn't consider explicitly the competitive reaction.

In some oligopolistic markets, cost-plus pricing can be considered as a means of tacit collusion among oligopolists. If all competitors apply the same or a similar conventional industry markup rate and if their costs are influenced by the same factors, which is frequently the case, then there is a good chance that the price will be close to the one that maximizes the joint profit. The reason will become clear in our later analysis.

While this situation may be desirable for the oligopolists, it is certainly undesirable from the customers' point of view because the price doesn't come down as close to cost as possible. However, such a market offers a good chance for entry to newcomers who do not adhere to the cost-plus procedures but pursue a more aggressive pricing strategy.

### Price-Leadership and Price-Followership

We can observe the phenomenon of price-leadership and price-followership in many oligopolistic markets (e.g., automobiles, cigarettes, gasoline).

Nicholls (1970) investigated successful and unsuccessful price-leaderships in the United States cigarette industry in the years 1917–1950. Table 4.2 shows the findings. In 11 out of the 17 successful cases (i.e., where competitors followed the move of the price leader), Reynolds was the price leader. American took the price leader role seven times including two unsuccessful cases. Four failure cases involved price increases. This picture is not atypical even though there are differences from industry to industry.

A prerequisite for the success of price-leadership is a certain trust in the price-leader's price management. This strategy presupposes not only the similarity of cost structures but also the price follower's assumption that the price leader's strategy is not aimed at damaging him.

Table 4.3
Cross-Price Elasticities in Different Price Ranges

| Price Range of the Brand | Deviation from the Median Price | Cross-Price Elasticity |
|---|---|---|
| High brand 4 | +7% | −1.34 |
| Medium brand 1 | +0.6% | −6.28 |
| brand 2 | 0 | −3.58 |
| brand 3 | −2.7% | −5.61 |
| Low brand 5 | −8.9% | −1.73 |

Since the pricing policy is tacitly coordinated, competitive intensity is reduced and a situation which is favorable for all oligopolists may result. Therefore, oligopolists who operate in such a system do better not disturb this equilibrium. Such systems usually collapse if new competitors enter the market, e.g., foreign entrants, generic companies, etc., or if market conditions develop unfavorably, e.g., overcapacities, declining demand, etc.

A company should not pursue the strategy of "follow the leader" naively but consider the differences in cost, quality, and perceived value of its product when setting the price. Particularly for new products this strategy can lead to highly sub-optimal results. This pricing behavior generally favors the incumbents.

*Niche Strategy*

The niche strategy aims at a deliberate differentiation from the competitors' prices. Price is set at a level where a price vacuum exists. This strategy can be effective when a sufficiently big market potential exists in the price niche not covered by competitors. If this strategy stimulates primary demand, competitors will not be appreciably affected and thus will probably not react.

Table 4.3 shows such a case from a consumer product category. The cross-price elasticities of the brands that served the high-end and low-end of the market (brand 4 and 5) are both distinctly lower than the elasticities of the brands in the middle. Within certain limits the price actions of these niche brands will not significantly affect the sales of other brands and thus competitive reactions will be less likely.

The situation is completely different when the niche price strategy attracts consumers from the segments currently served by other competitors. If the niche brand is of comparable quality but sold at a price considerably lower than that of competing brands, consumers would switch over to the new cheaper brand. The competitors would lose market share and most likely react.

# 4.3 Oligopolistic Price Management with Analytic Procedures

## 4.3.1 General Optimality Condition

*The Reaction Function*

In oligopoly the price should be set in such a way that it is optimal after the competitive reactions. Besides the price response function we must, therefore, consider the reaction function

$$p_i = r_i(p_1, ..., p_{i-1}, p_{i+1}, ..., p_n),$$ (4.1)

The reaction function $r_i$ describes how oligopolist $i$ reacts to the prices $p_1, ...., p_n$ set by his competitors. Such a competitive reaction function can be set for each individual competitor or we can adopt an aggregate form of the reaction function. Then for oligopolist $j$ the average price of competitive brands $\bar{p}_j$ (usually weighted by market share, see Chapter 2) depends on his own price $p_j$

$$\bar{p}_j = r(p_j).$$ (4.2)

In the aggregate case we have only to determine one reaction function, but possibly reactions of individual brands are not captured. A compromise between (4.1) and (4.2) would be to group the brands according to reaction pattern (e.g., private vs. manufacturer brands, branded vs. generic products, brands in the same segments vs. brands in other market segments). This is useful in markets where such sub-groups exist.

Substituting the reaction function (4.2) into the price response function (without product index)

$$q = f(p, \bar{p}),$$ (4.3)

we get

$$q = f(p, \bar{p}(p)).$$ (4.4)

*The Optimal Price*

To determine the optimal price, we derive the profit function with respect to p and set the derivative to zero

$$\frac{\delta G}{\delta p} = q + p^* \frac{\delta q}{\delta p} - C' \frac{\delta q}{\delta p} = 0,$$ (4.5)

where $C'$ is marginal cost with respect to volume.

The principle of "marginal revenue = marginal cost" remains the same in the oligopolistic case. The derivative $\delta q/\delta p$ in (4.5) differs from its counterpart in the monopolistic case in that it has an additional term that incorporates the competitive reaction. Inserting the competitive reaction term into (4.5) leads to

$$q + (p^* - C')\left(\frac{\delta q}{\delta p} + \frac{\delta q}{\delta \bar{p}}\frac{\delta \bar{p}}{\delta p}\right) = 0. \tag{4.6}$$

Multiplying (4.6) by p/q and simplifying yields

$$p + (p^* - C')\left[\frac{\delta q}{\delta p}\frac{p}{q} + \frac{\delta p}{\delta \bar{p}}\frac{p}{\bar{p}}\frac{\delta p}{\delta \bar{p}}\frac{\bar{p}}{q}\right] = 0. \tag{4.7}$$

Substituting the expressions for direct and cross-price elasticity and reaction elasticity into (4.7), we get

$$p^* + (p^* - C')[\varepsilon + r\varepsilon_k] = 0, \tag{4.8}$$

where $\varepsilon = \delta q/\delta p \cdot p/q$ direct price elasticity; $\varepsilon_k = \delta q/\delta \bar{p} \cdot \bar{p}/q$ cross-price elasticity of the brand in question with respect to the competitive price; $r = \delta \bar{p}/\delta p \cdot p/\bar{p}$ reaction elasticity of the competitive price with respect to the price of the brand in question.

The reaction elasticity $r$ represents the percentage change of the competitive price caused by a 1%-change in one's own price.

Modification of (4.8) leads to

$$p^* = \frac{\varepsilon + r\varepsilon_k}{1 + \varepsilon + r\varepsilon_k}C'. \tag{4.9}$$

Optimality condition (4.9) is a modified version of the Amoroso-Robinson Relation (3.16) where the price elasticity is adjusted for the competitive reaction. We can interpret the numerator in (4.9) as "price elasticity after competitive reaction".

If the reaction elasticity $r$ is zero or no competitive reaction is expected, the optimal price at the given competitive price can be determined via the simple Amoroso-Robinson Relation. This is the case under monopolistic competition, i.e., competition without competitive reaction. In the context of oligopoly, this price is called the Cournot- or Launhardt-Hotelling price (the no reaction-case).

The reaction elasticity $r$ is usually positive. It is particularly interesting to know how the reaction elasticity influences the optimal price $p^*$. Taking the derivative of $p^*$ with respect to the reaction elasticity

$$\frac{\delta p^*}{\delta r} = \frac{\varepsilon_k}{(1 + \varepsilon + r\varepsilon_k)^2}C' > 0, \tag{4.10}$$

we can see that the optimal oligopoly price $p^*$ moves in the same direction as the reaction elasticity $r$, i.e., the higher the reaction elasticity $r$ is, the higher is the optimal price.

Summary: The condition for the optimal price in the oligopolistic case is a modified version of the Amoroso-Robinson Relation where the price elasticity is adjusted for the competitive reaction. The markup on marginal cost is the higher, ceteris paribus,

- the smaller the direct price elasticity is in absolute terms,
- the smaller the cross-price elasticity is,
- the greater the reaction elasticity is.

### 4.3.2 Specific Functions

*Linear Price Response Function, Linear Reaction Function*

In the following discussion we specify the functions to derive concrete decision rules. First we consider the case where both price response and reaction functions are linear. The cost function is assumed to be linear.

Substituting the linear reaction function

$$\bar{p} = \alpha + \beta p \tag{4.11}$$

into the price response function

$$q = a - bp + c\bar{p}, \tag{4.12}$$

we get a price response function that is structurally similar to the monopolistic one

$$q = (a + c\alpha) - (b - c\beta)p. \tag{4.13}$$

Consequently, the monopolistic decision rule can be applied to this reaction-adjusted function, i.e., optimal price = $\frac{1}{2}$(maximum price + marginal cost). Since the reaction-adjusted maximum price is

$$p^{max} = (a + c\alpha)/(b - c\beta), \tag{4.14}$$

the optimal price is

$$p^* = \frac{1}{2}\left(\frac{a + c\alpha}{b - c\beta} + k\right). \tag{4.15}$$

Equation (4.15) shows that the optimal price rises linearly with the absolute term $\alpha$ of the reaction function and rises more than proportionally with the reaction coefficient $\beta$.

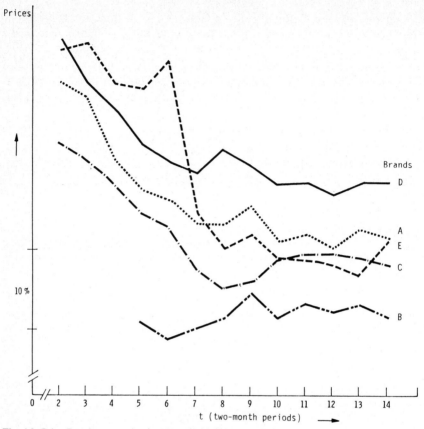

Fig. 4.2. Price Developments in the Household Cleanser Market

*Empirical Application*

Our example of the linear case is from the household cleanser market which is characterized by heavy price competition. Fig. 4.2 illustrates the price paths of five major brands. The prices of brands A, C, D, and E have developed similarly.

Table 4.4 shows the estimated coefficients of the reaction function (4.11) for these brands.

For the new brand B, the relation between $p_B$ and $\bar{p}_B$ is negative and not significant. The existing brands reacted little to the pricing actions of this new and small brand.

For an illustration, we optimize the price of brand E whose reaction coefficient $\beta$ is significantly different from one. We choose a linear price response function whose independent variable is the price difference. E's price response function is

$$q_E = 3373 - 8624( p_E - \bar{p}_E)$$
(4.16)

Table 4.4
Linear Reaction Functions for Four Household Cleaner Brands

| Variable | | $\alpha$ | $\beta$ | $R^2$ |
|---|---|---|---|---|
| dependent | independent | | | |
| $p_A$ | $\bar{p}_A$ | 0.131 | 0.927 | 0.9462 |
| $p_C$ | $\bar{p}_C$ | −0.306 | 1.284 | 0.8882 |
| $p_D$ | $\bar{p}_D$ | −0.184 | 1.037 | 0.8464 |
| $p_E$ | $\bar{p}_E$ | 0.876 | 0.436 | 0.7180 |

This function explains 59.21% of the variance in E's sales. The maximum price of E is

$$p^{max} = \frac{a + c\alpha}{b - c\beta} = \frac{3373 + 8624 \cdot 0.876}{8624(1 - 0.436)} = 2.25. \tag{4.17}$$

Since marginal cost is DM 0.85 the optimal price is

$$p^* = 0.5(2.25 + 0.85) = 1.55 \; DM. \tag{4.18}$$

If competitors react according to the estimated reaction function, they will set their average price at

$$\bar{p} = 0.876 + 0.436 \cdot 1.55 = 1.55. \tag{4.19}$$

Thus the (average) competitive price happens to be equal to $p_E$. Under these circumstances, 3,373 tons of brand E will be sold, and its contribution will be DM 2,361,000. We can check the optimality of this price using the reaction-adjusted Amoroso-Robinson Relation (4.9). Direct price elasticity and cross-price elasticity have the same absolute value of 3.96. The reaction elasticity is 0.436. Substituting these values into (4.9), we get

$$p^* = \frac{(0.436 - 1) \cdot 3.96}{1 + (0.436 - 1) \cdot 3.96} \cdot 0.85 = 1.81 \cdot 0.85 = 1.55.$$

It is interesting to compare the optimal price under competitive reaction with the result we would get if we don't consider the competitive reaction. We assume that the competitive price is given at DM 1.55. Then the maximum price for brand E is

$$p^{max} = (3373 + 8624 \cdot 1.55)/8624 = 1.94. \tag{4.20}$$

At marginal cost of 0.85, the optimal price would be

$$p^* = 0.5(1.94 + 0.85) = 1.40. \tag{4.21}$$

If competitors do not react, E would sell 4,666 tons at this price and would get a contribution margin of DM 2,567,000, which is higher than DM 2,361,000. However, if the estimated reaction function is valid, competitors would react and reduce their average price to $0.876 + 0.436 \cdot 1.40 = 1.49$. At this competitive price E sells only 4,118 tons. The contribution decreases to DM 2,265,000, which is lower than the optimal value of DM 2,361,000. This simple example thus shows that it is important to observe the competitive behavior in oligopolistic situations.

Another mathematically simple and tractable case is the case where both price response and reaction functions are multiplicative. Lambin et al. (1975) and Lambin (1976) have estimated numerous functions of this kind.

In general, we can say that simple reaction hypotheses (like the linear or multiplicative function) may simplify reality too much because they assume that competi-

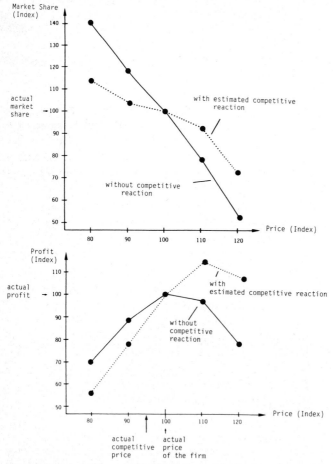

Fig. 4.3. Reaction-Adjusted Price Response and Profit Curve Derived via Subjective Judgment

tors react without considering whether the reaction is favorable or unfavorable for them. Competitors usually are not that stupid.

*Subjective Estimation of Competitive Reaction*
An alternative to econometric calibration of the competitive reaction function (based on historic price data) is to have managers subjectively estimate the competitive reaction for each price level under consideration. Based on these estimates we can then construct a reaction-adjusted price response functions.

Fig. 4.3 gives an example. Managers were asked to predict the most likely competitive price reaction for five alternative prices and then to estimate the market share response under this assumption. We see that no competitive reactions are expected if price is held constant or raised, whereas a full reaction is predicted if price is reduced to 90 or 80. As a result we get a reaction-adjusted price response with a rather steep slope for price increases and a flat slope ( = low price elasticity) for price reductions. The figure shows the market share estimates as well as the associated profits. We can see that a price increase to 110 is optimal under the most likely competitive reaction.

This subjective method is easy to apply and more flexible than the rigid reaction functions derived from market data. All aspects affecting the reactive behavior of competitors can be considered. On the other hand, the approach does not comprehensively address the problem of competitive reaction and managers tend to be more uncertain in predicting competitive reactions than in estimating sales response.

Summary: Simple reaction functions, such as the linear or the multiplicative ones, sometimes fit the empirical data well. Since they lack the theoretical foundations, however, managers should be very cautious in using them as an aid for pricing decisions. As an alternative subjective judgments can be used to include competitive reactions.

## 4.4 Reaction Hypotheses in Oligopoly Theory

The reaction models discussed so far lack theoretical foundation and are called heuristic. Normative oligopoly theories, on the other hand, do not postulate a specific reaction pattern but infer one by considering what would be optimal for the competitor in a specific situation. These theories have been heavily influenced by game theory. In order to predict a competitor's reaction, we have to put ourselves in his position and try to understand which reaction would be optimal for him. The situation is complicated further because we have to consider not only how our competitors think about their own position but also how they think about our behavior. The main purpose of the following analyses is to enhance the reader's understanding of these complex interdependencies. We first discuss only the first step, i.e., how our pricing actions affect competitors. We assume that their objective is profit maximization like ours.

### 4.4.1 Price Management in Oligopoly under Linear Price Response Functions

In order to clearly illustrate the oligopolistic relations and to obtain the analytic solutions, we posit a linear price response function in the following discussion. The oligopoly in question is assumed to be symmetric and consists of oligopolists A and B (duopoly). The price response function of oligopolist $i$ is

$$q_i = a - bp_i + cp_j, \quad i, j = A, B, \tag{4.22}$$

where $a$, $b$ are parameters, and $p_i$, $p_j$ are prices. The parameter values are $a = 1000$, $b = 50$, $c = 25$. The cost function is assumed linear, with $C_{fix} = 1000$ and marginal cost of $k = 5$. The initial price-combination is $p_{AO} = p_{BO} = 20$, with the result that sales $q_{AO} = q_{BO} = 500$ and profits $G_{AO} = G_{BO} = 6500$.

Duopolist A now reexamines his pricing policy. There are four major theoretic hypotheses about competitive reaction. We first discuss two of them from A's point of view.

*1) Cournot or Launhardt-Hotelling Hypothesis*
A assumes that B does not react and holds his price constant at $p_B = p_{BO} = 20$. A's price response function is

$$q_A = (a + cp_{BO}) - bp_A = (1000 + 25 \cdot 20) - 50p_A. \tag{4.23}$$

And A's optimal price is

$$p_A^* = 0.5((a + cp_{BO})/b + k) = 0.5(1500/50 + 5) = 17.50. \tag{4.24}$$

This price is called either Cournot price (Cournot 1838) or Launhardt-Hotelling price (Launhardt 1885, Hotelling 1929). At this price A would sell 625 units and his profit would be 6,812.5, if B did not react. Since, however, B's sales would decrease from 500 to 437.5 units and his profit would go down from 6,500 to 5,562.5, B will almost certainly react. If B reacts with a price reduction of the same magnitude as A's, i.e., from 20 to 17.50, A's price response function would become

$$q_A = a - (b - c)p_A = 1000 - 25p_A. \tag{4.25}$$

If B reacted this way, A's sales and profit would amount to only 565.5 and 6,031, respectively (worse than before the initial action). B would realize a profit of 6,031 (better than without reaction). Since B has an incentive to react and A knows this, A would not reduce his price.

Table 4.5
The Oligopoly Situation as Prisoners' Dilemma

| Options | B does not increase ($p_B = 20$) | B increases to $p_B = 22.50$ |
|---|---|---|
| A does not increase ($p_A = 20$) | $G_A = 6500$ $G_B = 6500$ | $G_A = 7437$ $G_B = 5562$ |
| A increases to $p_A = 22.50$ | $G_A = 5562$ $G_B = 7437$ | $G_A = 6656$ $G_B = 6656$ |

## 2) *Chamberlin Hypothesis*

This hypothesis, named after Chamberlin (1933), assumes that B would react to A's initial action with a price change of the same direction and magnitude. Then A's price response function is (4.25) and his optimal price becomes

$$p_A^* = 0.5(a/(b-c) + k) = 0.5(1000/25 + 5) = 22.50. \qquad (4.26)$$

At this price, A's profit is 6,656. If B reacted as assumed, he would also increase his price to 22.50 and realize an equal profit of 6,656. But if he did not react, his profit would be 7,437 and that of A only 5,562.5. If both competitors react according to the Chamberlin hypothesis, the joint profit is maximized. Note, however, that this combination does not yield the maximum profit for each individual competitor.

The situation is summarized in Table 4.5 and called Prisoners' Dilemma. If A increases his price and B doesn't follow (B has a strong incentive not to follow), A's profit decreases a lot. Thus A would rather not change his price. Only if he is sure that B will follow, he would increase his price. And if B follows suit indeed, both will end up earning higher profits than at the beginning. Still, B's incentive to follow is weak because he would do better by not following.

Only if both competitors increase the price, the joint profit is maximized. This outcome has a higher chance of happening if all oligopolists use cost-plus procedures or one is accepted as price leader and the others follow. Stigler (1947) therefore suggests that "price leadership" is a solution to this problem. It can lead to a situation satisfactory for every competitor at least when the competitors have similar cost structures and sales positions. Yet price leadership also presupposes a considerable mutual trust. These conditions are likely to be met in mature markets but hardly in growing or declining markets. Particularly, new aggressive competitors often do not adhere to well-established pricing rules and thus may disturb the equilibrium.

## *Iso-Profit Line Analysis*

To deepen our understanding of oligopolistic relations, we now use a methodology called "iso-profit line analysis" developed by von Stackelberg (1934) and refined by

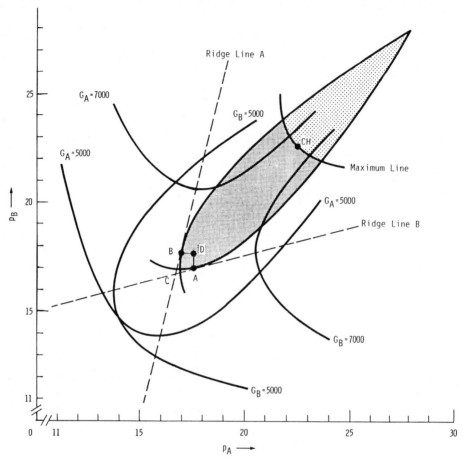

Fig. 4.4. Iso-Profit Line System for a Symmetric Duopoly with Linear Price Response and Cost Functions

Krelle (1969, 1976). This analysis is most useful for a duopoly. Iso-profit lines represent the set of price combinations ($p_A$, $p_B$) that yield the same profit for a supplier. Fig. 4.4 illustrates the situation for our example. For each supplier two iso-profit lines ($G_i = 5000$ and 7000) are shown. The great advantage of this technique is that it illustrates clearly the profit impact of each price combination ($p_A$, $p_B$) for both suppliers. Thus all consequences of a pricing move can be easily analyzed with this analytic tool.

As we said earlier, the Cournot price maximizes oligopolist $j$'s profit for a given price of oligopolist $i$, i.e., when $i$ doesn't react. The line that connects all Cournot prices is called "ridge line" and is drawn in Fig. 4.4 for A and B. It is determined via equation (4.24), i.e.,

$$p_i^C = 0.5\big((a + cp_j)/b + k\big), \quad i, j = A, B. \tag{4.27}$$

If both oligopolists behave according to the Cournot hypothesis, their prices are set at the Cournot point (also called Launhardt-Hotelling or Nash point). No supplier can increase his profit by deviating from this point as long as the other supplier sticks to it. We can get this price combination by equating the ridge line equations (4.27) of both oligopolists and solving for prices $p_A$ and $p_B$. In our symmetrical example, $p_A^C = p_B^C = 16.67$, each supplier sells 584 units and earns a profit of 5,803. This point is marked as C in Fig. 4.4.

If, on the other hand, both suppliers behave according to the Chamberlin hypothesis, the prices are determined via equation (4.26)

$$p_i^{CH} = 0.5\big(a/(b - c) + k\big) = 0.5(1000/25 + 5) = 22.50. \tag{4.28}$$

The Chamberlin point (marked as CH in Fig. 4.4) lies on the so-called "maximum line". This line represents the set of points at which supplier $j$'s profit is maximized for a given profit of supplier $i$. On this line, no supplier can improve his position without reducing his competitor's profit. This property is called Pareto-optimality.

### 3) Stackelberg Hypothesis

A third hypothesis was suggested by von Stackelberg (1934). This hypothesis postulates an asymmetric behavior. Duopolist $i$ knows that duopolist $j$ maximizes his profit under the assumption that $i$ will not react to changes in $p_j$. Thus at a given price $p_i$, $j$ rides along his ridge line. Supplier $i$ is in the "independent position", and supplier $j$ in the "dependent". Now $i$ sets his price in such a way as to maximize his profit $G_i$ after $j$'s reaction. This is at the point where $i$'s iso-profit line is tangent to $j$'s ridge line. Since supplier $j$ reacts on his ridge line, $p_j$ is a function of $p_i$. The "independent" supplier $i$ can determine his Stackelberg price by substituting the ridge line equation (4.27) for $p_j$ in his profit function and taking the derivative with respect to his price $p_i$. In the case of our example, this leads to a Stackelberg price for the "independent" supplier of $p_i^{ST} = 17.50$. The Stackelberg price of the "dependent" supplier $j$ is determined from the ridge line equation (4.27) by substituting $p_i^{ST}$ and is 16.87 in our example. Stackelberg points are marked as A and B in Fig. 4.4 (A = supplier A is in the independent position).

The profit of the "independent" supplier is 5,834, while the "dependent" oligopolist earns a profit of 6,051. The "dependent" supplier is better off than the "independent" one. This result generally holds when the ridge lines are positively sloped. Thus each oligopolist has an incentive to be in the "dependent" position. Since, however, he cannot force his competitors into the "independent" position (at least not by

Table 4.6
Prices and Profits under Different Reaction Hypotheses

| Reaction Hypothesis | Price | Profit |
|---|---|---|
| Cournot, no reaction | 16.67 | 5,803 |
| Chamberlin, full reaction | 22.50 | 6,656 |
| v. Stackelberg, independent | 17.50 | 5,834 |
| v. Stackelberg, dependent | 16.87 | 6,051 |

peaceful means), this hypothesis can hold true only in cases where an oligopolist is so small compared with his competitors that he (erroneously) assumes that they would not react to his pricing actions.

Table 4.6 summarizes the prices and profits that result from various reaction hypotheses.

### 4) Krelle Hypothesis

Krelle (1976) suggested a hypothesis that deserves attention because it explains the price rigidity in oligopoly through explicit assumptions about the actions and reactions of oligopolists. Whenever an oligopolist takes an "action" in order to maximize his profit, he takes the opponent's reaction into account. If as the result of the action his competitor is worse off after his own reaction than before, Krelle calls the action a "challenge", otherwise a "normal action". If the competitor is content with restoring his former profit position by his reaction, Krelle calls it "normal reaction". If, on the other hand, he reacts to maximize his profit, this is called "retaliation".

Unlike the classical heuristic reaction hypotheses we have discussed so far, Krelle's system of assumptions does not lead to uniquely determined solution points but to so-called equilibrium areas. An equilibrium area consists of all ($p_A$, $p_B$)-combinations at which it is not advantageous for any supplier to change his price because he would be worse off after the competitive reaction.

The actual boundaries of the equilibrium area depend on the assumptions made about action and reaction. If the oligopolists act and react according to the "normal action – normal reaction" scheme, the two ridge lines and the maximum line are the boundaries of the equilibrium area (see Fig. 4.4). If the competitors adopt the "challenge – normal reaction"-mode of behavior, the maximum line and the two iso-profit lines that go through the Stackelberg points define the equilibrium area. This area is shaded in Fig. 4.4. In the "challenge – retaliation"-case, the whole area between the two Stackelberg iso-profit lines (shaded plus dotted) consists of the equilibrium price combinations. Thus, depending on the actual behavior of the oligopolists we have smaller or wider areas of price rigidity where each player tries to avoid any action which may disturb the equilibrium.

Krelle's hypotheses are based on consistent assumptions about the behavior of oligopolists. His theory provides no guidance for the optimization of the price but it tells us under which conditions an oligopolist should refrain from touching the price. It thus convincingly explains the often observed price rigidity in oligopoly. While it is difficult to exactly determine these areas in practice, Krelle's theory makes it clear that any price move in oligopoly should be made with great care.

None of the above hypotheses is too helpful for concrete price decisions in practice. It was our goal to illustrate and to explain the extreme complexity of price management in oligopoly. In contrast to the monopoly case, there is no clear-cut and straightforward optimal solution. The competitive reaction is more difficult to predict than the response of consumers. Therefore, it is important that managers fully understand the interdependencies and the systems context of oligopolistic pricing.

*An Empirical Iso-Profit Line Analysis*

While the iso-profit line analysis is popular in price theory, we do not know of any empirical applications. The following empirical example is from a consumer goods market with five major brands. We consider the situation of the market leader A and lump together the other four brands as competitive brand B to make a two-dimensional representation possible. The competitive price $p_B$ is the market share-weighted average of the four brands' prices.

The linear price response functions are as follows:

for brand A:
$$q_A = 47540 - 29975p_A + 8400p_B, \tag{4.29}$$

for the aggregate "competitive brand" B:

$$q_B = 24857 - 33127p_B + 22745p_A. \tag{4.30}$$

Marginal cost is assumed to be $k = 1$ for all brands.

Fig. 4.5 illustrates the iso-profit line system. According to (4.27), the ridge lines are:

Ridge Line A:  $p_B = -9.235 + 7.14p_A,$ (4.31)

Ridge Line B:  $p_B = 0.875 + 0.343p_A.$ (4.32)

Table 4.7 lists the prices and profits that result from various reaction hypotheses.

The development of actual prices is marked by the arrow in Fig. 4.5. During the last five periods, prices moved only in the circled area. This circle lies between the Chamberlin point of joint profit maximization (point CH) and the Cournot point (point C). It is closer to point C and near the Stackelberg point when A is in the independent position. The circle is part of the equilibrium area for each of Krelle's hypotheses.

Supplier A could reach a higher iso-profit line by unilaterally lowering his price. Since, however, this would worsen the competitors' situation, as is clear from the

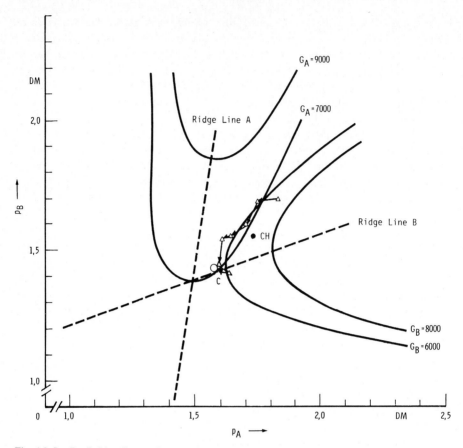

Fig. 4.5. Iso-Profit Line System for an Empirical Example

figure, competitive reaction would follow and prices would move closer to the Cournot point. On the other hand, competitors would probably not follow a price increase by A because they would be better off by not reacting. Therefore, A has little incentive to change his price. The situation is similar for B.

### 4.4.2 Price Management in Gutenberg Oligopoly

In Chapter 2 we discussed the Gutenberg price response function as an empirically particularly relevant model. It postulates an underproportional price response for small price differentials and an overproportional one for large differentials (see Figure 2.7). In Figure 3.8 we demonstrated that this hypothesis may lead to two local

Table 4.7
Price and Profit Combinations under Different Reaction Hypotheses for an Empirical Example

| Reaction Hypothesis | Prices | | Profits | | |
|---|---|---|---|---|---|
| | A | B | A | B | Total |
| Cournot, no Reaction | 1.48 | 1.38 | 7,089 | 4,866 | 11,955 |
| Chamberlin, A assumes full Reaction by B | 1.60 | 1.60 | 7,812 | 4,947 | 12,762 |
| Chamberlin, B assumes full Reaction by A | 1.70 | 1.70 | 7,603 | 5,045 | 12,648 |
| Joint Profit Maximiz. | 1.73 | 1.56 | 6,414 | 7,015 | 13,429 |
| Stackelberg with A in Independent Position | 1.51 | 1.39 | 7,130 | 5,166 | 12,296 |
| Stackelberg with B in Independent Position | 1.48 | 1.38 | 7,089 | 4,866 | 11,955 |

profit maxima each of which can be the global maximum. The case where the global profit maximum is attained at a very low price is particularly interesting. In order to show the implications of such situations we use the following price response function for Duopolists A and B

$$q_i = a - bp_i + c_i \cdot \sinh(c_2(p_j - p_i)), \quad i, j = A, B. \tag{4.33}$$

In order to facilitate the comparisons with the linear case discussed above we choose the same parameter values: $a = 1000$, $b = 25$, $c_1 = 25$, $c_2 = 0.45$, variable cost $k = 5$, $C_{fix} = 1000$. The current prices $p$, sales $q$, and profit $G$ are

$$p_A = 17, \qquad q_A = 586, \qquad G_A = 6036,$$
$$p_B = 17.50, \qquad q_B = 551, \qquad G_B = 5889.$$

Fig. 4.6 illustrates the situation.

We now assume that A reduces his price $p_A$ and B does not react. The dashed lines in Fig. 4.6 show the results:
- sales $q_A$ go up increasingly sharply (bottom part of figure),
- A's profit first goes down and then goes up (middle part),
- B's profit decreases sharply (top part).

The global profit maximum for A is attained at $p_A = 8.16$. As compared to the initial situation A's profit increases from 6,036 to 6,798 so that – if B does not react – this price move is very attractive for A. Fig. 4.5a shows, however, that the non-reaction would be disastrous for B.

Therefore, it is highly likely that B reacts with his own price reduction. Consequently the profits of both duopolists decrease to a much lower level than before. It is

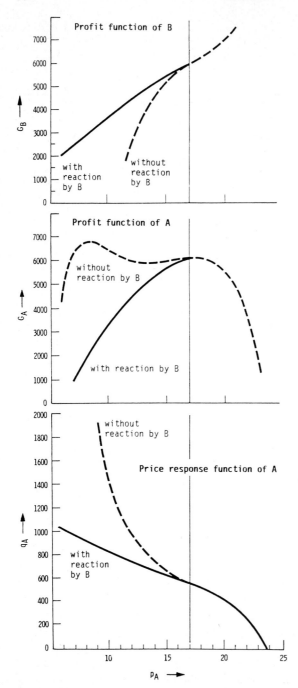

Fig. 4.6. Effects of Reaction and Non-Reaction in Gutenberg Oligopoly

very difficult to recover from such a collapse of the price structure because then the players are caught in the Prisoners' dilemma (see Table 4.5).

Summary: In the Gutenberg oligopoly, a dangerous situation can arise if not all oligopolists fully understand the complex interdependencies. If a global profit maximum exists at a low price level, the temptation to attain that profit through massive price cuts may be strong. But the competitors are forced to react in such a situation and everybody's profits will probably go down. The whole price structure collapses. It is difficult to get out of such situations (price warfare!).

Chapter 5

# Determinants of Dynamic Price Management

## 5.1 Special Problems of Dynamic Price Management

This and the next chapter are concerned with the time dimension of price management. The inclusion of dynamic aspects adds to the complexity of analysis and makes the practical implementation more difficult. On the other hand, it captures important pricing phenomena better and thus it is often a must.

Dynamics can and typically do affect various pricing determinants:
- the objective function,
- the market and competitive situation,
- the price response,
- the cost.

Firms usually strive for long-term rather than short-term profit maximization. A product's current position is not independent of the firm's past marketing activities; and current prices, in turn, influence the product's future prospects. The competitive position of a new product changes over its life cycle. New products continually come and go and existing products become obsolete. The diffusion process and the life cycle of a new product have to be considered in pricing.

Productivity and cost also change over time. Production processes typically become more efficient. Managers and workers learn from their experience in production. Due to these effects the average unit cost of a new product declines as its cumulative production volume increases. This experience or learning effect has important implications for pricing.

The complex interactions between dynamic objective function, market dynamics, price response dynamics, and cost dynamics can hardly be analyzed intuitively, making the use of analytic methods inevitable. The next four sections discuss these dynamics.

## 5.2 The Dynamic Objective Function

Our planning horizon consists of $T$ discrete periods, for each of which a price $p_t$, $t = 1, ..., T$ should be set. We call this set of prices $(p_1, ..., p_T)$ the "pricing strategy".

Under a long-term or "strategic" perspective, the firm wants to maximize the total discounted profits, i.e.,

$$\Pi_0 = \sum_{t=1}^{T} (p_t q_t - C_t)(1 + i)^{-t}. \tag{5.1}$$

If dynamic price effects exist, all prices $p_t$, $t = 1, ..., T$ should be considered simultaneously when the decision on $p_t$ is made. Wied-Nebbeling's survey (1985) suggests that the long-term profit maximization is the most relevant objective in reality. It is often critized that Western and, in particular, American companies lack this long-term orientation (see e.g., Hayes and Abernathy 1980), while Japanese companies are deeply committed to the long-term.

In (5.1) $i$ denotes the discount rate. Basically, it is determined by the return that would result from the best alternative use of the funds. Discounting has the following effects:
- the later a cash flow is generated, the less worth it is,
- the higher the discount rate $i$ is, the less valuable the cash flows in future periods are.

Thus the lower the discount rate $i$ is, the more strongly the optimal pricing strategy will favor long-term profits (et vice versa).

## 5.3 Market Dynamics

This section is concerned with two closely related dynamic processes that take place in the market: life cycle dynamics and competitive dynamics.

### 5.3.1 Life Cycle Dynamics

The product life cycle (PLC) concept is probably the most well-known and widely accepted concept to describe and explain the sales history of products or brands over time. The concept is based on the extensive empirical results from diffusion research, which suggest that individuals differ in their adoption of innovations. The hypothesis of Rogers (1983) says that the individuals are approximately normally distributed in terms of timing of innovation adoption. If we assume that each individual buys one unit of the new product, this hypothesis translates into a "typical" product life cycle which we generally divide into four stages: introduction, growth, maturity, and decline.

The PLC concept has provoked conflicting comments. Kotler (1980, p. 302) describes it as "the major concept used by marketers to interpret product and market dynamics". Many researchers, however, find little practical relevance in the concept (e.g., Meffert 1974). Others even consider it dangerous because it can easily mislead the managers to wrong decisions such as premature elimination of a product (Dhalla and Yuspeh 1976).

Most authors agree that the hypothesis of a general, s-shaped PLC is wrong. There is ample empirical evidence that no general but various life cycle types exist (e.g., Polli and Cook 1969, Cox 1967, Brockhoff 1967, Hoffmann 1972). The shape of each individual PLC is determined by situation- and product-specific causal factors. Thus general recommendations which don't adequately consider product/situation-specific conditions can be misleading (Dhalla and Yuspeh 1976). The empirical examples in Fig. 5.1 underline this point. The diverse PLC shapes in Fig. 5.1 can be explained only through a careful analysis of the underlying processes.

We should also note that some products or brands never enter the decline stage. A classic example is Aspirin, which has held a leading position for more than 70 years. In some product categories, creative marketing policies can prevent a brand from falling into obsolescence.

Two more points should be emphasized before we complete our short discussion of the life cycle dynamics. First, we need to distinguish between product and brand life cycle. Both cycles are the same only in monopoly. Typically, however, product and brand life cycles differ from each other (see a and b in Fig. 5.1). This distinction is very important because the object of marketing control and of pricing is not the product category but the brand. Second, the life cycle of a product/brand should not be viewed as a function of time but as a result of specific marketing actions as well as of competitive and environmental influences.

Summary: The life cycle concept becomes useful only when it is based on the analysis of situation-specific conditions. A strict distinction between product and brand life cycle is essential. In order to use the concept meaningfully for managerial purposes, the sales development of a product (brand) should be considered as dependent on marketing factors and not on time alone.

### 5.3.2 Competitive Dynamics

*Life Cycle and Number of Competitors*

Many authors have associated the stages of the life cycle with certain typical competitive situations. Table 5.1 summarizes some of these statements. According to these statements, the number of competitors or alternatively the competitive intensity steadily rises until the maturity stage and drops in the decline stage.

Although these claims lack empirical support in a strict scientific sense, they are plausible. Fig. 5.2 shows, as an example, how the number of suppliers for a chemical product has developed over a period of 11 years. It is noticeable that only one new supplier entered the market in the first four years, while 12 firms entered in the last two years when the product reached its maturity stage.

We observe similar patterns of entry in many innovative markets, e.g.,

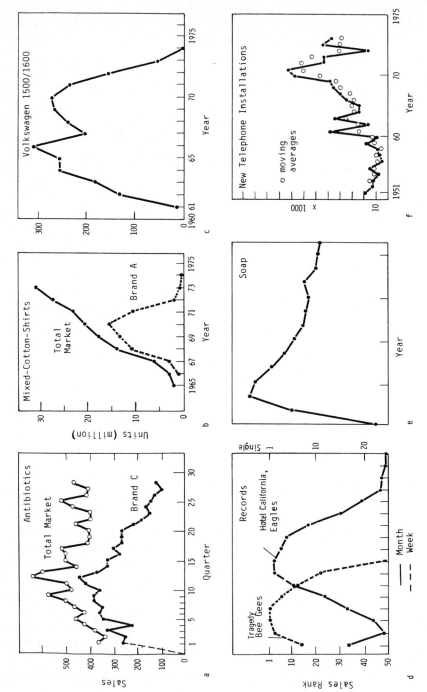

Fig. 5.1. Examples of Product Life Cycles

Table 5.1
Product Life Cycle and Competitive Dynamics

| Author | Criterion | Introduction | Growth | Maturity | Decline |
|---|---|---|---|---|---|
| Doyle (1976) Kotler(1980) | number of competitors | few | increases | many | decreases |
| Smallwood (1973) | number of competitors | few | many | many | few |
| Meffert (1974) | number of competitors | few | several | many | fewer |
| Scheuing (1970) | market form | quasi-monopoly | oligo-poly | polypoly | oligopoly |
| GfK (1973) | competitive intensity | low | intense | very intense | relaxes |

pharmaceuticals, electronics, computers, etc. A wave of new entrants typically follows such events as the expiration of patents, dissemination of know-how, or the removal of other barriers to entry.

Such an increase in the number of entrants almost always causes sharp changes in competitive intensity and pricing conditions. Frequently the competitive pressure is

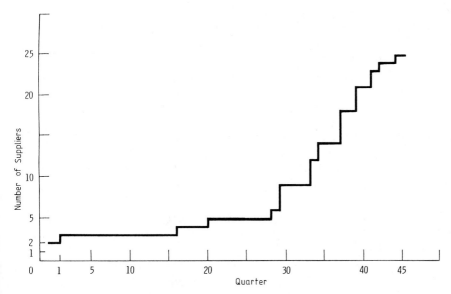

Fig. 5.2. Development of the Number of Suppliers for a Chemical Product from Introduction to Maturity Stage

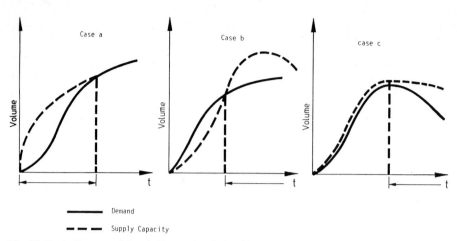

Fig. 5.3. Basic Patterns of Supply-Demand Relationships over PLC

enhanced by the aggressive pricing policies of the newcomers. This is particularly true for new foreign entrants and for companies selling generic products.

*Supply-Demand Relations*

It is important to recognize that competitive intensity does not depend solely and directly on the number of competitors but rather on the supply capacity relative to demand. When the industry capacity exceeds demand, the pressure on prices increases. This situation can happen in all PLC stages. Fig. 5.3 shows three basic patterns. Phases of high competitive intensity are marked by horizontal arrows.

Case a: Here capacity increases faster than demand, and overcapacity exists from the beginning of the PLC. Competitive pressure remains high throughout and may relax only after industry shakeout which typically results after a heavy price warfare. Examples are microwave ovens and video recorders.

Case b: Demand increases faster than capacity. Manufacturers can achieve full capacity utilization, price pressure is typically low and prices remain high in the growth stage. This situation often leads manufacturers to overestimate future demand and to expand the capacity beyond the maximum demand level in the maturity stage. Thus fierce competition characterizes the maturity stage. Examples are synthetic fibers, steel, automobiles, etc.

Case c: Here the balanced development of supply and demand is maintained until the maturity stage. A noticeable increase in competitive price pressure is expected only after the product enters the decline stage.

The relation between supply capacity and demand is probably the single most important determinant of price competition. It is, therefore, crucial that managers understand the competitive dynamics and anticipate them when developing pricing strategies.

Summary: The number of competitors and/or the competitive intensity change over the product life cycle. The price competition increases when a product moves from its introductory stage to the maturity stage. The intensity of price competition depends less on the absolute number of competitors than on the supply-demand relationship. Imbalances between industry capacity and demand can occur in all stages of the PLC. The resulting changes in price pressure must be anticipated.

## 5.4 The Dynamic Price Response Function

### 5.4.1 Dynamic Dimensions of Price Response

The inclusion of the time dimension requires a modification of the static price response function since the current price can have effects on future sales. Two possible effects are shown in Fig. 5.4. On the one hand, for many customers the past prices serve as a base of price comparison and, thus, affect the current price response. The current price assumes the same role with respect to future prices. The effect of price changes may be influenced by this initial base of comparison. On the other hand, the sales in the current period have an impact on future sales via brand loyalty and/or word-of-mouth. This dynamic relation is generally called "carryover". A sales increase in the current period due to a current price reduction may lead to higher sales in the future.

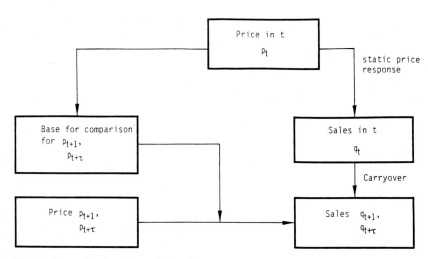

Fig. 5.4. Dynamic Dimensions of Price Response

### 5.4.2 Response Dynamics of Price Changes

There are only two kinds of pricing decisions: 1) the decision on the introductory price of a new product and 2) the decision on changes in the current price. The first decision occurs only once for each product or brand. All subsequent price decisions concern price changes. Thus managers face decisions on price change much more frequently than those on initial price.

*Price Change Response*

In static analysis, the price response depends solely on current prices. This assumption is not always realistic. In many cases the effect of a price is influenced by its relation to the price in the previous period. If consumers remember historical prices, a current price of 10 monetary units is likely to have different effects depending on whether the product's price in the previous period was 15, 10, or 5 monetary units. In the first case, the current price represents a reduction of 33%. In the second, the price has remained stable and in the last case, the consumers are faced with a price increase of 100%.

According to adaptation theory, the response to a stimulus is determined by the strength of the stimulus and its relation to the preceding stimulus. This hypothesis has been validated in numerous behavioral studies (Helson 1964, Massaro 1975). The basic principle of this theory holds also for prices. The preceding stimulus – in our case the price in the previous period – becomes the "anchor", or the reference point with which the current price is compared. The importance of the price in the previous period as anchor point is the greater and the effect of the price change is the stronger, the fewer other ways of comparison exist for consumers. This tends to be the case when there are few brands offered in the market or when the products or services are difficult to compare. For a pioneering brand, its past price is probably the only anchor point. The same is true of custom-made products and services. According to the author's experience, when the customer-supplier relationship is of an ongoing nature, current price is always evaluated against past price. This is likely to be different in mature mass markets. When there are many similar brands, consumers rather compare the prices of competitive brands and the importance of past prices decreases.

*Response Proportional to Price Change*

If we assume a linear response to the price change, we get

$$q_t = a_t - c(p_t - p_{t-1}).\tag{5.2}$$

The parameter $a_t$ captures all effects other than that of price change. The relative price change rather than the absolute one could also be the independent variable

$$q_t = a_t - c(p_t - p_{t-1})/p_{t-1}.\tag{5.3}$$

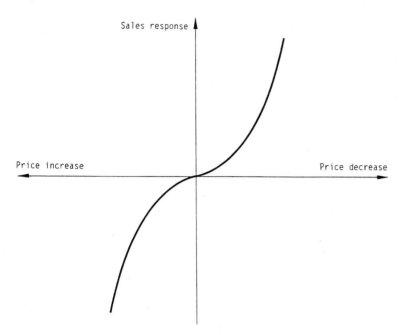

Fig. 5.5. Non-Proportional Response to Price Change

These formulations postulate a sales response which is proportional to the absolute and relative price change, respectively.

*Non-Proportional Response to Price Change*
    In many cases, it seems that small price changes cause under-proportional responses and big price changes produce over-proportional responses. This phenomenon is often observed in the sale of new products. The empirical work by Abrams (1964) shows that price reductions of less than 10% had no significant effect, while the sales increased strongly when price reductions were more than 15%. The hypothesis of non-proportional response to price changes is similar to the Gutenberg hypothesis for price differentials between competitive products (see Chapter 2). Formally a sinus-hyperbolic function can generate the shape of the curve. If we choose the relative price change as the independent variable, we get

$$q_t = a_t - c_1 \cdot \sinh\big(c_2 (p_t - p_{t-1})/p_{t-1}\big),$$  (5.4)

where $c_1$ and $c_2$ are parameters. Fig. 5.5 shows such a function with a non-proportional response to price change.

*Asymmetric Response to Price Change*

In models (5.2)–(5.4) we assume that sales respond symmetrically to price changes, i.e., price increases and price reductions have the same absolute effect on sales (with opposite signs). Empirical evidence indicates, however, that price change response may be asymmetric in some cases. This hypothesis leads to the following function

$$q_t = a_t - c_1(p_t - p_{t-1})^+ - c_2(p_t - p_{t-1})^-, \tag{5.5}$$

where $c_1(p_t - p_{t-1})^+$ and $c_2(p_t - p_{t-1})^-$ measure the sales effect of price increases and price reductions, respectively.

The following example provides an empirical illustration. Since advertising played an important role in this case, a logarithmic advertising variable $\ln A_t$ was also included and the following function was estimated.

$$q_t = 2866 + 1249.5 \ln A_t - 39.57 p_t - 40.48(p_t - p_{t-1})^-. \tag{5.6}$$
$$\quad\ (0.60)\ \ (3.75)^a \qquad\qquad (-2.36)^b (-3.12)^a$$

a, b significant at 1%- and 5%-level.

The response to price increases was not significant (it is captured by the absolute price variable). The function explained 66.4% of the variance. Fig. 5.6 illustrates this asymmetric price response function. The asymmetry of price change response can possibly be explained by marketing-mix interactions (see Chapter 12).

The calibration of price change response is difficult because the price change effect has to be separated from the effect of the absolute price level. The separation of both effects requires that there are enough data points and the correlation between the price change variable and the price level variable is not too high. For new products for which there are not enough data points, a subjective estimation is suggested.

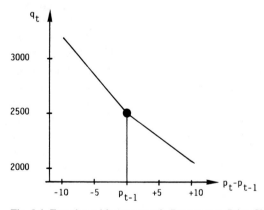

Fig. 5.6. Function with Asymmetric Response to Price Changes

*Price Expectation Effects*

Besides the effects of price changes, there is another kind of dynamic price effect which we call consumers' price expectations. We often observe situations where consumers apparently form expectations about future prices of a product.

In many consumer durables markets, a price decline is interpreted as a signal for further price declines. Consumers have observed such continuous price declines with enough regularity in the past. Actual price reductions reinforce or confirm these anticipations and do not lead to immediate purchases on the part of consumers but postponement of purchases in anticipation of even lower prices. Examples are personal computers, video recorders, calculators, compact disc players, and camcorders.

This development of price expectations is an important phenomenon for manufacturers to understand. Kucher's model (1985) includes a component that captures the expectation effect. His comprehensive analysis of scanner data shows that the expectation effect exists also with consumer nondurables. More recently Moorthy (1988) dealt with consumer durable goods and studied the effect of consumer expectations on the pricing policy of a monopolist. Yoo (1986) was the first to examine the expectation and its pricing implications for consumer durables.

*Yoo's Model*

Suppose consumers are completely certain about their predicted future prices. Then they would buy the product in the current period if the cost of waiting for one period is greater than the gain they can get by postponing the purchase of the product by one period. Mathematically expressed, they would buy when

$$U_{i,t} - U_{i,t+1}/(1+r) > p_t - p_{t+1}/(1+r), \qquad (5.7)$$

where $U_{i,t}$ consumer $i$'s utility for the product at time $t$, $r$ consumers' discount rate.

Since the present value of $U_{i,t+1}$ equals $U_{i,t}/(1+r)$, we substitute this value for $U_{i,t+1}$ and rearrange equation (5.7) to get

$$U_{i,t} > p_t + (p_t - p_{t+1})/r. \qquad (5.8)$$

When consumers have no expectations, the right hand side of (5.8) is just $p_t$.

In many cases, consumers may not be completely certain about future prices but still expect some price changes. Such uncertainty would be gradually overcome as more information necessary to predict price changes is spread and accumulated. In those cases, the right hand side of (5.8) changes to $p_t + w(p_t - p_{t+1})/r$, where $w$ represents the consumers' degree of confidence in their predicted future prices and ranges between 1 and 0; $w = 1$ represents the case of complete certainty about future prices and $w = 0$ represents the complete uncertainty case. Yoo calls $w$ "price expectation parameter".

In addition, he proposes three alternative distributions of consumers' utilities for a product. The distributions considered are exponential, uniform, and Weibull. Combining the three expectation hypotheses (complete certainty, partial uncertainty, and complete uncertainty) with the three utility distributions he develops nine alternative price-dependent diffusion models. His analysis shows that price expectations were important for three out of five product categories he examined.

Summary: In the dynamic real market, both the absolute price and its relation to the past price affect the sales. Non-proportional sales response to price changes is often observed. Consumers' expectations of future prices are an important phenomenon to be considered in strategic pricing (particularly for durables).

### 5.4.3 Carryover Effects

Carryover effects are said to exist when sales in period $t$ influence sales in future periods. The presence of these effects has important implications for strategic price management. Carryover effects operate differently for consumer nondurables than for durables because of differences in the repeat purchase patterns. Thus we discuss each category separately.

*Carryover Effects for Consumer Nondurables*
The most important determinant of carryover effects for consumer nondurables is repeat purchase behavior. Depending on the nature of the product, the motive for variety seeking and word-of-mouth are also operative. Demonstration effects generally play a minor role.

The sign and the strength of the carryover effect for a product are mainly determined by the consumers' experience with it. A satisfied consumer is more likely to make a repeat purchase than one who is not. Since such behavior takes place over time, it presupposes that consumers can remember and identify the products over time. The most important means of identification is the brand.

Formally the carryover effect for consumer nondurables can be expressed as follows:

$$q_t = \alpha q_{t-1} + \beta(Q - q_{t-1}),    \qquad (5.9)$$

where $q_t$ unit sales in period $t$, $Q$ total demand, $\alpha$ repeat purchase rate, $\beta$ rate of switch to the brand under consideration.

Equation (5.9) can be transformed into

$$q_t = \beta Q + (\alpha - \beta)q_{t-1} = a_t + \mathscr{L}q_{t-1}.    \qquad (5.10)$$

We denote the parameter $\mathscr{L} = \alpha - \beta$ as "carryover coefficient". It corresponds to the difference between the probability of repeat purchase $\alpha$ and the probability of switching $\beta$. A variety of terminology has been used for the carryover coefficient ("brand loyalty", Buzzell 1964, Wittink 1977; "repeat purchase probability", Lambin 1972, Dhalla 1978; "new buyer holdover", Kotler 1971).

The multiplicative carryover function

$$q_t = a_t q_{t-1}^{\mathscr{L}} \tag{5.11}$$

has been tested empirically as often as the additive version (5.10). The exponent $\mathscr{L}$ measures the carryover elasticity.

The carryover coefficients in models (5.10) and (5.11) are constant. This implies that brand loyalty or repeat purchase behavior does not change over time. Such an assumption is realistic only in mature markets where the market share relations are relatively stable. Since new and improved products continue to appear in the market over a brand's life cycle, the brand's ability to retain current customers and attract new ones would decrease over time and so would the carryover coefficient.

If we assume an exponential decline at the rate $(1 - r)$ first for the carryover coefficient and then for both the carryover coefficient and the base demand term $a_t$, the linear version becomes

$$q_t = a_t + \mathscr{L} r^t q_{t-1}, \tag{5.12}$$

and

$$q_t = (a_t + \mathscr{L} q_{t-1}) r^t, \tag{5.13}$$

respectively. We can interpret the parameter $(1 - r)$ as the "obsolescence rate". These time-varying carryover models are simple but flexible enough to reproduce highly different forms of life cycles (see Fig. 5.7).

### Empirical Findings

The empirical findings presented here should be viewed cautiously because their causal validity has not been completely established. Nevertheless, it is noteworthy that in almost all of the studies the carryover effect is highly significant and contributes to the variance explanation more than the marketing instruments. Table 5.2 summarizes the values of the carryover coefficient reported in the literature. The table includes time-constant as well as time-varying estimations. In the latter case, mean values were used (for details see Simon 1985).

The table suggests that the carryover coefficients are the higher
- the more "personal" the product is (cosmetics),
- the higher the perceived risk is (pharmaceuticals),
- the higher the perceived differences in taste are (beverages, cigarettes, coffee).

Summary: Carryover effects for consumer nondurables result mainly from repeat purchase behavior and brand loyalty. The carryover coefficient, which measures the

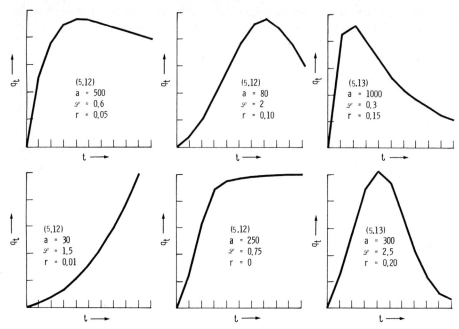

Fig. 5.7. Alternative Life Cycles Produced by Time-varying Carryover Models

Table 5.2
Empirical Values of Carryover Coefficients

| Product Category | Econometrically Estimated | | Computed from Panel Data | |
|---|---|---|---|---|
| | $n^*$ | $\mathscr{L}$ | $n$ | $\mathscr{L}$ |
| Cosmetics | 9 | 0.6344 | | |
| Pharmaceuticals | 25 | 0.6272 | | |
| Beverages | 22 | 0.6080 | | |
| Cigarettes | 48 | 0.5680 | | |
| Gasoline | 14 | 0.5630 | | |
| Coffee | 16 | 0.5044 | 12 | 0.5294 |
| Orange juice | 7 | 0.4940 | 12 | 0.3839 |
| Margarine | 25 | 0.4603 | 12 | 0.5139 |
| Detergent | 29 | 0.3832 | 12 | 0.4195 |
| Flour | | | 9 | 0.4885 |
| Ketchup | | | 8 | 0.3948 |
| Toothpaste | | | 12 | 0.3749 |
| Shampoo | | | 12 | 0.3084 |

* $n$ = number of brands

strength of this effect, can be either constant or time-varying. Empirical values of the coefficient typically range between 0.3 and 0.6 and differ substantially from one product category to another.

## Carryover Effects for Consumer Durables

Sales of new consumer durables consist mostly of initial purchases for a pretty long time after introduction. Nevertheless, the current sales affect the future sales through two mechanisms: 1) each unit sold today reduces what can be sold in the future when the market potential is considered as given and 2) the consumers who have already purchased the product actively or passively disseminate information about it, and this word-of-mouth influences the purchase decisions of those who haven't yet bought the product.

These two distinct types of influences were integrated into a diffusion model by Bass (1969). His model is given by:

$$q_t = \alpha[\overline{Q} - Q_{t-1}] + \beta Q_{t-1}[\overline{Q} - Q_{t-1}] \tag{5.14}$$

or

$$q_t = [\overline{Q} - Q_{t-1}][\alpha + \beta Q_{t-1}],$$

where $q_t$ sales in period $t$, $\overline{Q}$ market potential, $Q_t$ cumulative sales to period $t$, $\alpha$ coefficient of innovation, $\beta$ coefficient of imitation.

Equation (5.14) is to be contrasted with two older models, the pure innovation model by Fourt and Woodlock (1960) and the pure imitation model by Mansfield (1961), which are shown as below:

Fourt and Woodlock (1960): $q_t = \alpha[\overline{Q} - Q_{t-1}],$
Mansfield (1961): $q_t = \beta Q_{t-1}[\overline{Q} - Q_{t-1}].$

The basic premise of the Bass model is that the sales rate as a percentage of the untapped market potential is an increasing linear function of the number of previous adopters. In each period, innovators and imitators buy the product. Innovators purchase whether or not others buy because they are particularly interested in the new product. They are not influenced by persons who have already bought, but they may be influenced by the flow of product information. As the diffusion process continues, the relative number of innovators decreases with time. Imitators, on the other hand, buy because others have bought. It is not of any concern to them whether the earlier purchasers are innovators or imitators. The growing diffusion of a new product may give potential imitators a feeling of security with respect to the product quality, which, in turn, would strengthen their desire to acquire it. So they are influenced by the number of previous buyers and tend to increase in number relative to the number of innovators as the process continues. The shape of the resulting sales curve depends on the relative rates of these two opposite tendencies measured by two parameters, $\alpha$ and $\beta$. Here we see that the Fourt-Woodlock model is a special case of the Bass model where the coefficient of imitation, $\beta$, is zero, while the Mansfield model is another special case where the coefficient of innovation, $\alpha$, is zero.

The major drawback of these basic diffusion models is that they consider diffusion as a function of time only and the marketing program of the firm does not enter explicitly as a variable. The managers, however, would like to evaluate the effects of various marketing strategies on new product growth.

### 5.4.4 Price-Dependent Life Cycles for Nondurables

The shape of the life cycle of a brand is determined by price and non-price factors. We present several alternative dynamic price response functions which incorporate both components and discuss their effects on the life cycle. While these models are relatively simple they capture most of the essential phenomena.

*Models for Established Products*
In markets where prices and the demand level are relatively stable, carryover effect and price response change little over time. In this case, the use of a time-constant price response and carryover model is justified.

$$q_t = a + \mathcal{L}q_{t-1} - bp_t. \tag{5.15}$$

The analogous multiplicative version is also used frequently.

$$q_t = aq_{t-1}^{\mathcal{L}} p_t^{-b}. \tag{5.16}$$

If competitive influences are to be included, the price term should be represented by either the price differential or a relative price term.

If $p_t$ remains constant, the linear model (5.15) approaches an equilibrium quantity $q^e$. The level of $q^e$ can be determined by setting $q_t$ and $q_{t-1}$ equal to $q^e$ and solving for $q^e$.

$$q^e = \frac{a - bp_t}{1 - \mathcal{L}}. \tag{5.17}$$

Fig. 5.8 illustrates such an adjustment process for a price increase and a price reduction by one unit ($q_0 = 80$, $p_0 = 6$, $a = 100$, $\mathcal{L} = 0.5$, $b = 10$). Such a model is called a "partial adjustment" model. The smaller the carryover coefficient is, the faster the adjustment takes place.

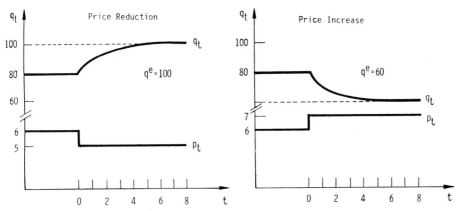

Fig. 5.8. Dynamic Price Response in a Time-Constant Carryover Model

For this function we obtain the following price elasticity values:

short-term price elasticity $-0.75$,
long-term (equilibrium) price elasticity $-1.50$.

This elasticity is related to the equilibrium quantity $q^e$. Thus, for the partial adjustment model the long-term price elasticity is greater (in absolute terms) than the short-term elasticity. The biggest advantage of a function with time-constant carryover is its simplicity. But such a function is usually applicable only for mature markets.

### Models for New Products

Time-varying carryover is particularly important for new products/brands. Parameterization in this case often has to rely on managerial judgments because of the lack of data.

A simple time-varying carryover model is:

$$q_t = a + \mathscr{L} r^t q_{t-1} - b p_t, \tag{5.18}$$

where $r$ is the "obsolescence factor".

As we said earlier, besides the absolute price level price change can have an effect on sales. If we add a non-proportional price change term (as in 5.4) to (5.18), we get

$$q_t = a + \mathscr{L} r^t q_{t-1} - b p_t + c_1 \sinh\left(c_2 (p_t - p_{t-1})/p_{t-1}\right). \tag{5.19}$$

The adjustment process of such a function is different from that of the partial adjustment model (5.15). For example, Fig. 5.9 shows the adjustment forms which result if we use the same parameter values as in Fig. 5.8 and $c_1 = c_2 = 10$, $r = 1$.

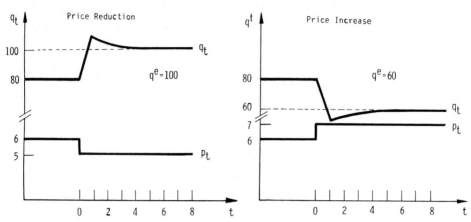

Fig. 5.9. Dynamic Price Response in a Carryover Model with Price Change Effects

Immediately after the price change a strong sales response takes place only to weaken over time. If the price is kept constant at the new level, sales approach the new equilibrium level.

Here the price elasticities are:

short-term price elasticity $-2.97$,
long-term (equilibrium) price elasticity $-1.50$.

Due to the additional price change effect the short-term elasticity is greater than the long-term elasticity.

Fig. 5.10 illustrates two adjustment processes of this kind, one for a food product and the other for a household cleanser product. Similar processes were observed for gasoline price rises and for telephone toll changes (Simon and Sebastian 1987). Based on a slightly different model and on weekly scanner data Kucher (1985) found similar dynamic response pattern for all eleven brands which he investigated. The adjustment process took usually five to seven weeks in his examples.

### A Model for Changing Markets

The time-constant price change response assumed in (5.19) is realistic only when the total market volume is stable. In a growing or declining market, however, the effect of the price change may vary with the market volume. If we assume that the price change effect is proportional to the previous sales volume $q_{t-1}$, (5.19) is modified to

$$q_t = a + \mathscr{L}r'q_{t-1} - bp_t - c_1 \sinh\left(c_2(p_t - p_{t-1})/p_{t-1}\right)q_{t-1}. \qquad (5.20)$$

This dynamic price response function is extremely flexible and can still be handled

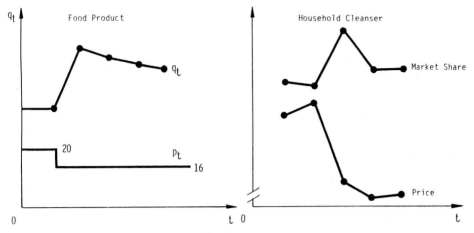

Fig. 5.10. Empirical Price Response after Price Changes

with available estimation techniques. It considers all essential effects relevant for changing markets (especially consumer nondurables), namely
- carryover,
- obsolescence,
- price level response,
- price change response,
- time-variation of various effects.

The influence of competitive prices can be incorporated by using relative prices or price differentials. As for the estimation of function (5.20), we suggest that parameters $r$ and $c_2$ be set exogenously and the function be estimated linearly. Our experience suggests that this procedure is better than the non-linear estimation. Table 5.3 shows the estimation results of this function for two new food products which were little affected by competitive products.

Table 5.3
Estimation Results for Two Food Products

| Product | $a$ | $\mathscr{L}$ | $r$ exo-genous | $b$ | $c_1$ | $c_2$ exo-genous | $R^2$ |
|---------|------|-------|------|------|--------|------|--------|
| A | 4207 | 0.56 | 0.98 | 122 | 0.035 | 10 | 0.9403 |
|   | (3.70)[a] | (3.30)[a] |  | (3.22)[a] | (2.89)[a] |  |  |
| B | 1845 | 1.33 | 0.95 | 28.0 | 0.027 | 10 | 0.9868 |
|   | (2.69)[b] | (7.28)[a] |  | (2.83)[a] | (2.21)[b] |  |  |

[a,b] significant at 1%- and 5%-level, respectively.

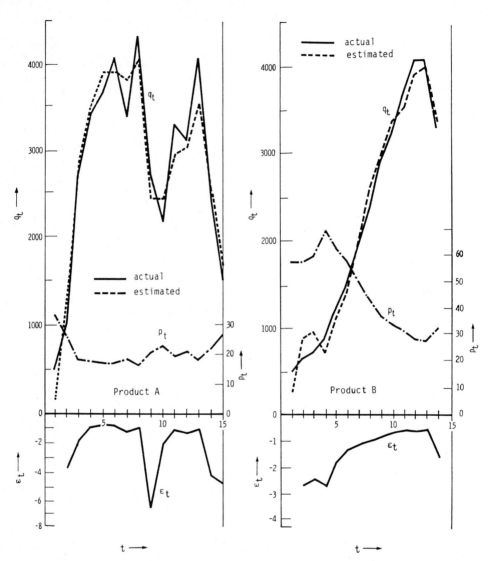

Fig. 5.11. Developments of Price, Sales, and Elasticity for Two Food Products

Fig. 5.11 shows the actual and estimated sales as well as the movements of price and short-term price elasticity. Both the table and the figure suggest that function (5.20) describes the sales history of these two products very well.

*Models for Dynamic Competitive Markets*

Many new products are only marginally better than existing products and face competition from the very beginning. In such cases, the influence of competitive prices should be incorporated in the price response function.

The Gutenberg function describes the price response under competitive situations better than other alternative functions (see Chapter 2). We suggest to combine the Gutenberg hypothesis with time-varying carryover and linear price level response to get

$$q_t = a_t + \mathcal{L}r^t q_{t-1} - bp_t - c_1 \sinh(c_2(p_t - \bar{p}_t)/\bar{p}_t), \tag{5.21}$$

where the competitive influence is captured by the relative deviation of $p_t$ from the (market share-weighted) average competitive price $\bar{p}_t$.

In (5.21), the price-deviation response is independent of the total market volume. If the total market volume changes, it is more reasonable to make the price-deviation response vary proportionally to the total market volume in the previous period $Q_{t-1}$ (analogously to 5.20). Then (5.21) changes to

$$q_t = a_t + \mathcal{L}r^t q_{t-1} - bp_t - c_1 \sinh(c_2(p_t - \bar{p}_t)/\bar{p}_t)Q_{t-1}. \tag{5.22}$$

Functions (5.21) and (5.22) as well as modified versions have been tested for many products/brands (see Simon 1979c, 1982c). The major findings can be summarized as follows:

1. In more than 80% of the tests, the results were economically plausible and econometrically satisfactory.
2. For most established products, the price level response was insignificant but the relative price to competition was important.
3. The time-varying price response function (5.22) yielded better results in 75% of the applications, which suggests that a time-constant version is too inflexible for dynamic markets.
4. More than 80% of the estimated parameters were significant at 10% or higher level.
5. $R^2$'s were higher than 0.60 in 83% of the tests and higher than 0.75 in more than 50% of the cases.

Summary: Price-dependent life cycle models for consumer nondurables must be flexible enough to be able to capture different market conditions. Two points are important in this regard: 1) which effects are to be included and 2) whether they are time-constant or time-varying. Table 5.4 shows a taxonomy of the models we discussed with regard to these two criteria. An important conclusion is that dynamic price response functions should be tailored to individual situations. Markets and products differ from each other so markedly in their response patterns and in their dynamics that each case needs to be treated specifically. In each individual case,

Table 5.4
Price-Dependent Life Cycle Models for Consumer Nondurables

| Product Situation | Carryover | | Price Response | | | | |
|---|---|---|---|---|---|---|---|
| | time-constant | time-varying | level | change | devia-tion | time-constant | time-varying |
| established product, stable market | × | | × | | | × | |
| established product, stable market, strong competition | × | | | | × | × | |
| new product, no big price change potential | | × | × | | | × | |
| new product with big price change potential and without competition | | × | × | × | | | × |
| new product with competition | | × | × | | × | | × |

several alternative hypotheses should be tested. The models we discussed should be interpreted as such alternative hypotheses and not as "master solutions".

### 5.4.5 Price-Dependent Life Cycles for Durables

There have been two major approaches to modeling the effect of price on the diffusion of consumer durables. The first approach assumes that price influences the purchase probability, whereas the second approach postulates that price affects the market potential. The first approach introduces the price effect into the diffusion model by multiplying the basic Bass model (5.14) by $f(p_t)$, a function of price to be specified, the result being equation (5.23).

$$q_t = [\overline{Q} - Q_{t-1}][\alpha + \beta Q_{t-1}] \, f(p_t). \tag{5.23}$$

We use the same notations as defined in equation (5.14).

The first characteristic of equation (5.23) is that the innovation coefficient $\alpha$ and the imitation coefficient $\beta$ are identically affected by price $p_t$. This is not intuitively appealing and contradicts the hypothesis by Rogers and Shoemaker (1971) who suggest that imitators and innovators have sharply different profiles with regard to income and price sensitivity (see also Schmalen 1979). The second characteristic is that the market potential $\overline{Q}$ is not a function of price. The market potential is assumed to be constant regardless of price changes.

An alternative approach assumes that the market potential $\overline{Q}$ depends on price (Kalish 1980, 1985). The notion that price affects the size of the market seems intuitively appealing. Prices of most new consumer durables change in real terms over time (normally decrease) and the market potential changes accordingly.

A third option is to consider the innovation and/or the imitation coefficient in the Bass model as price dependent (Simon and Sebastian 1987). This version allows for differences in price elasticities of both groups and is, thus, more versatile than (5.23).

All alternatives face the inherent difficulty of the ex ante-calibration of the parameters and, in particular, the price response.

Table 5.5 gives an overview of price dependent diffusion models. Since these models consider demand and/or cost dynamics, they are a step toward realism and managerial relevance.

The main theoretical findings from these works can be summarized as follows:
- the models provide structural insights into how price influences diffusion processes,
- depending on the form and the parameter values of the dynamic price response function highly different diffusion patterns and pricing implications are generated,
- due to the experience curve effect prices tend to decline over time.

The diversity of assumptions and implications suggests that price-dependent diffusion models be used cautiously. The models in Table 5.5 are confined to the monopolistic situation. As competition is another major influence on a brand's diffusion, the inclusion of competitive influences would significantly expand the usefulness of the analysis. The empirical investigation of price-dependent diffusion models is still in a very early stage. Generalizations are not yet feasible. Nevertheless, the available models provide valuable insights into the interactions between pricing strategy and diffusion processes.

## 5.5 Dynamics of Price Elasticity

In Chapter 3, we established that (short-term) price elasticity and marginal cost determine the (static) optimal price. The influence of these two factors remains valid under dynamic conditions and determines the development of optimal prices over time. It is, therefore, important to investigate how these two determinants change over time. In this section we discuss the dynamics of price elasticity. The next section addresses cost dynamics.

Table 5.5
Monopolistic Diffusion Models that Include Price

| Model | Demand Dynamics | Cost Dynamics | Price Response/ Major Features |
|---|---|---|---|
| Robinson and Lakhani (1975) | + | + | (5.23) |
| Spremann (1975) | + | + | general framework |
| Schmalen (1979) | + | − | price response different for innovators and imitators |
| Kalish (1980) | + | + | market potential function of $p_t$ |
| Bass (1980) | | + | (5.23) |
| Dolan and Jeuland (1981) | + | + | (5.23) |
| Jeuland (1981b) | + | − | individual uncertainty-adjusted reservation prices |
| Bass and Bultez (1982) | + | + | (5.23) |
| Jeuland and Dolan (1982) | + | + | (5.23) |
| Clarke, Darrough, and Heineke (1982) | + | + | general framework |
| Kalish (1983) | + | + | general framework |
| Kalish (1985) | + | + | market potential function of $p_t$ |
| Yoo (1986) | + | − | price expectations |
| Simon and Sebastian (1987) | + | − | only imitators' demand price-dependent |

*Some General Thoughts on Price Elasticity*

To examine how the price elasticity changes over time, it is useful to analyze its components. The price elasticity

$$\varepsilon_t = \frac{\delta q_t}{\delta p_t} \frac{p_t}{q_t}$$

consists of three components:
– the absolute price response $\delta q_t / \delta p_t$,
– the (unit) sales $q_t$,
– the price $p_t$.

If $\delta q_t / \delta p_t$ and $p_t$ remain constant, $\varepsilon_t$ would decrease as long as sales $q_t$ increase and vice versa. Price tends to decrease over the life cycle (experience curve!). This would accelerate the fall of the elasticity.

Some authors (e.g., Mickwitz 1959) contend that price elasticity increases (in absolute terms) during the upswing stages of the life cycle. If this is to be true,
- the price response $\delta q_t / \delta p_t$ should rise faster than the sales when price remains constant. At typical sales increase rates (often sales rise 10, 20, or 100 times), this is unrealistic;
- when price falls, $\delta q_t / \delta p_t$ should go up faster than $p_t / q_t$ goes down. This is also unlikely particularly when experience curve effects are strong (the prices of calculators and quartz-watches fell by factors of 100 and more in less than five years).

It is often ignored that the price elasticity is a relative measure. If a price reduction of 10% causes sales to increase from 10 to 14 units in the introduction stage, then the price elasticity is $-4$. Later when the unit sales amount to, say, 1,000, the same price reduction should increase sales by 400 units, if price elasticity is to remain $-4$. Such a development is – at least under a stable market structure – unlikely.

When the market structure and the competitive intensity change strongly, which typically happens over the life cycle of new product categories, the above statement should be modified. For a pioneer product/a genuine innovation, the price elasticity is equal to the primary demand elasticity. After competitive entries, the price elasticity becomes the sum of primary and cross price elasticity (see Chapter 2) and is probably bigger than the (primary) price elasticity in the monopolistic stage. In addition, over the life cycle the products are continuously being improved and standardized. The products are viewed as more homogeneous by consumers. The consumers' willingness to pay a premium for a specific brand goes down, i.e., the cross-price elasticity goes up.

*Empirical Findings*

Simon (1979c) reports the developments of price elasticities of 35 brands over their life cycles. The elasticities are calculated on the basis of the estimated price response functions using the actual price and sales data. After demarcating each stage in the life cycle based on the visual inspection of the sales curves, he did two kinds of analysis: i) cross-sectional analysis, i.e., comparison of the elasticity change rates for those brands which were in the same (life cycle) stage in the last observation period and ii) longitudinal analysis, i.e., how the price elasticity of the same brand develops in two consecutive life cycle stages.

The cross-sectional analysis revealed:
- price elasticity fell for all growth products,
- price elasticity rose for all declining products,
- price elasticity changed less for mature products than for both growth and decline products (2 exceptions).

The longitudinal analysis showed that (absolute) price elasticity:
- was greater in the introduction than in the growth stage in 95% of the cases,
- was greater in the growth than in the maturity stage in 71% of the cases,
- was smaller in the maturity than in the decline stage in 100% of the cases.

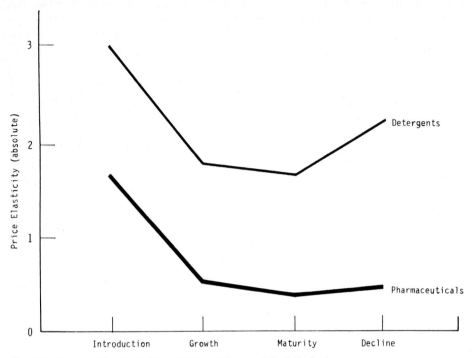

Fig. 5.12. Average Price Elasticities at Different Stages of the Life Cycle

Fig. 5.12 illustrates the findings. In short, these findings show that the elasticity goes down in the introduction and growth stages to reach its minimum in the maturity stage and goes up again in the decline stage. This pattern conflicts with what is suggested in the literature (Mickwitz 1959). But this result is not surprising considering what we said above on the development of the price elasticity components. Since this analysis was done for markets whose competitive structure remained relatively stable during the data periods, it is not clear whether the findings would hold for those products which experience bigger changes in the competitive structure. We presume that for real innovations the price elasticity increases when the product goes from the monopolistic introductory/growth stage into the competitive maturity stage. In the decline stage, price elasticity should increase further.

Summary: An empirical analysis shows that in almost all cases the price elasticity decreases in the growth stage, reaches its minimum in the maturity stage, and increases again in the decline stage. These results hold when competitive conditions remain relatively constant. We expect a pattern of increasing price elasticity from introduction to maturity when the number of competitors and the competitive pressure increase over time. This issue is empirically not well researched.

## 5.6 Cost Dynamics

Costs are affected by changes in the sales and production volume over the life cycle. If sales volume increases in the upswing stage of the life cycle and economies of scale exist, the unit variable cost goes down. According to the Amoroso-Robinson Relation (3.16), this leads, ceteris paribus, to a decline of the optimal price. The reverse is true for the decline phase of the life cycle. Larger volumes also lead to lower fixed costs per unit. However, this phenomenon does not affect the optimal price, since the latter is independent of the fixed costs.

For dynamic pricing, the intertemporal cost effects are of greater relevance than the (static) economies of scale. As a company gains experience in manufacturing and marketing, the unit costs typically go down. Unlike the economies of scale, which is basically a static phenomenon achievable simply by installing and operating a sufficiently large and efficient capacity, the experience effect is directly associated with time. Learning requires time and an experience advantage over competition is essentially a time advantage.

The best proxy variable for learning/experience is the cumulative production volume. The relationship between the cumulative volume and (deflated) unit cost is called the learning or experience curve. These two terms are not always used in the same sense (Yelle 1979). Though detected already back in 1936 for airplane production, it was not until the 1970's that the experience curve concept gained wide acceptance in the management world. The Boston Consulting Group (1970) put the concept in a simple form: Each time cumulative production volume of a product doubles, (deflated) unit costs fall by a constant percentage $\alpha$, the learning rate. This concept of the experience curve has had a strong impact on management thinking in the 70's and early 80's. It is known that companies like Texas Instruments, National Semiconductor, and particularly Japanese firms have successfully based their strategies on this concept. Reportedly National Semiconductor "has made a fetish of forcing down production costs...and it moves with lethal speed to slash prices, gobble up market share and drive competitors from the field" (Fortune, January 12, 1981, p. 92). Another article calls the experience curve "one of the most reliable relationships in industrial economics" and "the most powerful of all industrial weapons" (Fortune, July 28, 1980, p. 55).

The experience curve effects have the greatest strategic importance in the introduction and growth stage of the product life cycle because in these stages cumulative production grows most rapidly. Strategically this means that a company should strive to gain a cost advantage in the early stages of the PLC. Once the leading cost position is lost to competitors, it is very difficult to catch up. Thus the competition can be very heavy in these stages just to attain a superior cost position.

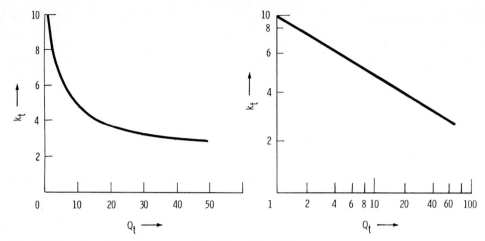

Fig. 5.13. Experience Curve in Exponential and Logarithmic Form

*Mathematics of the Experience Curve*

The simplest form of the experience curve is the log-linear model:

$$k_t = k_0'(Q_t/Q_0)^w,  \tag{5.24}$$

where $Q_t$ = cumulative production to period $t$, $Q_0$ = pilot production at $t = 0$, $k_0'$ = start-up unit cost at pilot production $Q_0$, $k_t$ = (deflated) unit cost in period $t$ at cumulative production of $Q_t$, $w$ = parameter, $w < 0$.

The parameter $w$ corresponds to the elasticity of unit cost with respect to the cumulative production $Q_t$. It represents the percentage decrease in unit cost when cumulative production increases by one percent. Since $Q_0$ is a constant, (5.24) can be simplified to

$$k_t = k_0 Q_t^w,  \tag{5.25}$$

where $k_0 = k_0'/Q_0^w$. Taking the logarithm, we get the linear function

$$\ln k_t = \ln k_0 + w \ln Q_t.  \tag{5.26}$$

Fig. 5.13 illustrates the exponential and logarithmic version of the experience curve for a learning rate $\alpha$ of 20% and $k_0 = 10$ ($Q_0 = 1$).

The relationship between the cost elasticity $w$ and the learning rate $\alpha$ becomes clear when we substitute $Q_t = 2Q_0$ and $k_t = (1 - \alpha)k_0$ into (5.25). For $Q_0 = 1$ we get $(1 - \alpha)k_0 = k_0 2^w$. After taking the logarithm and solving for $w$, we obtain

$$w = \ln(1 - \alpha)/\ln 2  \quad \text{or} \quad \alpha = 1 - 2^w.  \tag{5.27}$$

Table 5.6
The Relationship between the Learning Rate $\alpha$ and the Cost Elasticity $w$ of the Experience Curve

| Learning Rate $\alpha$ | Cost Elasticity $w$ |
|---|---|
| 0.05 | $-0.0740$ |
| 0.10 | $-0.1520$ |
| 0.15 | $-0.2345$ |
| 0.20 | $-0.3219$ |
| 0.25 | $-0.4150$ |
| 0.30 | $-0.5146$ |

Table 5.6 lists some numerical examples of the learning rate $\alpha$ and the corresponding cost elasticity $w$.

## Determination of Parameters

The first step in applying the experience curve concept is to determine the parameters $k_0$ and $w$ (or the learning rate $\alpha$). We can consider several procedures to do that.

If no historical cost data are available (as in the case of a new product), the simplest way is to have managers estimate the parameters directly. This method should present few problems for start-up cost $k_0$. The cost elasticity $w$ and the learning rate $\alpha$, however, are abstract concepts, so that their direct estimation may be difficult. Thus it is suggested that managers first derive unit cost estimates for various production volumes. On the basis of these estimates the parameters are then calibrated using the formulas given above. Important information sources in such cases are historical data on comparable products.

When historical cost data for the product under consideration are available, these data can be used to estimate the parameters $k_0$ and $w$. As only two parameters are to be estimated, two data points are sufficient for the computation, i.e., the straight line in Fig. 5.12 is determined by only two points. With more than two data points, parameters can be estimated econometrically. Reliability increases with the number of available data points (see also Womer 1984).

The estimation procedure can be demonstrated using the example of the Airbus. Table 5.7 provides the data. Assembly hours are a proxy for real cost measurements. Three data points are available.

The cost elasticity is $w = -0.3233$, so that the learning rate $\alpha$ is 20.08%. Assembly hours decrease by about 20% for each doubling of the cumulative production volume.

Table 5.8 shows empirical values of the learning rate $\alpha$ for various product categories. The information in the table is based on data in Henderson (1979), Abell and Hammond (1979), and Bass (1980).

The high $R^2$'s suggest that the development of cost (prices) is well explained by the experience curve hypothesis. Learning rates range from 6.5% for color televisions

Table 5.7
Data for Determining the Experience Curve of the Airbus

| Index $i$ | Cumulative Units $Q_i$ | Assembly Hours $k_i$ | Year |
|-----------|------------------------|----------------------|------|
| 1 | 1 | 340,000 | 1976 |
| 2 | 104 | 65,000 | 1980 |
| 3 | 860 | 40,000 | 1989 |

to 31.0% for viscose rayon, the average being 18.7%. Most of the estimated values are in good accord with the results of Hirsch (1956) who established learning rate values between 14.1% and 25.6%. Table 5.8 also suggests that learning rates may be higher for intermediary industrial products than for end-products. The mean for the six intermediary products is 24.3% and that for the eleven end-products is 15.6%.

One should note that the above learning rate estimates are based on price data and not on cost data. The authors defend the use of price as a proxy for costs with the argument that it is close to impossible to determine the costs in the remote past. However, actual price changes reflect not only cost changes but also competitive influences and the supply-demand relation. Thus one should be cautious when learning rates are calibrated on the basis of price data.

Table 5.8
Cost Elasticities and Learning Rates for Various Product Categories

| Product Category | Cost Elasticity $w$ | Learning Rate $\alpha$ | $R^2$ | Number of Data Points |
|------------------|---------------------|------------------------|-------|------------------------|
| Germanium Transistors | −0.3728 | 0.228 | 0.8848 | 19 |
| Silicon Transistors | −0.4699 | 0.278 | 0.8969 | 19 |
| Integrated Circuits | −0.4706 | 0.278 | 0.9992 | 9 |
| Polyethylene | −0.3473 | 0.214 | 0.8946 | 21 |
| Polypropylene | −0.2296 | 0.147 | 0.9556 | 14 |
| Gas Ranges | −0.2726 | 0.172 | 0.6171 | 22 |
| Electric Ranges | −0.1799 | 0.117 | 0.4623 | 22 |
| Viscose Rayon | −0.5353 | 0.310 | – | 32 |
| Long-Distance Tariffs | −0.4739 | 0.280 | – | 10 |
| Large Air Conditioners | −0.3219 | 0.200 | – | 18 |
| Electric Razors | −0.3771 | 0.230 | – | 13 |
| Refrigerators | −0.0987 | 0.066 | 0.83 | 19 |
| Home Air Conditioners | −0.1897 | 0.123 | 0.87 | 29 |
| Dishwashers | −0.1832 | 0.119 | 0.85 | 28 |
| Black and White TVs | −0.3641 | 0.223 | 0.73 | 27 |
| Electric Clothes Dryers | −0.1930 | 0.125 | 0.83 | 25 |
| Color TVs | −0.0972 | 0.065 | 0.73 | 14 |

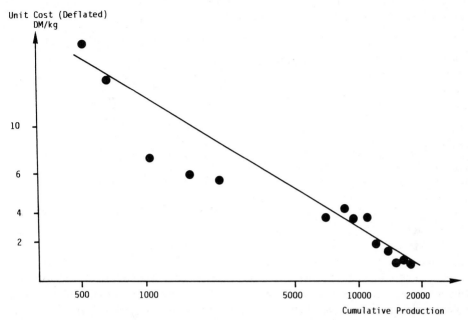

Fig. 5.14. Experience Curve for a Chemical Product Based on Actual Costs (Years 1971–84)

In Fig. 5.14, we show an experience curve for a chemical product based on actual (deflated) costs. The observation period covers 14 years (1971-1984). The learning rate in this case is 29%.

*Experience Curve and Life Cycle*

Henderson (1974) demonstrated the relationship between sales growth and unit cost decreases based on the experience curve. Yelle (1980) has shown its explicit relationship over the life cycle. A change in the growth rate has a greater impact on costs, the higher the learning rate is. Conversely, any increase of the learning rate is more effective when accompanied by a higher growth rate.The time needed to double the cumulative production is directly related to the growth rate of sales and, thus, to the life cycle. The highest growth rates are usually attained in the early stages of the life cycle but can hardly be retained for an extended period of time. Therefore, the time needed to double the cumulative production typically increases over the life cycle. Empirical observations support this hypothesis. Table 5.9 gives several examples.

These observations demonstrate the decisive importance of the experience curve for pricing strategy and competitive advantage during the introduction and growth stages of the life cycle.

Table 5.9
Empirical Time Periods for Doubling Cumulative Production

| Doubling of Cumulative Production | Chemical Product (months) | Automobiles (Germany) (years) | Polyvinyl-Chloride (years) | Black and White TVs (years) |
|---|---|---|---|---|
| First | 4.5 | 1 | 2.2 | 0.2 |
| Second | 5 | 1.5 | 2.7 | 0.4 |
| Third | 9 | 3.5 | 3.5 | 0.5 |
| Fourth | 11 | 4.8 | 4.5 | 0.5 |
| Fifth | 12 | 6.8 | 5 | 0.5 |
| Sixth | 14 | – | 5 | 0.7 |
| Seventh | 20 | – | – | 2.1 |
| Eigth | – | – | – | 3.5 |
| Ninth | – | – | – | 7 |

*Relative Market Share and Experience Curve*

Relative market share becomes a crucial determinant of the (relative) cost position when experience curve effects are strong. We demonstrate this relationship with a simple example involving two firms, A and B. Firm A has a market share of 60% in all periods and Firm B's market share is 40%. Thus A's relative market share is $60/40 = 1.5$. Total sales amount to 100 units and remain constant in all periods. Both firms have the same pilot production volume $Q_0 = 50$ and start-up cost $k_0 = 10$. Table 5.10 shows the development of unit costs at a learning rate of 30% and how the gap between A and B grows.

Competitor A's relative cost position improves with each period. In Period 5, A's unit cost is 16% lower than that of B. While the pace of the improvement of the relative cost position slows down, the time lag between A and B continues to grow.

Table 5.10
Development of Unit Costs and Time Lag at a Relative Market Share of 1.5 (A:B)

| Period | Firm A | | Firm B | | Difference | |
|---|---|---|---|---|---|---|
| | Cumulative Production | Unit Cost | Cumulative Production | Unit Cost | Unit Cost | Time Lag |
| 0 | 50 | 10.00 | 50 | 10.00 | 0.00 | 0 |
| 1 | 110 | 6.66 | 90 | 7.39 | 0.73 | 0.5 |
| 2 | 170 | 5.33 | 130 | 6.11 | 0.73 | 1.0 |
| 3 | 230 | 4.55 | 170 | 5.33 | 0.78 | 1.5 |
| 4 | 290 | 4.05 | 210 | 4.77 | 0.72 | 2 |
| 5 | 350 | 3.67 | 250 | 4.36 | 0.69 | 2.5 |

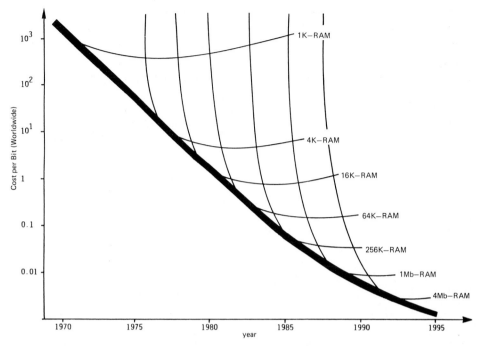

Fig 5.15. Cost Forecast Based on Experience Curve for Dynamic MOS-RAMs

## The Experience Curve and Price-Forecasting

It is obvious by now that the experience curve can be extremely useful as a price-forecasting tool. If the learning rate is established, the decline of unit cost can be extrapolated to predict future price levels. This method is frequently applied in such industries as airplanes, electronics, etc. The forecasting period could even cover the life cycles of follow-up products. Fig. 5.15 gives an example of such a cost- (and implicit price-) forecast for electronic components (dynamic MOS-RAMs).

This kind of forecast is very useful for the determination of the long-term pricing strategy and, of course, for the decision on whether a company should stay in a business or not.

## Problems of the Experience Curve

Although the experience curve concept is rather simple, managers should apply it carefully keeping its problems in mind. We discuss just one problem which deserves special mention. Details of other problems of experience curves are discussed by Yelle (1979) and Wacker (1980). Almost all estimates of the experience curve reported in the literature are based on price data and not on cost data. Learning rates estimated on this basis, however, are valid measures of cost decline only if prices change in proportion to unit costs. This is a very strong assumption. Even the proponents of the experience curve concept consider the disproportionate development of price and cost as more typical (Henderson 1974, Abell and Hammond 1979).

Price always reflects the interactions between demand, competitive situation, and cost position. It can be misleading to attribute the development of price to a single factor like cost. Simon (1982) and Devinney (1987) show that price and cost movements over time can be strongly affected by the entry of new competitors. Great caution is indicated. The experience curve concept should not be applied naively and mechanically. Note that this is a measurement problem and doesn't concern the validity of the concept itself. In the context of pricing, however, this problem deserves special attention.

### Recent Trends

While the belief in the quasi-automatic correlation between cumulative volume and unit cost may have been weakening over the recent year the pressure to bring costs down has been ever increasing. Many companies (particularly in Japan, but also in Europe and in the U.S.) set today targets of 4 to 6% real cost reduction per year. Our experience shows that, with commitment and determination, these targets can be achieved. Japanese companies even go that far to mark off $X\%$ of factory space which is to be saved next year as a physical symbol for the need to permanently cut costs. This will be a never-ending race. Management in industries where these attitudes prevailed are well advised to observe these developments and to act accordingly. At the end of the day the relative cost position determines price competitiveness and profitability.

Summary: The experience curve concept is of strategic importance in business planning and pricing. Due to the accumulation of experience the (deflated) average unit cost of the product falls by a percentage called "learning rate" with each doubling of the cumulative production volume. According to the available empirical studies, the learning rates are in the range of 5 to 30%. The experience curve effect is particularly important in the early stages of the PLC because growth is fastest in these stages. Although there are some measurement and other problems associated with the experience curve concept, they do not fundamentally affect its relevance for strategic pricing. The pressure to bring costs down over time has become even stronger in recent years. Many companies set targets of 4–6% real cost reductions year after year. Management in industries where this attitude prevails must very keenly observe these developments to remain cost and price competitive.

Chapter 6

# *Strategic Price Management*

## 6.1 Systems Context

Strategic price management is distinguished by two characteristics: (i) the objective is long-term rather than short-term profit maximization and (ii) the manager considers the impact of price on both current and future sales and profits. The existence of dynamic relations requires the consideration of multiple periods and makes strategic pricing very complex. Fig. 6.1 demonstrates the complexity of strategic pricing. For clarity, it shows the monopoly case. The thick arrows represent behavioral relations which result from the behavior of relevant variables (price, sales, etc.). The dotted arrows, on the other hand, stand for definitional relations (e.g., Profit = Revenue-Cost). Fig. 6.1 shows that current price affects sales and costs in future periods, thereby affecting future prices also. The current price is, in turn, influenced by future prices through feedback. Optimal strategic pricing, therefore, requires simultaneous determination of prices in every period within the planning horizon.

Due to the complexitiy and importance of these pricing issues, managers are interested in models to assist in this decision. We begin with simple rules of thumb for strategic pricing and then discuss analytic models.

## 6.2 Strategic Price Management with Rules of Thumb

Strategic pricing of new products is one of the most challenging decisions facing marketing managers. Some well-known rules of thumb address this problem.

### Skimming and Penetration Strategy

In his early pioneering works, Dean (1951, 1969) presents arguments for the skimming and penetration approaches to new product pricing. Under a skimming strategy, the new product is introduced at a relatively high price which is successively lowered over time. Dean did not precisely define the high introductory price. We define a skimming price as a price which is greater than the price which maximizes the short-term profit in the introductory period (Cournot or myopic price). Cournot

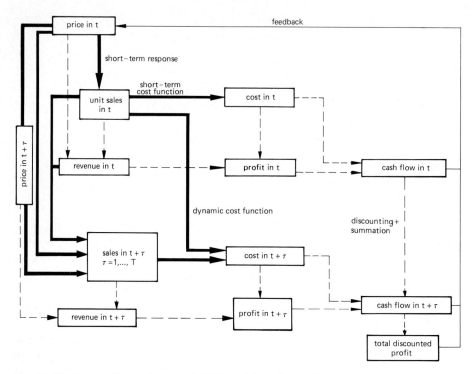

Fig. 6.1. The Systems Context in Strategic Pricing without Competitive Reaction

price is the price that maximizes the short-term profit when no competitive reaction is assumed in an oligopolistic situation (see Chapter 3). In contrast, the penetration strategy has a low introductory price. We define a penetration price as a price which is lower than the myopic price in the introductory period. In penetration strategy, the price can be increased, decreased, or held constant in later periods (see Fig. 6.2).

The skimming strategy is recommended for "products that represent a drastic departure from accepted ways of performing a service" (Dean 1951, p. 419), i.e., real innovations.

The most important arguments for using either one of these two strategy options are listed in Table 6.1. While these recommendations provide valuable insights of a directional kind, they are less useful when factors favoring skimming and penetration are both present. This is often the case in reality, e.g., an innovative product with a low price elasticity but a high learning rate. Such a problem can be solved only by quantitative methods.

Experience curve pricing is a special kind of the penetration strategy. But the motivation is different. It aims to bring cost down through increased cumulative production and to gain a competitive cost advantage. The introductory price may be

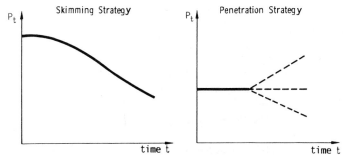

Fig. 6.2. Skimming and Penetration Strategy in their Ideal Form

Table 6.1
Arguments for Skimming and Penetration Strategies

| Skimming Strategy | Penetration Strategy |
|---|---|
| – high short-run profits little affected by discounting. | – high total contribution through fast sales growth in spite of low unit contribution margins. |
| – quick pay back for real innovation during the period of monopolistic market position, reduces long-run competitive risk, quick amortization of R&D expenses. | – takes advantage of positive intrapersonal (consumer goods) or interpersonal (durable goods) carryover effects, builds up a strong market position (with the potential of higher prices and/or higher sales in the future). |
| – high profit in early life cycle phases, reduces the risk of obsolescence. | |
| – allows for price reduction over time. | – takes advantages of short-run cost reductions through (static) economies of scale. |
| – avoids the necessity of price increases. | |
| – high price implies positive prestige and quality. | – allows fast increase of the cumulative quantity by accelerating the experience curve effect. Achieves a large cost advantage that competitors will find difficult to match. |
| – requires fewer financial resources. | |
| – requires lower capacity. | – reduces the risk of failure; low introductory price gives some assurance of low probability of failure. |
| | – deters potential competitors from market entry, or delays their entry. |

Table 6.2
Market Share-Oriented Pricing Strategy in the Life Cycle

| PLC Stage | Market Share Objective | Pricing Strategy |
|-----------|------------------------|------------------|
| Introduction | build up | aggressive |
| Growth | expand | undercut market price, if possible |
| Maturity | maintain | maintain or increase price, small suppliers are advised to undercut the market leader or to position themselves in a niche |
| Decline | harvest, prepare for the phase-out of the product | keep price relatively high |

well below the initial cost. Prerequisites for the success of this strategy are that experience curve effects are strong and that customers are price sensitive. Experience curve pricing is closely related to the market share-oriented rules of thumb which we discuss below.

*Market Share-Oriented Rules of Thumb*

The market share plays a crucial role in strategic planning (Abell and Hammond 1979). First, as a rule the supplier with the largest market share has accumulated the most experience and thus holds the most favorable cost position. Second, because of the carryover effect firms with a higher market share have better sales prospects in the future and they seem to enjoy economies of scale in marketing (Buzzell et al. 1975, 1987).

Given these dynamic relations, the market share represents a very important determinant of future profit potential, or in Brock's words (1975, p. 105), "market share can be thought of as a form of capital that is purchased through competitive actions and that can be sold through raising prices and gradually allowing customers to slip to competitors". The issue is then how to balance the short-term profits and the "investment" in market share.

Table 6.2 summarizes the conventional recommendations concerning the investment in market share at each life cycle stage (see Fogg and Kohnken 1978, Abell and Hammond 1979). These recommendations are theoretically rather well-founded, as we will see later. The market share can be considered a good proxy variable for long term profit. This view is particularly shared by Japanese companies.

In the more recent literature on competitive strategy, the value of market share as such is viewed more skeptically (Porter 1985). It is necessary to analyze thoroughly the factors which determine the value of market share before one draws conclusions on the optimal pricing strategy. In this context, it is particularly important to integrate long-term pricing into the overall competitive strategy which includes positioning, segmentation, and gaining competitive advantages.

Summary: Several rules of thumb have been developed for strategic pricing decisions. Skimming and penetration strategy are recommended for pricing of new products under certain conditions. These recommendations are generally useful but of limited help in the realistic situations where the determinants interact in a complex way. Market share-oriented pricing rules favor penetration strategy in the introduction stage and provide general guidelines for pricing in later PLC stages.

A naive market share-oriented approach should, however, be avoided. Pricing has to be considered as an integral part of the overall competitive strategy.

## 6.3 General Optimization Rules for Strategic Price Management

This section discusses (1) the general relationship between the optimal strategic price and its determinants as well as (2) the differences between this price and its static counterpart. For this purpose we derive general optimality conditions for the dynamic case. Initially we do not consider competitive effects.

### 6.3.1 The Optimal Strategic Price for the General Case

The dynamic price response function can be written in general form as

$$q_t = f(p_t, ..., p_{t-\tau}). \tag{6.1}$$

Substituting $q_t$ into the objective function (5.1), taking the derivative with respect to $p_t$, and setting the derivative to zero, we get

$$\frac{\delta \Pi_t}{\delta p_t} = q_t + p_t \frac{\delta q_t}{\delta p_t} - C_t' \frac{\delta q_t}{\delta p_t} + \sum_{\tau=1}^{T} (p_{t+\tau} - C_{t+\tau}') \frac{\delta q_{t+\tau}}{\delta p_t} (1+i)^{-\tau} = 0. \tag{6.2}$$

From (6.2) we can derive the general optimality condition (see the appendix to this chapter for technical details).

$$p_t^* = \frac{\varepsilon_t}{1 + \varepsilon_t} C_t' - \frac{\varepsilon_t}{1 + \varepsilon_t} m_t = \frac{\varepsilon_t}{1 + \varepsilon_t} (C_t' - m_t), \tag{6.3}$$

where

$$m_t = \sum_{\tau=1}^{T} \frac{\varepsilon_{t+\tau,t}}{\varepsilon_t} (p_{t+\tau} - C_{t+\tau}') \frac{q_{t+\tau}}{q_t} (1+i)^{-\tau}. \tag{6.4}$$

$\varepsilon_{t+\tau,t}$ is the dynamic price elasticity and denotes the effect of pricing action in $t$ on sales in $t + \tau$. It is defined as

$$\varepsilon_{t+\tau,t} = \frac{\delta q_{t+\tau}}{\delta p_t} \frac{p_t}{q_{t+\tau}}. \tag{6.5}$$

Note that (6.3) generally does not represent a solution for $p_t^*$ because some or all terms on the right-hand side depend on price.

Equation (6.3) shows that the optimal strategic price depends on three factors:
- the short-term price elasticity $\varepsilon_t$,
- the marginal cost $C_t'$, and
- $m_t$.

The difference of (6.3) from the static Amoroso-Robinson Relation (3.16) is the term $m_t$. This term represents the present value of the future contribution margins attributable to a change in price in $t$. If $m_t$ is positive, the optimal strategic price is lower than its static counterpart (myopic price) and vice versa. From (6.3) and (6.4) we can also readily verify that the difference between strategic price and myopic price is, ceteris paribus, the bigger,
- the greater $\varepsilon_{t+\tau,t}/\varepsilon_t$ is (in absolute terms),
- the greater the future contribution margins are,
- the lower the discount rate $i$ is,
- the greater $q_{t+\tau}/q_t$ is, and
- the longer the planning horizon $T$ is.

In short, the difference is the bigger, the greater the impact of the current pricing action on future profits is.

The essence of strategic pricing is to maximize the long-term rather than the short-term profit. We can interpret the sacrifice of short-term profit as "marketing investment": $G_t^s - G_t^*$, where $G_t^s$ and $G_t^*$ denote the profit in period t under static (myopic) and strategic optimization, respectively.

### 6.3.2 The Optimal Strategic Price with Carryover Effects

Price response dynamics depend on carryover and/or price change effects. We first analyze the carryover effect. Carryover effects represent the impact of current sales on future sales through such factors as brand loyalty, brand switching, or word-of-mouth (see Chapter 5). The price response function with carryover effects has the following form.

$$q_{t+\tau} = f(q_t, p_{t+\tau}). \tag{6.6}$$

In this case, the partial derivative $\delta q_{t+\tau}/\delta p_t$ in (6.2) can be rewritten as

$$\frac{\delta q_{t+\tau}}{\delta p_t} = \frac{\delta q_{t+\tau}}{\delta q_t} \frac{\delta q_t}{\delta p_t}, \tag{6.7}$$

Table 6.3
Cumulative Sales Effects of a Price Reduction of 1 Unit under Different Carryover Coefficients

| Case | $\mathscr{L}$ | $t$ | $t+1$ | $t+2$ | $t+3$ | $t+4$ | Sum $t+1,...,\infty$ | Marketing Multiplier |
|------|------|------|------|------|------|------|------|------|
| A | 0.60 | 100 | 60 | 36 | 21.60 | 12.96 | 150 | 1.5 ( $=150/100$) |
| B | 0.20 | 100 | 20 | 4 | 0.80 | 0.16 | 25 | 0.25 ( $=25/100$) |

and the decision rule for the optimal strategic price becomes

$$p^* = \frac{\varepsilon_t}{1 + \varepsilon_t}(C_t' - m_t),$$  (6.8)

where

$$m_t = \sum_{\tau=1}^{T} (p_{t+\tau} - C_{t+\tau}')\frac{\delta q_{t+\tau}}{\delta q_t}(1 + i)^{-\tau}.$$  (6.9)

As in (6.3), $m_t$ represents the present value of the future carryover effects. Compared to (6.4) $m_t$ now has a very simple form and can be considered as a *multiple* of the short-term price response $\delta q_t/\delta p_t$. We, therefore, call $m_t$ "marketing multiplier" (see Simon 1979c, 1981).

We illustrate this concept with the simple carryover model of the following form

$$q_t = a + \mathscr{L}q_{t-1} - bp_t.$$  (6.10)

We consider two cases. In case A, $b = 100$ and $\mathscr{L} = 0.6$. In case B, $b = 100$ and $\mathscr{L} = 0.2$. Table 6.3 shows the sales effects of a price reduction by one unit in each case. Due to the different carryover coefficients a big difference in the cumulative sales effects between the two cases results.

In the case of model (6.10), the marketing multiplier is given by

$$m_t = \sum_{\tau=1}^{T} (p_{t+\tau} - C_{t+\tau}')\left(\frac{\mathscr{L}^\tau}{(1 + i)^\tau}\right).$$  (6.11)

If the future unit contribution margins are constant and equal to $(p - C')$, then the marketing multiplier can be further simplified to

$$m_t = \left(\frac{1}{1 - \mathscr{L}/(1 + i)} - 1\right)(p - C').$$  (6.12)

Table 6.4
Results of Strategic vs. Myopic Pricing

| Optimization | Optimal Prices | | Profits | | Net Present Value |
|---|---|---|---|---|---|
| | Period 1 | Period 2 | Period 1 | Period 2 | |
| Myopic | 8.40 | 8.27 | 115.60 | 106.60 | 220.11 |
| Strategic | 7.64 | 8.44 | 109.82 | 118.20 | 225.70 |

We illustrate the principle of strategic pricing with a simple two-period case. We want to maximize the total discounted profit for the two periods

$$\Pi_1 = (p_1 - C')q_1 + (p_2 - C')\, q_2(1 + i)^{-1}. \tag{6.13}$$

The dynamic price response function is (6.10). We assume the following parameter values:

$$\mathscr{L} = 0.45, \ i = 0.02, \ a = 100, \ b = 10, \ C' = 5, \ q_0 = 40.$$

We set the partial derivatives of (6.13) with respect to $p_1$ and $p_2$ to zero and solve them. Table 6.4 shows the results. The table compares strategic and static optimization. We can see that by pursuing the strategic rather than the myopic (static) pricing policy the company can improve its profit. The profit in Period 1 is, however, lower than what it would be under myopic policy (marketing investment).

The difference between the strategic and the myopic price optimization is illustrated in Fig. 6.3.

### Heuristic Multipliers

In Table 5.2, we have established that for most consumer nondurables the value of the carryover coefficient lies between 0.3 and 0.6. If we assume that the future contribution margins remain constant, then we can estimate the empirically relevant range of the value of the marketing multiplier via (6.12). Table 6.5 shows the values of the marketing multiplier at different combinations of the carryover coefficient and unit contribution margin. The underlying discount rate is 10%. To determine the optimal strategic price, the (static) marginal costs have to be reduced by the percentage rates in the table.

### Time-Varying Carryover

As we discussed in Chapter 5, carryover coefficients may decline over the life cycle and this phenomenon can be captured by weighting the carryover coefficient $\mathscr{L}$ with an obsolescence term $r^t$, $0 < r < 1$, so that $\mathscr{L}_t = \mathscr{L}r^t$. The basic form of the optimality

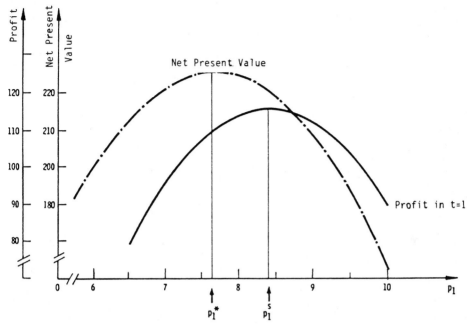

Fig. 6.3. Strategic and Myopic Optimal Price in a Two-Period Carryover Model.

condition (6.8) is not affected by this change. The marketing multiplier, of course, takes a different form:

$$m_t = \sum_{\tau=1}^{T} \left( p_{t+\tau} - C'_{t+\tau} \right) \left( \frac{\mathscr{L}^\tau}{(1+i)^\tau} \right) r^{\tau t + \tau(\tau-1)/2}. \tag{6.14}$$

This formula shows that $m_t$, cet. par., decreases over time as a result of obsoles-

Table 6.5
Marketing Multipliers for Different Carryover Coefficients and Contribution Margins

| Carryover Coefficient $\mathscr{L}$ | Relative Contribution Margin $(p - C')/C'$ | | |
|---|---|---|---|
| | 10% | 25% | 50% |
| 0.30 | 3.8% | 9.4% | 18.4% |
| 0.40 | 5.7% | 14.2% | 28.5% |
| 0.50 | 8.3% | 20.8% | 41.6% |
| 0.60 | 12.0% | 30.0% | 60.0% |
| 0.70 | 17.5% | 43.8% | 87.5% |

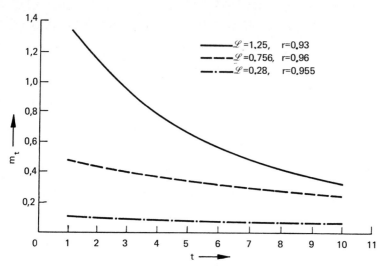

Fig. 6.4. The Development of $m_t$ over Time (Empirical Examples from Three Different Product Classes)

cence. Fig. 6.4 shows three empirical examples of the developments of $m_t$. The calculations are based on an assumed future contribution margin of 30% of marginal cost and a discount rate of 10%. The upper curve shows that $m_t$ may temporarily be greater than $C_t'$ when the carryover coefficient is very high.

The implication of the (over time) decreasing marketing multiplier for pricing strategy is that the optimal strategic price differs a lot from its myopic counterpart in the beginning of the life cycle but this difference decreases over time. In other words, strategic pricing is more important in the early stage than in the decline stage of the life cycle. The "marketing investment" is relatively high in the early phase.

Summary: If positive carryover effects are present, a sales increase in period $t$ increases the sales in the future. The present value of these additional sales can be expressed as a multiple of the short-term price response and thus called marketing multiplier. The strategic price is determined on the basis of marginal cost reduced by the value of this multiplier. For typical consumer nondurables, the value of the multiplier is between 2% and 60% of marginal cost. If the carryover effect goes down over time, which is often the case in reality, so does the multiplier unless the unit contribution margin goes up sharply.

### 6.3.3 The Optimal Strategic Price with Price Change Response

Another important dynamic price determinant is the price change effect.

*Symmetric Price Change Response*
As we said in Chapter 5, the simplest way to model this phenomenon is to

postulate a linear effect of price change. If we combine such a linear effect of price change and the price level effect, we get

$$q_t = a - bp_t - c(p_t - p_{t-1}),$$ (6.15)

which can be simplified to

$$q_t = a - (b + c) p_t + cp_{t-1}.$$ (6.16)

Equation (6.16) shows that a higher price in $t - 1$ promotes sales in $t$ if price goes down in $t$ (and vice versa). The price effect is here limited to two periods, so that a two-period model captures all effects.

Maximizing the corresponding profit function leads to the following condition:

$$p_t^* = p_t^s - \tfrac{1}{2}m_t,$$ (6.17)

where $p_t^s$ = optimal static (myopic) price, $m_t = -c/(b + c)(p_2 - C')(1 + i)^{-1}$.

We compare the results under strategic and static (myopic) pricing in a two-period case. The assumed parameter values for (6.15) are as follows: $a = 100$, $b = 8$, $c = 4$, $p_0 = 10$, $C' = 5$, $i = 0.02$.

Table 6.6 summarizes the results under both strategies. The company sacrifices 3.05 profit units in Period 1 (= marketing investment) to achieve an overall profit improvement of 3.12 units.

Such a price change effect favors a skimming strategy followed by subsequent price reductions – as long as the initial price is not too low.

*Asymmetric Price Change Response*

If we have an asymmetric sales response to price changes, i.e., a stronger response for price reductions than for price increases (as illustrated in Figure 5.6), the optimal pricing strategy is of the "pulsation type". Optimal prices pulse between a lower and a higher level.

We illustrate this strategy with the empirical example (5.6). For marginal cost of $C' = 180$ and a discount rate of zero, we get the following optimal prices:

$$p_t^{low} = 233.40,$$

$$p_t^{high} = 269.48.$$

Table 6.6
Strategic vs. Myopic Pricing with Asymmetric Price Change Response

| Optimization | Optimal Prices | | Profits | | Net Present Value |
|---|---|---|---|---|---|
| | Period 1 | Period 2 | Period 1 | Period 2 | |
| Myopic | 8.33 | 8.06 | 133.32 | 111.99 | 243.12 |
| Strategic | 8.84 | 8.14 | 130.27 | 118.29 | 246.24 |

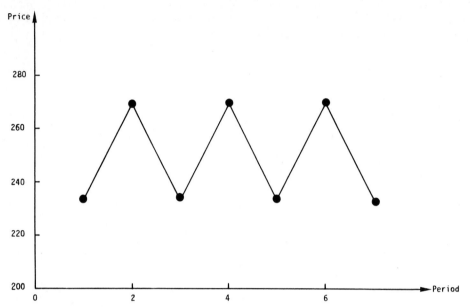

Fig. 6.5. Price Pulsation Strategy with Asymmetric Price Change Response

Fig. 6.5 shows the optimal pricing strategy. The average profit per period is 176.15. The strategy of optimal uniform prices, which neglects the price change response, would lead to a price of 242.26 and a profit of 153.39, which is 12.9% lower than the optimum.

Thus the asymmetric price change response provides a theoretical underpinning for pulsation strategy. Actual price promotion strategies resemble this pattern.

*Response Non-Proportional to Price Change*

In Chapter 5, we saw that sales response may be underproportional for small price changes and overproportional for large price changes (Figure 5.5). In this case it becomes advantageous to repeat the pattern of reducing the price once in a big step and then increasing it several times in small amounts. This pricing strategy is illustrated in Fig. 6.6. Since many empirical studies reveal a non-proportional price change response, this strategy deserves particular attention. It should, however, be applied with care. If price increases provoke resistance from the customers, this strategy is not recommended. But in such a case the underlying response function is different anyway.

*Effects of Price Expectations*

In Chapter 5, we have discussed Yoo's model (1986) which addressed the issue of consumers' expectations of future prices. Given evidence of the development and

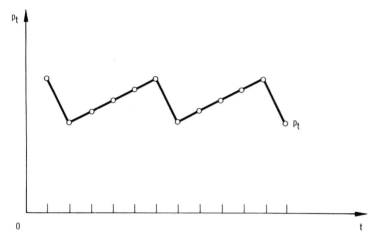

Fig. 6.6. Price Pulsation Strategy with Non-Proportional Price Change Response

impact of price expectations established by his empirical analysis, he developed a heuristic optimization model that can help managers develop pricing recommendations for the cases where price expectations are important. Specifically, he examined and compared the price paths and profits generated in Cell I through Cell VII in Table 6.7.

Fig. 6.7 shows price paths under seven cases generated using realistic parameter values. His model results suggest two broad guidelines for managers confronted with situations where consumers form expectations.

1) Managers should consider optimal uniform pricing strategy at a relatively low price level if they believe i) consumers form very strong price expectations, and ii) their anticipation of future prices is chiefly based on their observed past prices.

2) The pricing strategy should be that of a slowly declining price path, with the overall price level being higher than under the myopic pricing if managers believe that i) consumers' expectation formation is not very strong but still strong enough to

Table 6.7
Pricing Strategies under Alternative Price Expectations

| Pricing Strategy | Expectation Formation | | |
|---|---|---|---|
| | No $w = 0$ | Complete $w = 1$ | Partial $w = x(t)$ |
| Myopic | I | II | III |
| Optimal Uniform | IV | | V |
| Optimal | | VI | VII |

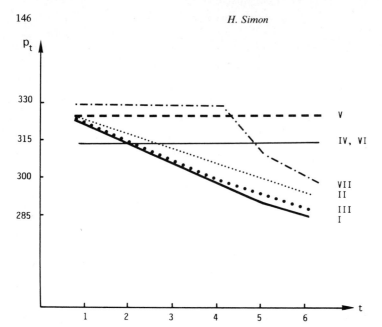

Fig. 6.7. Price Paths under Alternative Price Expectations

warrant managerial action, and ii) their anticipation of future prices is chiefly based on their observed past prices.

Summary: The optimal strategic price is higher than the optimal myopic price when price reductions promote additional sales. In such cases, an introductory skimming price followed by price reductions is suggested. Setting a relatively high initial price creates a "price reduction potential" that can be later used to stimulate sales. If we have an asymmetric price change response, i.e., a stronger response to price reductions than to price increases, a price pulsation strategy is optimal. Yoo's research (1986) established three major findings:

1) There are situations where consumers form expectations about the future prices of some products and act on these expectations.

2) Understanding consumers' price expectations can make a substantial difference in profitability.

3) Managers can reduce the extent of suboptimality in profits caused by expectation formation to a substantial degree by pursuing a well-conceived pricing strategy.

### 6.3.4 The Optimal Strategic Price with Dynamic Cost Function

In this subsection, we assume that current costs depend on past sales and, therefore, on past prices, while the price response is static. For simplicity, we further assume that $k_t$, the unit cost in $t$, is influenced by the activities until the beginning of $t$ and is constant within a period $t$.

Then the general dynamic cost function can be written as

$$k_{t+\tau} = f(p_t, ..., p_{t+\tau-1}).$$ (6.18)

The optimality condition for this cost function takes the following form (see the appendix to this chapter for details):

$$p_t^* = \frac{\varepsilon_t}{1+\varepsilon_t}(k_t - z_t),$$ (6.19)

where

$$z_t = -\sum_{\tau=1}^{T} \frac{u_{t+\tau,t}}{\varepsilon_t} k_{t+\tau} \frac{q_{t+\tau}}{q_t}(1+i)^{-\tau},$$

$$u_{t+\tau,t} = \frac{\delta k_{t+\tau}}{\delta p} \frac{p_t}{k_{t+\tau}}.$$

$u_{t+\tau,t}$ is the elasticity of the unit cost in $t+\tau$ with respect to the price in $t$ and it is proportional to $w$, the elasticity of the unit cost with respect to the cumulative production volume (see Chapter 5). The $z_t$ term in (6.19) represents the present value of the future cost reductions attributable to the pricing action in $t$.

We can see that if $u_{t+\tau,t}$ is positive (this is the normal case), $z_t$ is also positive, so that the optimal strategic price is, cet. par., lower than the optimal myopic price. The difference between the two prices is, cet. par., the bigger,
- the greater the unit cost elasticity with respect to the price (or cumulative volume) is,
- the greater the unit cost $k_{t+\tau}$ is,
- the greater $q_{t+\tau}/q_t$ is,
- the lower the discount rate $i$ is,
- the smaller the absolute value of the price elasticity $\varepsilon_t$ is.

These statements hold for any kind of dynamic cost function.

*Application of the Experience Curve*

We now specify the dynamic cost function in the form of the experience curve and analyze its impact on pricing strategy using a two-period example.

Since we assumed that $k_t$ is influenced by the activities until the beginning of $t$, $k_1$ and $k_2$ look as below.

$$k_1 = k_0(Q_0/Q_0)^w = k_0,$$ (6.20)

$$k_2 = k_0(Q_1/Q_0)^w,$$ (6.21)

where $Q_1$ = cumulative production to 1, $k_0$ = start-up unit cost, $w$ = cost elasticity.

We assume a linear price response function without dynamics

$$q_t = a - bp_t. \tag{6.22}$$

Even for the two-period case, $p_1^*$ cannot be determined analytically and thus has to be found by means of a search procedure. On the other hand, we can apply the static decision rule to determine $p_2^*$ because the planning horizon is only two periods. Substituting (6.22) into (6.21) and applying the static decision rule, we get

$$p_2^* = 0.5 \left( a/b + k_0 \left( \frac{a - bp_1}{Q_0} \right)^w \right). \tag{6.23}$$

We can see that $p_2^*$ is the lower, the greater the cost elasticity $w$ ($w < 0$) is in absolute terms.

For illustrative purposes, we assume the following parameters:
– cost function: $k_0 = 6$, $Q_0 = 1$,
– price response function: $a = 100$, $b = 10$,
– discount rate $i = 0.1$.

The optimal myopic price in period 1 is thus

$$p_1^s = 0.5(10 + 6) = 8.$$

Therefore, the optimal strategic price $p_1^*$ must be lower than 8. Table 6.8 shows the optimal strategy for alternative values of the learning rate $\alpha$ (the cost elasticity $w$).

The example confirms the general conclusion that the difference between the optimal strategic and myopic prices increases as the learning rate $\alpha$ goes up. The marginal effect on price, however, falls as the learning rate $\alpha$ increases. Fig. 6.8 illustrates this phenomenon clearly.

Table 6.8
Optimal Strategic Prices under Different Learning Rates

| Learning Rate $\alpha$ | Cost Elasticity $w$ | $p_1^*$ | $p_2^*$ | $k_2$ | Marketing Investment | Improvement of Tot. Discounted Profit over Myopic Strategy |
|---|---|---|---|---|---|---|
| 0%  | 0        | 8    | 8    | 6    | 0    | 0    |
| 5%  | -0.0740  | 7.81 | 7.39 | 4.77 | 0.36 | 0.41 |
| 10% | -0.1520  | 7.66 | 6.86 | 3.71 | 1.14 | 1.39 |
| 15% | -0.2345  | 7.56 | 6.42 | 2.84 | 1.94 | 2.44 |
| 20% | -0.3219  | 7.51 | 6.07 | 2.13 | 2.40 | 3.12 |
| 25% | -0.4150  | 7.50 | 5.79 | 1.58 | 2.50 | 3.31 |

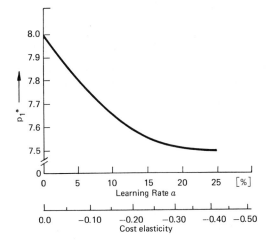

Fig. 6.8. The Dependence of the Optimal Strategic Price on the Learning Rate

The last two columns in Table 6.8 demonstrate that the marketing investment and the magnitude of profit improvement increase as the learning rate goes up.

Summary: If a price reduction in the current period (or the sales increase associated with it) causes the unit cost to fall in future periods, the optimal strategic price is lower than the myopic price. The difference between the two prices is the bigger, the higher the unit cost elasticity (in absolute value) and the level of the unit cost are. The cost dynamics have the effect of reducing the current unit cost. As the unit cost elasticity goes up, the unit cost falls at a slower rate. Undercutting the myopic price means again that short-term profits are sacrificed (marketing invest-ment) to achieve higher long-term profits.

### 6.3.5 The Existence of Dynamic Price Floors

Under dynamic conditions, no general price floors exist for individual periods. The carryover as well as the experience curve effect can cause the optimal strategic price to be lower than marginal cost. This can be easily shown via the general optimality conditions (6.3) or (6.19), both of which can be written as

$$p_t^* = \frac{\varepsilon_t}{1 + \varepsilon_t}(C_t' - m_t),$$

where $m_t = z_t$ in the case of (6.19).

The optimal strategic price is lower than marginal cost $C_t'$, if

$$\frac{\varepsilon_t}{1 + \varepsilon_t}(C_t' - m_t) < C_t'. \tag{6.24}$$

This case is relevant only for $m_t > 0$. (6.24) can be transformed into (note that $1 + \varepsilon_t < 0$)

$$-\varepsilon_t > C_t'/m_t. \tag{6.25}$$

The optimal strategic price is lower than marginal cost, if (at the optimal point) the ratio of marginal cost to the present value of dynamic effects (carryover or cost dynamics/experience curve) is smaller than the (absolute) price elasticity. In this case, the loss in $t$ is more than compensated by the positive effects in the future.

This is the more likely to happen, cet. par.,
- the smaller the difference between the optimal myopic price and marginal cost is,
- the higher the carryover coefficient $\mathscr{L}$ is,
- the higher the learning rate $\alpha$ is.

Since these conditions are frequently met for new products, the strategy of undercutting marginal cost is often used for new products in the introductory stage to achieve rapid penetration (e.g., free samples of new pharmaceuticals).

### 6.3.6 Summary of the Strategic Optimization Rules

We have discussed the impact of each individual dynamic effect on the optimal strategic price. Table 6.9 summarizes the findings. Two comments deserve special mention here.

First, we suggest that managers determine the optimal myopic price and then analyze how much and in which direction the optimal strategic price deviates from the myopic price. The deviation is the greater, the greater the present value of the future effects caused by current actions.

Second, in reality the dynamic effects listed in Table 6.9 often appear simultaneously and reinforce or offset each other. Therefore, managers should carefully

Table 6.9
Dynamic Effects and Their Impact on the Optimal Strategic Price

| Type of Dynamic Effects | Optimal Strategic Price Relative to the Optimal Myopic Price |
|---|---|
| Positive carryover | lower |
| Positive, time-degressive carryover | lower, but difference decreases over time |
| Price change response | higher<br>pulsation (alternating between a higher and a lower level), if asymmetric price change response |
| Experience curve | lower |

analyze product- and market-specific conditions to determine which dynamic effects are relevant, how they interact with each other, and how they develop over time.

## 6.4 Strategic Price Management over the Life Cycle

Since strategic price management is by definition long-term oriented, the development of the optimal prices over the life cycle is of utmost interest to managers. This section addresses this topic. We first discuss the strategic price management in the monopoly case for both new consumer nondurables and durables and then analyze the strategic pricing of new products in the competitive case. Finally, we address the pricing problems of a brand which enters an existing market and thus faces competition from the beginning.

### 6.4.1 Strategic Price Management for New Products

When an innovative new product appears in the market, it faces no or little competition for a considerable period of time due to patent protection, entry barriers, etc. Since the dynamic conditions are different for nondurables and for durables, we discuss each category separately.

*6.4.1.1 Strategic Pricing of New Nondurables*
As we said in Chapter 5, the following dynamic effects are relevant for genuine nondurable innovations:
- obsolescence-dependent carryover,
- price change response,
- experience curve.
We explore the implications of each effect for pricing strategy. We use the same model as the one we adopted for changing markets in Chapter 5, i.e. (5.20).

$$q_t = a + \mathscr{L}r'q_{t-1} - bp_t - c_1 \sinh\left(c_2\left(p_t - p_{t-1}\right)/p_{t-1}\right)q_{t-1}. \tag{6.26}$$

Since an analytic optimization is no longer possible, we use a simulation procedure. The base parameter values are as follows:
- carryover coefficient $\mathscr{L} = 0.50$,
- obsolescence rate $(1 - r) = 0.05$,
- price change response $c_1 = 0.05$, $c_2 = 10$.
  The other parameter values are:
- absolute term $a = 1000$,
- price level response $b = 60$,
- marginal cost $C' = 4$,

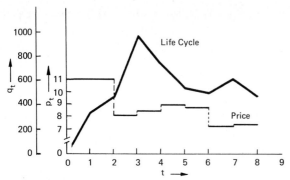

Fig. 6.9. Optimal Pricing Strategy for an Innovation when Carryover and Price Change Effects are Present

– discount rate $i = 0.1$,
– planning horizon $T = 8$ periods.

   With these parameter values and assumptions, we get the optimal price path shown in Fig. 6.9. The optimal strategy is of a skimming type. Because of the non-proportional price change response, price declines in big steps but goes up in small increments. By systematically varying the values of the parameters relevant to pricing strategy, we can examine the impact of each dynamic effect on pricing strategy over the life cycle.

*Strategic Impact of Individual Dynamic Effects*

   We begin with the carryover coefficient $\mathscr{L}$. From equation (6.11) we know that the rise of $\mathscr{L}$ increases the marketing multiplier $m_t$. In the early life cycle stages, this effect is particularly strong because the obsolescence of the carryover effect is negligible at these stages. Therefore, cet. par., a high $\mathscr{L}$ pushes the introductory price down and helps build a strong market position in later life cycle stages during which a higher price can be charged. Fig. 6.10 illustrates the impact of the carryover coefficient on pricing strategy for $\mathscr{L} = 2$ and $\mathscr{L} = 0$ (holding other parameters in (6.26) fixed).

   Since $\mathscr{L}$ tends to be higher for genuine innovations, a myopic pricing strategy can entail particularly big profit losses for truly new products. For new pharmaceutical products whose carryover coefficients are generally high, the strategy of low introductory price often takes the form of distribution of free samples.

   High obsolescence rates have the same effect as low $\mathscr{L}$'s, i.e., they favor skimming strategies. High obsolescence means that the market potential is rapidly depleted. Big marketing investments are not worthwhile. The decrease of market potential over time should be matched by price cuts.

   A strong price change response favors a skimming strategy. The stronger this effect is, the higher the optimal introductory price is and the earlier the price falls. If price change effects increase overproportionally with the magnitude of price changes, price cuts should be made in big chunks, whereas price increases have to be in small steps.

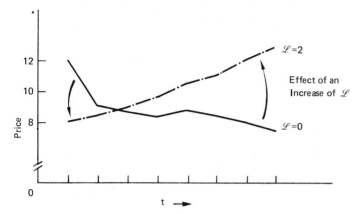

Fig. 6.10. The Impact of the Carryover Coefficient on the Optimal Price Path

As shown above, the experience curve lowers the introductory price. The higher the learning rate, the lower the introductory price is. Since experience curve and carryover effect generally reinforce each other, a penetration strategy is strongly suggested if these two effects operate simultaneously.

Table 6.10 summarizes our discussion of pricing recommendations for new consumer nondurables over the life cycle, which is divided into two stages. The table shows that in a number of cases the optimal pricing strategy is "undetermined" because the effects offset each other. This again suggests that managers should carefully examine the existence and strength of possible dynamic effects in each specific case.

### 6.4.1.2 Strategic Pricing of New Durables

In Chapter 5, we discussed alternative approaches to incorporating the price variable into monopolistic diffusion models. Spremann (1975) was the first to derive control theoretic optimality conditions for the pricing strategy. He maximizes the so-called Hamiltonian function

$$H(p_t, Q_t^*, v_t^*) = e^{-it}(p_t q_t(Q_t^*, p_t) - C_t(q_t)) + v_t^* q_t(Q_t^*, p_t). \qquad (6.27)$$

The term $e^{-it}$ is the discount factor for the continuous time model. The first sum term in (6.27) gives the discounted profit, the second term evaluates a change in the state variable $Q_t^*$. The "adjoint variable" $v_t$ measures the "future value" of the current sales position $q_t$. The adjoint variable $v_t$ is the continuous time-equivalent to our marketing multiplier $m_t$ from (6.4).

The general optimality condition can be written as

$$p_t^* = \frac{\varepsilon_t}{1 + \varepsilon_t}\left[C_t' - v_t^*/e^{-it}\right], \qquad (6.28)$$

Table 6.10
Life Cycle and Optimal Pricing Strategies for New Consumer Nondurables

| Strength of the Dynamic Effects | | | Optimal Strategic Prices | |
|---|---|---|---|---|
| Carryover | Price Change Response | Experience Curve (Learning Rate) | Early LC Stages | Late LC Stages |
| high | low | low = constant marginal cost | low | high |
| high | high | low = constant marginal cost | un-determined | un-determined |
| low | low | | | |
| low | high | low = constant marginal cost | high, possibly pulsation | low, possibly pulsation |
| high | low | high | very low | un-determined |
| low | high | high | un-determined | low |
| high | high | high | un-determined | un-determined |
| low | low | high | low | low |

with $v_T^* = 0$.

Condition (6.28) is structurally similar to (6.3). The adjoint variable $v_t^*$ plays a key role in the control theoretic model since it determines the difference between the optimal strategic price and the optimal static (myopic) price according to the Amoroso-Robinson Relation (3.15). Condition $v_T^* = 0$ says that future effects are only considered up to the planning horizon $T$.

In (6.28) the demand dynamics are reflected both in the price elasticity and in the adjoint variable whose value and development depend on the diffusion model's form and parameter values.

If the adjoint variable is positive in all periods, i.e., if an increase in current sales increases future profits, the strategic price is smaller than the myopic price (et vice versa). However, for most diffusion models the sign of the adjoint variable cannot be unequivocally determined. The following statements hold for the diffusion models presented in Chapter 5:

- Fourt-Woodlock-Model (pure innovation): the optimal strategic price is always higher than the optimal myopic price,
- Mansfield-Model (pure-imitation): in the first half of the life cycle the relation between the two prices is undetermined, after penetration has attained half the market potential the strategic price is higher than the myopic price,

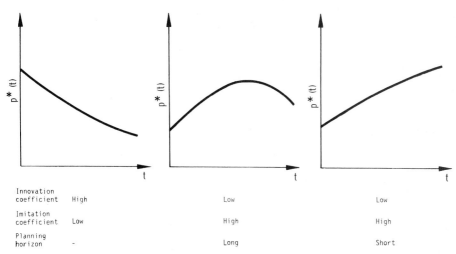

| Innovation<br>coefficient | High | Low | Low |
|---|---|---|---|
| Imitation<br>coefficient | Low | High | High |
| Planning<br>horizon | - | Long | Short |

Fig. 6.11. Optimal Pricing Strategies in Price-Dependent Diffusion Models

– Bass-Modell (innovation and imitation): the relation of the two prices depends on the magnitudes of the innovation and imitation coefficient, only in the last part of the life cycle is the strategic price higher than the myopic price.

The development of absolute price levels depends on the development of the price elasticity so that general conclusions are not feasible. A third factor which influences the pricing strategy is the planning horizon. The size of the optimal "marketing investment" ( = sacrifice of short-term profits) increases with the length of the planning period. Fig. 6.11 summarizes the most relevant pricing strategy options and the conditions under which they are indicated.

Roughly speaking, strong innovation and imitation effects tend to favor skimming and penetration strategy respectively. The real message of Fig. 6.11 is, however, that these two effects interact with one another and also with other relevant variables (e.g., planning horizon, discount rate) in special ways which can lead to fundamentally different optimal pricing strategies and thus no simple and general pricing recommendations can be made for new durables. Kalish (1988) comes to a similar conclusion.

Of equal importance as the demand dynamics are the cost dynamics. The experience curve plays a major role in the manufacturing of many consumer durables (e.g., calculators, video recorders) and experience curve oriented pricing is typical for the most-aggressive competitors in such markets.

The various models differ in detail but the main findings can be summarized as follows:

1. Experience curve effects cause the optimal strategic price to be lower than the myopic price (Bass and Bultez 1982, Kalish 1983).

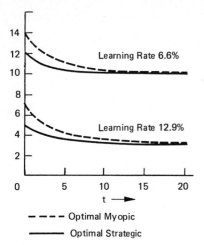

Fig. 6.12. Time Paths of the Optimal Strategic vs. Myopic Price under Different Learning Rates

2. The higher the learning rate is the greater is the relative difference between the two
   prices. Fig. 6.12 gives numerical examples of the time paths of these two prices
   under different learning rates.
3. Experience curve effect alone, with no diffusion dynamics, causes price to decline
   over time (Kalish 1983), i.e., prices follow costs.
4. The optimal pricing strategy should not be oriented to the current cost level but to
   the cost level to be achieved in the long run (Simon 1976).
5. Experience curve effects and carryover/imitation effects work into the same
   direction, i.e., they favor relatively low introductory prices (penetration strategy).

*Empirical Examples*

In many real cases, skimming strategy is widely adopted for new durables.
Examples are personal computers, video recorders, digital watches, new books, etc. In
all such cases, it is very difficult to separate the effects of demand and cost dynamics.
We should not, however, infer from the prevalence of skimming strategies that this
strategy is optimal in most cases (like Bass and Bultez 1982). It is quite probable that
firms frequently do not understand the complex dynamic relations or are short-term
profit oriented. This is particularly true for American companies – as compared to
Japanese firms (Hayes and Abernathy 1980).

The anecdotal evidence of penetration strategy is interesting: Many Japanese car
manufacturers enter a new market with low prices and then later raise the prices after
their reputation is established. As of mid 80's, Korean manufacturers seem to follow
the same pattern. Even Daimler-Benz, certainly not known as a "penetration pricer",
adopted this strategy for the U.S. market as Fig. 6.13 shows. The relative price of
Mercedes models has gone up steadily over the observation period.

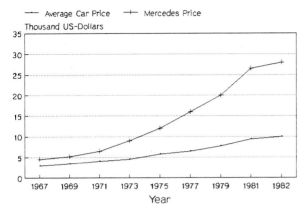

Fig. 6.13. Mercedes vs. Average Car Price in the U.S. Market

Penetration strategies are also popular for new airplane models. The airline which first adopts a new model (called "launching carrier") is usually given a considerable price discount. The strong imitation (demonstration) as well as the experience curve effect favors this strategy.

The penetration strategy is also frequently observed in the prefabricated-house market. The early buyers of a new house model are given favorable price terms. Given the importance of the high visibility (imitation and demonstration effect) in this market, this strategy makes a lot of sense.

In the electronics industry, price is frequently employed as a means of accelerating the diffusion process and "riding" the experience curve. Such experience curve oriented pricing strategies have been a favorite of Texas Instruments (Bird 1979), National Semiconductors, Intel (Fortune Jan. 12, 1981), and most Japanese companies in this industry. Fig. 6.14 shows an extreme example of this strategy. The accompanying advertising text reads as follows: "Bubble Price Break ... On August 11th (1980), Intel lowered its 100-unit price for the BPK 72 Bubble Memory Kit by 40% to $995. By August 1981, the price of bubble memories will be an unprecedented $595... Not 'projected'. Not 'expected'. Guaranteed. One year later, for 25,000-piece orders, the unit price will be $295 – cutting the per bit price in half once more. Again we guarantee it."

Note that linking the lower price to high order quantity is an additional means of accelerating the diffusion.

Before concluding this section we would like to warn against a careless application of penetration pricing. Low introductory prices are an effective and tempting way to get a new product or service off the ground. They involve, however, the risk that price increases planned in the later stages meet with the buyers' resistance. A "penetration-skimming-strategy" is often very difficult to implement particularly if repeat business plays an important role and prices have to be negotiated with

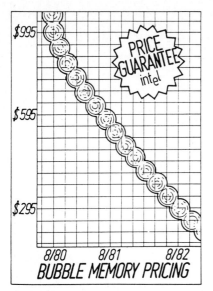

Fig. 6.14. Example of an Experience Curve Oriented Pricing Strategy (Source: Electronics Design, October 25, 1980, p. 10)

individual customers. According to our own experience it may take years to attain the proper price level if one started too low. Implementing price increases can be a challenging task.

### 6.4.2 Strategic Price Management in the Competitive Case

With very few exceptions, the manufacturer of a new product loses his monopolistic position sooner or later as new competitors enter the market. In a competitive market, not only the consumers' behavior but also competitive prices and reactions should be considered in pricing decisions. How the existing and future competitors would react to the manufacturer's pricing strategy is highly uncertain. Table 6.11 shows a taxonomy of strategic pricing papers that consider the competitive case and Table 6.12 summarizes these papers in chronological order. Table 6.11 tells us that there have been three distinct approaches to incorporating competition in the strategic pricing framework and that we find little empirical research in this area. It should be emphasized that under the application aspect the competitive reaction is much less a mathematical than an empirical problem. Therefore, more empirical work on the competitive case is needed.

Since a detailed review of these papers is available elsewhere (Yoo 1986), we confine ourselves to a discussion of a specific model as well as the empirical examples which seem to support the validity of this model. We consider the pricing problem

Table 6.11
A Taxonomy of Competitive Strategic Pricing Literature

| Empirical Test | Methodology | | |
|---|---|---|---|
| | Game Theory | Simulation | Managerial Judgments |
| Yes | Rao and Bass (1985) | | Simon (1982b) |
| No | Thompson and Teng (1984) Yoon (1984) Eliashberg and Jeuland (1986) | Simon (1977c) Clarke and Dolan (1984) | |

facing a pioneer firm which introduces a new product. Although the pioneer firm faces no competition now, it expects that one or several competitors will enter the market within the planning horizon. The market structure will change from monopoly to oligopoly. The pioneer firm has realistically three options for its pricing strategy with regard to the competitive entry:

- proactive price reduction: price is reduced before the competitor enters,
- reactive price reduction: price is reduced after the competitor has entered with the resulting loss in market share,
- keeping price constant: this usually amounts to a harvesting strategy if the new competitor is price aggressive, which is often the case.

Theoretically a fourth option would be to increase the price before or after the competitive entry. But this option is of little empirical relevance unless the pioneer decides to go into a price niche, e.g., the premium segment (see Chapter 8).

The decision situation and the three realistic options are illustrated in Fig. 6.15.

The price response function is naturally not the same in monopoly and in oligopoly. Table 6.13 summarizes the price response function adopted by the author for both situations. $t_i$ denotes the introduction period of brand $i$.

We consider ten sensible pricing strategies for a competitor entering the market at period 4. The planning horizon covers 8 periods. Each competitive strategy was run 12 times using varying parameter values. The strategy which, on the average, produced the maximum profits for the new entrant was considered the most likely to be adopted by him. The chosen strategy was that of short-term sales revenue maximization, i.e., a relatively aggressive strategy of the competitor. The pioneer firm then maximizes its profits assuming that the competitor chooses this strategy. The main result is: With realistic parameter values and the competitor's strategy of short-term sales maximization, the optimal strategy for the pioneer firm is to pursue

Table 6.12
Strategic Pricing Papers that Include the Competitive Case (Source: Yoo 1986)

|  |  | Simon (1977c) |
|---|---|---|
| I | Major Assumption | The competitor chooses the pricing strategy that yields the maximum profit for him. |
| II | Factors Considered<br>Demand Dynamics<br>Cost Dynamics | <br>Yes<br>No |
| III | Methodology | Simulation |
| IV | Major Results and/or<br>Managerial Implications | The skimming strategy followed by a sharp ("proactive") price reduction before the competitive entry is suggested as optimal. |

|  | Simon (1982b) | Thompson and Teng (1984) |
|---|---|---|
| I | Firm's sale depends on initial demand potential, carryover effect, price, and competitors' prices. | Firm's sale depends on its advertising, price, cumulative sales, and unsaturated market potential. |
| II | Yes<br>Yes | Yes<br>Yes |
| III | Managerial Judgments, Simulation | Game Theory |
| IV | The implications of strategic vs. myopic pricing are clarified by means of an empirically applied model. | In general, the optimal competitive price, decided by the price leader, starts high and steadily declines. |

|  | Yoon (1984) | Clarke and Dolan (1984) |
|---|---|---|
| I | Market potential is a function of price. | Firm's sale depends on brand prices and consumers' reservation prices. |
| II | Yes<br>Yes | Yes<br>Yes |
| III | Game Theory | Simulation |
| IV | Marginal cost pricing is rarely justified as an optimal policy in a dynamic duopoly situation. | Impact of three alternative pricing strategies (myopic, skimming, and penetration) is investigated by simulation. No generalizable results on superiority of skimming vs. penetration. |

|  | Rao and Bass (1985) | Eliashberg and Jeuland (1986) |
|---|---|---|
| I | Firm's output is the decision variable. | Firm's sale depends on the rate of diffusion, unsaturated potential, brand prices. |
| II | Yes<br>Yes | Yes<br>No |
| III | Game Theory | Game Theory |
| IV | Once competition is introduced, non-myopic strategies clearly dominate myopic strategies. Strategic thinking might better concentrate on actions before rival entry rather than after entry. | Optimal pricing strategies are investigated when the entry of a second firm is anticipated. |

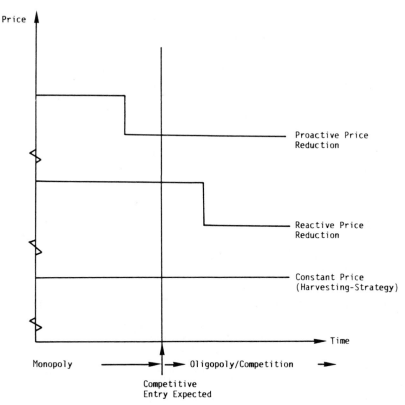

Fig. 6.15. Decision Situation and Strategic Options of a Pioneer Firm which Anticipates Competitive Entry

Table 6.13
Price Response Functions in a Strategic Pricing Model with Competitive Entry

| Determinants | Monopoly | Oligopoly |
|---|---|---|
| autonomous demand potential | | $a_t$ |
| carryover obsolescence | | $\mathscr{L}q_{i,t-1}\, r^{t-ti}$ |
| price level response | | $-bp_{i,t}$ |
| price change or price deviation response | $-c_1 \sinh\!\left(c_2 \dfrac{p_{it}-p_{i,t-1}}{p_{i,t-1}}\right) q_{i,t-1}$ | $-c_3 \sinh\!\left(c_4 \dfrac{p_{it}-\bar p_{it}}{\bar p_{it}}\right)\sum_i q_{i,t-1}$ |

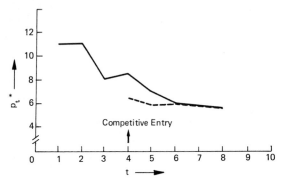

Fig. 6.16. Example of an Optimal Pricing Strategy when Competitive Entry is Expected

the skimming strategy during the early monopoly period but to lower the price to penetration level before the expected competitive entry (proactive price reduction). One typical strategy of this sort is shown in Fig. 6.16. The dashed line represents the pricing strategy of the new competitor.

The pioneer firm pursues first the skimming strategy in the monopoly period and thereby realizes a high short-term profit. It does not, however, maintain the high price over the whole monopoly period but reduces the price at such a timely moment that it strengthens its market position considerably before the competitive entry. We call this a "proactive price cut". Due to the carryover effect a higher profit accrues to the pioneer firm from its stronger market position. The following examples suggest the optimality of this strategy.

*Empirical Examples*

Between late 1967 and mid 1968, several competitors entered the plug compatible industry. IBM apparently underestimated the threats posed by these new entrants and didn't react until its market share declined considerably. In February, 1970, the company declared the plug compatible manufacturers problem as the "Key Corporate Strategic Issue". Since then, IBM embarked on a series of drastic price cuts until its market position finally stabilized. Brock (1975, p. 112) comments on IBM's actions as follows: "In retrospect, it appears that a substantial price cut early in 1969 would have largely prevented the plug compatible industry from developing – an advantage worth more than the temporary loss of revenue from IBM's point of view, .... However, at the time, IBM felt that the plug compatible competition would remain small in spite of IBM in action and that therefore a price cut was not needed."

A similar situation developed several years later when Amdahl and Itel entered the mainframe computer market. This time IBM reacted promptly with drastic price reductions. Reportedly Chairman Frank Cary started to push the company to more competitive pricing (Fortune, May 19, 1980, p. 107). Fig. 6.17 shows the development

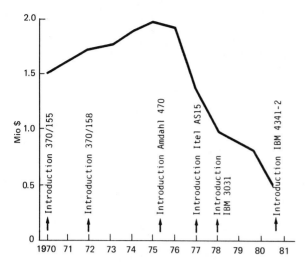

Fig. 6.17. Introductions and Price Developments of New Mainframe Computer Models (Source: Absatzwirtschaft, February, 1981)

of the system price (for System 370 until 1978). The introduction of System 4300 was part of a new strategy. For the first time, it was offered at a fully competition-oriented price. Thanks to this "penetration-price" the company received 42.000 orders within three weeks after the announcement. This was twice as many as forecast for the total life cycle of the product series. Because of this penetration-price IBM was criticized for pursuing a "predatory pricing" strategy, i.e., trying to drive the competitors out of the market with aggressive pricing. However, our model analysis suggests that such a pricing action is a perfectly sensible way of defending the pioneer firm's market position against competition.

The case of Gillette in its disposable razor business provides a classical example of proactive price cutting. Several months before the entry of BIC, a firm known for its aggressive pricing strategies, Gillette introduced a cheaper razor at a price 31% lower than that of its pioneer products. Although BIC entered the market shortly thereafter with an aggressive pricing strategy, Gillette's market share changed little. In the similar battles for market share where Gillette had cut the prices reactively, i.e., after the competitive entry (disposable pens and lighters), it lost its market leader status to BIC (see for details Fortune Feb. 25, 1980).

Interesting examples are found in the pharmaceutical industry. One of the most spectacular cases in Germany is Euglucon, until 1983 the best selling product in West-Germany co-marketed by Hoechst and Boehringer Mannheim. In spite of two big reactive (after competitive entry) price cuts, its sales continued to decline.

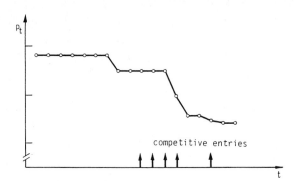

Fig. 6.18. Price Development in a Pharmaceutical Market

However, in the case of the brand shown in Fig. 6.18, the price was cut proactively. This brand experienced a further sales growth even after the entry of competitors and maintained its market leader position.

A few years later the patent of another major pharmaceutical brand expired. The company raised its price shortly before the entry of competitors because a price increase was considered feasible during the monopoly phase, but not later. It was a fatal mistake. Within a year it lost half of its market share.

However, our experience suggests, that a proactive price cut is difficult to implement in practice. Typically there is a strong resistance against sacrificing short-term profits before the competitive pressure becomes real. If anything, managers tend to try to "cash in" as much profit as possible before the competition breaks loose. This attitude totally neglects the strategic aspects. The balancing of short- and long-term profits is particularly delicate during the transition period from monopoly to oligopoly.

Summary: The pioneer firm which expects a competitive entry within its planning horizon must reach an optimal compromise between short-term and long-term profit-realization. Generally it appears optimal for a pioneer firm to pursue a skimming strategy in the monopoly period for the purpose of gaining short-term profits and then reduce the price before the competitive entry to strengthen its market position. If the product is to be phased out anyway, maintaining skimming prices well into the competitive period, i.e., a harvesting strategy, could be optimal.

Two concluding comments are in order. First, the competitive reaction is more an empirical than a mathematical problem and there has been relatively little progress in the empirical research on the competitive case. Second, although we have focused on pricing strategy, generally a long-term defensive strategy should also include product policy (innovations), as the IBM example shows, to be successful. Price is but one weapon in the arsenal that a company can draw on to defend its market position.

### 6.4.3 Strategic Price Management in Established Markets

In established markets, a brand faces competition from the moment of its introduction. There exists a more or less stable price structure with which the price of the new brand is inevitably compared. Because of this comparison possibilities a firm's ability to increase the price of its brand is limited. On the other hand, if a firm undercuts the competitive price strongly, the competitors would most likely react to defend their market positions (see Chapter 4). As for competitive behavior, it is extremely difficult to explain the actually observed reactive behavior by means of mathematically simple and econometrically measurable reaction functions.

*Life Cycle and Competitive Reactions*
A few examples may support this contention. In Fig. 6.19 the price developments of four products and the respective market share-weighted average prices of competing products are depicted. The variety of patterns is amazing.

Each reduction of product A's price is matched by a larger reduction of the competitive price (or is the causality reverse?). For product B, the competitors raise their prices while B's price is reduced. For products C and D, no reasonable or consistent reaction pattern seems identifiable.

None of the classical (static) hypotheses (like Cournot, Chamberlin, von Stackelberg, Krelle, etc.; see Chapter 4) is capable of adequately explaining such a variety of patterns. If we consider, however, the specific situations of the products (e.g., stage in the life cycle, relative competitive strength, market share shifts), many of the observed reaction moves are explainable.

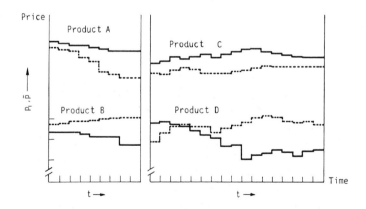

---- Competitive Price
____ Product's Price

Fig. 6.19. Actual Price Developments in Four Markets

Product A has a dominant position and is in the growth stage of its life cycle. Most of the competitors have only recently entered the market and attempt to take market shares from A by means of aggressive pricing. Rather moderate reductions of A's price were sufficient to compensate the effects and to retain the market share.

Product B has a minor market share. In spite of cumulative price reductions of 27%, its share did not increase. Obviously, competitors can behave without paying much attention to this weak product.

Product C has maintained a relatively high market share throughout the period under investigation. Slight losses occurred in the high-price phase but could be compensated by the subsequent price reductions. These price cuts affected the competitors only slightly so that no reactions occurred.

Product C and most of its competing products are in the maturity stage and the observed market share shifts were not dramatic nor were the reactions.

Product D has entered its decline stage. In spite of considerable price cuts, its market share decreased to 60% of the initial value. Evidently competitive products were perceived as superior by consumers, and despite price increases their accumulated share increased. It seems unlikely that competitors would react to any action of product D.

The issue becomes even more complex if, instead of the aggregate price, individual prices of competing products are considered. Such a disaggregation might be important since the competitors are likely to be affected in different ways by a certain action and thus should react differently.

The point is that i) empirical reaction patterns are very diverse and ii) these patterns cannot be explained by simple reaction hypotheses and most importantly iii) product- and market-specific information is extremely useful in explaining the real competitive behavior.

*A Simplified Procedure*

Although the product- and market-specific information is useful to explain the actually observed competitive behavior, it is very difficult to incorporate such information into quantitative and econometrically measurable functions. The problem is aggravated by the fact that no certain information on the cost situation of competitors is available. In a recent empirical study, we found that the biggest competitive information gap exists with respect to competitors' cost. In view of these problems, we suggest, for the time being and in particular under the aspect of managerial application, a simplified two-step procedure for the inclusion of the competitive reaction.

First step: The managers predict expected competitive prices for the periods under consideration. The optimization is run with these prices considered as given (No reaction-hypothesis in an oligopoly-theoretic context).

Second step: The managers reconsider their original estimate of competitive prices under the assumption that the "optimal" prices (obtained in the first step) will be realized. If the original estimates prove still realistic under this assumption, then the final optimal strategy is obtained. If not, the estimates are revised and a new optimization is run. Our experience suggests that a "sufficient convergence" is achieved after one or two re-estimations. This simplified procedure is certainly not fully satisfactory. It should, however, be emphasized that it is appealing to managers and that the input of their subjective judgment on possible competitive reactions increases their confidence in the model's results.

*The Pricing Strategy in Established Markets*

We can make inferences on the relative magnitude of the optimal strategic prices at different stages of the life cycle with the help of the general optimality condition. Since the optimality condition (without competitive reaction) according to (6.8) is

$$p_t^* = \frac{\varepsilon_t}{1 + \varepsilon_t}(C_t' - m_t),\qquad(6.29)$$

we need to know how the magnitudes of the price elasticity $\varepsilon_t$, marginal cost $C_t'$, and the marketing multiplier $m_t$ change over the life cycle of products which are not genuine innovations. Our knowledge of these magnitudes can be summarized as follows:

1. According to available empirical studies, the price elasticity decreases over the introduction and growth stage, reaches its minimum at the maturity stage, and increases during the decline stage (see Chapter 5). This pattern as well as the implied developments of the markup factor $\varepsilon_t/(1 + \varepsilon_t)$ are depicted in Fig. 6.20.

2. The marketing multiplier $m_t$ tends to decrease over time as the obsolescence effect comes into play, thereby reducing the difference between the optimal strategic and the myopic price.

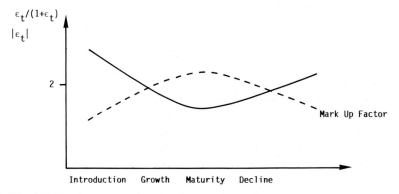

Fig. 6.20. Developments of the Price Elasticity and the Markup Factor over the Life Cycle

Table 6.14
Pricing Recommendations over the Life Cycle in Established Markets

| LC-Stage | Introduction | Growth | Maturity | Decline |
|---|---|---|---|---|
| price elasticity | high | medium | low | medium |
| markup factor | low | medium | high | medium |
| marketing multiplier | high | medium-high | low | very low |
| optimal strategic price relative to the optimal myopic price | low | relatively increasing | relatively high | very high (almost equal) |
| optimal strategic price relative to the marginal cost | low | relatively increasing | relatively high | decreasing |

3. Three hypotheses are economically reasonable for the development of marginal costs: (1) constant marginal cost, (2) marginal cost decreasing with sales volume per period (static economies of scale), and (3) marginal cost decreasing with accumulated sales volume (experience curve effect).

Table 6.14 summarizes the general pricing guidelines that result from the interactions of these three determinants. Note that general statements on the absolute levels of optimal prices at different life cycle stages are not feasible because these levels depend on marginal cost, which can develop in the three different ways described above. Nor can we make general statements about the level of the optimal prices relative to the competitive prices. The relative position of the optimal prices depends on the relative value of the individual product in question, which is reflected in the parameters of the response function. What matters is not the absolute but the relative price level, i.e., price level relative to the performance, quality, etc. The optimal price is always a result of the interaction of demand, cost, and competitive factors.

Fig. 6.21 illustrates three possible patterns of cost development and associated pricing strategies. We can see that the pricing guidelines point to a penetration strategy in the introductory stage (in the relative sense) followed by (relative) price increases. The highest relative price is reached in the maturity stage, where the product is in its strongest position and has the highest market share. If the product is to be retained in the decline stage for an extended period of time, the (relative) price has to fall. Alternatively the firm could pursue a harvesting strategy in this stage.

*Empirical Examples*

Many Japanese firms employ the suggested strategy when they enter new markets. Consequently they apply a very simple principle, which says that a firm should offer

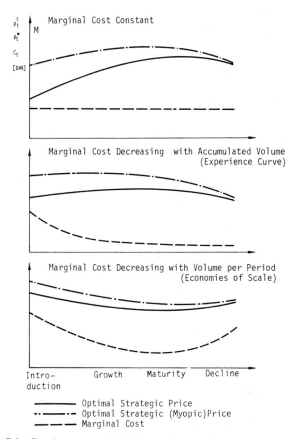

Fig. 6.21. Price Developments under Different Cost Behavior

consumers very strong incentives, i.e., substantially better price terms relative to performance, to motivate them to switch to new unknown products. This strategy is very costly in the short run, but it is the surest way to secure long-term success in the market.

In a less obvious form, this strategy has also shaped IBM's pricing policy until the late 70's. Although at first sight IBM's strategy was that of "holding prices constant", it really was a penetration strategy in the early years after the introduction and later became a harvesting strategy because the competitive prices fell over the life cycle. Fig. 6.22 illustrates this relationship.

Brock (1975, p. 100) describes this strategy for the system 370/135 as follows: "During the first two years of deliveries, the prices are below those of competitors, the third year is equal, and the last three years the price is higher than that of competitors... This procedure means that the company loses some customers toward

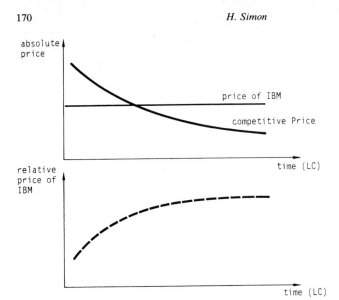

Fig. 6.22. The IBM-Strategy of Constant Prices – Actually a "Penetration-Harvesting Strategy"

the end of the product cycle, causing a need for extra low prices initially in order to win back the previous market share."

An important prerequisite for the harvesting strategy is the timely introduction of a follow-up product. "The knowledge that the company will soon be introducing a new, lower priced product will keep many customers from switching to competitive equipment" (ibid.). Since the late 70's as the competition in the computer industry intensified, substantial price cutting has been part of IBM's overall pricing strategy. This strategy is particularly pronounced for personal computers where the price pressure from the so-called "clones" has been very strong.

The introductory penetration strategy in consumer goods markets usually takes the form of relatively short-term actions, such as discount coupons or special introductory prices for a few weeks, etc. Considering the fact that most new consumer products belong to the "me-too" category, it seems doubtful whether such short-term actions would be enough to attract many consumers to the new product and to keep them. One of the main reasons for the high failure rate of new consumer goods are their high relative prices, which in turn result from overestimating the attractive power of the novelty.

One of the most instructive studies on the relationship between the introductory price and the probability of success was done by Davidson (1976). He examined 50 successful and 50 unsuccessful new brands introduced in Great Britain during 1960–1970. The most important determinant of success turned out to be the price-performance ratio relative to that of competitive brands. Cooper (1979) reports similar findings. These findings are consistent with our recommendations. A new brand which doesn't perform significantly better than the existing products can hope to be successful only with a low relative price. Only those new products which offer superior relative performance can be introduced at equal or higher relative prices. Product managers tend to regard their own new products very highly, which is understandable. But the affection for their new products should not be expressed in the form of unrealistically high prices.

### Pricing Strategy in Later Cycle Stages

The maturity stage of a product is more stable than other LC stages. In addition, more experience and data have been accumulated, which permit a better measurement of the price response. The product reaches its strongest position in terms of the absolute sales level and/or the market share. The markup factor is relatively high and at the same time the difference between the optimal strategic and the myopic price decreases. Marketing investments are rewarding only to a limited degree. This is the stage when the application of the static decision rules seems most permissible. The analytical rules of strategic price management can also be applied with fewer problems because in this stage the situation is in near equilibrium.

A more active pricing policy is typically needed when the product enters the decline stage. If we do not consider the follow-up products and focus only on the product being offered currently, usually it is optimal to reduce the markup factor because of the increasing price elasticity. At the same time, the firm can pursue a near myopic pricing policy.

The optimal pricing strategy for a product in the decline stage is shown in Fig. 6.23. The estimated dynamic price response function was

$$q_t = -393 + 0.397 \cdot 0.95^t \, q_{t-1} - 97.26 \, p_t/\bar{p}_t.$$  (6.30)
$$\quad\;\, (-5.87)\,(3.09) \qquad\qquad (-1.33)$$

The significance of the price response parameter is not very high in this example (significant at only 10%-level).

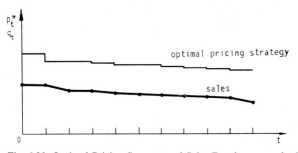

Fig. 6.23. Optimal Pricing Strategy and Sales Development of a Declining Product

Prices were lowered successively. Although the price reductions did not stop the sales decline, the pace of decline was slower than would have been the case if the price had been kept high.

It is generally not possible to prevent the decline of an obsolete product by means of pricing actions. The story of the American car manufacturers in the 1980s provides a good example for this. They offered very attractive price discounts, cash backs and financing terms for their cars without being able to stop the imports from increasing their market share.

The harvesting strategy is an alternative to price cuts in the decline stage. In most cases, this strategy makes sense only when the introduction of follow-up products is planned and/or when the production of the old product involves a lot of opportunity costs. When the company plans to replace the old product with a new one and the loss of market share of the old product doesn't have a negative impact on the introduction of the new one, this strategy could be a viable one (Simon 1985). It could also be considered when the company incurs opportunity costs because of the old product, i.e., part of the capacity is tied up (in the production of the old product) which could be put to better use. In this case, the company can set the price so high that either the opportunity cost is covered or the sales go down so sharply that the (old) product can be phased out.

In pricing products which enter into the decline stage the timing aspect is critical. According to our experience the downward adjustment of prices is typically done too late, i.e., after the market share has substantially declined. In such a situation, it is very difficult to recover. As in the case of competitive entry a proactive rather than a reactive price reduction is much more effective. But again the short- vs. long-term profit dilemma confuses managers in this situation.

Summary: Pricing in established markets is distinguished by two characteristics: (1) there exists a more or less fixed price structure with which the price of each brand is compared and (2) more and better information is available about consumers and competitors. These conditions are favorable for the use of econometric measurement techniques. Still, the measurement of competitive reaction is extremely difficult partially because the competitors' internal data are inaccessible.

The optimal price path in established markets begins with a low price (relative to the marginal cost and the myopic price) in the introductory stage and goes up (relative to these two) until the maturity stage and then goes down relative to the marginal cost. We can't make general statements about the absolute price level in different stages of the life cycle (this depends on how the marginal cost changes over time) nor can we establish general relations between the optimal and competitive prices (these relations depend on the superiority/inferiority of the product in question). Empirical studies on the relationship between the success probability and the prices support these recommendations.

# Appendix to Chapter 6

*Derivation of the Strategic Optimality Condition (6.3) under General Dynamic Price Response Function*

Multiplying the derivative (6.2) by $p_t/q_t$ and substituting $\varepsilon_t$ for the resulting price elasticity expression, we get

$$p_t + (p_t - C_t')\varepsilon_t + \sum (p_{t+\tau} - C_{t+\tau}') \frac{\delta q_{t+\tau}}{\delta p_t} \frac{p_t}{q_t} (1+i)^{-\tau} = 0.$$

Multiplying the summation term by $q_{t+\tau}/q_{t+\tau}$ leads to

$$p_t + (p_t - C_t')\varepsilon_t + \sum \varepsilon_{t+\tau,t}(p_{t+\tau} - C_{t+\tau}') \frac{q_{t+\tau}}{q_t} (1+i)^{-\tau} = 0,$$

where $\varepsilon_{t+\tau,t} = \dfrac{\delta q_{t+\tau}}{\delta p_t} \dfrac{p_t}{q_{t+\tau}}$.

Since the summation term can be expressed as $\varepsilon_t \, m_t$ (see equation 6.4), the derivative reduces to

$$p_t + (p_t - C_t')\varepsilon_t + \varepsilon_t \, m_t = 0,$$

which leads to (6.3) when solved for $p_t$.

*Derivation of the Strategic Optimality Condition (6.19) with Dynamic Cost Function*

The derivative of the objective function with respect to $p_t$ is

$$\frac{\delta \Pi_t}{\delta p_t} = q_t + (p_t - k_t)\frac{\delta q_t}{\delta p_t} - \sum_{\tau=1}^{T} \frac{\delta k_{t+\tau}}{\delta p_t} q_{t+\tau}(1+i)^{-\tau} = 0.$$

Multiplying by $p_t/q_t$ and substituting $\varepsilon_t$ for the price elasticity expression leads to

$$p_t + (p_t - k_t)\varepsilon_t - \sum_{\tau=1}^{T} \frac{\delta k_{t+\tau}}{\delta p_t} \frac{p_t q_{t+\tau}}{q_t} (1+i)^{-\tau} = 0.$$

Multiplying the summation term by $k_{t+\tau}/k_{t+\tau}$ and substituting

$$u_{t+\tau,t} = \frac{\delta k_{t+\tau}}{\delta p_t} \frac{p_t}{k_{t+\tau}}$$

as the elasticity of the unit cost in $t + \tau$ with respect to the price in $t$ into the
derivative and solving for $p_t$, we get

$$p_t^* = \frac{\varepsilon_t}{1 + \varepsilon_t} k_t - \frac{1}{1 + \varepsilon_t} \sum_{\tau=1}^{T} u_{t+\tau,t} \, k_{t+\tau} \frac{q_{t+\tau}}{q_t} (1+i)^{-\tau}.$$

This can be written as

$$p_t^* = \frac{\varepsilon_t}{1 + \varepsilon_t} (k_t - z_t),$$

where

$$z_t = -\sum_{\tau=1}^{T} \frac{u_{t+\tau,t}}{\varepsilon_t} k_{t+\tau} \frac{q_{t+\tau}}{q_t} (1+i)^{-\tau}.$$

Chapter 7

# *Price Management and Psychology*

## 7.1 Price and Psychology

Price response is influenced to a considerable extent by psychological factors. Without understanding these factors, a seller would have difficulty in making a rational pricing decision. Particularly relevant are price perception and evaluation processes, and the role of price as a quality indicator.

Some authors (e.g., Salcher 1977) claim that psychological influences are often inconsistent with economic rationality and that consumers behave irrationally. We do not share this opinion. Although it seems the case at first glance, we can explain many "psychological" phenomena in terms of "economic rationality".

## 7.2 Price Perception and Price Evaluation

This section discusses psychological factors that influence price perception and evaluation, the dynamics of these processes, and their implications for pricing.

### 7.2.1 The System of Price Perception and Evaluation

Table 7.1 shows a simple system of price perception and evaluation.

Price perception can be related either to the absolute price level or to reference prices, where past prices or competitive prices may be considered. The price of a

Table 7.1
System of Price Perception and Evaluation

| Price Perception | Absolute price level | Relative price level | |
|---|---|---|---|
| | | Relative to past prices | Relative to competitive prices |
| Price Evaluation | Price-value-evaluation | Price-value-evaluation | Price-advantage-evaluation |

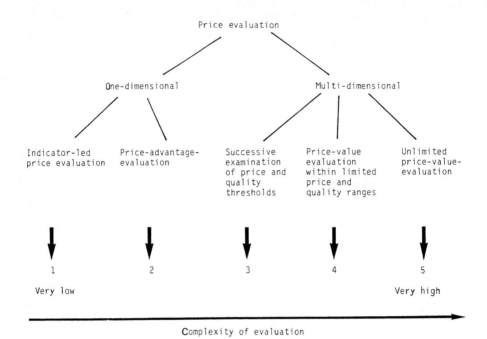

Fig. 7.1. Price Evaluations of Varying Complexity

product can be evaluated on its own merit, and/or relative to the prices of comparable products. The former is called price-value-evaluation and the latter price-advantage-evaluation (Diller 1985). Both forms of price evaluations can play a role in a purchase situation.

Diller (1985) classifies price evaluations along the degree of complexity. He distinguishes between one- vs. multi-dimensional and compensatory vs. non-compensatory price evaluations (Fig. 7.1). In price evaluations of type 1, the buyer relies on an easily accessible indicator (brand, manufacturer, special offer, highest price, etc.). In type 2 evaluations, the buyer compares only prices of products he considers more or less equal.

Types 3, 4, and 5 evaluations are multi-dimensional. Understanding of price evaluation structures is extremely important for price management. For instance, in the case of type 1 evaluations, the manager can control the indicator to cause a favorable impact on price evaluation: strengthen the brand name, choose particular distribution channels, modify packaging. Pure price-advantage-evaluations (type 2) are usually geared toward comparison of competitive prices.

Pricing is most complex, however, if demand is influenced by explicit price-value-evaluations (type 4 and 5), which can be modeled in two ways. One alternative is to have price enter into the utility index as an additional attribute with a negative weight. In a linear compensatory model (vector model), this alternative looks as follows

$$U_i = \sum_j a_j x_{ji} + a_p p_i, \qquad (7.1)$$

with $U_i$ utility index of product $i$, $x_{ji}$, $j = 1,...,n$ perceived value of attribute $j$ of product $i$, $a_j$ weight of attribute $j$, $a_p$ weight of price.

The weight of the price attribute is negative in this model. The ideal product model and the part-worth model are alternatives to the vector model. In the ideal product model, the difference between the ideal and the perceived value of the product's attributes determines a buyer's preference. In a part-worth model, $a_j x_j$ is replaced by $f_j(x_{ji})$ (see Green and Srinivasan 1978).

Another alternative is to compute utility $U_i$ of product $i$ without price and then relate it to price. We define the price-value-criterion $h_i$ as

$$h_i = U_i/p_i. \qquad (7.2)$$

$h_i$ expresses how many utility units are obtained for one monetary unit. The inverse, i.e., price per unit of utility, is called the hedonic price.

To use price-value or utility-oriented pricing techniques one has to know the weights that enter the utility functions. In principle, these weights can be determined by direct questioning. While this method can generate valid results for industrial goods, it is often inadequate for consumer goods. Better methods are multidimensional scaling, conjoint measurement, or analytic hierarchy process (see Green and Carmone 1970, Green and Srinivasan 1978, Thomas 1979, and Chapter 2). In the conjoint measurement technique, alternative product concepts or alternative combinations of two attributes are presented to the respondents. One of the attributes is price. Preferences are then elicited via comparisons of pairs, ranking, or scaling procedures. From these we can compute weights, ideal points and/or part-worths of individual attributes. After determining parameter values, a metrically scaled utility or preference index can be constructed. For more details on the conjoint measurement technique see Chapter 2.

### 7.2.2 Influences on Price Perception and Price Evaluation

We now focus on price perception and evaluation. Table 7.2 lists motivational, cognitive, and situational variables that may influence price perception and evaluation.

Since most of these variables are self-explanatory, we limit the discussion to a few variables for which empirical findings are available. Brown (1971) shows that the

Table 7.2
Variables which Influence Price Perception and Evaluation

| Motivational Variables | Cognitive Variables | Situational Variables |
|---|---|---|
| – personal involvement | – ability to compare quality | – way of exhibiting price (form and quantity, etc.) |
| – striving for • social recognition • quality • cognitive consistency • shopping convenience • saving | – ability to remember and compare prices | – mode of payment |
| | – experience | – time pressure |
| | – trust in the supplier | – competitive products and prices |
| | – self-confidence | – complexity of purchasing task |
| | – application of simplified decision rules (brand loyalty, etc.) | – variability of prices |
| | | – price labeling |
| | | – product use |
| | | – financial situation of buyers |
| | | – price image of the store |

more frugal the buyers are, the better they perceive prices. Gabor and Granger (1961, 1964) note that the knowledge of prices is better in lower social classes (with the exception of the lowest class). Müller and Hoenig (1983) could not confirm the hypothesis that price perception increases with the perceived risk of a purchase.

In most of these studies the knowledge of price turned out to be surprisingly good; on the average, about 50 to 70 percent of the prices stated by consumers were approximately correct. We would like to warn, however, against generalizations. The three empirical examples in Fig. 7.2 show wide variations. In market A the perceived prices reflect the actual prices very accurately, whereas in the case of market B perceived prices have no relation to actual prices. In market C two product categories exist: low-price generics and more expensive branded products. Consumers' perception clearly differentiates between the two categories and their price levels but not within categories.

These findings suggest that consumers' perception and knowledge of prices are highly situation-specific.

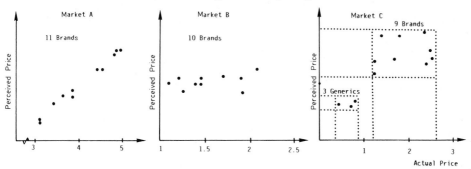

Fig. 7.2. Actual Prices and Perceived Prices in Three Markets

The reader should also note that most of these tests measure some form of price recall. However, Diller (1987) found that consumers in general, have a good awareness of price relations and price structure. He suggests a classification for consumers' price awareness. He distinguishes between knowledge of individual prices, of distribution characteristics and price anchors. He found in an empirical study in West Germany, that 80% of the respondents were aware of the median price of major product categories and had a clear notion of their individual willingness to pay. This finding shows that consumers have a rather high awareness of general price levels. Measuring price awareness by price recall may be a method of limited validity.

Particularly popular elements of price awareness in Diller's study were:
- 78.8% had a good knowledge about the frequency of price deals,
- 77.5% had a correct perception of the price differences between stores,
- 73.5% accurateley ranked specific brands according to price.

On the other hand only 9.4% of the respondents were able to give the price of their most favorite brand in different stores.

These results confirm that price awareness and its formation is an extremely complex process. While the detailed knowledge of individual prices may not be very accurate consumers seem to have a good overall perception and awareness of price structures and relations. The fact that a price is not remembered or not remembered accurately does not necessarily imply that it is not perceived at the time of purchase.

### Perceiving and Evaluating Price Differences

Of central significance for price management is how buyers perceive and evaluate price differences vis-à-vis competitive prices as well as past prices. Some researchers have extended Weber's and Fechner's psycho-physical laws to the perception of price differences and price thresholds (see Gabor and Granger 1964; Adam 1969; Monroe 1971a, 1971b). We find these analogies somewhat misplaced because the psycho-physical laws have to do with physical perceptions (warmth, light, sound, weight). Price, on the other hand, is a figure. We agree with Kaas (1980) that both kinds of stimuli are comparable, only "if weights were presented in terms of abstract numbers (kilograms) or if prices were presented as 'piles of coins'."

*Dynamic Aspects*

The theory of adaptation level provides some insights into the dynamics of price perception. Simply stated, it says that perception and evaluation of a new price are influenced by an adaptation level, which depends, on past prices. The price adaptation level, also called the "reference price", is defined as

$$A_t = p_t^{\alpha} \left[ \left( \prod_{\tau=1}^{n} p_{t-\tau} \right)^{1/n} \right]^{\beta} \tag{7.3}$$

with $\alpha$, $\beta$ as parameters and $\alpha + \beta = 1$. If $p_t$ is greater than $A_t$, the buyer regards the product as "expensive" or "more expensive" and vice versa. Simultaneously, $p_t$ brings the adaptation level closer to the current price level.

The principle of adaptation implies that price thresholds are not fixed but a function of actual prices, a view that is shared by Gabor and Granger (1964). It follows from the adaptation theory that any increase in price should be in small steps, while price reductions should occur in big steps. Readers are referred to Chapter 6 for further discussion of this suggestion.

## 7.2.3 The Control of Price Perception and Evaluation

The firm wants to control price perception and evaluation in such a way that the buyer perceives its products as inexpensive, or at least worth the price. This implies that price reductions should be perceived strongly while price increases should be perceived only weakly.

Managers can control price perception by means of any of the variables listed in Table 7.2. To influence these variables directly, the firm can use non-price marketing instruments (e.g., advertising, personal selling, distribution channels). It can also influence price perception and evaluation through alternative price structures, modes of payment, and tactics of price changes.

*Price Structure*

For numerous products and services, "price" actually has separate components. For example, prices for telephone services, electricity, and bank accounts often consist of a base and a variable rate. Prices of EDP systems consist of prices for hardware, software, and service. In such complex situations a buyer can evaluate a price correctly only after intensive calculation. Such calculations are rare in the case of consumer goods.

An example for telephone services illustrates this problem. Assume that a consumer in West Germany uses 300 units per month. Under the West German fee structure this costs DM 96 (DM 27 base fee + (300 · DM 0.23) = DM 69 variable fee). Any fee combination that satisfies the linear condition

base fee = 96 − 300 · fee per unit

(e.g., base fee = 96, fee per unit = 0; or base fee = 0, fee per unit = 0.32) would not change the total price of the same telephone service for this consumer. It is, however, likely that such alternative structures would create different price perceptions and evaluations even though the total bill doesn't change.

During inflationary periods, shifts in the price structure are frequently employed. One form is called "unbundling" (Guiltinan 1976). Instead of charging a single price for the main product (e.g., a computer) with additional services free of charge (software, test run, service parts), each system component is charged separately. Typically, the price of the main component decreases considerably, while the price of the total system increases (see also Chapter 3). Similarly, the total cost of a house or a car is determined by the purchase price and the financing terms. The relative importance of these two components varies over time. In one case, contractors offered an interest rate of 6.75% to buyers of new homes when the effective mortgage rate of banks was over 10%. The same method is frequently applied in the car market. The reduction in the financing cost is offset by a higher purchase price. Via conjoint measurement technique we can measure price perception and evaluation in such complex situations. Alternative price structures can be included in the research design.

The use of another method, mixed price bundling, has increased in recent years particularly in service industries (Guiltinan 1987). In mixed price bundling, a firm offers its customers the choice of buying one or more products/services individually or of buying a "bundle" of two or more products or services at a special discount. For example:

- Hotels are offering weekend packages that combine lodging and some meals at special rates.
- Airlines routinely bundle vacation packages combining air travel with car rentals and lodging.
- Physicians bundle diagnostic tests into their physical examinations.

Guiltinan (1987) presents a normative framework for determining the demand conditions required for success of each type of bundling. Bundling can be an efficient means of influencing the consumers' perception/evaluation of price.

Price perception and evaluation can be controlled by changing the price structure or individual price components. We need to have a good understanding of perception processes to make an effective use of price structure changes.

## Mode of Payment

Buyers' price perception is likely to be influenced by timing: timing of purchase decision, of consumption of the product, and of payment. A consumer has different price perceptions when he uses a public phone with coins than when he uses the phone at home. The price of travelling by train whose full cost we incur at the time of travel is not perceived in the same way as the costs of travelling by car. A substantial part of the costs of travelling by car was already paid earlier (purchase, tax, insurance). We tend to pay by check or credit card more easily than by cash. It is clear that we can control price perception and evaluation by mode of payment. All forms of credit can be used for this purpose: installment, payment postponement, "buy now, pay later", credit card, charging to bank account instead of paying cash, payment by usage instead of payment in a lump sum, leasing.

## Tactics of Price Changes

The firm prefers a rather strong perception of price decreases, and a weak perception of price increases (Exception: when price is a quality indicator). Thus price decreases should be conspicuously presented. They increase sales only if potential buyers perceive the price decrease. The announcement of a special offer by itself can stimulate sales even without actual price reductions (Diller 1985). Such a trick, however, will destroy the buyer's goodwill toward the supplier in the long run.

The recommendation to advertise price decreases is widely followed in the retail industry. A number of empirical studies show that the effect of a price reduction can be considerably increased by advertising it. In Chapter 12 we deal in more detail with this interaction between price and advertising. A number of tactics can be used to weaken the perception of price increases. The firm can counteract price increases with advertising that strengthens consumer preference, e.g., by emphasizing quality or improvements in quality. The empirical examples in Chapter 12 show that sales after a price increase decrease less if the price change is supported by heavy advertising. In this way, the consumer's attention can be diverted from the price.

Price increases can be realized through changes in package sizes. This alternative is especially useful if one wants to avoid exceeding a certain price threshold, or if one needs round-numbered prices to sell through vending machines. Under conditions of high inflation requiring frequent price adjustments, price increases through package reduction becomes less attractive. Package reduction can provoke undesirable publicity as well. Montblanc, the writing instruments manufacturer, was criticized in a consumer journal (Test, June 1981, p. 80) for keeping the prices of its pencils constant, while shortening them and substituting plastic for the shortened part. Price increases often coincide with product modifications, causing buyers to re-evaluate price and quality all over again. In countries with price controls for existing products, new product introductions may be the only way to implement price increases.

## Price Thresholds

We distinguish absolute and relative price thresholds. There is a widespread belief that sales will decrease sharply if price exceeds certain absolute price thresholds, particularly round figures. The problem of exceeding such a threshold for the first time is of major concern for the price-leader, i.e., the product with the highest price, in inflationary times. The risk of losing market share seems especially great during a transition period, when some of the prices are above the threshold, while other prices are below it.

The existence of such thresholds has not yet been proved. The following arguments for the existence of price thresholds have been put forward:

– consumers divide the price scale into discrete categories (2.98 is seen as "between 2 and 3", 4.95 as "below 5", see Emory 1969),
– consumers tend to define their reservation price in terms of round numbers ("below 3", "at most 5", see e.g., Lange 1972, Theisen 1960),
– consumers feel they are saving when they buy below a round price (Leitherer 1969), consumers are underestimating prices below round figures (Müller and Hoenig 1983),
– the first figure of a price exerts a strong influence on price perception, i.e., a price of 9.95 is perceived "as 9 and something" (Schmitz 1964) or, more generally, the intensity of perception of price digits decreases from left to right (Müller and Hoenig 1983).

In practice, "odd" prices or prices just below round figures play an immense role. Twedt (1965) observed that "9" was the last price digit in 64% of the cases he investigated, Wisniewski and Blattberg (1983) report a percentage of 44.3%. Kucher (1985), analyzing scanner data, found "9" as last digit in 43.5% of several thousand cases.

Research on this policy since Ginzberg (1936) has so far failed to establish its usefulness. Dean (1951) reports several experiments where mail order firms varied prices systematically. "The results were shockingly variable ... sometimes moving a price from $2.98 to $3.00 greatly increased sales, and sometimes it lowered them. There was no clear evidence of concentration of sales response at any figure" (Dean 1951, pp. 430–431).

These ambiguous findings support Gabor and Granger (1964) who suggest that such pricing practice is mainly a product of conventional marketing practices. Kaas and Hay (1984, p. 345) see price threshold effects "as the result of a self-fulfilling prophecy." These views are consistent with the theory of adaptation level used to explain price thresholds, which suggests that the price threshold goes up as actual prices do.

Price thresholds may pose a problem when, under inflationary conditions, the brand with the highest price surpasses the threshold while the other brands' prices are still below the threshold. In such a case, Kaas and Hay (1984) suggest to surpass the threshold with a substantial rather than a marginal price increase. If a negative threshold effect exists at all, it will be offset by the higher contribution margin.

Another situation where price thresholds may have a certain significance are purchases of high price items where consumers often apply a two step decision procedure. In the first step they decide on the maximum amount they want to spend and then confine their choice to products whose prices do not surpass the predetermined price threshold. The same structure applies sometimes to industrial purchasing decisions. Certain budgets are predetermined or the person who decides on the purchase may only be authorized to spend a certain amount. The seller should try to identify such price thresholds and consider them in his pricing.

Summary: The sales effect of a price depends mainly on how the price is perceived and evaluated by potential buyers. Price evaluation can depend on the price-value-judgment (relative to quality) and/or the price-advantage-judgment (relative to competitive prices). Price perception and evaluation are influenced by motivational, cognitive, and situational factors, and thus are situation-specific. The price structure and mode of payment as well as tactics of price change can be used to influence price perception and evaluation. The theory of adaptation level helps explain price perception and evaluation processes. The importance of price thresholds is probably overestimated, but they can be important in specific situations.

## 7.3 Price Management under the Situation of Price-Dependent Quality Evaluation

### 7.3.1 Price as a Quality Indicator

The role of price as a quality indicator represents one of the most important psychological aspects of pricing. Classical price theory assumes that consumers have perfect information and thus their evaluation of product quality is independent of price. Within the budget limits the consumers buy the more, the lower the price is and vice versa (Exception: Giffen's paradox).

*Price-Dependent Quality Evaluation as a Simplified Decision Rule*
In reality, consumers are not generally in the position to correctly judge the quality of products. In many cases, the consumer has to make a purchase decision based on incomplete quality information. The consumer tries to reduce the perceived quality risk and the cognitive dissonance resulting from it, by evaluating quality based on criteria or indicators which are easily accessible and which he assumes are closely related to "objective" quality. Significant indicators of this kind are brand name, manufacturer, the store, and price. Such simplified decision techniques (called "limited problem solving" by Howard and Sheth (1969), and especially price-dependent quality evaluation may be quite rational. The search for objective quality information entails direct costs (e.g., literature, telephone calls, etc.) and/or opportunity costs (time loss). Total cost of a product is the sum of its price and such information costs. A consumer who posits a positive price-quality correlation may find it cheaper to buy a more expensive product considering the underlying trade-off (see Ferguson and Maurice 1978).

A number of intuitively plausible arguments suggest that price is an important quality indicator:
1. Past experience may show that high prices guarantee good quality more often than do low prices.

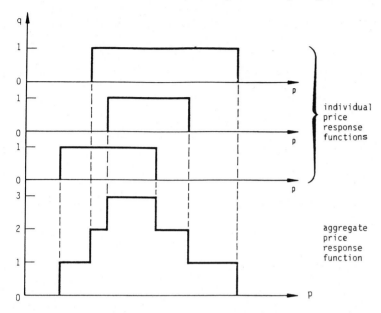

Fig. 7.3. Price Response Functions under Price-Dependent Quality Evaluation

2. Products can be directly compared with respect to price, particularly in the case of consumer goods. When prices are determined via negotiation (e.g., industrial goods), generally they do not serve as quality indicators.
3. Price is a signal of high credibility unlike the advertising messages. Consumers think that price is closely related to cost. A buyer often believes what costs a lot is worth a lot.

*Static Price Response Function under Price-Dependent Quality Evaluation*
The price response function under price-dependent quality evaluation can be modeled in a simple way. We assume that each consumer has an individual "range of acceptable prices". Below the lower limit of the range, quality is regarded as unacceptable. Above the maximum price, the product is considered qualitatively good, yet too expensive. Within the range each consumer buys one unit of the product (for the sake of simplicity).

Fig. 7.3 illustrates the individual price response functions of three consumers and the resulting aggregate price response function. The difference to Fig. 2.3 is apparent.

Gabor and Granger (1966, see also Gabor 1977) have measured price response functions of the type illustrated in Fig. 7.3. They suggest two alternative methods to measure such price response functions. In the direct method, one asks a potential buyer for the minimum and the maximum price he is willing to pay. Using the indirect method, one states a price and asks the respondent if he would purchase the

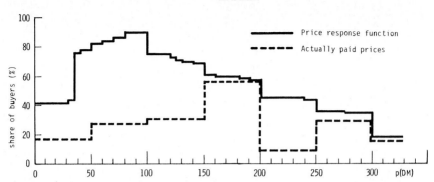

Fig. 7.4. Price Response Function Elicited through Questioning and Actually Paid Prices of Eyeglasses

product at this price. The respondent can answer with "yes", "no, too cheap", or "no, too expensive".

The results from both methods can be used in the same way. Fig. 7.4 shows one result obtained via the direct method. In a study on the purchase of eyeglasses, two questions were asked:
1. What is the maximum price you would pay for a pair of glasses?
2. Is there a bottom price below which you would not buy?

Only about 40 percent of the respondents are willing to buy a pair of glasses at less than DM 35. The mode value of the price response function lies between DM 80 and 100. To the right of this range the curve is "normal" with some disjunctions at specific price thresholds (round numbers).

Of particular interest for price management is the discrepancy between the elicited price response function and the prices actually paid (Fig. 7.4). Fig. 7.4 confirms past research results (Gabor and Granger 1966, Sowter 1973): the mode value of actually paid prices is higher than that of the price response function. This disparity has important implications for the pricing strategy.

Sales or market share distributions of similar shape are observed in many markets. The champagne market is one example (Fig. 7.5). Such a distribution does not necessarily imply the existence of a price-dependent quality evaluation. After all price differences may reflect objective quality differences. Similar relationships have been observed in product categories such as furniture, rugs (Shapiro 1973, Stafford and Enis 1969); shampoo, floor wax (Leavitt 1954); toothpaste, instant coffee (Lambert 1972); table salt (Tull, Boring, and Gonsior 1964) and radios (Schreiber 1960). Actual cases of sales increases after a rise in price were reported for nasal spray, stockings, and ink (Ferguson and Maurice 1978, p. 152). In Germany such an effect was observed for an electric shaver brand (Krups) when its price moved closer to that of the market- and price-leader (Braun).

Price-dependent quality evaluation is not limited to consumer goods. In the Harvard Business School case "Deere Industrial Equipment Operations", the Japanese

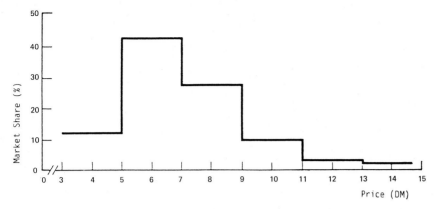

Fig. 7.5. Distribution of Market Shares for Champagne along Price Classes (Source: Spiegel-Verlag)

competitor Komatsu offers comparable machines at lower prices. "This made dealers and customers wonder what "was wrong" with the product" (Shapiro 1977, p. 9).

These findings should, however, be viewed with some reservations.

– Many of them are not based on actual purchase data but on survey data.
– The influence of price is particularly strong if it is the only stimulus (e.g., see Peterson 1970, Jacoby et al. 1971). Such a situation is rather unrealistic.
– The influence of price on quality evaluation is not a static but a dynamic phenomenon, i.e., consumers learn. In many product categories, the consumers' initial reluctance to buy low-priced generic products has disappeared.

In light of these limitations and the contradictory evidence found by Zeitham (1988) in her recent review of studies done on the price-quality relationship, it is necessary to clarify the conditions under which a price-dependent quality evaluation is expected.

*Conditions of Price-Dependent Quality Evaluation*

We expect the phenomenon to occur most frequently in product categories with the following characteristics:

1. Brand and manufacturer names do not play an important role, e.g., rugs, furniture.
2. Consumers have little or no experience,
   – because the product is new. Note that the quality indication is effective only if the new product is not a genuine innovation which is beyond the existing reference system.
   – because the purchase interval is long; that is, for infrequently purchased "low involvement" products.
   – because it is not usual for people to share their experience with the product.
3. Objective quality is difficult to evaluate,
   – because of technical complexity,

   – because of the particular importance of such attributes as durability, reliabil-
     ity, etc.
 4. Considerable quality differences are perceived.
 5. Price itself is an important product attribute
     – prestige products (Snob, Veblen effect),
     – use or display of the product are associated with social risk (wine, liquor,
       cosmetics, fashion products, clothing, gifts, etc.).
 6. Absolute price is not too high. For very expensive products, the search for
     objective quality information can be rewarding. In other words, the reliance on
     price alone can be costly.
   With respect to situational conditions, the role of price as a quality indicator is the
greater,
 7. the greater the time pressure is during the purchase,
 8. the more complex the purchase task is,
 9. the lower the price transparency is (e.g., with respect to the variation of prices for
     the same product),
10. the more the buyer trusts the supplier of the price information.
   With respect to personal characteristics, price-dependent quality evaluation should
be the more important,
11. the less self-confident the buyer is,
12. the less frugal the buyer is,
13. the stronger the desire is to purchase quickly and conveniently,
14. the stronger the desire is to avoid cognitive dissonance,
15. the better the economic situation of the household is,
16. the less product-related information the buyer has.
   Shapiro (1973) examined several of the above hypotheses. Hypotheses 4, 5, 10, and
13 as well as the influence of perceived risk proved to be significant. Influences of
personal characteristics such as self-confidence and frugality showed the expected
signs, but were not significant. Empirical support is lacking for most of the proposi-
tions above.


*Empirical Findings on Price-Quality Relations*
   Diller (1985) examined the actual correlation of "objective" quality and price. The
reader should keep in mind that there are problems in measuring "objective" quality.
Diller calculated the correlations between medium prices and quality evaluations of
Stiftung Warentest (a public foundation which tests products) for 269 product
categories with a total of 4006 items. Table 7.3 shows the median correlation
coefficients for the product categories examined. The results somewhat contradict the
popular price-dependent quality evaluation. This means either that consumers let
themselves be fooled or that the quality measures of Warentest do not fully correspond to the ways consumers evaluate quality. We believe in a third explanation. The

Table 7.3
Median Correlation between Price and Quality (Source: Diller 1985)

| Product Category | Tested Products per Product Category | Mean Correlation Coefficient |
|---|---|---|
| Articles for children | 9 | 0.230 |
| Furniture | 3 | 0.293 |
| Small appliances | 51 | 0.149 |
| Food | 22 | 0.108 |
| Detergents | 17 | 0.575 |
| Textiles | 17 | 0.058 |
| Leisure/hobby/sport | 40 | 0.273 |
| Phono/radio/TV | 23 | 0.299 |
| Photo/optical/watches | 26 | 0.325 |
| Cosmetics | 8 | 0.007 |
| Major household appliances | 29 | 0.183 |
| Automobiles and auto-parts | 24 | 0.002 |
| Sum/median | 269 | 0.190 |

data show that if the consumers choose the most expensive item:
– a product with the highest quality grade is chosen 51 percent of the time,
– a product ranked satisfactory or better is chosen 83 percent of the time,
– a product whose quality is at least as good as that of the cheapest one is bought 81 percent of the time.

The simple decision rule "buy the most expensive product", therefore, offers a certain insurance against the risk of obtaining inferior quality. Whether the premium for this insurance, i.e., the price difference compared to products of equal value, is reasonable or too high, can be said only for each individual case. Diller shows that often we can get good quality more cheaply. But without the information on search costs, it cannot be said whether the consumer behaves rationally or not.

### Dynamics of Price-Dependent Quality Evaluation

Price-dependent quality evaluation is not constant over time. Consumers learn and/or exchange their experience. We can consider the dynamics from three partly interactive aspects
– learning processes of a single consumer,
– developments during the product life cycle,
– general economic developments.

Consumers' uncertainty about quality is the highest at the first purchase and goes down with the use of the product. As experience is accumulated, i.e., the learning process progresses, the individual minimum acceptable price may approach zero. If such a learning process takes place for many buyers, the aggregate price response

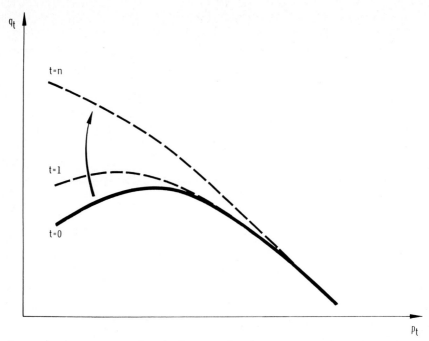

Fig. 7.6. The Development of the Price Response Function over Time with Quality Learning

function shifts over time (see Fig. 7.6). This explains why the sales of well-known brands increase more than those of lesser-known ones when their prices are marked down as special offers. The learning process for such brands has progressed more than for the lesser-known ones. If the purchase interval is long and/or if there is little motivation to store experience, the learning process does not become effective. In such a case, a repeat purchase is little different from the first purchase as far as the information is concerned; quality evaluation remains price-dependent.

Quality evaluation during the life cycle (1) runs parallel to the individual learning processes described and (2) is influenced by quality changes over time. Over the life cycle, the quality of the new product improves constantly. As a result, the quality-related risk diminishes and quality evaluation is likely to depend less on price.

The dynamics of cost and competition have a considerable impact on this process. Falling prices due to the experience curve effect and new competitors with aggressive pricing strategies shatter the existing price-quality relationship. The case of IBM-compatible personal computers (so-called clones) offers an illustrative example. Yet, as the example of Japanese automobiles shows, this process can take a lot of time. Market entry is made difficult for aggressive newcomers by price-dependent quality evaluations. In the extreme case, it may be possible that a product-related cost advantage cannot be passed on to the market. In a long-term study of the Intermarket Institute, Benad (1975) reports a decreasing importance of price-dependent quality evaluation. A similar finding is reported by Meffert and Bruhn (1984) for the West German Market. Reasons may include better consumer education, rising consumerism, availability of more information, etc.

In many countries, so-called no name, generic, or white products have made major inroads into the markets of long-established "classical" brands. Generally these products are sold at prices 25% to 40% below the leading brands. Many empirical studies show that consumers are less concerned about inferior quality of these products (Meffert and Bruhn 1984). The pharmaceutical market is another example where aggressively priced generics play an increasingly important role. In the West German pharmaceutical market, a generic company became the largest competitor as of 1986 in terms of prescription volume.

Summary: Consumers often view price as a quality indicator. Price-dependent quality evaluation is not necessarily irrational and may represent a simplified decision rule that helps to save search costs. As a consequence, the price response function may include some positively sloped segments, as has been shown for a number of products examined. Price-dependent quality evaluation is particularly significant when other indicators are absent, consumers have no experience with the product, big differences in quality are suspected, or price itself is an important attribute. Situational (e.g., time pressure) and personal (e.g., self-confidence) variables also influence this role of price. Dynamic aspects are important because individual experiences and learning processes change the dependence of quality evaluation on price. Typically the product quality also changes over the life cycle. Also influential are such developments as consumer attitudes, consumerism, better consumer education, etc. These factors may have reduced the price-dependency of quality evaluation in the last decade.

### 7.3.2 Strategic Implications of Price-Dependent Quality Evaluation

The presence of price-dependent quality evaluation has strategic implications for the choice of the relevant price range, market entry, and market segmentation.

*Relevant Price Ranges*
We focus on the single product-single price case. Price differentiation and competition are not considered. Assume a price response function of the type illustrated in Fig. 7.3. Independent of cost-related price floors, the relevant pricing range is limited to prices $p > p^m$, where $p^m$ represents the price at which the price response function is at its maximum. To the right of $p^m$, "normal" price response conditions exist, and the optimal price can be determined in the way we discussed in previous chapters.

We demonstrate the procedure with the eyeglasses example (Fig. 7.4). Fig. 7.7 shows the empirically determined price response values and the approximated response lines (to the left of $p^m$ as a dotted, to the right of $p^m$ as a solid line). The price response function to the right of $p^m$ is $q = 113 - 0.2916p$. The revenue-maximizing

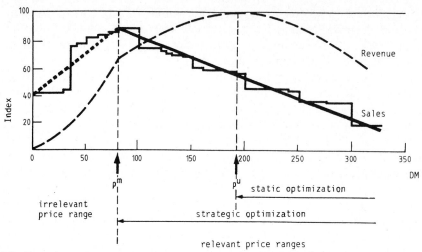

Fig. 7.7. Relevant Price Ranges under Price-Dependent Quality Evaluation from an Empirical Example

price is $p^u = 113/(2 \times 0.2916) = $ DM 194. The revenue curve is given by the dashed line.

There is a difference between static and strategic pricing. Under static pricing, the revenue-maximizing price defines the market-oriented price floor. It corresponds to the optimal price if marginal cost is equal to zero. For marginal cost $C'$ greater than zero, the static optimal price is the same as in the usual linear case (see Chapter 3). For $C' = 50$, we obtain an optimal static price $p^s$ of 219.

Under strategic optimization the relevant price range is extended by the interval $(p^m, p^u)$. The strategic optimal price lies in this interval if the marketing multiplier (= present value of carryover effects) is higher than static marginal cost. If the example is based on a carryover coefficient of 0.5, an expected unit contribution margin of DM 80, and a discount rate of $i = 0.10$, then the marketing multiplier is $m = $ DM 66.66 (see Chapter 6). The strategic optimal price $p^* = p^s - m/2 = 219 - 33 = 186$ would be to the left of the revenue-maximizing price $p^u$. Under strategic optimization, $p^m$ remains the price floor. Thus, there exists always an absolute price floor under the situation of price-dependent quality evaluation, which is not the case under the situation of a "normal" dynamic price response function.

*Competitive Orientation*

So far we have not considered competitive influences. It is particularly instructive to contrast the price response function determined by surveys with the distribution of competitive prices on the one hand, and actually paid prices on the other. The latter distribution is reproduced from the example of glasses in Fig. 7.4. There we showed that the highest prices paid lie to the right of the mode value of the price response

Sales

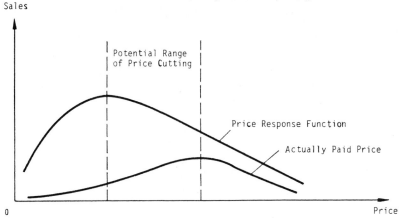

Fig. 7.8. Price-Dependent Quality Evaluation with Price Cutting Potential

function (see also Gabor and Granger 1966). Such a finding suggests that most consumers don't yet consider a slightly falling price as a sign of reduced quality. Only if price-cutting exceeds a certain level it will have negative impact on quality perception. As Fig. 7.8 demonstrates, this situation implies that some potential for price-cutting exists. For a "moderate" price cut below the current price level to be successful, the objective quality standard should be undercut only slightly. If "moderate" price-cutting causes sales increases, competitive reactions will follow. This should be considered in the pricing decision (see Chapter 4).

### Market Segmentation under Price-Dependent Quality Evaluation

So far we have dealt with the market as a whole. Such an undifferentiated view can be dangerous under the situation of price-dependent quality evaluation. Consumers may differ in their behavior, e.g., experts are likely to evaluate quality more objectively than amateurs. Fig. 7.9. illustrates such a situation. Segment 1 shows a "normal" price response, that is, quality is evaluated independently of price, while segment 2-buyers make a price-dependent quality evaluation. The aggregate response function (dashed line) is similar to that in previous examples.

Table 7.4
Price Optimization for a Market with Two Segments with Differing Quality Evaluation

| Segment | Price Response Function | Relevant Range | $p^s$ | $G^s$ |
|---|---|---|---|---|
| 1 | $q_1 = 7 - p_1$ | 0– 7 | 4.5 | 6.3 |
| 2 | $q_2 = 10.2 - 0.85p_2$ | 5–12 | 7 | 19.1 |
| Total | $q = 17.2 - 1.85p$ | 5– 7 | 5.65 | 24.6 |

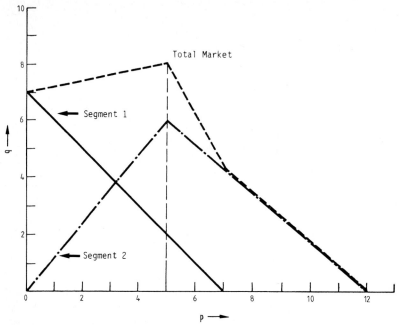

Fig. 7.9. Segment Specific and Aggregate Price Response Functions for a Market with Two Segments and Differing Quality Evaluation

Table 7.4 shows the data as well as the optimal values from static optimization at marginal cost of $k = 2$.

This example shows, first, that price differentiation under segment-specific quality evaluation leads to better results; and second, that a segment-specific price to the left of the total market's sales-maximizing price (here $p = 5$) can be optimal.

### Price-Image Consistency

When price affects quality perception, it becomes an important instrument for image control. It is then crucial to achieve price-image consistency. If we measure image one-dimensionally and label the extremes of this dimension "exclusive" and "simple", respectively, the relations shown in Fig. 7.10 result.

When price affects quality evaluation:
1. It determines the position of the product on the image dimension.
2. Consumers are attracted to those products whose position is close to their ideal product image or high on their preference vector.
3. If the image and quality expectations of these consumers are met, they become regular customers. Price-image consistency exists, and the product has a good chance of success.

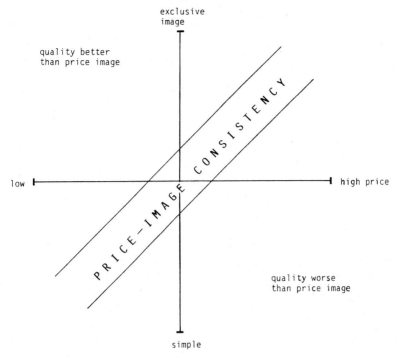

Fig. 7.10. Price-Image Consistency

4. If expectations are not met, the consumers will switch to other brands. There is a high probability of failure. Consumers who would accept the lower quality are not reached because the price is too high.
5. If expectations are more than met, there can be two consequences: consumers remain loyal, although they would be content with lower quality. Or they switch to cheaper products, hoping to find the quality that matches their ideal level. Consumers whose ideal level matches the quality, on the other hand, are not attracted in the first place.

In any case, price-image consistency is desirable. Gabor and Granger (1965) estimate that about 20 percent of the new product failures are due to price-image inconsistencies (see also Köhler 1973). The consistency model explains why many manufacturers object to having their brands discounted. First, such an action would shift the position of an item from the upper right to the upper left in Fig. 7.10. Then, there is the danger of slipping to the lower left. Here is a conflict of interest between manufacturer and retailers. Retailers are interested in price promotions for those items for which price reduction is not interpreted as a sign of low quality. This is often the case for strong brands, and in practice only these brands generate a strong "pull" effect.

*Price-Dependent Quality Evaluation and Market Entry*

Price-dependent quality evaluation has ambivalent implications for the market entry of new brands. On the one hand, it extends the price range upward, so that it becomes easier for the newcomer without a cost advantage to achieve an introductory price that covers cost. On the other hand, a price-dependent quality evaluation limits the chance to use price as a weapon to achieve quick penetration. In this way it protects the established products against price-aggressive newcomers.

Strategic recommendations vary. If quality perception based on price remains constant over time, the only option is to adjust price to quality standards (Sabel 1973). In this situation, it is advisable to keep price constant, or to adjust it only in inflationary periods. This "fixed price strategy" for branded products is supposed to have a stabilizing effect on image and quality evaluation (e.g., Gutenberg 1966, p. 367).

Strategically more challenging is the situation where a learning process takes place, and quality evaluation depends less and less on price. In the earlier stages of the life cycle, the situation is not much different from the one where the price-dependent quality evaluation remains constant. But after a certain period of time, depending on the speed of the learning process, the firm faces the option to either maintain the high price or to expand the market share by pursuing a more aggressive pricing strategy.

Fig. 7.11 shows the division of the life cycle into a price-inactive phase and a potentially price-active phase. In the first phase, the major objective is to establish a strong quality image. Advertising plays a central role here. For example, Pepsi Cola entered the market with the advertising campaign whose main message was that most consumers preferred Pepsi to Coca Cola in a blind test (see Fortune, June 1, 1981, p. 32).

These considerations suggest that it would be better to introduce a new brand to the champagne market shown in Fig. 7.5 in the price range of DM 5 to 7 rather than below DM 5. After many consumers have become familiar with the quality by consuming it and are less affected by price, a price reduction could be considered to increase consumption and to tap new market segments. Such a strategy would be better than an introductory penetration strategy.

Some pricing strategies seem too aggressive. For example, in the eyeglasses market German companies such as Foto-Quelle and others offer eyeglass frames at about DM 40. The quality perception shown in Fig. 7.4 suggests that higher prices (something like DM 70-100) could lead to faster penetration.

Summary: When price serves as an indicator of quality, a part of the price response function is positively sloped. The relevant price range is then limited to the right side of the sales maximizing price. In this case, an absolute price floor exists even under strategic optimization. We can get a clue to room for price cuts by contrasting the price response function with actually paid prices. If a price-dependent quality evaluation is suspected, the manager should determine whether it is general or segment-specific. Depending on the result, market segmentation based on price

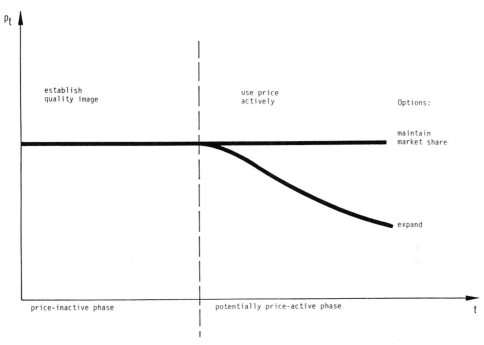

Fig. 7.11. Pricing strategy under Decreasing Price-Dependent Quality Evaluation

and/or product differentiation might be advisable. Under price-dependent quality evaluation, price is an important instrument for image control. It is desirable to strive for price-image consistency. There are ambivalent implications for market entry: room for upward price moves is bigger and room for downward price moves is smaller. Depending on the consumer learning process, we can divide the life cycle into a price-inactive and into a potentially price-active phase.

Chapter 8

# *Price Management and Market Segmentation*

## 8.1 Problem Definition

In the previous chapters we have mostly treated the demand side as if the buyers were homogeneous in their reactions towards price. Frequently, however, the buyers differ in income, preference structure, price sensitivity, reservation price, etc. Such heterogeneity suggests that firms should treat buyers differently. On the other hand, sub-groups of buyers are typically homogeneous enough in their behavior, so that they can be served with the same marketing program.

The idea of segmentation is to divide the market in such a way that the segments are maximally homogeneous within themselves and maximally heterogeneous across themselves. Then the firm is in the position to address one or several segments with segment-specific marketing programs and pricing strategies.

Thus the whole task of market segmentation consists of two parts:
1. Identification of market segments.
2. Developing (normative aspect) and implementing (operational aspect) segment-specific strategies.

We discuss each of these topics in turn in the context of price management. For a more general discussion of the segmentation concept we refer to the literature (e.g., Frank, Massy, and Wind 1972; Bonoma and Shapiro 1984; Grover and Srinivasan 1987). In the context of price management, segmentation is particularly useful. Recently powerful methods have been developed that can assist managers in segmenting the market and in developing segment-specific pricing strategies.

## 8.2 Identification of Market Segments

### 8.2.1 Segmentation Criteria

Good segmentation criteria should meet the following requirements:
– behavioral relevance, i.e., categorize customers with respect to differences in behavior,

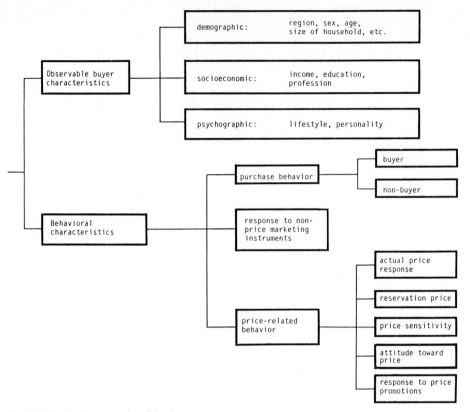

Fig. 8.1. Market Segmentation Criteria

– be measurable/easy to observe,
– be addressable by marketing actions.
Segmentation criteria can be structured as shown in Fig. 8.1.

   The practical dilemma is that the behaviorally relevant criteria are often hard to observe and/or the segments defined on such criteria cannot be addressed separately. On the other hand, segments solely based on observable criteria may be easy to address but are often of doubtful behavioral relevance. Table 8.1 summarizes this dilemma.

   Marketers can attempt to overcome this problem in the following way:

1. Segments are first defined on the basis of behavioral differences, e.g., price sensitivity, reservation price, preference structure, etc.
2. Correlations between the behavioral and the observable buyer characteristics (e.g., socio-demographic) are identified/measured.
3. Operational and addressable market segments are then redefined on the basis of the observable characteristics that strongly correlate with the behavioral criteria.

Table 8.1
The Evaluation of Different Market Segmentation Criteria

| Evaluation | Segmentation Criteria | |
| --- | --- | --- |
| | Observable Characteristics | Behavioral Characteristics |
| Observability/Measurability | relatively good | relatively poor |
| Addressability/Accessibility | relatively good | relatively poor |
| Behavioral Relevance | low, questionable | high |

Table 8.2
Seven Subjects Identified on Two Market Segmentation Criteria

| Subject | Income | Reservation Price |
| --- | --- | --- |
| 1 | 2000 | 100 |
| 2 | 4000 | 300 |
| 3 | 5000 | 100 |
| 4 | 3000 | 300 |
| 5 | 1800 | 170 |
| 6 | 1000 | 200 |
| 7 | 3500 | 400 |

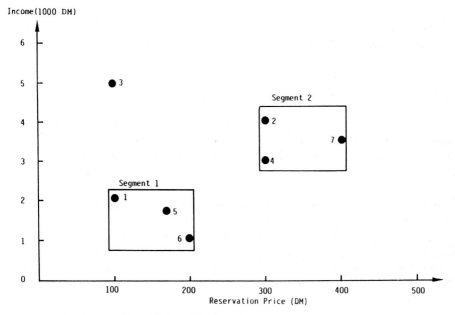

Fig. 8.2. Market Segmentation with Two Criteria

We demonstrate this procedure with a simple example. Suppose a survey produced the results in Table 8.2. The table shows for seven subjects the reservation price (= the maximum price a buyer is willing to pay for a product), a behavioral characteristic, and the income, a socio-demographic characteristic which is easy to observe because data on income are readily available.

While it is difficult to identify segments from the table, the visualization of the market as shown in Fig. 8.2 reveals two distinct segments. Three subjects are willing to pay DM 300–400, while the reservation prices of subjects 1, 5, and 6 lie in the range of DM 100–200. For these six subjects the reservation price is closely related to income. Subject 3 is an outlier.

In this market, it would be advisable to introduce two product versions, a cheaper one in the range of DM 100–200 and a more expensive model in the range of DM 300–400. Each segment would have to be reached via different media and distribution channels. The operationalization of the segmentation on the basis of the observable variable "income" is necessary to address the segments separately. Methodologically the approach applied in this example resembles cluster analysis.

We first discuss a series of empirical applications of price-related market segmentation. It should be noted that segmentation is not a method but a task (or rather a challenge) which can be tackled through many alternative methods.

### 8.2.2 Empirical Applications

*Market Segmentation According to Price Elasticities*

To be able to measure the price response for individual buyers or for sub-groups, data should be available at a corresponding disaggregate level. Such data often exist for regionally separated markets. Fig. 8.3 shows the price elasticity estimates for 14 sales districts (Wittink 1977). It would lead to sub-optimal results to set a uniform price in all districts.

Table 8.3 shows the price elasticities for a pharmaceutical brand in seven European countries. The values are based on a combination of customer surveys and expert judgments. The price elasticities differ considerably among these countries. It is obvious that such huge differences call for a differentiated pricing strategy.

Fig. 8.4 shows the result of a study on price response for diagnostic materials for laboratory use. Price elasticities differ sharply depending upon the annual purchase volume of customers. Information of this kind is a good base for price differentiation (e.g., quantity discounts).

The next example is based on scanner data collected for individual households. Based on these data, household (price) deal elasticities were econometrically estimated for two brands (A and B) and three income groups (low, medium, high). Fig. 8.5 shows that the price deal elasticities differ markedly across income groups and brands.

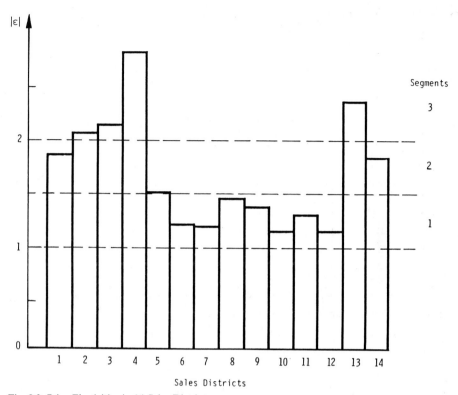

Fig. 8.3. Price Elasticities in 14 Sales Districts

High income households respond strongly to price deals of brand A, while price deals for brand B have a higher effect with low income earners. Households with medium income respond similarly to price deals for both brands. Therefore, price

Table 8.3
Price Elasticities for a Pharmaceutical Brand in Seven European Countries

| Country | Price Elasticity |
|---|---|
| France | −1.26 |
| Germany | −0.63 |
| UK | −0.89 |
| Holland | −0.53 |
| Italy | −0.78 |
| Spain | −1.07 |
| Switzerland | −0.47 |

Price Elasticity (absolute)

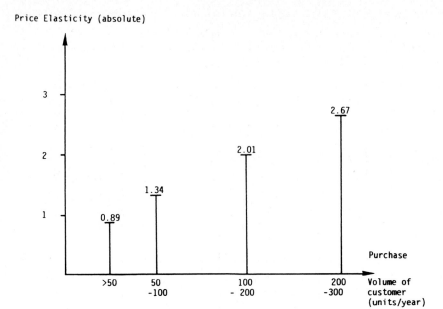

Fig. 8.4. Price Elasticity According to Purchase Volume of Customers

Price Deal Elasticity (absolute)

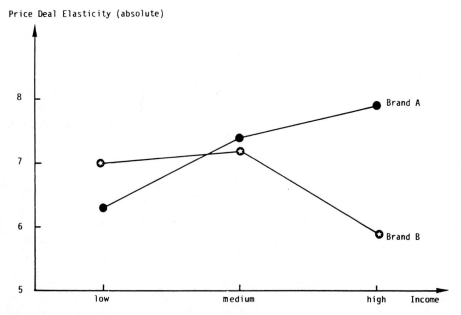

Fig. 8.5. Price Deal Elasticities for Three Income Groups and Two Brands

deals for the two brands should aim at different income classes. In a similar vein, Blattberg et al. (1978) studied whether households that heavily purchase products on deals could be identified on the basis of socio-demographic characteristics. They found that households are especially deal prone, if they
– own a house (have more space),
– own a car (have easier transportation).
Their results show that households which have both a house and a car were 66% higher than those without both in the deal-proneness measure defined by the authors.

### Market Segmentation Based on Multivariate Techniques

Numerous multivariate techniques, such as conjoint measurement, analytic hierarchy process, multidimensional scaling, cluster analysis, etc..., can be used to segment markets and to detect differences relevant to price management.

### Analytic Hierarchy Process

The analytic hierarchy process (Saaty 1980, 1986) enables us to measure the relative importance of various factors. The measurement is based on paired comparisons and a constant sum scale, i.e. the weights add up to 100.

In Fig. 8.6 we reproduce the result of a study for light industrial vehicles. Two

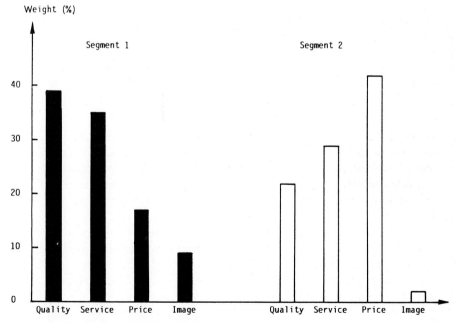

Fig. 8.6. Market Segmentation with Analytic Hierarchy Process

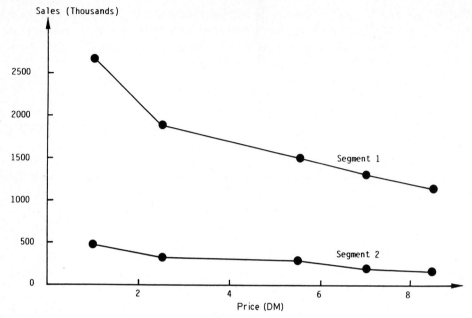

Fig. 8.7. Price Response Functions for Two Segments Derived via Conjoint Measurement

highly distinct segments were identified. Segment 1 is very quality- and service-oriented, whereas price is the most important factor for segment 2.

The company must decide which segment it will address and with what kind of marketing strategy. It would be very inefficient in this case to pursue a strategy which appeals to the "average" customer.

*Conjoint Measurement*

Similar results can be derived via conjoint measurement (see Chapter 2). The difference between analytic hierarchy process and conjoint measurement is that in the former the stimuli consist only of the factors, whereas in conjoint measurement we have to provide alternative levels for each factors. This additional feature allows us to derive individual or segment-specific price response functions based on individual part worths.

Fig. 8.7 shows an example of a chemical product where price response functions were derived via conjoint measurement technique for two segments of customers. Both the levels and the slopes of the two functions are highly different.

The results have far-reaching implications for segment-specific strategies.

In a second example we show individual price response functions for a consumer nondurable. These functions apply to the "variable-quantity-case" (see Chapter 2). Such functions serve as the basis for the so-called non-linear (or quantity-dependent)

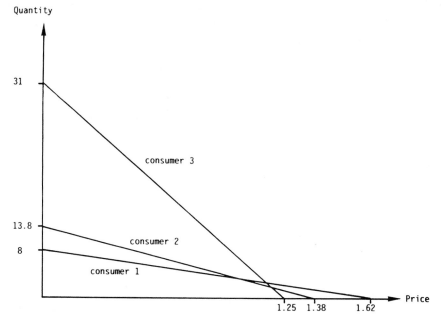

Fig. 8.8. Individual Price Response Function for Chocolate Derived via Conjoint Measurement (Source: Tacke 1988)

pricing, which we discuss later in this chapter. The product under consideration is chocolate and the price response functions for three consumers are

$$q_1 = 8.12 - 5p,$$
$$q_2 = 13.86 - 10p,$$
$$q_3 = 31.44 - 25p.$$

These functions are shown in Fig. 8.8.

The figure shows that consumer 3 is very price-sensitive and consumer 1 reacts little to changes in price. Consumer 2 is in-between. Managers can take advantage of such strong heterogeneity of consumers by charging different prices to each consumer group.

*Multidimensional Scaling*

Multidimensional scaling is another technique which provides interesting opportunities for market segmentation (see Green and Tull 1978). Perception and preference data are represented in a so-called mapping or joint space. By means of this technique differences between customer segments can be detected and illustrated.

Two preference models are used in this context, the vector model and the ideal-point model. In most price situations, the vector model is more relevant since

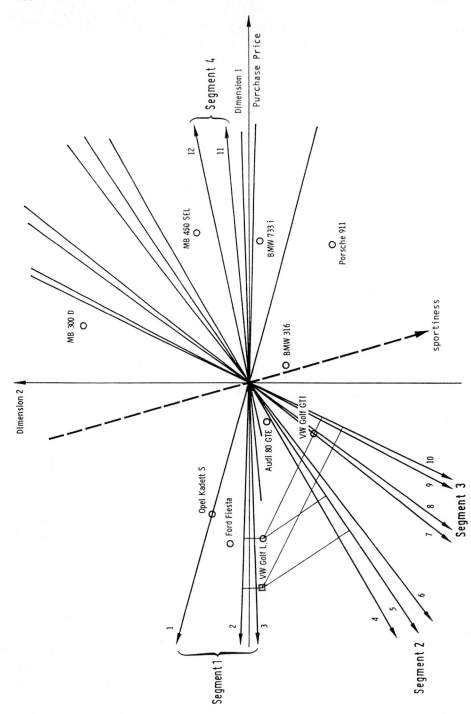

Fig. 8.9. Market Segmentation on the Basis of Preference Vectors Derived via Multidimensional Scaling

customers, cet. par., typically prefer a lower price to a higher one. However, if price affects the quality perception or the prestige value of a product, the ideal-point model may be more valid. We present three applications.

Fig. 8.9 shows the positions of ten automobile models in the German market. The horizontal axis represents the attribute "purchase price" which is highly correlated with "prestige". The vertical axis strongly correlates with the attribute "sportiness".

The other (solid) arrows represent the preference vectors of 12 customers who are representative of various segments in this market. The direction of the arrow symbolizes an increase in preference. A person's preference for a specific model is measured by the projection from the model's position to the customer's preference vector. Such lines are shown for VW Golf L and for customers 2, 5, and 10.

Four distinct segments are identified:
- Segment 1: customers 1, 2, and 3
  This segment is very price-sensitive. A price increase reduces the preference substantially (and vice versa).
- Segment 2: customers 4, 5, and 6
  To this segment sportiness is as important as price.
- Segment 3: customers 7, 8, 9, and 10
  Here sportiness is more important than price.
- Segment 4: customers 11 and 12
  In this segment, preference goes up as price does, which can be explained by the extremely strong correlation of price with the attributes "prestige" and "exclusiveness". This segment values these attributes highly and is willing to pay a high price to get them.

Fig. 8.9 also shows the effect of a hypothetical price reduction for VW Golf L. Suppose the car's position moves to the one marked by a square because of a price reduction. As a result of this, the preference of customer 2 (segment 1) increases more than that of customer 5 (segment 2) whose preference in turn rises more than that of customer 10 (segment 3).

The second example shown in Fig. 8.10 concerns an industrial product. In this study nine competitors were included in the analysis whose positions are marked by dots in the figure. The two most important dimensions are "high quality/know-how" and "low price". Three preference segments (1,2, and 3) are identified.
- Segment 1: very quality- and know-how-oriented customers, mostly large and technologically sophisticated firms.
- Segment 2: firms in this segment attach similar weights to quality/know-how and price, mainly medium-sized companies with an intermediate technology.
- Segment 3: price sensitive customers with low interest in quality and know-how, companies with low technology and/or of small size and low purchase volume.

We see from the figure that competitor C has the strongest preference position in segment 1, while B and A are the preference leaders in segment 2 and 3, respectively. This analysis was done for company C and later C stopped serving segment 3. C is

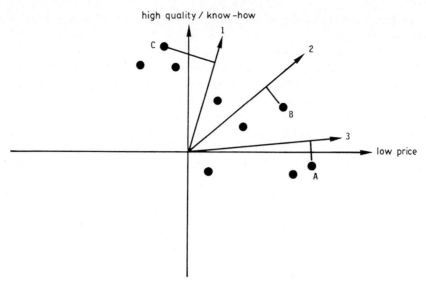

Fig. 8.10. Market Segmentation for an Industrial Product Based on Preference Vectors

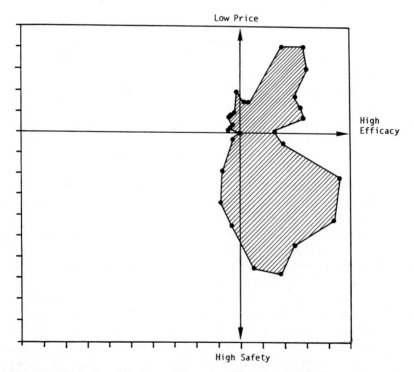

Fig. 8.11. Distribution of Preference Vectors in a Pharmaceutical Market

the technology leader with a high cost position and cannot be competitive in segment 3 where only price counts.

Fig. 8.10 does not show the size of the segments. A method developed by Kucher enables us to visualize this information. In this method, each individual preference vector is calculated and then vectors which point to the same direction (e.g., the same 5°-sector) are added so that the length of a vector represents the size of a segment. Then the end points of these vectors are connected and the preference surface is shaded. In this way a managerially helpful visualization of the segment structure is obtained. Fig. 8.11 gives an example for a pharmaceutical market.

One should note that the surface provides only a rough approximation of the segment sizes. In this case the majority of the 200 doctors surveyed are not price-sensitive but mainly interested in efficacy and safety. Thus a price reduction would appeal to only the minority group. This kind of illustration is very well received by managers because it helps them understand the market structure.

### The Defender Model

In multidimensional scaling we usually treat price as a product attribute and include it as a dimension in the perceptual map. Hauser and Shugan (1983) suggest an alternative scaling procedure. They divide each attribute by the product's price and derive "per dollar" perceptual maps. This concept is similar to the price-value criterion and the price-performance ratio we discuss in Chapter 7 and 11, respectively.

Fig. 8.12 illustrates the procedure. The horizontal dimension represents "Efficacy/$", while the vertical axis measures a brand's position with regard to "Mildness/$". It is assumed that consumers maximize "Utility/$" which is the weighted sum of a brand's value on the two attributes. Thus, this model is a preference vector model. Consumers are heterogeneous, i.e. they apply different weights for "Efficacy/$" and "Mildness/$". The figure shows the preference vector for a specific consumer. "Joy" has the highest preference value for this consumer followed by "Ivory".

The model provides three basic repositioning options:
– a (pure) price change: the brand moves along the ray emanating from the origin and passing through its current position,
– a (pure) change in efficacy moves a brand horizontally,
– a (pure) change in mildness moves a brand vertically.

All three options can, of course, be combined. The impact of such changes on the preference position can be visually verified. Hauser and Shugan (1983) employ the model to derive optimal defense strategies which depend on the distribution of the individual preference vectors. Defender is a market share model. Its unique feature is that attributes are measured "per dollar". This assumption is rather controversial (Sen 1982, Gavish et al. 1983, Rao 1984). The empirical evidence suggests that the Defender model may be superior to comparable models in predicting market share

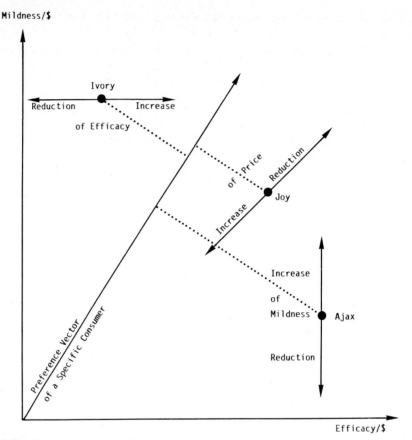

Fig. 8.12. The Defender Model with Three Repositioning Options

(Hauser and Gaskin 1984). Under the pricing perspective the inclusion of the price variable is extremely interesting. The preference distribution/segmentation and the competitive structure and their implications for pricing are explicitly considered.

Many other methods can be employed to segment markets according to differences in price response and other variables. Other techniques not discussed here are cluster analysis, discriminant analysis, automatic interaction detection, and multiple regression. We would like to emphasize again that market segmentation is not a method but a task which can be accomplished by many different methods. Both creativity and methodological knowledge are essential. A unique advantage of multivariate techniques is that here price is viewed in the marketing mix- and the competitive context. Such a way of incorporating price is managerially realistic and relevant.

Summary: The identification of market segments is the first step in the process of market segmentation. It presupposes the determination of segmentation criteria which are behaviorally relevant, observable, and addressable. There is no "optimal" solution to the segmentation problem. Creativity and imagination are as important as methodology. The potential rewards of good segmentation are, however, enormous.

## 8.3 Segment-Based Price Discrimination

Segment-based price discrimination involves the determination of segment-specific prices (normative aspect) and the implementation of the price discrimination (operational aspect). We discuss these two aspects in the next two subsections.

### 8.3.1 Normative Aspects of Price Discrimination

Suppose a certain number of market segments are identified and segment-specific price response functions

$$q_i = f(p_i) \tag{8.1}$$

are known ($i$ = segment index). Sales in segment $i$ are assumed to depend only on price $p_i$. This implies that segments can be addressed separately and arbitrage does not exist. The cross-price elasticity between two segments is zero.

We do not consider the cost of price discrimination nor competitive influences. Under these conditions, the optimal price in each segment is very simply determined by the segment-specific Amoroso-Robinson Relation

$$p_i^* = \frac{\varepsilon_i}{1 + \varepsilon_i} C_i', \tag{8.2}$$

where $\varepsilon_i$ price elasticity in segment $i$, $C_i'$ marginal cost in segment $i$.

When both price response and cost functions are linear, this can be modified to

$$p_i = \tfrac{1}{2}(a_i/b_i + k_i), \tag{8.3}$$

where $a_i$ and $b_i$ are price response parameters and $k_i$ represents the unit variable cost.

We demonstrate the potential of price discrimination with a simple case of two segments. The linear price response functions are

$$q_1 = 100 - 10p_1, \quad q_2 = 84 - 6p_2.$$

The variable cost per unit is 4 for both segments. If we do price discrimination, we get the following optimal values:

|              | segment 1 | segment 2 |
|--------------|-----------|-----------|
| optimal price | 7        | 9         |
| sales volume  | 30       | 30        |
| profit        | 90       | 150       |

The total profit is 240. If we set a uniform price, the aggregate price response function is

$$q = 184 - 16p$$

and we obtain an optimal price of 7.75. The sales are 60 and the profit is 225, which is 6.25% lower than the optimal value of 240.

An important case is regional price discrimination. How should different transportation costs be incorporated in pricing? There are three common practices:
- Uniform fob prices: The delivered price is equal to the factory price plus actual transportation costs,
- Zone prices: A uniform delivered price is applied throughout a given region (zone),
- Uniform price: A uniform delivered price is applied in all regions.

We illustrate the difference between the conventional practice where transportation costs are fully added to the price and the optimal price obtained according to (8.3) with a simple example. Suppose a company in Boston serves three regional markets: Boston, Providence, and New York. The (fully variable) transportation cost per unit is

$$TC_B = 0,$$
$$TC_P = 50,$$
$$TC_{NY} = 100.$$

Variable production cost amounts to 500 and the price response function is the same in all three markets.

$$q_i = 10000 - 10p_i.$$

The maximum price is, therefore, 1000. If we don't consider transportation cost, the optimal ex factory-price is 750. Table 8.4 shows the results under the "conventional" and the optimal strategy.

In conventional strategy, the transportation cost is fully charged to the customer so that (with equal price response functions) the unit contribution margin is held constant. In our example this strategy yields a total contribution of 1,500,000. Under the theoretically optimal price structure where only 50% of the transportation cost is passed on to the buyer, the total contribution is 1,531,250. Even if the company gives up price discrimination and charges a uniform price, it would be better off in this

Table 8.4
Comparison of Conventional and Optimal Strategy

|  | Price | Unit Contribution | Sales | Total Contribution |
|---|---|---|---|---|
| Conventional: | | | | |
| Boston | 750 | 250 | 2500 | 625,000 |
| Providence | 800 | 250 | 2000 | 500,000 |
| New York | 850 | 250 | 1500 | 375,000 |
| Total | | | | 1,500,000 |
| Optimal: | | | | |
| Boston | 750 | 250 | 2500 | 625,000 |
| Providence | 775 | 225 | 2250 | 506,250 |
| New York | 800 | 200 | 2000 | 400,000 |
| Total | | | | 1,531,250 |

example. The optimal uniform price would be 775 and a total contribution of 1,519,000 would be obtained.

Many companies refrain from regional price discrimination due to legal, competitive, and cost reasons. One should note that substantial profits may be lost by doing so.

*Classical Price Discrimination*

We have so far discussed the price optimization for given market segments. In the classical price discrimination model, on the other hand, optimal prices and segments are determined simultaneously on the basis of a single price response function. Without loss of generality, we present the classical model using the linear price response function (von Stackelberg 1939).

The prerequisite for price discrimination on the basis of this function is a uniform distribution of individual reservation prices (the "yes:no-case" from Chapter 2). If, on the other hand, the linearity of the aggregate demand function is due to the linearity of the individual price response functions, i.e., each individual customer buys more at a lower price (the "variable quantity-case" in Chapter 2), then price discrimination is not feasible. Thus the application of the classical model is confined to the yes:no-case. The left portion of Fig. 8.13 illustrates the situation without price discrimination for a numerical example. The underlying price response function is

$$q = 100 - 10p$$

and the constant marginal cost $k$ equals 4. Then we get $p^{max} = 10$, $p^* = 7$, Sales = 30, Profit = 90. The shaded rectangle represents the profit. Under "perfect" individual

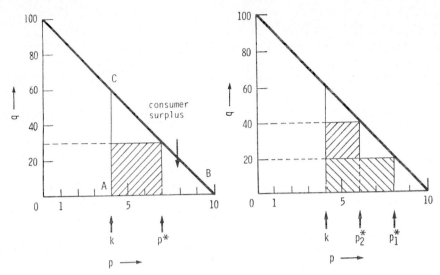

Fig. 8.13. The Classical Model of Price Discrimination

price discrimination, not only this rectangle but the whole triangle ABC represents the profit. The profit potential not exploited by the firm is called "consumer surplus".

The effect of dividing the market into two segments is illustrated in the right portion of Fig. 8.13. The optimal price and sales for Segment 1 are 8 and 20, respectively. For Segment 2 we get $p_2^* = 6$ and $q_2 = 20$, so that the total profit amounts to $4 \cdot 20 + 2 \cdot 20 = 120$ (shaded area). The more segments are formed in this way, the more profits can be realized. The generality of this relationship can be easily inferred from the figure.

We have so far assumed that market segmentation and price discrimination entail no costs. This assumption is, of course, unrealistic. Identifying market segments as well as implementing the price discrimination is not only costly but the costs tend to rise more than proportionally to the number of segments. Conversely, the marginal

Table 8.5
Number of Segments and Profits in an Empirical Study

| Number of Segments | Profit Index | Marginal Profit |
|---|---|---|
| 1 | 0 | – |
| 2 | 65.9 | 65.9 |
| 3 | 72.8 | 6.9 |
| 4 | 87.6 | 14.8 |
| 5 | 90.0 | 2.4 |
| 6 | 90.3 | 0.3 |

increase of benefits usually goes down as the number of segments increases. In reality, it is hard to estimate the benefits and costs of segmentation. A study by Elrod and Winer (1980) sheds some light on this issue. If one sets the profit without segmentation equal to zero and that with perfect individual price discrimination equal to 100, then the profit indices at different numbers of segments are as shown in Table 8.5.

The profit potential is almost exhausted with four segments. We believe that this result is rather typical and conclude that the optimal number of segments is small in practice.

## Price Discrimination through Non-linear Pricing

While classical price discrimination concerns the "yes:no-case", non-linear pricing is relevant for the "variable quantity-case" as defined in Chapter 2. In this case a consumer buys fewer or more units of a product depending on its price. Since the marginal utility decreases with the number of units, the consumer's willingness to pay for an additional unit decreases as well. He is willing to pay more for the first than for the second unit, and so on (Law of Gossen). If consumers are heterogeneous in this regard (which is almost always the case), the seller can increase his profit – as compared to a uniform price – by setting a higher price for the first than for the second unit a consumer buys, and so on. This is called non-linear pricing, i.e., the average unit price decreases with purchase volume (see Phlips 1983).

We illustrate the non-linear pricing approach with a numerical example. We have three consumers whose willingness to pay for the first, second, etc. unit is given in Table 8.6.

We assume (without loss of generality) that marginal cost $C'$ is zero. We derive the optimal price scheme by setting the profit-maximizing price for each product unit separately. For the first unit we have the following options:

- $p_1 = 12$ only C buys $\qquad q_1 = 1$ $\qquad$ Profit$_1 = 12$,
- $p_1 = 10$ C and B buy $\qquad q_1 = 2$ $\qquad$ Profit$_1 = 20$,
- $p_1 = 9$ C, B, and A buy $\qquad q_1 = 3$ $\qquad$ Profit$_1 = 27$.

Table 8.6
Non-Linear Pricing in an Example with Three Heterogeneous Consumers

| Product Unit | Willingness to pay per consumer and product unit | | | Optimal price for $n$-th unit | Unit Sales | Profit |
|---|---|---|---|---|---|---|
| | A | B | C | | | |
| first | 9.0 | 10.0 | 12.0 | 9.0 | 3 | 27.0 |
| second | 6.0 | 7.5 | 10.0 | 6.0 | 3 | 18.0 |
| third | 3.5 | 5.5 | 8.0 | 5.5 | 2 | 11.0 |
| fourth | 2.0 | 4.0 | 6.0 | 4.0 | 2 | 8.0 |
| fifth | 1.1 | 1.5 | 3.5 | 3.5 | 1 | 3.5 |

Table 8.7
Comparison of Non-Linear and Uniform Pricing

|  | Optimal Uniform Price | Optimal Non-Linear Price Scheme |
|---|---|---|
| Price | 6.18 | 9 for the first unit down to 3.5 for the fifth unit, average price 6.14 |
| Unit Sales | 7.85 | 11.0 |
| Profit | 48.52 | 67.5 |

Obviously $p_1 = 9$ is the optimal price for the first purchase unit, etc. In the case of the fifth unit we can either set a price of $p_5 = 1.1$ to get $profit_5 = 3.3$, or $p_5 = 1.5$ with $profit_5 = 3$, or $p_5 = 3.5$ with $profit_5 = 3.5$. With the optimal scheme total sales are 11 units and profit is 67.5.

This profit should be compared with the one obtained through uniform pricing. Aggregating the three individual price response functions as demonstrated in Figure 2.3 and calibrating the aggregate response function econometrically, we get

$$q = 15.7 - 1.27p,$$
$$(53.26)(-30.36)$$
$$R^2 = 0.990,$$

where $p$ uniform price, $q$ total unit sales.

Since $C' = 0$, the optimal uniform price is $0.5 \cdot 15.7/1.27 = 6.18$ and total sales are 7.85 units yielding a profit of 48.52. Table 8.7 compares the two price schemes.

Fig. 8.14 demonstrates that non-linear pricing exploits the profit potential of this market much more effectively than uniform pricing. The shaded area represents the profit with uniform price while the much larger surface below the step curve gives the profit with non-linear pricing.

There are several common forms of non-linear pricing schemes (Dolan 1987). $R(q)$ denotes the charge for a quantity $q$.

1) A two-part tariff (Fig. 8.15a): A fixed charge $F > 0$ is imposed if any good is purchased and a uniform price $p$ is then paid for all units.

$$R(q) = \begin{cases} F + pq, & \text{if } q > 0 \\ 0 & \text{if } q = 0 \end{cases}.$$

2) A two-block tariff (Fig. 8.15b): A per-unit price $p_1$ is charged for any units up to quantity $q'$, then per-unit price changes to $p_2$ for all units greater than $q'$.

$$R(q) = \begin{cases} p_1 q & \text{if } 0 < q < q' \\ p_1 q + p_2(q - q') & \text{if } q > q' \end{cases},$$

where $p_1 > p_2$.

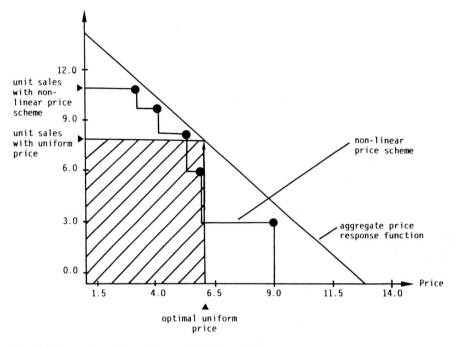

Fig. 8.14 Comparison of Non-Linear and Uniform Pricing

3) All-units quantity discount (Fig. 8.15c): If a certain quantity level $q'$ is exceeded, the price applies to all units, not just those incremental to the break point.

$$R(q) = \begin{cases} p_1q & \text{if } 0 < q < q' \\ p_2q & \text{if } q > q' \end{cases},$$

where $p_1 > p_2$.

We apply four alternative schemes to an empirical example. For this, we must know the structure of the individual price response functions in the "variable quantity-case" (= "willingness-to-pay functions"). Using a conjoint design Tacke (1988) measured such "willingness-to-pay functions" for chocolate bars. Based on the knowledge of these functions he developed optimal non-linear price schemes under alternative non-linear tariffs. Table 8.8 shows the results. The percentage profit increases over uniform pricing are given in the last row of the table. The superiority of non-linear pricing is clearly demonstrated.

Thus, through non-linear pricing a seller can transform a substantial part of the consumer surplus into his own profit. In addition, consumers are given the incentive

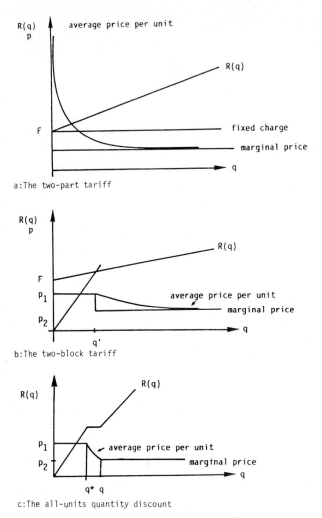

Fig. 8.15. Common Forms of Non-linear Pricing Schemes

to remain loyal to his brand if the discount applies to the cumulative purchases in a given period. If the consumer has bought a specific brand, he is motivated to buy the same brand again within a period of time to qualify himself for the discount (e.g., frequent flyer program). In this context, the experience of American Airlines is suggestive which called its frequent flyer program "the single most successful marketing tool we've ever had" (Newport 1985).

Summary: If market segments can be separated, optimal prices are determined by segment-specific Amoroso-Robinson Relations. In the case of regional price dis-

*Price Discriminati*

In the U.S., tl
promotion in co
amount specified
from the newspap

Coupon is noi
Little, and Kleir
According to Na:
tivity than non-u:
the sales in the
coupons to prom
realize optimal p:
buyers are willing

*Price Discriminat.*

Segmentation
Examples are:
– age: special ad
– income and ec
  azine subscrip
  tions to organi
– profession: di:
  public officials
– membership:
  discounts for e

*Support of Price .*

If market segn
implement a "pu
prices. In such a
non-price market
parency and mak
ated prices are
supporting price
Differentiatioi
prices in differen
Product differ
less than the pri
(1980, p. 211) rej
differences of up
only the package
Brand differei

Table 8.8
Different Price Structures for Chocolate Bars (Source: Tacke 1988)

|  | Uniform Price | All-Units Discount | Two-Part Tariff | Two-Block Tariff with Fixed Charge |
|---|---|---|---|---|
| Price | $p = 1.12$ | $p_1 = 1.27$ $p_2 = 1.10$ $q' = 8$ | $F = 0.57$ $p = 1.03$ | $F = 0.57$ $p_1 = 1.37$ $p_2 = 1.03$ $q' = 1.676$ |
| Sales | 788 | 1206 | 1168 | 1186 |
| Profit | 134.13 | 200.96 | 212.00 | 219.56 |
| Profit Increase over Uniform Price |  | 49.8% | 58.0% | 63.7% |

crimination transportation costs should be considered as additional marginal costs and thus should not be simply added to the factory price, as is customarily done. In the classical model of price discrimination, segments are not given ex ante. Instead, prices and segments are determined simultaneously. This type of price discrimination is applicable to the "yes:no-case" (Chapter 2) when individual reservation prices are known. Non-linear pricing is a particularly powerful method of price discrimination and widely applied in practice. It is applicable in the "variable quantity-case" with heterogeneous price response functions.

### 8.3.2 Implementational Aspects of Price Discrimination

This subsection discusses the implementation of price discrimination. Critical issues in this context are how the market segments can be separated from each other and how the price discrimination can be supported by other marketing instruments.

#### Regional Price Discrimination

Since geographic distance or international borders serve as natural barriers against arbitrage, regional price discrimination may seem easy to implement. If arbitrage costs are higher than the price differential, this may be the case. In reality, due to the reduced transportation costs regional price discrimination is difficult to realize even at the international level. "Grey imports" of automobiles and other durables, "parallel imports" of pharmaceuticals across EEC-countries or computer imports from the U.S. into Europe are good examples of the (partial) failure of international price discrimination. For many internationally operating companies these re-, parallel-, or grey imports pose serious problems. Even if the arbitrage costs are taken into account when the initial prices are set, problems are likely to develop over time due to differences in national inflation rates and fluctuations in exchange rates.

Com⌐
substan⌐
were in
process⌐
market
home m
may be
the pro⌐
compan
price st⌐
would ⌐
quantit⌐

*Tempor*
    Tem
often a
profitat⌐
    Exar
– time
    dorf⌐
– day
    stau⌐
– seas⌐
In mos⌐
making
for fas⌐
system⌐

*Price L*
    In g
– the
    then
– the ⌐
    disc⌐
– legal
The m⌐
produc
recomr⌐
tariff.

sometimes highly different prices. This strategy is particularly popular in consumer durables, e.g., video recorders. Some manufacturers have added generics to their traditional lines of branded products.

Use of multiple differentiated instruments: Often multiple instruments are differentiated. A certain product version is distributed only through a specific channel under a specific brand or generic name.

It is often necessary to support price discrimination with such measures. However, the implementation costs go up as more marketing instruments are employed to support price discrimination, which makes a careful cost-benefit analysis essential.

### Price Discrimination and Information

The implementability of price discrimination strongly depends on the information situation. This is particularly true when prices are individually negotiated between seller and buyer – the extreme case of price discrimination.

In such situations, price discrimination is often possible only if certain buyers are not aware that the product can be bought elsewhere at a lower price. While most of the approaches described above are public in the sense that the price discrimination scheme is known to everybody, some discrimination schemes depend on a confidential treatment of the price information for their success. Customers can become extremely annoyed if they learn that other customers (particularly if those are their own competitors) have got a more favorable price deal. This is often a hot issue in price negotiations between manufacturers and retailers.

We know of several cases where the whole price level collapsed because price concessions, explicitly characterized as "exceptional" were given to an individual customer. In spite of the promises to keep such deals secret, sooner or later the truth becomes known and the concessions have to be extended to more and more customers. Even the most sophisticated kinds of discounts, rebates, and bonuses which are used to disguise the true size of the price concessions hardly work in the long run. This is the opposite of the skillful exploitation of consumer surpluses. Such risks should be taken into account when prices are differentiated.

Another important aspect that has to be born in mind in price discrimination are legal constraints. In most countries, price discrimination is limited by law. In the U.S., the Robinson-Patman Act of 1936 forbids to charge different prices to two buyers under identical circumstances unless the supplier can justify the price differences (see Monroe 1979, Scherer 1980). In Germany, price discrimination is not generally prohibited but companies which are in a dominant position are subject to restrictions.

Chapter 9

# *Vertical Price Management*

## 9.1 The Problem

We have so far assumed that the manufacturer deals directly with the end-users of his product and he determines the end-price. This is the case for many industrial goods, banking and insurance, and so on. In other industries, both direct and indirect distribution channels coexist (e.g., automobiles, furniture, electric appliances). Some companies use both types of channels (e.g., coffee, office machines, electric appliances). For many other products selling through retailers is the typical or the only form of distribution (e.g., food, textiles, books). The manufacturer who sells indirectly has to consider the behavior of intermediaries in his pricing policy.

Important factors in this context are:
– sales response to end-price,
– pricing policy of retailers,
– relative power positions of manufacturers and retailers.

Fig. 9.1 shows a simple illustration of the system. The following cases are of interest:

1. The manufacturer sets both the ex factory- and end-price and thus determines the trade margin.
2. The manufacturer sets the ex factory-price, but has no influence on the end-price.
3. The retailer determines the ex factory-price, and the manufacturer can either accept or refuse this price.
4. Manufacturer and retailer cooperate in pricing and try to maximize the profit. The division of profits is determined via the ex factory-price and thus subject to negotiation.

## 9.2 Vertical Price Management of the Manufacturer

### 9.2.1 The Manufacturer Sets the Ex Factory- and End-Price

Two action parameters – the ex factory-price $p_H$ and the end-price $p$ – are at disposal to the manufacturer. These two parameters determine the trade margin $s$,

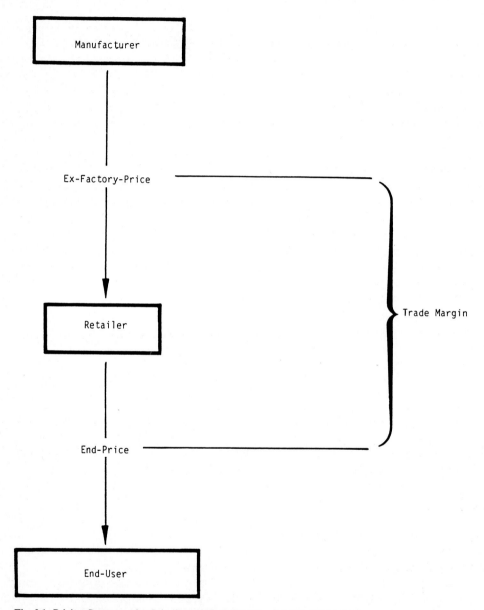

Fig. 9.1. Pricing System under Sale through Retailer (One Intermediate Level)

according to the equation

$$s = p - p_H. \tag{9.1}$$

It should be noted that this decision situation is determined by the actual behavior of manufacturers and retailers and not by the legal conditions. While in most countries and for most product categories the classical resale price maintenance (RPM) has been abandoned, there are still major markets where RPM prevails. Cigarettes, pharmaceuticals, published materials, gasoline are typical cases.

Non-binding price recommendations have the same effect if they are observed by the retailers. A study in West Germany produced some interesting findings (Batzer et al. 1976):
- small retailers appreciate recommended prices and tend to observe them, about 60% of the respondents stick entirely to the recommendations,
- the retailer price-recommendation under which the recommended price is only known to the dealer but not to the end-customer is about twice as frequent as the consumer price-recommendation, under which the recommended price is typically printed on the package,
- small retail firms value the price-recommendation as a decision and marketing support. Price-aggressive retailers appreciate the positive sales effect which supposedly results from undercutting the recommended price.

*Optimization of End-Price and Margin*
Under these assumptions, the response function for the manufacturer is of the following type

$$q = q(p,s), \tag{9.2}$$

with $q$ as sales, $p$ as end-price, and $s$ as trade margin. Margin $s$ determines the extent to which retailers push the product. The higher the margin is, the more eagerly the retailer pushes the product (active selling support, shelf space, promotion). We can define the margin elasticity as

$$\gamma = \frac{\delta q}{\delta s} \frac{s}{q}. \tag{9.3}$$

It represents the percentage change in sales (holding end-price $p$ constant) when the margin changes by 1%.

Margin and end-price have opposite effects. An increase in end-price leads to a negative end-user response, but increases – holding ex factory-price constant – the retailer's incentive to push the product because of increased margin. The optimal combination of end-price and margin balances these two opposing tendencies. In order to maximize the manufacturer's profit we differentiate the profit function

$$G = (p - s)q(p,s) - C(q),$$                                          (9.4)

with respect to $p$ and $s$ and obtain

$$\frac{\delta G}{\delta p} = q + (p - s)\frac{\delta q}{\delta p} - C'\frac{\delta q}{\delta p} = 0,$$                (9.5)

$$\frac{\delta G}{\delta s} = -q + (p - s)\frac{\delta q}{\delta s} - C'\frac{\delta q}{\delta s} = 0,$$               (9.6)

where $C'$ denotes marginal cost with respect to quantity.

If we multiply equation (9.5) with $p/q$, equation (9.6) with $s/q$, and substitute price elasticity $\varepsilon$ as well as margin elasticity $\gamma$, we can solve for $p^*$ or $s^*$ to get the following two equations.

$$p^* = \frac{\varepsilon}{1 + \varepsilon}(C' + s),$$                          (9.7)

$$s^* = \frac{\gamma}{1 + \gamma}(p - C').$$                               (9.8)

Since $p_H^* = p^* - s^*$, it follows

$$p_H^* = \frac{\varepsilon + \gamma}{1 + \varepsilon + \gamma}C'.$$                             (9.9)

From equations (9.7)–(9.9), we draw the following (cet. par.) conclusions:
- the smaller the absolute price elasticity $\varepsilon$, the larger $p^*$, $s^*$ and $p_H^*$ are (and vice versa),
- the larger the margin elasticity $\gamma$, the larger $p^*$, $s^*$, and $p_H^*$ are (and vice versa),
- the existence of intermediaries, compared to the case of direct sales, leads to a higher end-price,
- as price elasticity goes down, the margin $s^*$ goes up more than the ex factory-price $p_H^*$ and the unit contribution margin, if the margin elasticity $\gamma$ is greater than one. If the margin elasticity is smaller than one, the opposite result holds,
- as margin elasticity $\gamma$ goes up, $s^*$ increases more than $p_H^*$, if price elasticity is greater than two (and vice versa).

If retailers incur variable distribution cost of $k$ per unit, the gross margin $(p - p_H)$ should be changed to the net margin $(p - p_H - k)$. The above statements concerning the effects of price and margin elasticity are not affected.

Table 9.1 summarizes the suggestions concerning end-price and margin strategy.

Table 9.1
Qualitative Suggestions for a Manufacturer's End-Price and Margin Strategy

| Price Elasticity $\varepsilon$ | Margin Elasticity $\gamma$ | |
| --- | --- | --- |
| | low | high |
| low | end-price high<br>margin low | end-price high<br>margin high |
| high | end-price low<br>margin low | end-price low<br>margin high |

*Numerical Example*
Assuming constant elasticities, i.e., a response function of the type

$$q = ap^{\varepsilon}s^{\gamma} \qquad\qquad (9.10)$$

and constant marginal cost $C'$, we can apply the decision rules (9.7) to (9.9) directly.
Fig. 9.2 shows the optimal end- and ex factory-prices as a function of $\varepsilon$ and $\gamma$ when
$C' = 1$. The difference between the two curves represents the margin $s^*$.

*Manufacturer's and Retailer's Share*
    Of particular interest is the question of how the total margin ($p^* - C'$)) is divided
between the manufacturer and the retailer. The manufacturer's share of the total

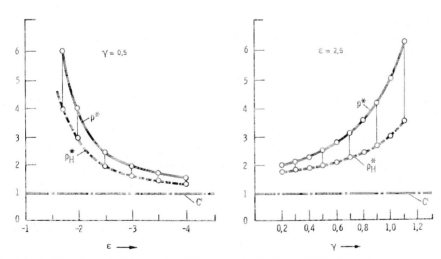

Fig. 9.2. The Effect of Changes in Elasticity on Optimal Prices and Margins

margin is $(p_H^* - C')/(p^* - C')$. Substituting $p_H^*$ and $p^*$ from (9.9) and (9.7), respectively, and simplifying lead to $1/(1 + \gamma)$ as manufacturer's share and $\gamma/(1 + \gamma)$ as retailer's share. Manufacturer's margin and retailer's margin are the same when margin elasticity equals one. When it is greater than one, the retailer receives the larger portion of the total margin and vice versa. This result is conclusive since for a margin elasticity greater than one a reduction of the manufacturer's margin is overcompensated by the additional sales induced by the increased retailer's margin.

### The Margin as Competitive Weapon

If several brands compete at the retail level, margin can be an effective competitive weapon. The dealer would push the brand that yields him the highest margin, ceteris paribus. The above analyses are applicable to the competitive case.

In practice, private brands and generic products generally yield higher margins than branded products. Since margin is much less transparent than price, manipulations of this instrument are hard to detect by competitors. Thus margin can be an important element of a pricing strategy which tries to avoid or delay competitive reactions. They allow selective-covert measures to increase one's market share in the hope that the competitors will only detect them after some delay and thus will react late.

### Empirical Aspects of Margin Elasticity

The empirical measurement of margin elasticity is difficult because of insufficient variation of margin data. One alternative is to estimate the elasticities of action budgets. Since the manufacturer here gives the retailer additional monetary incentives, the effect is similar to that of a margin increase and we can expect a similarity of elasticities. Action budget data have the advantage of sufficient variation. The problem is the short-term nature of the effect of action budgets. Table 9.2 shows an estimate of action budget and price elasticities for three consumer goods.

If we express the optimal margin $s^*$ as a function of ex factory-price $p_H^*$ by

Table 9.2
Econometrically Estimated Elasticities of Action Budgets (as proxy of the margin elasticity) and Price Elasticities.

| Product | Action Budget Elasticity | Price Elasticity |
|---------|-------------------------|------------------|
| A | 0.742 | −2.19 |
|   | (8.65) | (−1.78) |
| B | 0.401 | −4.13 |
|   | (2.49) | (−1.68) |
| C | 0.363 | −1.157 |
|   | (3.85) | (−2.64) |

Table 9.3
Implied Values of the Margin Elasticity for Different Price Elasticities and Markup Rates

| Markup Rate ($s$ as % of $p_H$) | Implied Margin Elasticity $\gamma$ | | |
|---|---|---|---|
| | $\varepsilon = -2$ | $\varepsilon = -3$ | $\varepsilon = -4$ |
| 10% | 0.18 | 0.27 | 0.36 |
| 25% | 0.40 | 0.60 | 0.80 |
| 50% | 0.33 | 0.50 | 0.67 |
| 100% | 1.0 | 1.5 | 2.0 |

combining (9.8) and (9.9), we obtain the following markups on $p_H^*$ for the three products:
- product A: 51.2%,
- product B: 29.3%,
- product C: 45.7%.

Since these retail markups are realistic (see Tables 10.1 and 10.2), the elasticity values of Table 9.2 are plausible. Remember, however, the problem of the short-term nature of the action elasticity.

Another alternative is to estimate the margin elasticity subjectively. The difficulty here is that the concept of margin elasticity is still unfamiliar to many retail and industrial managers.

We can derive the implied margin elasticities for different price elasticities and markup rates (markup percentage) on $p_H$. They are given in Table 9.3.

Thus we expect the range of margin elasticity to be between 0.2 and 1.5.

Summary: We have derived the conditions for the optimization of end-price and trade margin. The optimal values there depend on the price and margin elasticities. The division of the total margin between the end-price and manufacturer's marginal cost is exclusively determined by the margin elasticity. The margin can be an important competitive weapon. Its low transparency has implications for competitive reaction. The measurement of margin elasticity is difficult and empirical results are not yet available. Some reasonable analyses suggest that its realistic values are between 0.2 and 1.5.

### 9.2.2 The Manufacturer Sets only the Ex Factory-Price

Today the typical situation for most consumer goods is as follows: The manufacturer sets an ex factory-price and the retailer decides on the end-price. To fix the profit-maximizing ex factory-price, the manufacturer needs information on
- the price response function of the end-users,
- the retailer's price-setting behavior as a function of the ex factory-price.

The following hypotheses deserve special attention:
- the retailer adds a fixed percentage to the ex factory-price (cost-plus calculation),
- the retailer sets his profit-maximizing price based on the given ex factory-price $p_H$.

Considering the widespread cost-plus calculation (Preston 1963, Nagtegaal 1974), the first hypothesis is empirically more relevant. The increasing use of scanners, however, which enable the retailers to set profit-maximizing prices for major products, will increase the importance of the second hypothesis.

*Optimization of Ex Factory-Price under Cost-Plus Calculation by Retailers*

Here the end-price is obtained as

$$p = \alpha p_H, \tag{9.11}$$

where $\alpha$ is the markup factor or, if retailers incur variable distribution cost $k$

$$p = \alpha(p_H + k). \tag{9.12}$$

If we substitute equation (9.12) for $p$ in the end-price response function $q = q(p)$, the profit function of the manufacturer to be maximized becomes

$$G = p_H \, q[\alpha(p_H + k)] - C(q) \tag{9.13}$$

and from this we can derive the optimality condition for the ex factory-price

$$p_H^* = \frac{\varepsilon(\alpha)}{1 + \varepsilon(\alpha)} \left[ C' - \frac{k}{\varepsilon(\alpha)} \right]. \tag{9.14}$$

For $k = 0$ this formula reduces to the Amoroso-Robinson Relation. However, price elasticity can depend on the markup factor $\alpha$. In the special case of the multiplicative price response function, price elasticity is constant and the optimal ex factory-price of the manufacturer is independent of whether he sells directly or indirectly. This is not the case for other end-price response functions. Via the markup rule (9.12), we obtain as end-price

$$p = \frac{\alpha \cdot \varepsilon(\alpha)}{1 + \varepsilon(\alpha)} [C' + k]. \tag{9.15}$$

Under multiplicative price response, the end-price is higher than under direct sale and the same marginal distribution cost.

We can make specific statements for linear end-price response functions:
- the ex factory-price $p_H$ is smaller and the end-price $p$ is greater than the optimal price under direct sale and the same distribution cost,

– the ex factory-price is the lower and the end-price the higher, the higher the markup is.

*Optimization of Ex Factory-Price under Profit Maximization by Retailers*
    Retailers set their profit-maximizing end-price

$$G_H = (p - p_H - k)\, q(p) \tag{9.16}$$

and here the Amoroso-Robinson Relation is applicable.

$$p^* = \frac{\varepsilon}{1+\varepsilon}(p_H + k). \tag{9.17}$$

The manufacturer optimizes the ex factory-price based on equation (9.17). Substituting equation (9.17) for $p$, we can get the condition of the optimal ex factory-price by deriving the profit function with respect to $p_H$.

$$p_H^* = \frac{\varepsilon}{1+\varepsilon}\left[C' - \frac{k}{\varepsilon}\right]. \tag{9.18}$$

This condition is analogous to equation (9.14) in form. If $k = 0$ and price elasticity is constant, the manufacturer sets his ex factory-price without considering retailers. Positive distribution cost increases the ex factory-price when price elasticity remains constant. The resulting end-price is higher than the optimal price under direct sale and the same distribution cost.

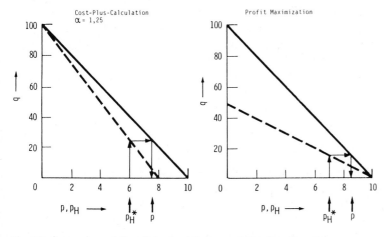

Fig. 9.3. Comparison of Two Behavioral Patterns of Retailers ($k = 0$)

The optimal ex factory-price under the linear price response function is

$$p_H^* = \tfrac{1}{2}(a/b + C') - k/4. \tag{9.19}$$

If $k = 0$, $p_H^*$ is identical with the optimal price under direct sale and the manufacturer sets his price without considering the retailers. If $k$ is positive, the manufacturer absorbs $\tfrac{1}{4}$ of it. The end price $p$ is higher than the optimal price under direct sale/same distribution cost. The end-users, the manufacturer, and the retailer incur $\tfrac{3}{8}$, $\tfrac{2}{8}$, and $\tfrac{3}{8}$ of the distribution cost, respectively.

### Comparison of Both Patterns of Behavior

Based on linear price response functions, we compare the consequences of both behavioral patterns in more detail. Fig. 9.3 shows the difference between the two situations for a linear price response function. The solid and the broken lines represent the response function with respect to the end-price and the ex factory-price, respectively, the markup factor is 1.25. The arrows show how end-prices are derived from ex factory-prices ($C' = 4$, $q = 100 - 10p$).

Under cost-plus calculation, the retail markup goes down as ex factory-price $p_H$ goes down and vice versa. The reverse is the case under retailer's profit maximization. Here the retailer optimally exploits the difference between the ex factory-price and the price the end-users are willing to pay. Table 9.4 shows the optimal prices/profits for this example as well as the case when unit distribution cost $k = 1$.

In these numerical examples, both retailer and manufacturer are worse off if the retailer pursues profit-maximization. This statement, however, cannot be generalized. For a high markup factor (e.g., $\alpha = 2$), the cost-plus calculation brings worse results for both parties. It is generally true, however, that under both cost-plus calculation and profit-maximization the end-price is higher and the total profit lower than under direct sale.

Summary: To set the ex factory-price optimally, the manufacturer needs information on the price response of end-users as well as on how the retailers set the

Table 9.4
Prices and Profits under Different Behavioral Patterns of Retailers

| Behavior of Retailers | $k = 0$ | | | | $k = 1$ | | | |
|---|---|---|---|---|---|---|---|---|
| | $P_H^*$ | $p$ | Profit | | $P_H^*$ | $p$ | Profit | |
| | | | Manufac-turer | Retailer | | | Manufac-turer | Retailer |
| cost-plus, markup = 1.25 | 6 | 7.50 | 50 | 37.50 | 5.50 | 8.13 | 28.1 | 30.5 |
| profit-maximization | 7 | 8.50 | 45 | 22.50 | 6.75 | 8.88 | 19.6 | 12.7 |
| direct sale | – | 7 | 90 | – | – | 7.50 | 62.5 | – |

end-price. Cost-plus calculation and profit maximization are two important ways retailers set the end-price. In both cases, end-prices are higher than the optimal end-price under direct sale and the same distribution cost.

### 9.2.3 Joint Profit Maximization of Manufacturer and Retailer

Given the mutual dependence of manufacturer and retailer, they have some incentive to form a "collective monopoly" vis-à-vis end users (Krelle 1976, p. 642) and pursue joint profit-maximization. There are two decision-making stages. In stage one, both parties set the profit maximizing end-price. Interests are here congruent since both parties have the incentive to make the total profit as big as possible.

In stage two, the total profit is divided between manufacturer and retailer. Now the interests of both parties conflict with each other. Since the amount to be divided is fixed, this is a zero-sum game: one can gain only at the expense of the other. In practice, profit sharing is achieved through the negotiation of the ex factory-price.

The empirical significance of joint profit maximization is hard to evaluate. In principle, this is the most sensible solution for both parties and, interestingly, also the most favorable outcome for the end-user. However, it is rather difficult to realize.

*Price Optimization*

Setting of the optimal price in stage one is very simple if we ignore competition. The term $p_H q$ ($p_H$ = ex factory-price) appears twice in the joint profit function. Since it is revenue of the manufacturer and cost of the retailer, it has opposite signs and, thus, cancels out. Total profit depends only on end-price $p$. This is a simple price optimization problem for which the Amoroso-Robinson Relation holds as the optimality condition (including distribution cost $k$). Logically, the optimal end-price $p^*$ must be identical with the optimal price under direct sale and same distribution cost.

It turns out that the optimal end-price under joint profit maximization is lower than in the other three cases. If industry and retail cooperate, end-users are better off than if both parties set prices independently or the manufacturer sets the price alone.

*Division of Profits*

Profit division is achieved through negotiation of the ex factory-price. The issue is where the ex factory-price should lie between the manufacturer's marginal cost $C'$ and the retailer's net revenue $p - k$ (Fig. 9.4).

This is a zero-sum game. The relative power position of manufacturer and retailer and personal characteristics (negotiation skill, willingness to make concessions) determine the negotiation results within this range. Opportunity costs may further narrow the room for negotiation.

*The Relationship between Manufacturers and Retailers*

Our discussion has revealed the structural and inherent conflict of interests between manufacturers and retailers. This phenomenon exists not only when both

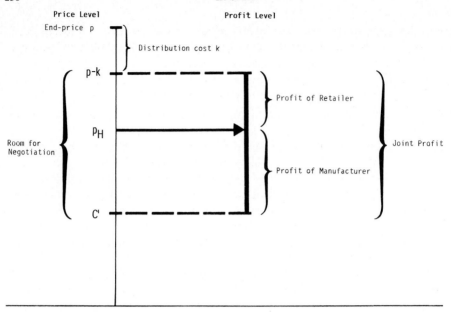

Fig. 9.4. Division of Joint Profit

sides pursue joint profit maximization but generally when the total profit has to be divided between the two sides. It underlies the conflict between industry and trade which has intensified over the years (Meffert and Steffenhagen 1976, Sandler 1981). Considering the weakened relative power position of the manufacturers, it is not surprising that recent developments are deplored mostly by them. The weakening of their power and the strengthening of the retailers' relative power position is not only due to the increasing concentration of retail firms but also because access to the consumer in general has become a bottleneck factor.

### Practical Problems of Joint Profit Maximization

Although joint profit maximization makes everybody better off (manufacturer, retailer, consumer), there are some difficulties that inhibit its implementation.

1. An intensive joint preoccupation with the problem is necessary. For a manufacturer with many retail customers, this is possible only with major customers. Conversely, the retailer has an extensive assortment, which limits his time available for each supplier.
2. Joint profit maximization presupposes a similar estimate of the price response function by manufacturer and retailer. This estimate, however, differs from retailer to retailer, which causes problems to the manufacturer.
3. Interests can diverge, e.g., when retailers want to use a product as a bait to attract customers (traffic building), while the manufacturer wants to use the price as a means of promoting the product image (price-image consistency).

4. Joint profit maximization presupposes a high degree of trust in the cost data provided by the other party. In fact, each party is tempted to overstate the cost data. Suppose the price response function is $q = 100-10p$, the manufacturer's marginal cost $C' = 4$, and the retailer's marginal cost $k = 1$. Each party is supposed to get one half of the total profit. The optimal price is $p^* = 7.50$; the resulting total profit amounts to 62.50 and the individual share is 31.25. If now the manufacturer claims that his marginal cost is 5 instead of 4, the optimal price becomes $p^* = 8$ and the "official" total profit would be 40. Thus the manufacturer receives 20. In addition, he gets a hidden profit of 20, making him better off than he would be if he didn't cheat. An analogous situation exists for the retailer with respect to the distribution cost. Thus there is an incentive for both parties to overstate costs.

In short, joint profit maximization with all its potential advantages for both sides presupposes conditions which are hardly met in reality.

Summary: Joint profit maximization of manufacturer and retailer requires in stage one setting the optimal end-price, and in stage two division of the joint profit, which involves negotiating the ex factory-price. The optimal end-price is lower than it would be if the price (ex factory- and end-price) were set independently by the manufacturer and the retailer or by the manufacturer alone. As for the negotiation, the manufacturer's marginal cost and the retailer's net revenue constitute the lower and the upper limit, respectively. The final outcome within this range depends on the power relations and personality factors. Joint profit maximization presupposes such a high degree of mutual trust and information sharing that it is not widely spread despite its advantages for all parties.

Chapter 10

# *Retail Price Management*

## 10.1 Special Problems in Retail Price Management

For many wholesale and retail companies, price is the most important marketing mix instrument. For years price-aggressive retail companies have been growing rapidly and increasing their market share. Despite of the importance of price management in retailing, intuition, experience, and rules of thumb still prevail.

The academic research has not been very helpful for retail price management (see Holton 1957, Humbel 1958, Holdren 1960, Theisen 1960, Preston 1963, Nystroem 1970). Particularly, promotion policy has been widely researched without producing generalizable results (e.g., Hinkle 1965, Welzel 1975, Eckhardt 1976, Glinz 1978, Blattberg et al. 1981, Diller 1979). Since the basic concepts discussed so far are also applicable to retail price management, we focus on retail-specific pricing problems, particularly

– assortment,
– cross-product effects,
– price promotions,
– price image of stores.

### Assortment

A typical "mom and pop store" carries several thousand articles. Medium-sized supermarkets have about 10,000 articles, and large supermarkets/department stores over 100,000. Such huge assortments preclude the precise measurement of price response and price optimization for individual articles, making the use of simple decision rules/rules of thumb inevitable.

### Multi-Item Purchases

Typically customers buy more than one item during the same shopping trip (one-stop-shopping, impulse purchases). This suggests that the cross-elasticities of price are not zero between many products. Retail managers should consider this fact in their pricing decisions.

## Price Promotions

Price promotions, i.e., temporary price reductions, are heavily used by retailers, particularly by grocery stores. Since price promotions produce complex demand effects (dynamic, substitute, complementary), it is very difficult to rigorously examine their overall impact on profits.

## Price Image of Stores

Price image plays an important role in the customers' choice of stores. Only a store with a favorable price image can be successful in the long run. Price image, therefore, is a very important element of the competitive strategy of a retail company.

## 10.2 Pricing of Individual Items in Retail

### Rules of Thumb

Rules of thumb and cost-plus calculations are prevalent in retail pricing. The procurement price serves as the basis for markup. Markups are usually differentiated according to various criteria. The following are such differentiated rules of thumb (see Holton 1957, Holdren 1960, Preston 1963, Gabor 1977, Monroe 1979):
1. The lower the absolute price, the higher the markup rate.
2. The higher the turnover rate, the lower the markup rate.
3. For those products whose prices are strongly perceived by consumers, markup rates should be very low (e.g., bread, milk, butter, gasoline, "political" prices).
4. Markups should be lower for mass products than for specialty goods.
5. Markups should be geared to competition.
These are just a few of the rules of thumb mentioned in the literature (see also Sweeny 1973, Cassady 1962, Lynn 1967, McClelland 1966). Other rules of thumb are geared to such criteria as target rate of return, revenue per unit of sales floor/shelf space, etc.

### Empirical Evidence

Table 10.1 shows the markup rates for various product categories in the United States. Table 10.2 gives the distribution of markup rates for food and beverages in France. Together these two tables prove that retailers do not apply standard markup rates but differentiate markups for various product categories.

### Theoretical Evaluation

The pricing of a single item corresponds to the classical static single product case for which the optimal price is determined by the Amoroso-Robinson Relation (3.16)

$$p^* = \frac{\varepsilon}{1 + \varepsilon} C'. \tag{10.1}$$

Table 10.1
Cost-Plus Markup Rates for Selected Product Categories in Two United States Studies (Source: Preston 1963).

| Product Category | Super Value Study | Preston Study | |
|---|---|---|---|
| | | Mean Value | Range of Markups |
| Small Items | 100% | – | – |
| Canned Tuna | 25% | 40% | 23–59% |
| Jam | 31% | 33% | 23–64% |
| Canned Soup | 18% | 25% | 18–36% |
| Canned Milk | 18% | 11% | 9–32% |
| Sugar | 9% | 15% | 12–29% |
| Coffee | – | 12% | 8–18% |
| Soap, Detergent | 12% | – | – |

Equation (10.1) – and therefore the cost-plus calculation – becomes the optimal decision rule if price elasticity $\varepsilon$ and marginal cost $C'$ are constant (see Chapter 3).

The question is whether these conditions are met in retailing. The bulk of a retail company's cost consists of prices of procured products, which are variable costs. The other costs (personnel, rent, utilities) are typically fixed. The requirement of constant marginal cost is met for a wide range of quantity intervals whose limits are determined by quantity discount schemes. In evaluating the assumption of isoelasticity as implied by the multiplicative price response function, we note that this response function differs very little from other price response hypotheses within a certain range (see Chapter 2). Second, this assumption is generally consistent with the reports by many researchers that retail price reductions seem to attract more customers than comparable price increases scare away customers (see Preston 1963, Peckham 1973). The reason for this asymmetry is that the number of customers of a retail firm is smaller than the number of potential customers who might be attracted by a price

Table 10.2
Distribution of Markup Rates for Food and Beverages in the French Retail Market (Source: Ninth Report on Competition, European Commission 1980)

| Markup Rates | Percentage of Products |
|---|---|
| > 80% | 1.1 |
| 60–80% | 3.0 |
| 40–60% | 10.5 |
| 20–40% | 27.8 |
| 10–20% | 22.6 |
| 0–10% | 31.5 |
| < 0% | 3.5 |

reduction. The assumption of a multiplicative response function for individual items, therefore, is a reasonable approximation to reality.

If we accept these arguments concerning marginal cost and price elasticity and consider the need for simple pricing rules (because of huge assortments), we can say that the Amoroso-Robinson Relation constitutes a useful theoretical foundation for cost-plus calculation in retailing.

### The Amoroso-Robinson Relation as a Rule of Thumb

The five rules of thumb we listed above are supported by this relation:

1. Higher markup rates at low absolute prices:
   If we assume that price elasticity increases as prices go up in absolute terms, the rule holds.
2. Lower markup rates at higher turnover rates:
   Higher turnover rates are often associated with frequent purchases by individual consumers. Presumably consumers are more sensitive to the price of frequently purchased products than to that of infrequently purchased ones.
3. Lower markup rates for products whose prices are strongly perceived:
   Here the higher price elasticity is well explained by the strength of perception.
4. Lower markups for mass products than for specialties:
   Mass products are less differentiated and have, therefore, a higher price elasticity.
5. Lower markups under intensive competition:
   Intensive (price) competition is associated with higher price elasticity.

Since all rules of thumb are related to the fundamental Amoroso-Robinson Relation, it makes sense to substitute this elasticity-related basic rule for the various rules of markup differentiation: The higher the product's price elasticity, the lower its markup rate.

Considering the huge product assortments, the precise measurement of price elasticity should be confined to major products. Retail managers often have a very good idea of relative price effects/elasticities. The Amoroso-Robinson Relation can be a big help if managers have such an idea. If the manager thinks Product A is more strongly affected by changes in price than Product B, its markup should be lower than B's. Such an explicit and elasticity-oriented calculation is still exceptional in retailing, although such calculation is implicit in the rules of thumb we listed.

The elasticity-oriented markup calculation can be also useful for decentralized pricing according to product groups or departments. In such a system, management can provide the department managers with average product group-specific markup rates based on "product group price elasticities". The department manager could then adjust markups within the product group for individual items while observing the overall average rate.

### Scanner and Retail Pricing

Optimal retail pricing can be made possible for major products by the use of scanners. The scanner provides the information necessary for price determination at very low cost. Using scanners, we can identify the profit-maximizing price by experimenting with alternative prices within the relevant range and measuring their effects on sales and profits.

We demonstrate the optimization with the example from Figure 2.14 where a scanner price experiment was carried out for a nondurable brand. The estimated price response function was $m = 0.205 - 0.169p$, where $m$ is market share and $p$ is relative price. We obtain a maximum relative price of $0.205/0.169 = 1.213$. Excluding competitive reaction and assuming constant relative marginal cost of 0.72, we get an optimal relative price of 0.967 (see Fig. 10.1). Thus, this brand should be priced about three percent below the market average. The market share at this price is 4.17%. Such a small market share makes the assumption that competitors will not react realistic. The price elasticity is $-3.91$, a value which is plausible for the product category under consideration.

Today only few retail companies apply such sophisticated price optimization techniques. Often the necessary know-how is lacking in retail companies. But some firms have achieved considerable profit increases by using such techniques.

Summary: Retail pricing is mostly based on cost-plus calculations. Retailers follow numerous rules of thumb to differentiate markup rates. The conditions in the retailing sector suggest that a cost-plus calculation leads to the near-optimal price via the Amoroso-Robinson Relation. Since individual rules of thumb are supported by this relation, it makes sense to employ only this general rule for markup differentiation. The implementation of this rule can be successful if retail managers have a good idea of relative price elasticities. The increasing use of scanners will enable retailers to price their products more rigorously and objectively.

## 10.3 Price Management and Cross-Product Effects

Table 10.3 gives an example recorded by means of a scanner. It shows multi-item purchases by 9 consumers in 6 product categories. The figures are the amounts in DM spent on the various categories.

Multi-item purchases (one-stop-shopping) which save the consumers cost and time are prevalent in many retail sectors. As a result, the cross-price elasticities between many products are not zero. A price reduction for product $j$ attracts new customers, who buy not only this product but other products as well.

*Price Optimization under Cross-Product Effects*
Under multi-item purchases, the price of product $j$, $p_j$, influences not only the sales of product $j$ but also the sales of another product $i$, whose price response function has the following form

$$q_i = q_i(p_i, ..., p_j, ..., p_n). \tag{10.2}$$

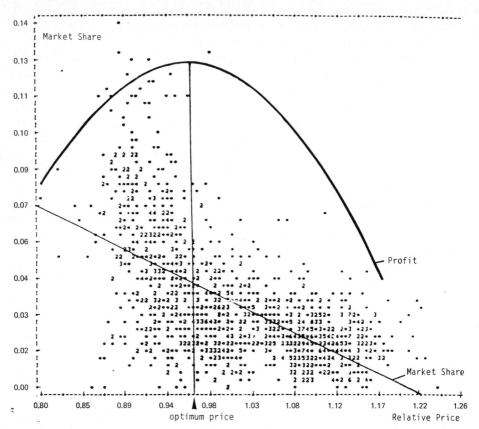

Fig. 10.1. Retail Price Optimization with Scanner Data

Table 10.3
Multi-Item Purchases Recorded by a Scanner

| Con- sumer | Household Cleanser | Fabric Softener | Candy Bar | Choco- late | Deter- gent | Coffee |
|---|---|---|---|---|---|---|
| 1 | 0.00 | 5.98 | 1.48 | 0.00 | 9.88 | 0.00 |
| 2 | 0.00 | 0.00 | 5.30 | 2.88 | 0.00 | 0.00 |
| 3 | 0.00 | 11.16 | 0.00 | 0.00 | 32.94 | 0.00 |
| 4 | 0.00 | 0.00 | 0.00 | 8.90 | 17.96 | 0.00 |
| 5 | 3.65 | 0.00 | 0.00 | 2.44 | 0.00 | 31.92 |
| 6 | 0.00 | 0.00 | 0.00 | 2.31 | 0.00 | 7.98 |
| 7 | 0.00 | 0.00 | 0.00 | 0.00 | 4.45 | 11.79 |
| 8 | 0.00 | 3.35 | 0.00 | 0.00 | 9.98 | 0.00 |
| 9 | 0.00 | 0.00 | 4.46 | 2.38 | 0.00 | 0.00 |

Differentiating the profit function of the retail firm with respect to $p_j$, we obtain

$$\frac{\delta G}{\delta p_j} = q_j + (p_j - C_j')\frac{\delta q_j}{\delta p_j} + \sum_{\substack{i=1 \\ i \neq j}}^{n} (p_i - C_i')\frac{\delta q_i}{\delta p_j} = 0. \tag{10.3}$$

This condition can be simplified to

$$p_j^* = \frac{\varepsilon_j}{1 + \varepsilon_j}C_j' - \sum_{\substack{i=1 \\ i \neq j}}^{n} (p_i - C_i')\frac{\varepsilon_{ij}}{1 + \varepsilon_j}\frac{q_i}{q}, \tag{10.4}$$

where $\varepsilon_j$ is the direct price elasticity and $\varepsilon_{ij}$ is the cross-price elasticity of product $i$ with respect to $p_j$ ($\varepsilon_{ij} < 0$ for complementary goods and $\varepsilon_{ij} > 0$ for substitutes). Niehans (1956) derived equation (10.4) for the first time (see also Selten 1970).

The first term of (10.4) is the Amoroso-Robinson Relation, which defines the optimal price without cross-product effects. If we take these effects into consideration, we get the optimal price by adding a corrective term to reflect the effect of price $p_j$ on all other products. Included in the corrective term are unit contribution margins of other products as well as the elasticities and the sales volume.

Product $i$, which is complementary to product $j$, contributes positively to the second term since $(1 + \varepsilon_j) < 0$ and $\varepsilon_{ij} < 0$ and thus reduces the optimal price of product $j$. The optimal price $p_j^*$ is therefore the lower (relative to the price that does not consider the cross-product effects),
- the more products are complementary to product $j$,
- the higher the cross-price elasticities of complementary products are,
- the higher the ratio of the unit sales of complementary product $i$ to those of product $j$ is.

The reverse is true for substitutes. Simply speaking, equation (10.4) says that the more a product contributes to the contribution margin of the total assortment, the lower its price should be. This is a mathematical expression of the principle of "mixed calculation" which is well familiar to retail managers. In a retail firm (as in multi-product firms), the objective is not to maximize the contribution margin of each product, but to realize the maximum contribution for the assortment as a whole.

Equation (10.4) makes clear that a product's price can be lower than its marginal cost (loss leader). This is an analogue to our dynamic optimization in Chapter 6. Similar phenomena underlie both cases. Cross-product effects concern the impact of one product on the other products in the same period, whereas the dynamic case is concerned with the intertemporal effect of current period's price.

*Simplification*
Since the empirical estimation of the elasticities required in equation (10.4) is very complex, we suggest a simplified procedure to implement (10.4) in practice. Our

procedure is not based on elasticities but on the quantity of joint purchases. If the consumers buy $a_{ij}$ units of product $i$ when they buy product $j$ (on the average) and the purchase of $j$ prompts the purchase of $i$ and not the other way around, the optimality condition is (see Simon 1985)

$$p_j^* = \frac{\varepsilon_j}{1+\varepsilon_j}(C_j' - m_j), \tag{10.5}$$

where

$$m_j = \sum_{\substack{i=1 \\ i \neq j}}^{n} a_{ij}(p_i - C_i'). \tag{10.6}$$

$m_j$ represents the sum of contribution margins that accrue to other products from the purchase of $j$. The marginal cost of product $j$ is reduced by this amount. The more product $j$ prompts the sale of other products and the more profitable these sales are, the lower the optimal price of $j$ is.

Suppose 0.8 shirts and 1.2 ties (on the average) are purchased with each purchase of a suit in a clothing store, and the average unit contribution is DM 15 and DM 10 for shirts and ties, respectively. The price response function for suits is as follows:

$$q = 1000 - 2p. \tag{10.7}$$

At marginal cost of DM 200, the optimal price is DM 350 in the absence of cross-product effects. 300 suits are sold, which leads to sales of 240 shirts and 360 ties. Total contribution is

DM 45,000 for suits,
DM   3,600 for shirts,
DM   3,600 for ties,

or a total of DM 52,200.

If we incorporate the cross-product effects in pricing, the marginal cost of a suit, according to (10.6), is reduced by $0.8 \cdot 15 + 1.2 \cdot 10 = $ DM 24. The new optimal price is DM 338. This price is lower than the isolated optimal price by DM 12 when we neglect cross-product effects. 324 suits, 259 shirts, and 389 ties are sold. Contribution margins are

DM 44,712 for suits,
DM 3,885 for shirts,
DM 3,890 for ties.

The sum of DM 52,487 is higher than in the previous case. The lower contribution margin of the main product (suits) is more than offset by higher contribution margins of the other products.

*Measurement of Cross-Product Effects*

With traditional cash registers, it is very costly to measure cross-product effects (Böcker 1978). The use of scanners improves the situation dramatically because it can relate the purchase incidence to purchase timing with extreme efficiency as demonstrated in Table 10.3. Considering the measurement/analysis problems, quantitative analysis of cross-product effects is feasible only for major products. Nevertheless, the understanding of these effects helps the retail managers at least qualitatively in their pricing of assortments.

Summary: Cross-product effects are very important in retail price management. The theoretical optimality condition suggests that the more a product prompts the sale of other products and the higher the unit contribution margins of these other products are, the lower the product's price should be. To incorporate these effects in pricing, we recommend to simplify the theoretical concepts. The use of scanners makes the measurement of cross-product effects easier and less costly.

# 10.4 Price Promotions in Retail

We define price promotions as short-term temporary price reductions for selected products. Although these price reductions are frequently offered by retailers, we do not have a solid knowledge about their overall effects. Due to the lack of such a solid knowledge, different philosophies on price promotions coexist. Most food retailers use promotions very frequently, whereas other firms offer such price reductions infrequently. We know of a large supermarket that increased its revenue by a factor of 40 within fifteen years without any price promotions (and advertising), and this despite the fierce attacks by several price aggressive firms in the same local market. Given the lack of well-founded knowledge about the effects of price promotions, we confine ourselves to a general discussion.

*Analysis of the Effects*

In formulating his policy on price promotions, a retailer should ask the following questions:
- Is the promotion necessary in the first place?
- Which products are appropriate for promotion?
  Popular or less-known brands?
  New or mature brands?
  Perishable or non-perishable products?
  Non-durable goods or durables?
- How much should the prices be reduced?
- When should the promotion period begin, and how long should it last?
- How frequently should promotions be used?

Table 10.4
Short- and Medium-Term Effects of Price Promotions

| Product Category | Regular Customers | | PP*-Customers | |
|---|---|---|---|---|
| | PP-period $t$ | Subsequent Periods $t + \tau$ | PP-Period $t$ | Subsequent Periods $t + \tau$ |
| Product on promotion | +/0    + | +/0    − | +    + | +    0 |
| Substitutes of the product on promotion | 0    − | 0    − | 0    0 | +    0 |
| Rest of the assortment | 0    −/0 | 0    0 | +    0 | +    0 |

PP*: price promotion

For most of these questions there are no conclusive and empirically supported answers. The total effect of price promotions consists of many subeffects in three product categories:
- the product on promotion,
- the products that belong to the same category as that on promotion (substitutes),
- the rest of the products in the assortment.

Some effects may be dynamic, i.e., they may affect sales in several periods. In addition, it is necessary to differentiate between the regular customers (who would buy the product even without the promotion) and the customers attracted by the promotion (deal-prone customers). Table 10.4 shows a categorization of the effects of price promotions. Besides these short- and medium-term effects, price promotions can have a long-term impact on the store's price image.

Symbols in the upper left corner of each cell represent the changes in sales when product A is on promotion. Symbols in the lower right corner apply when product B is on promotion ("+" means sales growth, "0" no change, "−" sales reduction).

When Product A is on promotion, the following effects result:

Regular customers:    – buy A as much as or more than usual in $t$ and $t + \tau$,
            – substitutes are not affected,
            – the rest of the assortment is not affected,

PP-customers:    – buy A in $t$ and $t + \tau$,
            – buy substitutes in $t + \tau$ because they become regular customers,
            – buy other products from the assortment in $t$ (cross-product effects) and $t + \tau$ (become regular customers).

When product B is on promotion, the picture is as follows:

Regular customers: – buy B more than usual in $t$ and less in $t + \tau$ (purchases are "borrowed" from future, B is stored),

– more purchases of B in $t$ result in less purchases of substitutes in $t$ and $t + \tau$,

– the rest of the assortment is either unaffected or sold less in $t$ because the customers buy B more than usual in $t$ and thus less budget is available for other products,

PP-customers: – buy B only in $t$, and no other effects occur.

The overall effect of price promotion of A is positive, while B is not appropriate for price promotion.

This example illustrates the extreme complexity of the effects of price promotions. Although a comprehensive quantitative analysis of the effects of price promotions is very difficult, the main effect (i.e., sales of PP-products during the PP-period and subsequent periods) can be measured easily with the help of scanners. Table 10.4 provides a structure for the qualitative analysis of the complex effects beyond the main effect. We illustrate the problems of price promotions with a simple example. The example is for one period and does not consider the substitutions within the product category to which the PP-product belongs.

The underlying assumptions are as follows:

1. 1000 customers come without the price promotion (regular customers); 10% more come with the price promotion (PP-customers).
2. The margin for normal products is 15%, and 0% for PP-products.
3. Each customer spends $ 50.
4. PP-products represent 10% of the purchases for regular customers, and 30% for PP-customers.

Table 10.5 shows the calculations of the contribution margins with and without the price promotion. This example illustrates a typical effect of price promotions: In order to attract a smaller number of PP-customers, profit margins are sacrificed for a considerably larger number of regular customers. An empirical study by Diller (1981)

Table 10.5
Calculation of Contribution Margins (CM) with and without Price Promotion

|  | Without price promotion | With price promotion |
|---|---|---|
| Regular Customers | 1000 | 1000 |
| CM/regular customer | $0.15 \cdot 50 = 7.50$ | $0.15 \cdot 45 = 6.75$ |
| PP-customer | – | 100 |
| CM/PP-customer | – | $0.15 \cdot 35 = 5.25$ |
| Total contribution | 7500 | 7275 |

Table 10.6
Selective Empirical Results on the Effects of Price Promotions

| Statement | Confirmed | Not Confirmed |
|---|---|---|
| Strong sales effect for PP-products (sales increase in PP-periods > 100%) | Chevalier 1975<br>McCurry 1980<br>Neale 1980<br>Dyer 1980<br>Eckhard 1976 | Diller 1981<br>Dyer 1980<br>Peckham 1973 |
| Effect depends significantly on the extent of price reduction | Gabor 1977<br>McCurry 1980 | Chevalier 1975<br>Diller 1981<br>Eckhardt 1976 |
| Purchases are borrowed from the future | Blattberg et al. 1981<br>Hodock 1981 | Dyer 1980<br>Klein 1980 |
| PP-products are sold at the expense of substitutes | Eckhardt 1976<br>Dyer 1980 | – |
| Frequent price promotions reduce their effect | Hinkle 1965<br>Novich 1981 | – |
| Price promotions have no impact on long-term trends | Peckham 1973 | – |
| The effects of price promotions are stronger for new products | Hinkle 1965 | Chevalier 1975 |
| Price promotions in the off-season are more favorable | Hinkle 1965 | – |
| Consumers who have been buying a product before respond more strongly to the price promotion of that product than those who have not | | Guadagni and Little 1983 |

suggests a more pessimistic effect of price promotions than that shown in this example. We note again that this example doesn't consider static and dynamic substitutions.

*Empirical Findings on the Effects of Price Promotions*

The empirical work in this area underscores the difficulties of evaluating the effects of price promotions. They are based on various kinds of data sets (e.g., experiments, scanner data), and the validity of each finding is hard to evaluate (Table 10.6).

The results are mixed. The direct effect on PP-products (statement 1) ranges from small sales increases to a 2,000% increase! It seems that the effects of (sufficiently large) price reductions are particularly strong for well-known high-priced branded products (Humbel 1958, Eckhardt 1976). This effect causes many conflicts between retailers and manufacturers who want to prevent the damage to the image of their brands done by low prices. Conflicting results on the influence of the extent of price reductions (statement 2) could possibly be explained by the fact that the mere announcement of a price promotion generates a considerable attention (Neale 1980, Eckhardt 1976). Sometimes this effect tempts retailers to declare some products to be on promotion when in fact their prices are not really favorable (Diller 1985, Guadagni and Little 1983).

The conflicting results on borrowing from the future (statement 3) can be explained by different product characteristics (e.g., whether or not the product can be stored).

We also note that different segments respond to price promotions in different ways (Blattberg et al. 1978). Thus the structure of the population in the store's business area has a strong impact on the effects of price promotion. No generalizable statements are possible.

Summary: Price promotions are implemented regularly by many retail firms. Their policy, however, is not based on theoretical foundation. Since it is very difficult to evaluate the total effects of price promotions, we proposed a structure that could help retail managers evaluate the various effects of a price promotion at least qualitatively. Empirical findings are partly conflicting and not generalizable.

## 10.5 The Price Image of Stores

We define the price image of a store as the consumers' evaluation of the store as to whether it sells products at favorable prices or not (Nystroem 1970, Welzel 1975, Eckhardt 1976). The price image is important in retail price management because consumers do not remember the prices of all products relevant to them. If a customer plans to purchase a product whose price he does not know, the price images of stores would often influence his choice of stores. From the perspective of price management, the following questions are of interest:
- How are price images formed?
- How do price images change over time?
- What kind of impact has the price image on the choice of a store?

*The Formation of Price Images*
The simplest operationalization of a price image *PI* is a weighted average of prices (price index):

$$PI = \sum_{j=1}^{n} w_j p_j, \tag{10.7}$$

where $w_j$ is the weight attributed to product $j$.

Price indices for an average basket of goods are another way to make price comparisons among stores (Holdren 1960, Preston 1963, Gabor 1977). Nystroem (1970) operationalizes the price image in another way

$$PI = \frac{n^+}{n}, \tag{10.8}$$

where $n^+$ number of favorable price evaluations by a consumer, $n$ number of all price evaluations.

In equations (10.7) and (10.8), the central question is which prices or which prices with how much weight $w_j$ influence the price image. This question has important strategic implications.

There are two competing hypotheses:

Hypothesis 1: Consumers' price image of a store is affected by prices of a few products, particularly those that are on price promotions and/or advertised.

Hypothesis 2: Consumers consider the prices of many products in their price image formation.

Hypothesis 1 is prevalent in the older literature. Geiger (1968) reports that 46% of the respondents were influenced mainly by price promotions in evaluating the price image of several stores. A West German court ruled that price promotions of well-known branded products give the impression that the rest of the store's products are low-priced as well. Hypothesis 1 assumes basically that consumers can be misled for a long time and that their price perception is selective, possibly to their disadvantage.

Recent research tends to support Hypothesis 2. Eckhardt (1976, p. 29) states, "image is less a result of promotional campaigns than of actual purchases." At another point (p. 98) he concludes "purchases actually made are decisive for the formation of price image because price evaluation processes have little impact on image formation unless they are perceived to bring cost savings by consumers." Diller (1981, p. 58) suggests that although the consumers attracted by price promotions had "strong positive price experiences" they "do not generalize their price evaluation but recognize promotion prices as such and differentiate them from normal prices." Lenzen (1983, 1984) found that consumers are not deceived by price deals but perceive overall price levels of stores accurately. In a study of ten stores, all stores above and below the average price level were correctly classified by consumers (Müller-Hagedorn 1983). This result indicates that the perception of the overall price level of stores tends to be rather accurate. Such results may be country- or situation-specific. If the discrepancy between promotional prices and regular prices is too wide, two price images can emerge. A store can be viewed as favorable for products on promotion but less favorable for other products.

*Dynamics of Price Image*

The static operationalization of price image in (10.7) and (10.8) is incomplete to the extent that price image is formed through a dynamic learning process. Nystroem (1970) suggests to capture this learning process through a partial adjustment model. If such a model is valid, consumers need to compare/evaluate only a few prices in each period. Thus, even the presence of large assortments does not overburden consumers. Every new piece of price information is attached to the existing image, which may be considered as an "information chunk" (Simon 1974, Bettman 1979).

The concept of information chunk provides another supportive argument for Hypothesis 2 that many prices contribute to the formation of price image. The partial adjustment model has a number of interesting implications:
– the price image changes only gradually,
– the mistakes made in the past have a lasting impact, it takes time to correct the image,
– there exists a trade-off between short-term and long-term pricing policy.
The dynamics of price image is important for strategic pricing in retailing. The strategic thinking should be geared not toward individual products but toward building a good price image of the store.

*The Influence of Price Image on the Choice of Stores*

Price image influences the consumers' choice of stores in many situations. In an empirical study of ten stores Lenzen (1984) found highly significant positive correlations between price images and actual purchases in each store. The influence is particularly strong when consumers have incomplete information on the prices charged for the same product by different stores. In this situation, they must either rely on the price image of the store or explicitly compare prices in different stores. The information search cost can exceed the expected benefit so that relying on price image can be a rational behavior.

Since the size of the assortment in most stores is growing, consumers will increasingly rely on the price image of the store in their choice of stores, thereby increasing the strategic importance of price image in retailing. If Hypothesis 1 holds, a strategy of selectively favorable prices is recommended. In this situation, it is important to emphasize favorable prices through advertising, display, etc. Note that the strategy of selectively favorable prices presupposes a certain homogeneity concerning reference products on consumers' part. If each consumer's price image is based on different products, this strategy would work for only a small part of the consumers. In this case, as when Hypothesis 2 holds, a strategy of generally favorable prices is suggested. Recall here that the strategy of selectively favorable prices might generate two price images (based on promotion prices and normal prices).

The dynamics of price image has the following implications. Since the price image changes only gradually, a long-term orientation becomes crucial. The more slowly the price image changes, the more important the marketing investment perspective is. The dynamics of price image seems to suggest a stable pricing. Price reductions have only a limited impact because the price image shaped by high prices in the past discourages many consumers from visiting the store. Price increase disillusions the consumers because their price image of the store has been shaped by the low prices in the past. A penetration strategy followed by a slowly rising price level seems appropriate for market entry.

Summary: Price images influence the consumers' store choice particularly when they lack detailed information on prices. There are two competing hypotheses concerning the formation of price image. The hypothesis that price image is formed by a number of actual prices enjoys stronger empirical support. From this, a strategy of generally favorable prices is suggested. The strategy of selectively favorable prices, which is recommended if the other hypothesis holds, involves the risk of generating two price images (based on promotion prices and normal prices). The dynamics of price image favors a long-term orientation and suggests a stable pricing over time.

Chapter 11

# Price Management in Industrial Markets

## 11.1 Special Aspects of Price Management in Industrial Markets

In industrial markets the buyers of products or services are not the individual consumers but business firms, private and public institutions (e.g., hospitals, schools, and other organizations). In the recent literature, these markets are often referred to as "business markets". The range of industrial or business markets is very wide and the demarcation between these markets and consumer markets is not always clear as far as pricing policy is concerned. Pricing for simple standardized industrial goods (e.g., office supplies, typewriters, or standard software) is similar to that for consumer goods. Conversely, pricing for some consumer goods shows a pattern similar to that for industrial goods (e.g., price negotiation for expensive items). This chapter discusses some aspects of price management that are unique to pricing in industrial markets. Important characteristics of industrial markets that are relevant for pricing include:
- the performance of industrial goods is often measurable and quantifiable,
- purchasing decisions are often made after intensive information gathering and explicit comparison of alternatives,
- decisions are jointly made by several people who do not necessarily have the same interests ("buying center").

Thus pricing should be geared toward the product performance and the customer's evaluation process.

Other characteristics are:
- direct selling is typical,
- bilateral oligopoly is a common market form in industrial markets. Sometimes there is only one supplier and one buyer (bilateral monopoly),
- frequently products are custom-made,
- often the number of projects a company sells (or buys) is very small, but each project is very big (e.g., a nuclear reactor).

When one or more of these characteristics exist, a contract is usually concluded after a negotiation that covers every aspect of the transaction (price, payment,

schedule, etc.). We discuss the issues that arise from the negotiation of price in section 11.3.
– particularly in public sector, orders are often placed via bidding.
   Pricing under competitive bidding is the subject of section 11.4.


## 11.2 Value-Pricing

We define value-pricing as price-setting where a benefit or performance index, measured technically or economically, is used as a guideline for pricing. Using IBM-terminology, Brock (1975, p. 101) talks about "functional pricing", i.e., "charging for the product according to its performance rather than according to its costs for production."

The way "performance" or "value" is defined/measured is critical in value-pricing. What matters is the value as perceived by the customers. The prerequisite for value-pricing is therefore to find out how the customers evaluate the product. This necessitates an intimate knowledge of the customer's internal situation (costs, objectives, decision processes, attitude toward risk, liquidity, etc.) as well as the market conditions (e.g., competition, capacity utilization) under which the customer organization operates. What is important is not to develop an "objective", "rational", or "sensible" value-index but to find out how the customer explicitly or implicitly evaluates the product. The following examples are meant to illustrate some procedures common in practice.

There are two ways to relate price to the performance of the product. One way is to construct a price-performance ratio (PPR) which measures how many monetary units must be paid for one unit of performance or value, i.e.,

$$PPR = \frac{price}{performance}. \tag{11.1}$$

A price-performance ratio can be computed for any performance dimension. It is particularly helpful for pricing or for price comparison when the monetary value of the product to the customer cannot be calculated. The alternative is to measure the monetary value of the product to the customer and then to compare it to the price. As a result we get a "net value". This method is feasible only if the monetary value of the product to the customer can be calculated.

### 11.2.1 Price Performance Ratio as a Pricing Tool

In the simplest case, performance in (11.1) is measured on a single dimension and this forms the basis for defining PPR. Such ratios are used for electric motors ($/hp), apartment rents ($/square meter), buildings ($/square meter), and so on.

Table 11.1
An Example of Simple Price-Performance Ratios (Source: Shapiro 1977)

| Product | List Price ($) | hp | Price/hp ($) |
|---|---|---|---|
| John Deere 450 c | 29,854 | 65 | 459 |
| Case 450 | 31,203 | 51 | 612 |
| Massey Ferguson 300 | 37,089 | 63 | 589 |
| International | | | |
| Harvester TD 7E | 32,802 | 65 | 505 |
| Caterpillar D3 | 30,146 | 62 | 486 |

Table 11.1 shows an example of PPR for tractors where the ratio of price to hp is considered important. In this case, John Deere introduced a new product with a superior price/hp-ratio.

*Multiple Performance Dimensions*

Customers typically consider several attributes in their product evaluation and weigh each attribute differently. Such evaluation processes can be described formally by the multi-dimensional attitude- and preference-models discussed earlier (vector model, ideal-point model, part-worth model).

For demonstration purposes, we confine our analysis to the linear-compensatory or vector model, where the performance index for product $i$ is given by

$$L_i = \sum_{j=1}^{k} \alpha_j x_{ij}, \tag{11.2}$$

where $\alpha_j$ = weight of attribute $j$, $x_{ij}$ = level of attribute $j$ at product $i$.

If perceptions and/or weights differ across customers in (11.2), which is often the case with weights, a customer index must be added. Equation (11.2) shows that a weak performance on one attribute can be compensated for by a strong performance on another (linear-compensatory).

We show an application of this model for a case concerning the purchase of a computer. Four products were considered as feasible by this customer. These four products were evaluated with respect to six attributes for which explicit weights were defined by the purchasing team. A constant-sum weighting scale (sum of weights = 100) was applied.

In Table 11.2, the six attributes and their weights are given in row 1 and row 2, respectively. The weighting scheme reflects the needs of this particular customer; it could be different for another customer. Different weighting schemes can be a basis for market segmentation (see Chapter 8).

Table 11.2
Computation of Price-Performance Ratios by a Buyer of a Computer

| Criterion | CPU Capacity KB | Performance Cycle N sec | Number of Monitors | Disc Drives MB | Compiler | Operating System | Sum of Points Performance = Index | Price | Price-Performance Ratio |
|---|---|---|---|---|---|---|---|---|---|
| Weighting Factor | 20 | 25 | 8 | 11 | 18 | 18 | 100 | | |
| Supplier A | 64 | 1200 | 3 | 18.4 | Cobol Fortran IV Basic | Timesharing (3 programs) | | 299.469 DM | 1.170 DM |
| | 2  40 | 1  25 | 4  32 | 3  33 | 4  72 | 3  54 | 256 | | |
| B | 72+12 | 1140 | 1 | 15 | Cobol Fortran IV RPG II, Algol Basic | DFÜ 1 Program | | 346.469 DM | 1.353 DM |
| | 3  60 | 2  50 | 2  16 | 2  22 | 4  72 | 2  36 | 256 | | |
| C | 40+72 | 1000 | 2 | 2×30 | RPG II, Cobol Assembler | Multitask Dual Programming | | 305.795 DM | 924 DM |
| | 4  80 | 3  75 | 3  24 | 4  44 | 2  36 | 4  72 | 331 | | |
| D | 64 | 980 | 1 | 18.8 | Fortran IV, Text Editor Macro Assembl. | Multitask Dual Programming | | 302.798 DM | 961 DM |
| | 2  40 | 4  100 | 2  16 | 3  33 | 3  54 | 4  72 | 315 | | |

In each cell, the following information is given:
- upper: attribute level,
- lower left: evaluation of the attribute ranging from 1 (worst) to 4 (best),
- lower right: product of weighting factor and evaluation point.

Performance Index (eighth column) is the sum of the figures in the lower right corner. Since C's PPR was the most favorable (DM 924), it received the order in this case.

## Strategic Implications

Let's consider the situation of the manufacturer of product D. Based on the information contained in Table 11.2, he could take the following corrective actions:
- he can lower his price to DM 291,060 so that his product's PPR would match that of *C*, he can decrease the price even more (say to DM 285,000) to offer a better PPR than *C* ( $\rightarrow$ DM 904 = DM 20 price advantage per performance unit),
- he can add a second or third monitor, which would lower his product's PPR to DM 937 or DM 914,
- he can offer compilers for Cobol and Basic so that his product's PPR would fall to DM 909,
- he could attempt to convince the customer that his weighting scheme is not adequate and that 15 points for the CPU and 30 points for the cycle time make more sense. This would make D's and C's PPR DM 932 and DM 938, respectively. But this option is the most difficult one to implement.

This example shows how information on the customer's evaluation of product performance can help pricing industrial goods. If the buyer's evaluation process is known in detail, it is possible to develop a product/pricing strategy that meets the customer's specific needs.

In this case a consensus on the weighting scheme, i.e., weights for each attribute, was reached among the purchasing team members. But it is often difficult to reach such a consensus among the members of the so-called "buying center". The price is usually very important for purchasing and finance people, whereas the engineers may put more weight an technical performance than on price (Choffray and Lilien 1980).

## Multivariate Techniques

The pricing of industrial goods provides particularly attractive opportunities for the application of sophisticated multivariate techniques. This is so because the key factors are normally easier to quantify than with consumer goods and the purchase decision process for industrial products tends to be more rational. In the context of market segmentation in Chapter 8 we have already discussed several examples. Therefore we confine ourselves to a few applications to industrial cases.

## Analytic Hierarchy Process

Fig. 11.1 shows an application of the Analytic Hierarchy Process (AHP) to construction machinery (for the method see Saaty 1980, 1986). On the first hierarchy

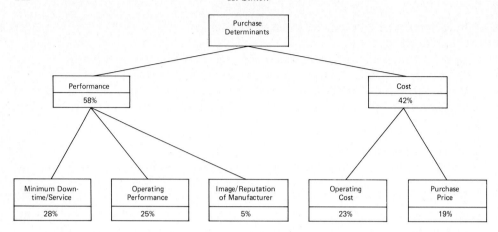

Fig. 11.1. Importance Weights for Construction Machinery at Two Hierarchical Levels Derived via AHP

level customers compare performance and cost, they attach weights of 58% and 42% (sum = 100%) to these two factors. On the second hierarchical level the two factors are split up into sub-factors. On this level it turns out that purchase price has only a weight of 19% and, thus, is of limited significance.

This result says that weaknesses in performance, service, and operating cost can hardly be compensated by lower prices. On the other hand, the customers are willing to pay a higher price if a company delivers superior performance. This does not imply that price is unimportant under competitive aspects. Because if several competitors offer similar or identical performance on the non-price factors (which is often the case), then price becomes the decisive criterion.

*Conjoint Measurement*

Another method which can be extremely useful for industrial products is conjoint measurement (see also Chapters 2 and 8). In Fig. 11.2 we demonstrate an application for a specific type of electric motors.

The factors included in the conjoint study were product quality/reliability, service interval, life duration, energy consumption, and price. The price response function was derived by means of the attraction model as described in Chapter 2. We see that the market share of the product goes down rapidly when price surpasses the threshold of DM 500. The profit curve attains its maximum at a price of DM 475, just below the average competitive price. Competitive reaction is not considered in the figure.

The unique value of the conjoint results is that product and performance characteristics can be directly translated into implications for pricing. Such implications in the present case are

– an increase of the service interval by 10% would have raised the optimal price to DM 525,

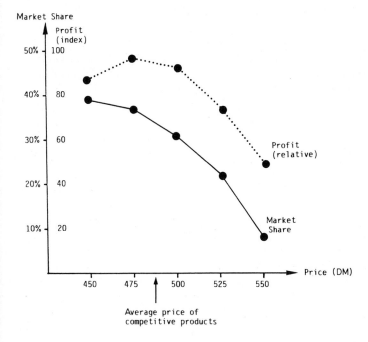

Fig. 11.2. Price Response Function for an Electric Motor Type Derived via Conjoint Measurement

- a reduction of energy consumption by 5% would have increased the optimal price to DM 550 (or possibly higher),
- a reduction of reliability (measured in mean breakdown time) of 5% would have reduced the optimal price to DM 450 (or below).

   Thus, conjoint measurement allows for a fine tuning of price and performance of industrial products.

   Another useful method is multidimensional scaling (MDS). It visualizes market and competitive structures and, thus, faciliates the understanding of the market. We refer the reader to the examples provided in Chapter 8 some of which are from the industrial sector.

### 11.2.2 Economic Evaluation of Industrial Goods

   The price of an industrial product represents a cost for the buying firm. On the other hand, the buyer may get additional proceeds from the use of the product as compared to competitive products. In such cases where the product brings a clearcut savings or additional proceeds, the monetary "net value" to the customer can be calculated. This value has to be divided between the seller and the buyer. The maximum price the customer is willing to pay for a product is the value he gets from it. The minimum price the seller is willing to accept is his cost plus margin.

Suppose a new plant pesticide increases the yield per acre by 100 kg of wheat as compared to the old pesticide. Application of the new product, however, costs DM 10 more per acre. If the price of wheat is DM 50 per 100 kg, the price of the new product could exceed the price of existing pesticides maximally by DM 50–DM 10 = DM 40. If the unit cost is the same for the new and the old pesticide, the feasible price range is between the old price and the old price plus DM 40. Typically the price will be set somewhere in the middle of this interval in order to induce farmers to adopt the new product.

Such calculations are much more complex for investment goods. In order to gauge the effect of price, the manufacturer should have a good information on how the customer evaluates the product. The price the manufacturer can charge would be different if the customer applies the return-on-investment criterion (ROI) than if he uses net present value as decision criterion.

Net present value (NPV) is defined as

$$\text{NPV} = -p + \sum_{t=1}^{T} CF_t(1+i)^{-t}, \tag{11.3}$$

where $CF_t$ is the cash flow in period $t$ and $i$ is the discount rate.

The purchase price of the investment good enters into the NPV in several figures:
– into purchase price $p$,
– into cash flow $CF_t$,
  – via depreciation,
  – via financing costs when the difference between equity and purchase price is financed by debt.

In order to demonstrate the implications for pricing we present a numerical example concerning a new truck model. The product under consideration is compared with the best competitive vehicle for which the following figures apply:

| | |
|---|---|
| Operating days per year | 200 |
| Proceeds per operating day | 500 DM |
| Operating cost per day | 250 DM |
| Purchase price | 100,000 DM |
| Economic life | 5 years |
| Salvage value | 0 DM |
| Equity available for financing | 50,000 DM |
| Income tax rate | 50% |
| Discount rate ( = Interest rate for debt) | 10% |
| Repayment of the loan after 5 years in a lump sum | |

To calculate the net present value for the competitive truck, we first compute the cash flow per year:

| | |
|---|---|
| Proceeds per year | 100,000 DM |
| Operating cost | − 50,000 |
| Interest | − 5,000 |
| Depreciation | − 20,000 |
| Profit before tax | 25,000 |
| Profit after tax | 12,500 |
| Cash flow | 32,500 DM |

The sum of the discounted cash flows for five years is DM 123,200 and the purchase price of the truck is DM 100,000, making the net present value DM 23,200.

The new truck model has a longer service interval and is more energy-efficient. Because of these improvements, it can be used 210 days per year and the operating cost decreases to DM 225 per operating day.

The net present value in this example can be expressed as a linear function of the truck price $p$

$$NPV = 118,936 - 0.8105p.$$

The purchase price at which the new truck's net present value is the same as the old one's ($= DM 23,200$) is DM 118,120. At this price for the new truck the buyer would get the same long-term profits as with the competitive truck. Thus, the technical improvements translate into a price difference of DM 18,120.

For other alternative prices of the new truck, we get

| Alternative Price | | Difference in Net Present Value from Competitive Truck | |
|---|---|---|---|
| | | absolute | relative |
| $p = 100,000$ | NPV = 37,886 | + 14,686 | 63.3% |
| $p = 110,000$ | NPV = 29,781 | + 6,581 | 28.4% |
| $p = 120,000$ | NPV = 21,676 | − 1,524 | − 6.6% |
| $p = 146,744$ | NPV = 0 | − 23,200 | − 100.0% |

These comparisons provide valuable support for the pricing decision. If the customers employ other criteria in their investment decision, the picture changes completely. Table 11.3 shows the corresponding values calculated for other criteria: return on equity, return on investment, and pay-back period. The last two columns give the criterion values at prices of DM 110,000 and DM 100,000 for the new truck. This example demonstrates that pricing implications differ depending upon which criteria the customers apply. The price at which the new truck provides the same

Table 11.3
Pricing Implications of Different Investment Decision Criteria

| Criterion | Value of Competitive Product | Competitive Neutral Price | Criterion Value at | |
|---|---|---|---|---|
| | | | $p = 110,000$ | $p = 100,000$ |
| Return on Equity | 25.0% | 125,833 | 29.7% | 32.8% |
| Return on Investment | 12.5% | 114,010 | 13.5% | 16.4% |
| Pay-Back Period | 3.08 years | 114,225 | 2.98 years | 2.75 years |
| Net Present Value | 23,200 DM | 118,120 | 29,781 DM | 37,886 DM |

value as the competitive product ("competitive neutral price") shows a wide variance depending upon which criterion is used.

The information on how the customer evaluates the product is extremely important for a manufacturer of investment goods. Forbis and Metha (1981, p. 50) put it as follows: "the value customers perceive depends so heavily on the way they evaluate it ... that management ought to be keenly concerned about how well and thoroughly these evaluations are made." Close contacts with customers are very important in this regard. Moreover, the manufacturer can approach this issue in an active way. He can, for instance, try to convince a customer who used to apply the pay-back period method that the net present value method is more appropriate because it takes interest into account. This change of criterion alone would justify a higher price differential (up to DM 3,895) in the example above.

Summary: Purchasing decisions for industrial goods depend to a large extent on explicit evaluations which are based on technical or economic criteria. A technical evaluation can produce a performance index, with which a price-performance ratio (PPR) can be computed. The economic evaluation is critical for investment goods. Depending on which criteria the customer chooses to apply, different pricing implications result. For optimal pricing in both cases, managers need good information on how customers evaluate the products. Such information is hard to come by in practice.

## 11.3 Pricing when Prices are Negotiated

Many industrial goods are sold direct. Only a few suppliers and customers exist in many industrial markets. A considerable proportion of industrial goods are custom-made. In such circumstances, price is typically negotiated between supplier and customer.

### 11.3.1 Theory of Price Negotiation

We first discuss the theory of price negotiation in the case of bilateral monopoly, i.e., when only one supplier and one customer exist. This case lends itself well to a rigorous analysis.

In order to make a deal in such a situation, the supplier and the customer have to agree upon price and sales (= purchase) volume. The interests of both parties conflict with each other, at least partly. If the quantity is given, the price negotiation represents a zero-sum game or, more precisely, a constant-sum game. Negotiation theory is important because its principles are applicable not only to the bilateral monopoly but also to all situations where transactions are completed only after the conclusion of an agreement. Such a situation is rather typical in industrial markets.

*The Negotiation Situation*

Suppose supplier A faces customer B, who sells his products to many end-users. No other firms exist besides A and B. Fig. 11.3 illustrates this situation.

The revenue of A represents the cost to B, the sale of whose end-product in turn determines the demand for supplier A's product. The object of negotiation is B's sales

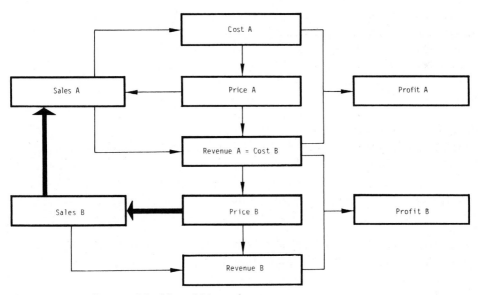

Fig. 11.3. Systems Context of the Bilateral Monopoly

volume ($q_B$) and A's price ($p_A$). All other numbers are either given or can be derived from these two variables.

Since the total joint profit depends solely on $p_B$ (or $q_B$), negotiation should proceed in two stages.

1. In stage 1, $p_B$ or $q_B$ are set in such a way that the joint profit is maximized. No conflict of interests exists here.
2. In stage 2, division of profit is negotiated. Here the interests of both parties conflict with each other.

*Quantitative Analysis*

Assuming linear cost functions, we get the profit functions of both firms as follows:

$$G_A = (p_A - k_A)q_A, \tag{11.4}$$

$$G_B = (p_B - p_A - k_B)q_B. \tag{11.5}$$

We assume, without loss of generality, that for each unit of $B$ one unit of $A$ is required, i.e., $q_A = q_B$. Total profit is then

$$G_T = G_A + G_B = (p_B - k_B - k_A)q_B. \tag{11.6}$$

Thus $G_T$ is not dependent on $p_A$. The optimal price $p_B^*$ (optimal quantity $q_B^*$) is determined independent of $p_A$ (negotiation stage 1).

We illustrate the situation with the example shown in Fig. 11.4. The underlying price response function and parameter values are as follows:

$$q_B = a - bp_B, \tag{11.7}$$

where $a = 100$, $b = 10$, $k_A = 3$, $k_B = 2$.

For each party two iso-profit lines are drawn. An iso-profit line represents the set of price combinations ($p_A$, $p_B$) that yield the same profit for one party. Agreement would be possible only if neither party incurs a loss. This condition is met within the triangle ABC. On line AB, $q_B = 0$, no business takes place. On line AC, firm A makes no profit because $p_A = k_A = 3$. On line BC, company B ends up empty-handed because $p_B = p_A + k_B$.

Let's consider point E ($p_A = 3.50$; $p_B = 6$). This point lies within the triangle ABC. At this price point the following profits result:

$$G_A = 20, \; G_B = 20, \; G_T = 40.$$

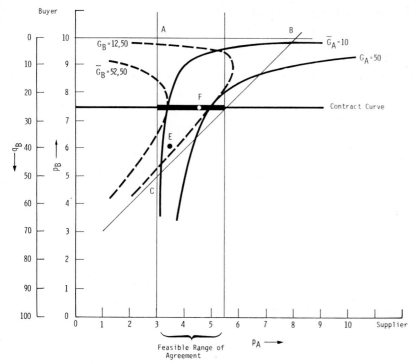

Fig. 11.4. Negotiation Situation Expressed as a System of Isoprofit Curves

Compared with this result, both firms will be better off by increasing $p_A$ to 4.5 and $p_B$ to 7.5 (point F). Here $G_A = 37.50$, $G_B = 25$, and $G_T = 62.50$.

*The Contract Curve*

At point F, the joint profit $G_T$ is maximized. This can be verified easily by deriving $p_B^*$ or $q_B^*$ from the joint profit function (11.6),

$$p_B^* = \tfrac{1}{2}\left(\tfrac{a}{b} + k_A + k_B\right) = 7.50, \tag{11.8}$$

$$q_B^* = \tfrac{1}{2}\left(a - bk_A - bk_B\right) = 25. \tag{11.9}$$

These figures correspond to the coordinate values of point F on the vertical axis. The line parallel to the $p_A$ axis at $q_B = q_B^*$ or $p_B = p_B^*$, i.e., the line of the maximum joint profit, is called the "contract curve". No party can become better off on the contract curve without making the other worse off by the same amount.

This property is called Pareto-optimality. The nature of Pareto-optimality becomes clear when it is pointed out that the contract curve represents the set of tangent points of the isoprofit curves of both parties. For each party two isoprofit curves are drawn in Fig. 11.4. Only the portion of the contract curve lying in the feasible range of agreement, i.e., within triangle ABC (thick solid line), is relevant for negotiation. Since $p_B$ is 7.50 on the contract curve and $k_B$ equals 2, the upper limit of $p_A$ is 5.50 ($G_B = 0$ here). The lower limit, which is determined by A's marginal cost, is 3. Krelle (1976) calls these two limits "exploitation points" because the profit of one of the parties is pushed down to zero at these points.

If both parties behave rationally, they will reach agreement within the interval between 3 and 5.50. A more precise specification of the outcome is possible only if we make further assumptions. The final result of the negotiation is usually not one of the exploitation points because one of the parties would lose interest in the transaction at these points.

### Threat Points

So far we have discussed the case of bilateral monopoly where the two parties have no choice but to make a deal with each other. If other options exist, say, A has another customer or B can order from another supplier, the picture changes.

In Fig. 11.5, A's profit is drawn on the horizontal axis and B's on the vertical. As in Fig. 11.4, $G_A = 0$ and $G_B = 62.5$ at $p_A = 3$, and at $p_A = 5.5$, $G_A = 62.5$ and $G_B = 0$. The negatively sloped 45°-line represents all possibilities of the division of the

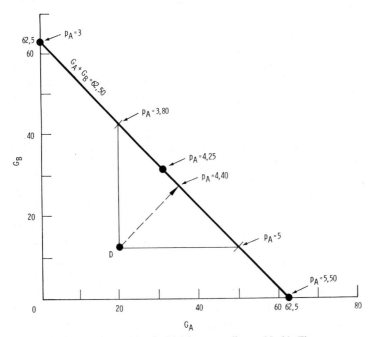

Fig. 11.5. Threat Point and Profit Division according to Nash's Theory

maximum joint profit. At $p_A = 4.25$, A and B receive the same amount of profit $(G_A = G_B = 31.25)$.

Now suppose A could sell 25 units of the product to another customer at a price of 3.80 and B could buy the product at a price of 5 elsewhere. These options narrow down the feasible range of agreement to prices between 3.80 and 5. If A and B cannot reach an agreement, A would make a profit of 20 and B a profit of 12.5 (point D). B would be hit harder than A if no agreement were reached; we can say that A has a greater threat potential. The relative strength of the threat potential is reflected in the position of point D. The more unequal the threat potential is, the farther D is located from the 45°-line.

According to the theory of Nash (1953), the incremental profit attainable through agreement is divided evenly between the two parties. Geometrically, a perpendicular line is drawn from the threat point D to the joint profit line. See the broken arrow in Fig. 11.5. In the example $p_A$ is set at 4.40.

Profits are divided as follows: $G_i$ = profit when the threat comes true + $\frac{1}{2}$ incremental profit,

$$G_A = 20 + 15 = 35 \ (56\%),$$

$$G_B = 12.50 + 15 = 27.5 \ (44\%).$$

The Nash solution thus considers the relative strength of threat potentials in profit division. Changing the threat point to $D = (30,10)$, which favors A, for example, would increase A's profit share to 66% of the total profit.

The concept of Nash provides an interesting conceptual framework because the ideas of threat potential and "fair division" always play a role in negotiations. Thus the model helps us better understand negotiation situations. The concrete applicability of the negotiation theory to real situations is limited because of intervening qualitative variables, incomplete/false information, bluffing, etc. Furthermore, real negotiations are strongly affected by the skills and personalities of the negotiators.

Summary: In the case of (near) bilateral monopoly, price and sales volume are usually negotiated. The negotiation takes place in two stages. First, the volume quantity that maximizes the joint profit is determined. In stage 2, the division of this profit is negotiated over the price. A portion of the contract curve represents the feasible range of agreement, at the limits of which the profit of one of the parties is reduced to zero. No general statement is possible concerning where the agreement will be reached within this range. Nash's solution considers the relative strength of the threat potentials.

## 11.3.2 Price Negotiation under Oligopolistic Interdependency

Price transparency is lower in a market where price is negotiated than in markets where actual prices are "public". This has important implications for oligopolistic reactions because these depend heavily on price transparency. List prices in most

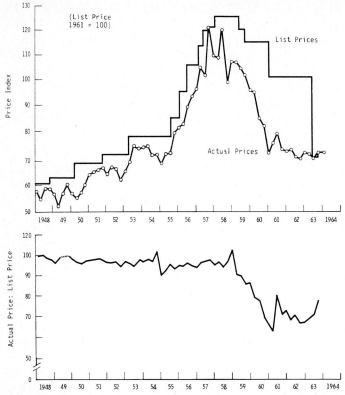

Fig. 11.6. Quarterly List Prices and Actual Prices of Steam Turbine Generators USA 1948–1963 (Source: Sultan 1974)

industrial markets often have little relationship to actual prices. "List prices may be a poor guide to the actual level of prices prevailing in an industrial market" (Burck 1973). The relation between list and actual prices changes with the firm's capacity utilization, the situation of the customer, the size of the order, etc., and it is highly unstable.

Fig. 11.6 gives an example of this relation. The top half of the figure contrasts the list prices with the actual prices of steam turbine generators. The bottom half shows the actual prices as a percentage of the list prices.

We can see that the actual prices fluctuate far more than the list prices. Flexible adjustments of prices to market conditions are often made by means of price negotiation. Such flexibility in pricing is extremely important in industrial marketing.

### Selective Price-Undercutting, Transparency, and Oligopolistic Reaction

In oligopolistic markets where prices are negotiated, competitive reactions can be delayed due to the lack of price transparency (Albach 1973). A supplier who

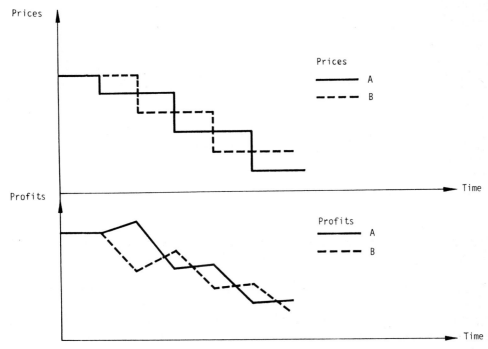

Fig. 11.7. Consequences of a Policy of Selective Price-Undercutting

undercuts price to attract individual customers can be temporarily successful because the price cutting is often not detected quickly by his competitors. The price-undercutting takes place in a selective and covert way. This policy is characterized by a potentially big discrepancy between short- and long-term effects. As soon as competitors realize what is happening, they are likely to react (possibly very strongly). Price warfare may break out in which everybody is caught in a downward price-profit spiral as illustrated in Fig. 11.7.

In markets where prices are individually negotiated and where price transparency is low, there exists a temptation to pursue such a policy of selective undercutting. This temptation is particularly strong if capacities are not fully utilized. For competitors, the situation is often very tricky. They cannot be sure whether or not the customers are switching over to other suppliers because their prices are being undercut. A customer may provide the supplier with false information to get price concessions. The business report of the sales force may be also misleading. Consider the following quotation: "The sales representative may assume that the spread between the company's price and the one offered by the successful competitor was, say, 10 percent instead of the actual 5 percent. At headquarters, this lost-business report showing a 10 percent premium over the successful competitor may be taken at

Table 11.4
Empirical Examples of Differentiation of Negotiated Prices across Customers

| Product/Service Category | Differentiation in Discounts |
|---|---|
| Personal Computers | 10–40% |
| Professional Services | 0–30% |
| Trucks | 20–55% |
| Electrical Components | 10–40% |
| Airline Services | 0–40% |
| Hotel Services | 0–50% |
| Passenger Cars | 0–25% |
| Optical Equipment | 0–50% |
| Advertising Space | 0–50% |

face value by sales management. Perhaps at the same moment, the successful competitor in this particular negotiation is receiving a similar lost-business report on another negotiation to which it had been a party in another section of the country. Sales management in each of the two companies by now may be roundly cursing the other for substantial price-cutting" (Tully 1978, p. 60).

Oligopolies where prices are negotiated represent very complex market structures, which have not been well researched. In view of the destabilizing factors inherent in such markets, management must price with finesse and caution.

*Price Negotiation and Price Discrimination*

Price negotiation allows for a covert discrimination of prices across customers. If list prices exist, the object of the negotiation is the discount which the individual customer gets. This discount can be strongly differentiated depending on the specific relation between supplier and customer. In Table 11.4 we list several examples from the author's experience which give an idea of the degree of such differentiations.

Important buyer characteristics which have an effect on the degree of differentiation are: purchasing volume, opinion leadership, history of business relation, negotiation skill, access to relevant information ("smart customers pay less"), toughness, economic situation, purchasing power, degree of dependence on the supplier, etc.

A low price transparency among the customers is the most important precondition for such an individual price differentiation. If the customers inform each other on the prices they actually pay, such differentiation is extremely dangerous because all prices can go down to the lowest level. This risk should not be underestimated. It is the greater, the more intensive the information flow and the more similar transaction situations are across customers. Therefore, the supplier should keep the differentiation confidential. But customers rarely keep silent in this regard. They even boast of the bargain they got. The covert price discrimination may be limited by law (e.g.,

Robinson-Patman Act, see also Chapter 8). In any case, this policy should be applied with great caution.

Summary: There is often little price transparency in markets where prices are negotiated. List prices are not a good guide to actual prices. Thus competitors cannot react to price cutting immediately because it is not easily detected. In this situation, some manufacturers are tempted to undercut their competitors. They run the risk, however, of getting caught in the downward price-profit spiral. Such markets are thus characterized by a sharp conflict between short- and long-term objectives.

Individual price negotiations provide an opportunity for price differentiation. If price transparency is low among customers, the supplier may differentiate the prices according to the individual customer's situation. Both covert price cutting and individual price discrimination involve the risk of destabilizing the overall price level. Great caution is therefore warranted.

### 11.3.3 Price Negotiation and Pricing Authority

Pricing authority typically rests with top management in markets where each pricing decision holds for a long time or is of a general nature. In markets where prices are negotiated, however, pricing decisions must be made case by case, so that the issue of delegating the pricing authority to decentralized units, particularly the sales force, arises.

### Types of Pricing Authority in Practice

We observe three basic types of pricing authority:
1. The sales force or other decentralized units have full authority in pricing.
2. The sales force has limited authority in pricing. Down to a certain price level, the salesperson can make a decision; if this level is to be undercut, he must get the approval of his superiors.
3. The sales force has no authority in pricing. Any undercutting of the list price has to be approved by management.

*Qualitative Arguments*

There are arguments both for and against delegation of pricing authority (Walker et al. 1977, Stephenson et al. 1979).

Arguments for delegation are:
- Since the salesperson is given more authority, his morale is boosted (Zarth 1981).
- The salesperson has the best information on the specific transaction and is, therefore, best able to evaluate the price the customer is willing to pay, making the optimal price differentiation possible (Lal 1986).
- The salesperson can quickly react to changing market conditions.
- In many negotiations, questions on product and price are interrelated. Product and

price decisions have to be made simultaneously. Negotiations can be hindered if the salesperson has no full authority.

- Decentralization of pricing authority leads to the optimum when the salesperson's commission is made proportional to the contribution margin.

Arguments for making superior units or top management fully or at least partially responsible for pricing are:

- The salesperson gives in too easily in price negotiations because he has a strong incentive to make a deal even when his commission is geared to the contribution margin. "There is the temptation always to 'play it safe' to get the order" (Nimer 1971, p. 48).
- Centralization of pricing authority relieves the salesperson of psychological pressures. According to Zarth (1981, p. 111), "most salespeople ... are afraid of the price talk".
- Centralization reduces the pressure from the buyer. An old purchasing axiom is: "Find out if the salesperson can reduce the price. If he can, insist that he do so" (Stephenson et al. 1979, p. 27).
- Only top management is in the position to look at each business in perspective and thus decide on the acceptable price.
- The pricing decision sometimes entails a complex cost analysis that can be done only in headquarters.

These pro- and contra-arguments suggest that the optimal practice is situation-specific. The following theoretical discussion is based on simplified assumptions and provides a framework for the decision on pricing authority.

*Theoretical Aspects*

The complete delegation of pricing authority to the salesperson is optimal under the following conditions (see Weinberg 1975):

1. The firm and salesperson strive to maximize profit.
2. The salesperson receives a commission proportional to the contribution margin.

At a commission rate of $s$, the firm's profit (contribution margin) is

$$G = (1 - s)[pq(p) - C(q)],\tag{11.10}$$

and the salesperson's commission (income) is

$$I = s[pq(p) - C(q)].\tag{11.11}$$

Since the firm and the salesperson have common interests, only the expressions in the brackets determine $G$ and $I$ and these are the same. The optimal price for both is determined by the Amoroso-Robinson Relation (see Chapter 3). If the salesperson can better gauge the price elasticity of the buyer than top management, it makes sense to delegate the pricing authority fully to him/her. More generally Lal (1986) suggests that delegation may be more profitable when the salesperson's information about the selling environment is superior to that of the sales manager or the headquarter. Weinberg (1978) shows that this policy remains optimal even when the salesperson is not striving for absolute income maximization but rather for a certain target income with minimum spending of time.

Delegation is not optimal, however, if the firm pays a commission proportional to revenue. In this case, the firm's profit after subtracting the commission is

$$G = (1 - r)pq(p) - C(q),$$ (11.12)

and the salesperson's commission is

$$P = rpq(p),$$ (11.13)

where $r$ is the commission rate.

Here the salesperson is interested in the revenue-maximizing price, which is attained when price elasticity is equal to $-1$ (see Chapter 3). The optimal price for the firm is, however,

$$p^* = \frac{\varepsilon}{(1 - r)(1 + \varepsilon)} C'$$ (11.14)

and this lies in the range where price elasticity is smaller than $-1$, i.e., the firm's optimal price is higher than the revenue-maximizing price. Delegation in this case leads to prices that are too low for the firm. Here it is better not to delegate the pricing authority.

It is not known to which extent the hypothesis that the salesperson consistently tries to maximize his income is realistic. The usefulness of the theoretical conclusions depends heavily on the validity of this hypothesis.

Stephenson et al. (1979) analyzed the relationship between the policy on pricing authority and the company's performance in 108 companies specializing in the distribution of medical products to hospitals. The study distinguishes between full, limited, and no delegation of pricing authority and calculates several performance measures for these categories. Table 11.5 shows the results.

A negative relationship between the degree of pricing authority of the sales force and the company's performance is observed for all performance measures except "revenue per salesperson". Only at "revenue per salesperson", limited pricing authority leads to the best performance. These results are surprising because in most of the companies the theoretical condition for delegation was met, i.e., commission was proportional to the contribution margin.

Since the significance level is better than 10 percent at only two criteria and the study is limited to one industry, the results should not be generalized. The authors themselves conclude that the salespeople's tendency to give in to customers'pressure

Table 11.5
Relationship between Pricing Authority of the Sales Force and Company Performance

| Pricing Authority of the Sales Force | $n$ | Performance Measures | | | | |
|---|---|---|---|---|---|---|
| | | Contribution Margin | | Revenue per Sales-person | Revenue Growth | Return on Investment |
| | | before Sales Cost | after Sales Cost | | | |
| none | 31 | 1.0570 | 1.0436 | 0.8697 | 1.3939 | 11.79% |
| limited | 52 | 0.9827 | 0.9978 | 1.2116 | 0.9905 | 10.49% |
| full | 25 | 0.9434 | 0.9537 | 0.7591 | 0.5605 | 9.65% |
| Signif-icance Level | | 9% | 28% | 17% | 8% | 62% |

for lower prices when they have pricing authority could explain the findings. The results suggest that the simple hypothesis of income-maximization does not capture the complexity of the salespeople's motivation (Walker et al. 1977). Our own experience suggests that centralisation of pricing authority usually leads to better results for the company.

Summary: In markets where prices are negotiated, the delegation of pricing authority is often at issue. We have discussed the arguments both for and against the delegation. Theoretically full delegation is optimal when the salesperson is better informed on the pricing conditions, strives to maximize his income, and receives a commission proportional to the contribution margin. When commissions are proportional to revenue, the pricing authority should remain with headquarters. An empirical study suggests that companies do the better, the less they delegate the pricing authority to the sales force. The optimal policy differs from case to case. Managers are urged to be cautious in their decision on delegation.

## 11.4 Price Management in Competitive Bidding

Competitive bidding is particularly important in sales to the public sector. The classical form of competitive bidding is characterized by the following conditions (Kempken 1980):
– the customer defines the product/service specifications,
– suppliers submit sealed bids independent of each other,
– all bids are opened simultaneously,
– the bid price cannot be changed.

Typical situations in which bidding is practiced are:
1. Delivery of products
   - military procurement,
   - procurement by other public institutions (hospitals, post offices, universities, etc.),
   - so-called "tender bids" through which governments procure pharmaceuticals, pesticides, fertilizer, etc. for whole countries (prevalent in third world countries).
2. Delivery of services
   - construction projects (airports, roads, buildings, etc.),
   - project management.

## Determinants of Price in Competitive Bidding

Determinants of price in bidding include:
- the objective function of the supplier,
- cost of the project,
- competitive behavior,
- decision criteria employed by the customer.

Friedman (1956) was the first to develop a quantitative model for pricing in bidding. Edelman's model (1965) has been widely applied. The basic model has been modified in later works. Some of the new solution concepts are based on game theory. Kempken (1980), after a comprehensive review of the relevant literature, concludes that decision theory is more helpful for competitive bidding in practice than game theory. Thus we confine our analysis to the basic decision-theoretic model.

## The Decision Model

We make the following assumptions:
- the supplier who bids lowest wins the bid,
- the bidding firm is risk-neutral, i.e., it maximizes the expected value of its profits.
  Profit $G$ of the firm is

$$G = \begin{cases} p - C - K & \text{if win} \\ -K & \text{otherwise,} \end{cases}$$

where $p$ bid price, $C$ variable cost of the project, $K$ bid preparation cost.
The probability of winning the bid at price $p$ is

$$\text{Prob}(p < \bar{p}),$$

where $p$ represents the lowest competitive price.
The expected value of profit is

$$E(G) = (p - C - K)\,\text{Prob}(p < \bar{p}) - K[1 - \text{Prob}(p < \bar{p})]. \tag{11.15}$$

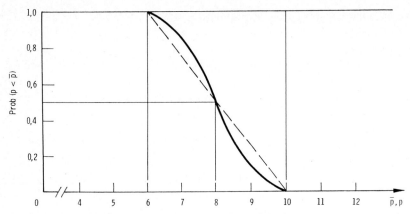

Fig. 11.8. Example of Distribution Functions of Competitive Prices

This is a problem of optimization under uncertainty, where the competitive behavior plays the key role. This behavior is reflected in probability distributions of the competitive bid prices. Such probability distributions can be either inferred from the bid prices in the past or estimated subjectively. Subjective estimates enable us to consider the specific situations of the competitors (e.g., capacity utilization).

Fig. 11.8 shows two hypothetical distribution functions of bid prices. The S-shaped (solid line) function is based on a bell-shaped probability distribution; the linear (dashed line) version is based on a uniform distribution of competitive prices.

The following probabilities of winning are associated with alternative prices:

Probability of Winning

| Bid Price | S-shaped Distribution Function | Linear Distribution Function |
|---|---|---|
| $\leqslant 6$ | 1.0 | 1.0 |
| $\leqslant 7$ | 0.86 | 0.76 |
| $\leqslant 8$ | 0.50 | 0.50 |
| $\leqslant 9$ | 0.14 | 0.24 |
| $\leqslant 10$ | 0 | 0 |

The expected value $E(G)$ in (11.15) is maximized when

$$\frac{\delta E}{\delta p} = \text{Prob}(p < \bar{p}) + (p - C - K)\frac{\delta\text{Prob}}{\delta p} + K\frac{\delta\text{Prob}}{\delta p} = 0. \tag{11.16}$$

Solving for the optimal bid price $p^*$ yields

$$p^* = C - \frac{\text{Prob}(p < \bar{p})}{\delta\text{Prob}/\delta p} \tag{11.17}$$

(11.17) is not a solution for $p^*$ because Prob and $\delta\text{Prob}/\delta p$ depend on $p^*$. Conditions (11.16) and (11.17) correspond to the competitive case without reaction (see Chapter 3). Prob simply replaces $q$.

The optimal bid price is the lower, ceteris paribus,
- the lower the variable cost of the project $C$ is,
- the more sharply the probability of winning increases with lower prices.

Theoretically $K$, the bid preparation cost, doesn't affect the optimal bid price. This is because $K$ is a sunk cost which the bidder incurs whether or not he wins the bid. In reality, however, we observe many cases where the decision maker feels the pressure from the sunk cost which he has already incurred. This pressure is presumably the stronger, the higher the sunk cost is. And the higher this pressure is, the stronger the psychological incentive to win the bid by lowering price. In this behavioral sense, $K$ might affect the final bid price in the form of "$p$ is the lower, the higher $K$ is".

We demonstrate the use of this model with the linear distribution function in Fig. 11.8. Within the interval (6, 10), the distribution function has the form

$$\text{Prob}(p < \bar{p}) = 2.5 - 0.25p, \text{ for } p \text{ in the interval } (6, 10). \tag{11.18}$$

Suppose variable cost $C = 5$, and bid preparation cost $K = 1$. Then the expected profit is

$$E(G) = (p - 5 - 1)(2.5 - 0.25p) - 1(1 - 2.5 + 0.25p). \tag{11.19}$$

The optimal price is $p^* = 7.5$. The win-probability at this price is 0.625, and the value of the expected profit 0.5625.

If the firm wanted to achieve a win-probability of 90 percent instead of the maximum expected value in this example, the price would be 6.4. For non-linear distribution functions, which are more realistic, the optimal price can be found only numerically.

This basic model has been modified/revised by several researchers. Edelman (1965) includes the customers' preferences for specific suppliers. Willenbrock (1973) introduces non-neutral risk preferences of the bidders. These modifications do not alter the basic structure of the competitive bidding model.

Summary: Competitive bidding is widely practiced in placing public orders. Competitors submit the sealed bids simultaneously, which cannot be corrected. Determinants of the bid price include the variable cost of the project, customer's decision criteria, and expected competitive behavior. Competitive behavior is reflected in the probability distributions of competitive bid prices; these are either inferred from the records of past bids or estimated subjectively. The optimal price that maximizes the expected profit lies at the point where the opposite profit effects of an increase in price and the probability to get the order exactly offset each other. The optimal bid price, ceteris paribus, is the lower, the lower the variable cost of the project is and/or the more sharply the win-probability goes up with lower prices.

Chapter 12

# Price Management and Price-Advertising Interaction

## 12.1 Introduction

So far we have implicitly assumed that pricing decisions are made independent of the decisions on other marketing mix instruments and that price response is not affected by the level of other instruments. Both assumptions are generally unrealistic.

Real world marketing activities are typically multi-instrument actions (Peckham 1973, Strang 1976). The promotion is a classical case. It could comprise a temporary price cut, an increase in advertising, a change in the package design, special sales force and distributor incentives, all sorts of in-store-activities, etc. (Hinkle 1965). An integrated approach of similar nature is used in the implementation of more permanent changes, e.g., a permanent price increase is often accompanied by a specific advertising campaign, a careful briefing of the sales force, a redesign of the product, etc.

These observations indicate that marketing mix interactions are of utmost practical relevance. In some cases, the interaction effects are likely to be more important than the main effects of the various instruments. There is further evidence that marketing instruments should not be viewed in isolation. A PIMS-study suggests that the consistency of the marketing mix may be a key determinant of a company's success (Farris and Reibstein 1979), another author contends that consistency is one of the three most crucial aspects of a marketing strategy (Levinson 1984).

In the context of price management, the influence of advertising on price response is managerially particularly relevant because pricing actions can be supported by advertising actions. This chapter focuses on this relationship.

We first define the concept of "marketing mix interaction". We then present our theory of price-advertising interaction and test this theory empirically. The final section discusses the strategic implications of our findings.

## 12.2 What is Marketing Mix Interaction?

In the literature the concept of marketing mix interaction is not precisely defined.

It is usually contended that the additive marketing mix response function

$$q_t = a - bp_t + c \ln A_t, \tag{12.1}$$

where $q_t$ sales in period $t$, $p_t$ price in period $t$, $A_t$ advertising in period $t$; $a$, $b$, $c$ parameters; does not incorporate interactions between price and advertising. On the other hand, the multiplicative response function

$$q_t = ap_t^b A_t^c \tag{12.2}$$

is said to represent such an interaction (see e.g., Kotler 1971).

If the objective is to maximize profit, the static objective function for these two models would be

$$G_t = (p_t - k_t) q_t, \tag{12.3}$$

where $G_t$ profit in period $t$, $k_t$ marginal cost (assumed constant).

If we substitute (12.1) or (12.2) into (12.3), and set the derivative of (12.3) to zero, we can get the conditions of optimal pricing for equations (12.1) and (12.2). These conditions reveal that the optimal price $p_t^*$ for the additive model depends on advertising, whereas that for the multiplicative model does not depend on advertising.

Obviously we have two kinds of interaction, which we define as follows:

– response interaction: the marginal sales response to the change in price depends on the level of advertising (sales response function), i.e., $\delta(\delta q_t / \delta p_t)/\delta A_t \neq 0$ (and vice versa),

– elasticity or decision interaction: the elasticity or the decision on the optimal value of price depends on the level of advertising (profit maximization model (12.3)), i.e., $\delta p_t^* / \delta A_t \neq 0$ (and vice versa).

Clearly, the two basic sales response models (12.1) and (12.2) are different with respect to these two interactions (see Table 12.1).

Naturally, a "true" interaction model should incorporate both kinds of interactions. This is the prevailing view of managers. The notion that advertising doesn't

Table 12.1
Price-Advertising Interactions for Two Basic Models

| Response Function | Response Interaction (Sales response function) | Decision Interaction (Objective function) |
|---|---|---|
| Additive (12.1) | No | Yes |
| Multiplicative (12.2) | Yes | No * |

* Note that the optimal advertising $A_t^*$ depends on price. This is not due to the interaction effect but to the contribution margin effect of price.

affect the optimal price nor the sales response to price changes is perceived as unrealistic.

## 12.3 A Theory of Price-Advertising Interaction

### 12.3.1 The Purpose of Advertising with Respect to Price Response

In order to develop a theory of price-advertising interaction, we first discuss an important issue: the purpose of advertising with respect to price response. Gatignon (1984) expresses a widely held view as follows: "To the marketer, one of the purposes of advertising is to make consumers less price sensitive" (p. 1). This statement is certainly true of any company which is selling at high (relative) prices or which is about to raise prices. Under these conditions a low price elasticity is highly desirable.

However, for a firm which sells at aggressive (low relative) prices or which cuts the price, the opposite is the case. For such a firm the main purpose of advertising is to increase price sensitivity. Only with a sufficiently high price elasticity, low prices or price cuts can be turned into profits.

Thus both positive and negative effects of advertising on (the magnitude of) price response can be desirable from the company's point of view. We would, however, expect to observe only price-advertising mixes which are consistent in the sense of Table 12.2, i.e., advertising which increases price sensitivity when prices are low or are being reduced (and vice versa).

### 12.3.2 Consumer Behavior

While the purpose of advertising may differ from company to company depending on the pricing strategy chosen, the interaction between price and advertising depends solely on the reaction of the consumers. According to Adaptation Level Theory (Helson 1964), consumers form adaptation levels for various variables like price and advertising. If confronted with a new stimulus, they compare the stimulus with the

Table 12.2
Consistent and Inconsistent Price-Advertising Mixes

| Relative Price Level/ Price Change | Effect of Advertising on (the Magnitude of) Price Response | |
|---|---|---|
| | Positive | Negative |
| High/Increase | Inconsistent | Consistent |
| Low/Reduction | Consistent | Inconsistent |

existing adaptation levels and judge accordingly, i.e., if the deviation is considered positive, they react positively and vice versa.

Recently the Adaptation Level Theory has gained wider attention (Rinne 1981, Winer 1986) in marketing. Strong empirical support for this theory was provided by Lattin and Buckling (1987) and by Kucher (1985, 1987). It was shown, that consumers form adaptation levels for prices of brands on the basis of the past prices. If presented with a new price, consumers react favorably if the new price is below the current adaptation level and vice versa. An analogous effect was found for advertising (Simon 1982a).

In order to develop hypotheses concerning the main and interaction effects of the changes in price and advertising, we assume for the moment that the system is in equilibrium, i.e., actual price and advertising levels are equal to the corresponding adaptation levels. We also assume that sales remain constant if both instruments are not changed.

Table 12.3
Main Effects and Interactions of Price and Advertising Changes

| Advertising | Price | | |
|---|---|---|---|
| | Constant | Increase | Reduction |
| Constant | Constant sales | negative sales response <br> * existing customers buy less and/or <br> * existing customers are lost | positive sales response <br> * existing customers buy more and/or <br> * new customers are attracted |
| Increase | positive sales response <br> * existing customers buy more and/or <br> * new customers are attracted | Interaction A <br> $(+ -)$ | Interaction B <br> $(+ +)$ |
| Reduction | negative sales response <br> * existing customers buy less and/or <br> * existing customers are lost | Interaction C <br> $(- -)$ | Interaction D <br> $(- +)$ |

Table 12.3 clarifies the main effects and four potential interactions. Note that the sales response to changes in price and advertising is defined as the slope of the respective response functions, i.e., $\delta q_t/\delta p_t$ and $\delta q_t/\delta A_t$.

In the table the signs in parentheses indicate the direction of the interaction effects. A twofold positive effect results from increased advertising and reduced price, whereas a twofold negative impact is generated by reduced advertising and increased price.

We first discuss hypotheses on the effect of increased advertising on the sales response to price changes. Fig. 12.1 illustrates the issue.

The sales response to a price change is represented by curve (1). The linearity is assumed only for ease of demonstration. If we increase advertising while keeping the price constant, sales increase from B to C, this is the main effect of advertising (no interaction).

If we now reduce the price and, at the same time, intensify advertising, we would expect a sales response which is at least as strong as the response (slope) with constant advertising. If, on the other hand, price and advertising are increased simultaneously, the sales decline due to the price increase should not be stronger than with constant advertising, i.e., the slope of the price response function should not be steeper. The shaded areas in Fig. 12.1 represent the hypothesized interactions. If the

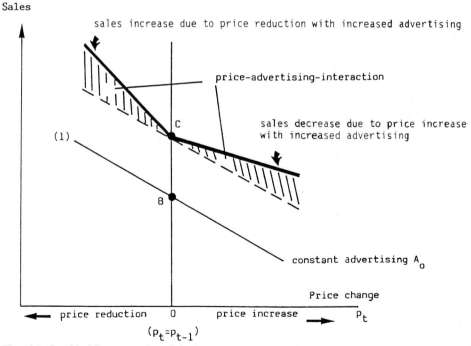

Fig. 12.1. Graphical Representation of the Interaction between Price Change and Advertising Increase

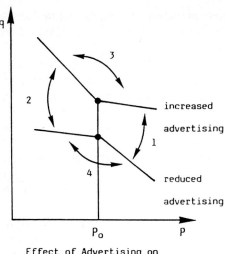

Effect of Advertising on
Price Response

Fig. 12.2. Graphical Representation of Four Hypotheses on Price-Advertising Interaction

reverse hypotheses were true, one should not observe intensified advertising efforts when prices are adjusted – as we do in the real world.

Obviously our hypotheses involve comparisons between slopes of response functions, of which two are vertical and two are horizontal comparisons (the numbers of the arrows in Fig. 12.2 refer to these comparisons):

1. Sales decrease due to price increase is not more with increased advertising than with reduced advertising (vertical).
2. Sales increase due to price reduction is not more with reduced advertising than with increased advertising (vertical).
3. Sales decrease due to price increase is not more than sales increase due to price reduction if accompanied by increased advertising (horizontal).
4. Sales increase due to price reduction is not more than sales decrease due to price increase if accompanied by reduced advertising (horizontal).

These four hypotheses concern the effect of advertising on price response. Note that we don't make cross-comparisons, i.e., we do not compare the response to "price reduction and reduced advertising" with the response to "price increase and increased advertising". Our theory allows for both negative and positive effects of advertising on price response.

### 12.3.3 Modeling the Interaction

In order to model the new theory, we introduce one variable for each of the branches in Fig. 12.2. Increases or decreases in price and advertising are modelled as deviations of current price and advertising from the corresponding adaptation levels. The adaptation levels of price and advertising are functions of past prices and advertising expenditures. According to Helson (1964), the anchor value is frequently formed by the last stimulus, but may also be determined by some weighted average of several preceding stimuli. The duration of the adjustment process is the crucial issue. From other research we know that the adaptation occurs rather fast (Simon 1982a). Kucher (1985) has shown that for frequently purchased branded goods the adjustment process lasts about 4 to 6 weeks. Given this information and the fact that our data set consists of either monthly or bimonthly data, we represent the adaptation levels of price and advertising as the price and the advertising expenditure in the last period.

The following model incorporates the influence of advertising changes on price response:

$$q_t = a + \mathscr{L}q_{t-1} + f_t(x_t) + b_1 \cdot \text{PRAR} + b_2 \cdot \text{PRAI}_t + b_3 \cdot \text{PIAR}_t + b_4 \cdot \text{PIAI}_t, \qquad (12.4)$$

where $f_t(x_t)$ function of various variables in period $t$; $\text{PRAR}_t$ price reduction, advertising reduction; $\text{PRAI}_t$ price reduction, advertising increase; $\text{PIAR}_t$ price increase, advertising reduction; $\text{PIAI}_t$ price increase, advertising increase; $a, \ldots, b_4$ parameters.

This model incorporates both response and decision (elasticity) interaction in the sense of Table 12.1. The synergistic effect of price and advertising changes (dummy variables) captures the response interaction.

Price reduction or increase is represented as the difference between $p_t$ and $p_{t-1}$. Advertising reduction or increase is included as a dummy (0-1) variable.

The function $f_t(x_t)$ captures all other relevant variables that explain the sales history of a specific brand under consideration. Note that a lagged sales effect is also included as an explanatory variable, which is commonly done in models of this kind to account for carryover effects (see Chapter 5).

## 12.4 Empirical Analysis

The model was tested for 10 frequently purchased nondurable brands. We present the results for one brand (Brand A) in some detail and summarize the findings for all 10 brands.

The model for Brand A is as follows:

$$q_t = 1543.1 + 0.2999q_{t-1} + 313.7A_t - 107.75\text{PRAI}_t - 46.05\text{PIAR}_t .$$
$$(4.59)^a \quad (2.64)^a \qquad (1.79)^c \quad (-5.31)^a \qquad (-2.00)^b \qquad\qquad (12.5)$$

The figures in parentheses represent $t$-statistics: a, b, c = significant at 1%-, 5%-, 10%-level.

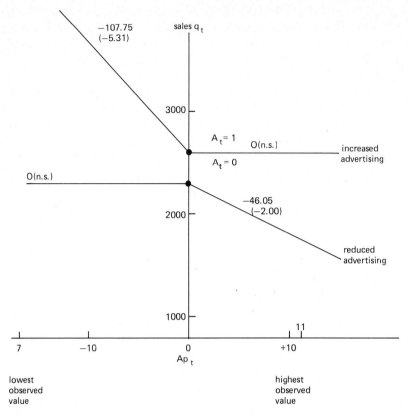

Fig. 12.3. The Effect of Advertising Changes on Price Response (Brand A)

The function $f_t(x_t)$ in 12.4 contains for brand $A$ only the advertising term, $A_t$. The main effect of price was not statistically significant. The main effect of advertising could be measured via the dummy $A_t$, which is 1 if the advertising budget in $t$ is above the median budget and 0 otherwise. The adjusted $R^2$ of this equation is 0.6650. In terms of the goodness of fit and the significance pattern, this model performs better than other models which represent the price response in different ways.

Fig. 12.3 illustrates the effect of advertising changes on the price response.

The figure demonstrates that a price reduction accompanied by intensified advertising has a very strong positive sales effect. However, if the price reduction is not supported by an increase in advertising, its sales effect is not significant (the coefficient of the omitted variable was $-4.06$ which is less than 4% of $-107.75$). A price increase, on the other hand, has strong negative sales effects if advertising is reduced concurrently, whereas sales are not significantly affected if the price increase is accompanied by increased advertising. Comparing Fig. 12.3 with the theory

Table 12.4
Summary of the Results on Price-Advertising Interaction for 10 Brands

| Number of Hypothesis (Fig. 12.2) | Comparison V = Vertical H = Horizontal | Hypothesis | Brands | | | | | | | | | |
|---|---|---|---|---|---|---|---|---|---|---|---|---|
| | | | A | B | C | D | E | F | G | H | I | J |
| 1 | V | Sales decrease due to price increase not more with increased than with reduced advertising | + | + | + | + | + | + | + | + | + | + |
| 2 | V | Sales increase due to price reduction not more with reduced advertising than with increased advertising | + | − | + | + | − | + | + | + | + | + |
| 3 | H | Sales decrease due to price increase not more than sales increase due to price reduction if accompanied by increased advertising | + | + | − | + | + | − | + | + | + | + |
| 4 | H | Sales increase due to price reduction not more than sales decrease due to price increase if accompanied by reduced advertising | + | − | + | + | + | + | + | + | + | + |

advanced in Fig. 12.2, we can see that in the case of brand A the findings are fully consistent with all four hypotheses.

Such a fully consistent price-advertising interaction pattern was not found for all brands which we investigated. The results for all 10 brands are summarized in Table 12.4. The "+ -sign indicates that the respective comparison is consistent with the hypothesis, whereas a "− -sign denotes an inconsistency.

Of the 40 comparisons (four comparisons for each of the 10 brands) five ($= 12.5\%$) are inconsistent with the theory. Though the sample is too small to allow for generalizations, these results suggest that our model is a reasonable representation of the price-advertising interaction. We now discuss the strategic implications of our model.

## 12.5 Strategic Implications

It is not our intention to investigate the optimality of price and advertising. Instead we are interested in the interactions which occur when these two instruments are concurrently changed. Therefore, the strategic implications of our model are concerned with the changes and not with the levels of the marketing variables. This does not mean that a change is always indicated. It is entirely possible that the profit is maximized at the current levels of price and advertising.

If price or advertising are, however, to be changed at all (e.g., due to changes in costs, competitive behavior or non-optimal past values, etc.), it would be generally optimal to change the two instruments simultaneously, i.e., both a reduction and an increase of price should be supported by an increase of advertising. Our recommendations are of a directional type, i.e., they suggest the directions of changes but do not specify the magnitude of the changes. This limitation is due to the use of dummy variables. Our recommendations are not of a general but of a "typical" nature. Table 12.4 shows that our model does not always provide an adequate representation of reality, so that a careful analysis is indicated in each individual case.

It is interesting that our recommendations to couple a price reduction with increased advertising is exactly the opposite of the implication derived from either a multiplicative or an additive price-advertising response model. Both models would tell us to cut advertising when the price is reduced. Our theory is more in line with reality where we observe that both price reductions and increases are often supported by intensified advertising (see Hinkle 1965, Peckham 1973). The new model can explain this phenomenon. Somewhat tentatively we may add that "price-advertising" is likely to be appropriate when the price is cut, whereas "quality- or image-advertising" is suggested for a price increase. Again this is not a generalizable statement. For example, if price serves as a quality indicator, one may be well advised to support a price reduction with "quality-advertising". The model can also be used to support a "pulsation strategy" for price. Since promotions are temporary price reductions supported by intensified advertising (and possibly other activities), the temporal pattern of a promotion/non-promotion sequence is of a "pulsation-type". In the literature no conclusive explanations for this behavior of manufacturers can be found. The new theory offers such an explanation.

# Bibliography

Abell, D.F. and J.S. Hammond: Strategic Market Planning: Problems and Analytical Approaches, Englewood Cliffs: Prentice Hall 1979.

Abrams, J.: A New Method for Testing Pricing Decisions, Journal of Marketing 28 (July 1964), 6–9.

Adam, D.: Consumer Reactions to Price, in: Taylor-Wills (eds.), Pricing Strategy, Princeton: Brandon 1969.

Adam, D.: Der Zusammenhang zwischen Gewinnmaximierung und Substanzerhaltung in statischen Entscheidungsfeldern bei frei verfügbaren Produktionsfaktoren, in: Coenenberg, A.G. (ed.), Unternehmensrechnung, München: Vahlen 1976.

Adams, W. (ed.), The Structure of American Industry, 6th ed., New York: MacMillan 1982.

Adams, W.J. and J.L. Jellen: Commodity Bundling and the Burden of Monopoly, Quarterly Journal of Economics 40 (1976), 475–488.

Addelman, S.: Orthogonal Main-Effect Plans for Asymmetrical Factorial Experiments, Technometrics 4 No. 1, (February 1962), 21–46.

Agarwala, R.: Price Policy in a Multi-Product Firm: A Case Study, Applied Economics 1 (August 1969), 161–167.

Albach, H.: Zur Sortimentskalkulation im Einzelhandel, in: Handelsbetrieb und Marktordnung, Festschrift für Carl Ruberg, Wiesbaden: Gabler 1962.

Albach, H.: Ansätze zu einer empirischen Theorie der Unternehmung, in: G.v. Kortzfleisch (ed.), Wissenschaftsprogramm und Ausbildungsziele der Betriebswirtschaftslehre, Berlin: Duncker & Humblot 1971.

Albach, H.: Das Gutenberg-Oligopol, in: Koch, H. (ed.), Zur Theorie des Absatzes, Wiesbaden: Gabler 1973.

Albach, H.: Market Organization and Pricing Behavior of Oligopolistic Firms in the Ethical Drugs Industry – An Essay in the Measurement of Effective Competition, Kyklos 32 (1979), 523–540.

Albers, S.: A Mixed Integer Nonlinear Programming Procedure for Simultaneously Locating Multiple Products in an Attribute Space, in: Henn, R. et al. (eds.), Methods of Operations Research, Vol. 26, Meisenheim am Glan: Hain 1977.

Albers, S.: Schätzung von Nachfragereaktionen des Tarif- und Leistungsangebots im öffentlichen Personennahverkehr, Zeitschrift für Verkehrswissenschaft 54 (April 1983), 207–230.

Alchian, A.: Reliability of Progress Curves in Airframe Production, Santa Monica (Calif.): Rand Corporation, April 1950 (Report 260-1) and in Econometrica 31 (October 1963), 679–693.

Alfred, A.M.: Company Pricing Policy, General Industrial Economics (November 1972), 1–15.

Allen, B.H., R.L. Tathem and D.R. Lambert: Flexible Pricing Strategies for High Inflation Periods, Industrial Marketing Management 5 (1976), 243–248.

Alpert, M.I.: Pricing Decisions, Glenview: Dryden Press 1971.

American Management Association: Pricing: The Critical Decision. New York 1961.

Angelmar, R. and R. Bagozzi: Typical Marketing Behavior over the Product Life Cycle, Working Paper, Insead, October 1982.

Anttila, M.: Consumer Price Perception, Dissertation: Helsinki, Helsinki School of Economics 1977.

Arbeitskreis Hax der Schmalenbach-Gesellschaft, Der Preis als Instrument der Absatzpolitik, Zeitschrift für betriebswirtschaftliche Forschung 22 (1980), 701–720.

Arora, R. and R.L. Vaughn: Product Life Cycle: A Synthesis of Recent Modeling Developments, Working Paper, Bradley University, Peoria (Ill.), June 1980.

Arrow, K.J.: The Economic Implications of Learning by Doing, Review of Economic Studies 29–30 (June 1962), 155–173.

Asher, H.: Cost-Quantity Relationships in the Airframe Industry, Santa Monica (Calif.): Rand Corporation, July 1956 (Report 291).

Askin, B. and R. Skinner: How British Industry Prices, Old Woking: The Gresham Press 1976.

Assael, H.: Segmenting Markets by Group Purchasing Behavior: An Application of the AID-Technique, Journal of Marketing Research 7 (May 1970), 153–157.

Assael, H. and A.M. Roscoe: Approaches to Market Segmentation Analysis, Journal of Marketing 40 (October 1976), 67–76.

Bachem, A. and H. Simon: A Product Positioning Model with Costs and Prices, European Journal of Operational Research 5 (July 1981), 362–370.

Baetge, J.: Ein Regelungsmodell für die Preispolitik, in: Hansen, H.R. (ed.), Computergestützte Marketing-Planung, München: Moderne Industrie 1974.

Bailey, E.L. (ed.): Pricing Practices and Strategies, New York: The Conference Board 1978.

Bain, J.S.: Barriers to New Competition, 4th Print, Cambridge (Mass): Harvard University Press 1967.

Balachandran, V. and A. Jain: A Predictive Model for Monitoring Product Life Cycles, Combined Proceedings, American Marketing Association, Chicago 1973.

Baldwin, H.R.: How to Assess Investment Proposals, Harvard Business Review 37 (May–June 1959), 3–9.

Balke, W.: Konkurrenzwerbung und Werbeerfolg, Wiesbaden: Gabler 1972.

Baloff, N.: Extension of the Learning Curve – Some Empirical Results, Operational Research Quarterly 22 (1971), 329–340.

Barclay, W.D.: Factorial Design in a Pricing Experiment, Journal of Marketing Research 6 (November 1969), 427–429.

Bass, F.M.: A New Product Growth Model for Consumer Durables, Management Science 15 (January 1969), 215–227.

Bass, F.M.: The Theory of Stochastic Preference and Brand Switching, Journal of Marketing Research 11 (January 1974), 1–20.

Bass, F.M.: The Relationship between Diffusion Rates, Experience Curves, and Demand Elasticities for Consumer Durable Innovations, Journal of Business 53 (July 1980), 51–67.

Bass, F.M. and A. Bultez: Optimal Strategic Pricing Policies with Learning, Paper No. 736, Krannert Graduate School of Management, Purdue University, August 1980.

Bass, F.M. and A. Bultez, A Note on Optimal Strategic Pricing of Technological Innovations, Marketing Science 1 (Fall 1982), 371–378.

Batzer, E., E. Greipl and E. Singer: Handhabung und Wirkung der unverbindlichen Preisempfehlung, Berlin: Duncker & Humblot 1976.

Bauer, E.: Markt-Segmentierung als Marketing-Strategie, Berlin: Duncker & Humblot 1976.

Bauer, H.H.: Die Entscheidung des Handels über die Aufnahme neuer Produkte, Berlin: Duncker & Humblot 1980.

Baumol, W.: Business Behavior, Value and Growth, New York: Harcourt & Brace 1959.

Baumol, W., R. Quandt and H. Shapiro: Oligopoly Theory and Retail Food Pricing, Journal of Business 37 (October 1964), 346–357.

Beckwith, N. et al. (eds.): Educators'Conference Proceedings, Chicago: American Marketing Association 1979.

Behrends, Ch.: Preise im Wettbewerb, Ein Leitfaden für die Kalkulation im Lebensmittel-Einzelhandel, Köln: Rationalisierungsgemeinschaft des Handels 1975.

Benad, G.: Das Verhalten des Verbrauchers, Veränderungen 1957/59–72, Düsseldorf: Intermarket-Institut 1975.

Bender, U.: Die Marketing-Konfrontation zwischen Industrie und Handel, Jahrbuch der Absatz- und Verbrauchsforschung 20 (1974), 280–291.

Bensoussan, A., G.E. Hurst and B. Näslund: Management Applications of Modern Control Theory, Amsterdam: North-Holland Publ. Co. 1974.

Bensoussan, A., A. Bultez and Ph.A. Naert: Leader's Dynamic Marketing Behavior in Oligopoly, in: TIMS Studies in the Management Sciences, Vol. 9, Amsterdam: North-Holland Publ. Co. 1978.

Benston, G.J.: Multiple Regression Analysis of Cost Behavior, Accounting Review 41 (October 1969), 659–672.

Bettmann, J.R.: Perceived Price a Product Perceptual Variable, Journal of Marketing Research 10 (February 1973), 70–80.

Bettmann, J.R.: An Information Processing Theory of Consumer Choice, Reading (Mass.): Addison-Wesley 1979.

Billon, S.A.: Industrial Learning Curves and Forecasting Production Requirements, Management International Review 6 (November-December 1966), 64–69.

Bird, R.: Managing High Technology Portfolio, Milks Cows, Kills Dogs, Marketing News, 13.7.1979, 6.

Bischof, P.: Produktlebenszyklen im Investitionsgüterbereich, Göttingen: Vandenhoeck & Ruprecht 1976.

Bitta, A.J.D. and K.B. Monroe: The Influence of Adaptation Levels on Subjective Price Perceptions, in: S. Ward and P. Wright (eds.), Advances in Consumer Research, Boston: Association for Consumer Research, 1984.

Blattberg, R., Th. Buesing, P. Peacock and S. Sen: Identifying the Deal Prone Segment, Journal of Marketing Research 15 (August 1978), 369–377.

Blattberg, R., D. Eppen and J. Lieberman: A Theoretical and Empirical Evaluation of Price Deals for Consumer Nondurables, Journal of Marketing 45 (Winter 1981), 116–129.

Böcker, F.: Die Bestimmung der Kaufverbundenheit von Produkten, Berlin: Duncker & Humblot 1978.

Böcker, F. and L. Thomas: Marketing, Stuttgart-NewYork: Fischer 1981.

Böhler, H.: Methoden und Modelle der Marktsegmentierung, Stuttgart: Poeschel 1977.

Bond, R.S. and D.F. Lean: Sales, Promotion, and Product Differentiation in Two Prescription Drug Markets, A Staff Report to the U.S. Federal Trade Commission, Washington 1977.

Bonoma, T.V. and B.P. Shapiro: Evaluating Market Segmentation Approaches, Industrial Marketing Management 13 (November 1984), 257–268.

Bonoma, T.V., V.L. Crittenden and R.J. Dolan: Can We Have Rigor and Relevance in Pricing Research?, in: Devinney, T.M. (ed.), Issues in Pricing – Theory and Research, Lexington Books 1988.

Bonus, H.: Die Ausbreitung des Fernsehens, Meisenheim am Glan: Hain 1968.

Bonus, H.: Untersuchungen zur Dynamik des Konsumgüterbesitzes, Berlin: Duncker & Humblot 1975.

Borchardt, K.: Preisbildung und Konkurrenz im Einzelhandel unter besonderer Berücksichtigung der Mehrproduktunternehmung, Jahrbücher für Nationalökonomie und Statistik 172 (1958), 32–57.

Boston Consulting Group: Perspectives on Experience, Boston: Boston Consulting Group, Inc. 1972.

Bowley, A.L.: Mathematical Groundwork of Economics, New York: Kelley 1924.

Bowman, W.S.: Tying Arrangements and the Leverage Problem, Yale Law Journal 67 (November 1957), 68–73.

Brand, E.: Der Lebenszyklus von Produkten und sein Einfluss auf die Preispolitik der Unternehmung, Dissertation, Universität Hamburg 1974.

Brede, H.: Lassen sich Preis-Absatz-Funktionen für neuartige Erzeugnisse durch Befragungen ableiten?, Zeitschrift für betriebswirtschaftliche Forschung 21 (December 1969), 809–827.

Brock, G.W.: The U.S. Computer Industry, A Study of Market Power, Cambridge (Mass.): Ballinger 1975.

Brockhoff, K.: A Test for the Product Life Cycle, Econometrica 35 (July 1967), 472–484.

Brockhoff, K.: On a Duopoly with a Doubly Kinked Demand Function, Zeitschrift für die gesamte Staatswissenschaft 124 (1968), 451–466.

Brodie, R. and C.A. de Kluyver, Attraction versus Linear and Multiplicative Market Share Models: An Empirical Evaluation, Journal of Marketing Research 21 (May 1984), 194–201.

Brown, F.E.: Price Image Versus Price Reality, Journal of Marketing Research 6 (May 1969), 185–191.

Brown, F.E.: Who Perceives Supermarket Prices Most Validly, Journal of Marketing Research 8 (February 1971), 110–113.

Brown, F.E. and A.E. Oxenfeldt: Should Prices Depend on Costs, MSU Business Topics 16 (Autumn 1968), 73–77.

Buchanan, I.M.: The Theory of Monopolistic Quantity Discounts, Review of Economic Studies XX (3/1953), 199–208.

Bultez, A.: La firme en concurrence sur des marchés interdépendants, Dissertation, Université Catholique de Louvain 1975 (1975a).

Bultez, A.: A Nonlinear Dynamic Model of Product Line Interdependencies. Working Paper No. 75-6, European Institute for Advanced Studies in Management, Brussels 1975 (1975b).

Bultez, A. and Ph.A. Naert: Estimating Gravitational Market Share Models. Working Paper 73-36, European Institute for Advanced Studies in Management, Brussels 1973.

Bultez, A. and Ph.A. Naert: Consistent Sum Constrained Models, Journal of the American Statistical Association 70 (1975), 529–535.

Bultez, A. and Ph.A. Naert: Does Lag Structure Really Matter in Optimizing Advertising Spending, Management Science 24 (May 1979), 454–465.

Burck, G.: The Myths and Realities of Corporate Pricing, in: Britt, S.H. – Boyd, H.W. (eds.), Marketing Management and Administrative Action, New York: McGraw Hill 1973.

Burstein, M.L.: The Economics of Tie-in-Sales, Review of Economics and Statistics 27 (February 1960), 68–73.

Busse von Colbe, W. and F. Eisenführ: Ermittlung von Preisuntergrenzen, in: Kosiol, E. (ed.), Handwörterbuch des Rechnungswesens, Stuttgart: Poeschel 1970, col. 1424.

Buzzell, R.D.: Predicting Short-Term Changes in Market Share as a Function of Advertising Strategy, Journal of Marketing Research 1 (August 1964), 27–31.

Buzzell, R.D.: Competitive Behavior and Product Life Cycles, in: Proceedings of the 1966 World Congress, Chicago: American Marketing Association 1966.

Buzzell, R.D., T.G. Bradley and R.G.M. Sultan: Market Share – A Key to Profitability, Harvard Business Review 53 (1975), 97–106.

Buzzell, R.D. and P.W. Farris: Marketing Costs in Consumer Goods Industries, Marketing Science Institute Report No. 76-111, Cambridge, MA 1976.

Buzzel, R.D. and B.T. Gale: The PIMS-Principles, New York, The Free Press 1987.

Cassady, R.: Competition and Price Making in Food Retailing, New York: Ronald 1962.

Cattin, Ph. and D.R. Wittink, Commercial Use of Conjoint Analysis: A Survey, Journal of Marketing 46 (Summer 1982), 44–53.

Chamberlin, E.H.: The Theory of Monopolistic Competition, Cambridge (Mass): Harvard University Press 1933.

Chapman, R.G. and R. Staelin: Exploiting Rank Ordered Choice Set Data within the Stochastic Utility Model, Journal of Marketing Research 19 (August 1982), 288–301.

Chevalier, M.: Increase in Sales Due to In-Store Display, Journal of Marketing Research 12 (November 1975), 426–431.

Choffray, J.-M. and G.M. Lilien: Market Planning for New Industrial Products, New York: Wiley & Sons 1980.

Chow, G.C.: Technological Change and the Demand for Computers, American Economic Review 57 (December 1967), 1117–1130.

Clark, F.H., M.N. Darrough and J. Heineke: Optimal Pricing Policy in the Presence of Experience Effects, Journal of Business 55 (November 1982), 517–530.

Clarke, D.G.: Econometric Measurement of the Duration of Advertising Effect on Sales, Journal of Marketing Research 13 (November 1976), 345–357.

Clarke, D.G. and R.J. Dolan: A Simulation Analysis of Alternative Pricing Strategies for Dynamic Environments, Journal of Business 57 (January 1984), 179–200.

Claycamp, H.J. and W.F. Massy: A Theory of Market Segmentation, Journal of Marketing Research 5 (November 1968), 388–394.

Clifford, D.K.: Leverage in the Product Life Cycle, Duns's Review and Modern Industry (May 1965), 62–70.

Coenenberg, A.G. (ed.): Unternehmensrechnung, München: Vahlen 1976.

Cole, R.: Increasing Utilization of the Cost Quantity Relationship in Manufacturing, Journal of Industrial Engineering 9 (May-June 1958), 173–177.

Conway, R. and A. Schultz: The Manufacturing Progress Function, Journal of Industrial Engineering 10 (January 1959), 39–53.

Cooke, E.F. and B.C. Edmonson: Computer Aided Product Life Cycle Forecasts for New Product Investment Decisions, Combined Proceedings, American Marketing Association, Chicago 1973.

Cooper, R.G.: The Dimensions of Industrial New Product Failure, Journal of Marketing 43 (Summer 1979), 93–103.

Corstjens, M. and D.A. Gautschi: Conjoint Analysis: A Comparative Analysis of Specification Tests for the Utility Function, Management Science 29 (December 1983), 1393–1413.

Cournot, A.: Recherches sur les principes mathématiques de la théorie des richesses, Paris 1838.

Cox, W., Jr.: Product Life Cycles as Marketing Models, Journal of Businesses 40 (October 1967), 375–384.

Crew, M.A. and P.R. Kleindorfer: Public Utility Economics, London: Macmillan 1979.

Davidson, J.H.: Why Most New Consumer Brands Fail, Harvard Business Review 54 (March–April 1976), 117–122.

Day, G.S.: The Product Life Cycle: Analysis and Application Issues, Journal of Marketing 45 (Fall 1981), 60–67.

Day, G.S. and D.B. Montgomery: Diagnosing the Experience Curve, Journal of Marketing 47 (Spring 1983), 44–58.

Deakin, M.D.: Pricing for Return on Investment, Management Accounting 57 (December 1975), 43–50.

Dean, J.: Managerial Economics, Englewood Cliffs: Prentice Hall 1951.

Dean, J.: Pricing a New Product, The Controller (April 1955), 163–165.

Dean, J.: Pricing Pioneering Products, The Journal of Industrial Economics 17 (April 1969), 165–179.

Dean, J.: Pricing Policies for New Products, Harvard Business Review 54 (November–December 1976), 141–153.

Devinney, T.M.: Entry and Learning, Management Science 33 (June 1987), 706–724.

Devinney, T.M. (ed.): Issues in Pricing – Theory and Research, Lexington (Mass): Lexington Books 1988.

Dhalla, N.K.: Assessing the Long-Term Value of Advertising, Harvard Business Review 56 (January–February 1978), 87–95.

Dhalla, N.K. and W.H. Mahatoo: Expanding the Scope of Marketing Research, Journal of Marketing 40 (April 1976), 34–41.

Dhalla, N.K. and S. Yuspeh: Forget the Product Life Cycle Concept, Harvard Business Review 54 (January–February 1976), 104–112.

Dichtl, E.: Die Bildung von Konsumententypen als Grundlage der Marktsegmentierung, Wirtschaftswissenschaftliches Studium 3 (Februar 1974), 54–59, (1974a).

Dichtl, E.: Die Marktsegmentierung als Voraussetzung differenzierter Marktbearbeitung, Wirtschaftswissenschaftliches Studium 3 (März 1974), 97–102, (1974b).

Diederich, H.: Leitsätze für die Preisermittlung auf Grund von Selbstkosten (LSP), in: Kosiol, E. (ed.), Handwörterbuch des Rechnungswesens, Stuttgart: Poeschel 1970, col. 1023.

Diller, H.: Der Preis als Qualitätsindikator, Die Betriebswirtschaft 37 (April 1977), 219–234.

Diller, H.: Verkäufe unter Einstandspreisen, Marketing-Zeitschrift für Forschung und Praxis 1 (März 1979), 7–12.

Diller, H.: Die Struktur von Produktpreisurteilen, Marketing-Workshop Schotten 11.5.1980.

Diller, H.: Die Variation des Preisniveaus von Sonderangeboten im Lebensmitteleinzelhandel, Eine empirische Wirkungsanalyse, Discussion Papers in Marketing Nr. 1, Hochschule der Bundeswehr, Hamburg 1981.

Diller, H.: Preispolitik, Stuttgart: Kohlhammer 1985.

Diller, H.: Preiskenntnisse von Konsumenten, Working Paper No. 19, Institut für Marketing, Universität der Bundeswehr, Hamburg 1987.

Dodson, J.A.: An Empirical Examination of Buyer Behavior: Individual and Brand Analysis, Unpublished Doctoral Dissertation, Purdue University 1975.

Dodson, J.A. and E. Muller: Models of New Product Diffusion through Advertising and Word-of-Mouth, Management Science 24 (November 1978), 1568–1578.

Dolan, R.J.: Quantity Discounts: Managerial Issues and Research Opportunities, Marketing Science 6 (Winter 1987), 1–22.

Dolan, R.J.: The Extent of Suboptimality of Myopic Pricing Rules, Discussion Paper, Graduate School of Business, University of Chicago, December 1979.

Dolan, R.J.: Pricing Strategies that Adjust to Inflation, Industrial Marketing Management 10 (1981), 151–156.

Dolan, R.J. and A.P. Jeuland: Experience Curves and Dynamic Demand Models: Implications for Optimal Pricing Strategies, Journal of Marketing 45 (Winter 1981), 52–62.

Doob, A.N. and M.J. Carlsmith: Effect of Initial Selling Price on Subsequent Sales, Journal of Personality and Social Psychology 11 (1969), 345–350.

Dorward, N.: The Pricing Decision, London: Harper & Row 1987.

Doyle, P.: The Realities of the Product Life Cycle, Quarterly Review of Marketing (Summer 1976), 1–6.

Dyer, L.W.: In-Store Research at Publix: Scanning the Selling Power of Merchandising, Progressive Grocer (November 1980), 98–106.

Ebisch, H. and J. Gottschalk: Preise und Preisprüfungen bei öffentlichen Aufträgen einschliesslich Bauaufträgen, 4th ed., München: Vahlen 1977.

Eckhardt, K.: Sonderangebotspolitik in Warenhandelsbetrieben – Eine empirische Studie, Wiesbaden: Gabler 1976.

Edelmann, F.: Art and Science of Competitive Bidding, Harvard Business Review 43 (July–August 1965), 53–66.

Edson, H.O.: The Application of Return on Investment to Product-Pricing, The Controller (October 1959), 464–469.

Ehrenberg, A.S.C. and L.R. England: Generalizing a Pricing Effect, Working Paper, London Business School 1987.

Ehrlinger, E.: Kundengruppen-Management, Die Betriebswirtschaft 39 (April 1979), 261–273.

Eichhorn, W.: Modelle der vertikalen Preisbildung, Mathematical Systems in Economics 6, Meisenheim am Glan: Hain 1973.

Eliashberg, J. and A.P. Jeuland: The Impact of Competitive Entry in a Developing Market upon Dynamic Pricing Strategies, Marketing Science 5 (Winter 1986), 20–36.

Elrod, T. and R.S. Winer: An Empirical Comparison of Aggregation Criteria for Developing Market Segments, Working Paper 299A, Graduate School of Business, Columbia University 1980.

Emory, F.: Some Psychological Aspects of Price, in: Taylor-Wills (eds.), Pricing Strategy, Princeton: Brandon 1969.

Engelhardt, W.H.: Mehrstufige Absatzstrategien, Zeitschrift für betriebswirtschaftliche Forschung 28 (Februar 1976), 175–182.

Engelhardt, W.H.: Erlösplanung und Erlöskontrolle als Instrument der Absatzpolitik, Zeitschrift für betriebswirtschaftliche Forschung 29 (Sonderheft 1977), 10–27.

Enis, B.M., R. La Garce and A.E. Prell: Extending the Product Life Cycle, Business Horizons 20 (June 1977), 46–56.

Erichson, B.: Probleme der Ermittlung von Wiederkaufwahrscheinlichkeiten bei der Testmarktsimulation, Vortrag gehalten vor der Marketingkommission, Schloss Gracht, Erftstadt Januar 1980.

Erichson, B.: TESI: Ein Test- und Prognoseverfahren für neue Produkte, Marketing-Zeitschrift für Forschung und Praxis 3 (August 1981), 201–207.

Eskin, G.J.: A Case for Test Market Experiments, Journal of Advertising Research 15 (April 1975), 27–33.

Eskin, G.J. and P.H. Baron: Effects of Price and Advertising in a Test Market Experiment, Journal of Marketing Research 14 (November 1977), 499–508.

Fandel, G.: Optimale Entscheidung bei mehrfacher Zielsetzung, Berlin-Heidelberg-New York: Springer 1972.

Farris, P.W. and D.J. Reibstein: How Prices, Ad Expenditures and Profits are Linked, Harvard Business Review 57 (November–December 1979), 173–185.

Fellner, W.: Competition Among the Few, New York: Kelley 1949.

Ferguson, C.E. and S.C. Maurice: Economic Analysis: Theory and Application, Homewood (Ill.): Irwin 1978.

Fiedler, J.: Condominium Design and Pricing: A Case Study in Consumer Trade-Off Analysis, Proceedings Third Annual Conference, Association for Consumer Research 1972.

Finerty, J.J.: Product Pricing and Investment Analysis, Management Accounting 53 (December 1971), 15–18.

Fischerkoesen, H.M.: Experimentelle Werbeerfolgsprognose, Wiesbaden: Gabler 1966.

Flämig, J. and G. Weyer: Zur Psychologie des Preises, Zeitschrift für Markt-, Meinungs- und Zukunftsforschung 3 (April 1972), 2413–2425.

Fölkers, D.: Monopolistische Preispolitik bei stochastischer Nachfrage, Göttingen: Vandenhoeck und Ruprecht 1975.

Fog, B.: Industrial Pricing Policies, Amsterdam: North-Holland Publ. Co. 1960.

Fogg, C.D. and K.H. Kohnken: Price-Cost Planning, Journal of Marketing 42 (March 1978), 97–106.

Forbis, J.L. and N.T. Metha: Value-Based Strategies for Industrial Products, The McKinsey Quarterly (Summer 1981), 35–52.

Fouilhé, P.: The Subjective Evaluation of Price: Methodical Aspects, in: Taylor-Wills (eds.), Pricing Strategy, Princeton: Brandon 1969.

Fourt, L.A. and J.W. Woodlock: Early Prediction of Market Success for New Grocery Products, Journal of Marketing 25 (October 1960), 31–38.

Frank, R.E. and W.F. Massy: Market Segmentation and the Effectiveness of a Brand's Price and Dealing Policies, Journal of Business 28 (April 1965), 186–200.

Frank, R.E., W.F. Massy and Y. Wind: Market Segmentation, Englewood Cliffs: Prentice Hall 1972.

Frankel, M.: Pricing Decisions under Unknown Demand, Kyklos 26 (1973), 1–23.

Friedman, L.: A Competitive Bidding Strategy, Operations Research 4 (February 1956), 104–112.

Freter, H.: Strategien, Methoden und Modelle der Marktsegmentierung bei der Markterfassung und -bearbeitung, Die Betriebswirtschaft 40 (Juli 1980), 453–463.

Frisch, R.: Monopole-Polypole, La Nation de Force dans l'Economie, in: Westergaard-Festschrift, Kopenhagen 1933.

Frisch, R.: On the Notion of Equilibrium and Disequilibrium, The Review of Economic Studies 3 (1935/36), 110.

Frohn, J.: Grundausbildung in Ökonometrie, Berlin-New York: de Gruyter 1980.

Funke, H. and K. Spremann: Preisbildung in Marktprozessen bei Zusammenschluss der Anbieter, Diskussionspapier Nr. 72, Institut für Wirtschaftstheorie und Operations Research, Universität Karlsruhe 1977.

Gabor, A.: Pricing, London: Heinemann 1977.

Gabor, A. and C.W.J. Granger: On the Price Consciousness of Consumers. Applied Statistics (November 1961), 170–188 and in: Taylor-Wills (eds.), Pricing Strategy, Princeton: Brandon 1969.

Gabor, A. and C.W.J. Granger: Price Sensitivity of the Consumer, Journal of Advertising Research 4 (December 1964), 40–44.

Gabor, A. and C.W.J. Granger: The Pricing of New Products, Scientific Business (August 1965), 141.

Gabor, A. and C.W.J. Granger: Price as an Indicator of Quality: Report on an Inquiry, Economica 23 (1966), 43–70.

Gabor, A. and C.W.J. Granger: The Attitude of the Consumer to Price, Revised Version of a Paper first given at the International Business Schools' Symposium – New Developments in Pricing Strategy – at the University of Bradford 1967.

Gabor, A. and C.W.J. Granger: The Attitude of the Consumer to Price, in: Taylor, B. and G. Wills (eds.): Pricing Strategy, Princeton: Brandon 1970.

Gabor, A., C.W.J. Granger and A.P. Sowter: Comments on "Psychophysics of Prices", Journal of Marketing Research 8 (May 1971), 251–252.

Gardner, D.M.: Is there a Generalized Price-Quality Relationship?, Journal of Marketing Research 8 (May 1971), 241–243.

Gaskins, D.W.: Dynamic Limit Pricing: Optimal Pricing under Threat of Entry, Journal of Economic Theory 3 (September 1971), 306–322.

Gatignon, H.A..: Competition as a Moderator of the Effect of Advertising on Sales, Working Paper, Wharton School, University of Pennsylvania 1984.

Gavish, B., D. Horsky and K. Srikanth: An Approach to Optimal Positioning of a New Product, Management Science 29 (November 1983), 1277–1297.

Geiger, H.: Sonderangebote werben für das gesamte Sortiment, Markenartikel 30 (September 1968), 414–419.

Gensch, D.H. and W.W. Recker: The Multinomial Multiattribute Logit Choice Model, Journal of Marketing Research 16 (February 1979), 124–131.

Gerstner, E. and P. Holthausen: Profitable Pricing when Market Segments Overlap, Marketing Science 5 (Winter 1986), 55–69.

GfK (ed.): Welchen Praxiswert hat der Produktlebenszyklus, Nürnberg 1973.

Ghemawat, A.: Building Strategy on the Experience Curve, Harvard Business Review 2 (March-April 1985), 143–149.

Ghosh, A., S. Neslin and R. Shoemaker: A Comparison of Market Share Models and Estimation Procedures, Journal of Marketing Research 21 (May 1984), 202–210.

Ginzberg, E.: Customary Prices, American Economic Review 26 (1936), 296.

Glinz, M.: Sonderpreisaktionen des Herstellers und des Handels, Wiesbaden: Gabler 1978.

Goldman, H.B., H.E. Leland and D.S. Sibley: Optimal Nonuniform Prices, Review of Economic Studies 52 (1984), 305–319.

Goodmann, D.A. and U.W. Moody: Determining Optimum Price Promotion Quantities, Journal of Marketing 34 (April 1970), 31–39.

Gossen, H.H.: Entwicklung der Gesetze des Menschlichen Verkehrs und der daraus fliessenden Regeln für Menschliches Handeln, Braunschweig: F. Vieweg 1854.

Granger, C.W.J. and A. Billson: Consumers' Attitudes Toward Package Size and Price, Journal of Marketing Research 9 (August 1972), 239–248.

Green, P.E.: An Application of Bayesian Decision Theory to a Problem in Long Range Pricing Strategy, Journal of the American Statistical Association 57 (June 1962), 490.

Green, P.E.: Bayesian Decision Theory in Pricing Strategy, Journal of Marketing 27 (January 1963), 5–14.

Green, P.E.: Application of Decision Theory in Pricing Strategy, in: Phillips-Williamson (eds.), Prices: Issues on Theory, Practice and Public Policy, Philadelphia: University of Pennsylvania Press 1967.

Green, P.E.: On the Design of Choice Experiments Involving Multifactor Alternatives, Journal of Consumer Research 1 (1974), 61–68.

Green, P.E. and F.J. Carmone: Multidimensional Scaling and Related Techniques in Marketing Analysis, Boston: Allyn and Bacon 1970.

Green, P.E., F.J. Carmone and D.P. Wachspress: On the Analysis of Qualitative Data in Marketing Research, Journal of Marketing Research 14 (February 1977), 52–59.

Green, P.E. and V. Srinivasan: Conjoint Analysis in Consumer Research: Issues and Outlook, Journal of Consumer Research 5 (September 1978), 103–123.

Green, P.E. and D.S. Tull: Research for Marketing Decisions, 4th ed., Englewood Cliffs: Prentice Hall 1978.

Griliches, Z.: Hybrid Corn – An Exploration in the Economics of Technical Change, Econometrica 25 (October 1957), 501–509.

Griliches, Z.: Distributed Lags: A Survey, Econometrica 35 (January 1967), 16–49.

Gröne, A.: Marktsegmentierung im Investitionsgütermarketing, Dissertation, Universität Münster 1976.

Gross, I.: Insights from Pricing Research, in: Bailey, E.A. (ed.): Pricing Practices and Strategies, New York: The Conference Board 1978.

Grover, R. and V. Srinivasan: A Simultaneous Approach to Market Segmentation and Market Structuring, Journal of Marketing Research 24 (May 1987), 139–153.

Guadagni, P.M.: Market Response Measurement Using the Multinomial, Multiattribute Logit Choice Model, Master's Thesis, Sloan School of Management, Massachusetts Institute of Technology 1980.

Guadagni, P.M. and J.D.C. Little: A Logit Model of Brand Choice Calibrated on Scanner Data, Marketing Science 2 (Summer 1983), 203–238.

Gümbel, R.: Die Sortimentspolitik in den Betrieben des Wareneinzelhandels, Köln und Opladen: Westdeutscher Verlag 1963.

Guiltinan, J.P.: Risk-Aversive Pricing Policies: Problems and Alternatives, Journal of Marketing 40 (January 1976), 10–15.

Guiltinan, J.P.: The Price Bundling of Services: A Normative Framework, Journal of Marketing 51 (April 1987), 74–85.

Gutenberg, E.: Anmerkungen zur Frage der Gestaltung industrieller Produktionsprogramme, Zeitschrift für Betriebswirtschaft 34 (1964), 667–675.

Gutenberg, E.: Zur Diskussion der polypolistischen Absatzkurve, Jahrbücher für Nationalökonomie und Statistik 177 (1965), 289–303.

Gutenberg, E.: Grundlagen der Betriebswirtschaftslehre, Band II, Der Absatz, 9th ed., Berlin-Heidelberg-New York: Springer 1966.

Gutenberg, E.: Grundlagen der Betriebswirtschaftslehre, Band I: Die Produktion, 21st ed., Berlin-Heidelberg-New York: Springer 1975.

Gutenberg, E.: Grundlagen der Betriebswirtschaftslehre, Band II, Der Absatz, 15th ed., Berlin-Heidelberg-New York: Springer 1976.

Haberstock, L.: Kostenrechnung II, Wiesbaden: Gabler 1977.

Hahn, D.: Planungs- und Kontrollrechnung, Integrierte und liquiditätsorientierte Planungs- und Kontrollrechnung als Führungsinstrument, Wiesbaden: Gabler 1974.

Haley, R.I.: Sales Effects of Media Weight, Journal of Advertising Research 18 (June 1978), 9–18.

Hall, G. and S. Howell: The Experience Curve from the Economist's Perspective, Strategic Management Journal 3 (1985), 197–212.

Hammann, P.: Entscheidungsanalyse im Marketing, Berlin: Duncker & Humblot 1975.

Hammann, P. and B. Erichson: Ansätze zu einer adaptiven Preispolitik, in: Köhler, R. and H.J. Zimmermann (eds.): Entscheidungshilfen im Marketing, Stuttgart: Poeschel 1977.

Hammann, P. and B. Erichson: Marktforschung, Stuttgart: Fischer 1978.

Hansen, P.: Die handelsgerichtete Absatzpolitik der Hersteller im Wettbewerb um den Regalplatz, Berlin: Duncker & Humblot 1972.

Hauser, J.R.: Pricing Theory and the Role of Marketing Science, Journal of Business 57 (January 1984), 65–71.

Hauser, J.R. and S.M. Shugan: Defensive Marketing Strategies, Marketing Science 2 (Fall 1983), 319–360.

Hauser, J.R. and S.P. Gaskin: Application of the "Defender" Consumer Model, Marketing Science 3 (Fall 1984), 327–351.

Hax, H.: Vertikale Preisbindung in der Markenartikelindustrie, Köln und Opladen: Westdeutscher Verlag 1961, (1961a).

Hax, H.: Preisuntergrenzen im Ein- und Mehrproduktbetrieb. Ein Anwendungsfall der linearen Planungsrechnung, Zeitschrift für betriebswirtschaftliche Forschung 13 (1961), 424–449 (1961b).

Hax, H.: Investitionstheorie, 2nd ed., Würzburg-Wien: Physica 1972.

Hax, H.: Preisuntergrenzen bei Ungewissheit über den Auftragseingang, in: Koch, H. (ed.): Zur Theorie des Absatzes, Wiesbaden: Gabler 1973.

Hayes, R.H. and W.J. Abernathy: Managing Our Way to Economic Decline, Harvard Business Review 58 (July–August 1980), 67–77.

Heertje, A.: On the Theory of Oligopoly, Economica Internazionale XIII (1960), 449.

Heertje, A.: Preis-Absatzfunktion beim Oligopol, Weltwirtschaftliches Archiv 89 (1962), 302–309.

Hefermehl, W.: Einführung zu Wettbewerbsrecht und Kartellrecht, in: Wettbewerbsrecht und Kartellrecht, München: Beck 1980.

Heidrich, H.: Konsumentenwissen und Wettbewerb, Freiburg: Haufe 1981.

Heine, Ch.: Die physische Veralterung von Gütern, Wesen, Ursachen und absatzwirtschaftliche Konsequenzen, Nürnberg: Spindler 1968.

Helson, H.: Adaptation-Level Theory, New York-Evanston: Harper & Row 1964.

Henderson, B.D.: Perspectives on Experience, Boston: Boston Consulting Group 1968.

Henderson, B.D.: Die Erfahrungskurve in der Unternehmensstrategie, Frankfurt: Herder & Herder 1974.

Henderson, B.D.: Henderson on Corporate Strategy, Cambridge (Mass.): Abt Books 1979.

Henderson, B.D.: The Application and Misapplication of the Experience Curve, Journal of Business Strategy 4 (Winter 1984), 3–9.

Hess, S.W.: The Use of Models in Marketing Timing Decisions, Operations Research 15 (July–August 1967), 720–737.

Hewitt, Ch.E.: Pricing – An Area of Increasing Importance, in: Mulvihill-Paranka (1967).

Hilke, W.: Der Preis als Marketinginstrument, in: Jacob, H. (ed.): Schriften zur Unternehmensführung, Band 16, Wiesbaden: Gabler.

Hilke, W.: Statische und dynamische Oligopolmodelle, Wiesbaden: Gabler 1973.

Hilke, W.: Dynamische Preispolitik, Wiesbaden: Gabler 1978.

Hilse, H.: Die Messung des Werbeerfolgs, Tübingen: Mohr-Siebeck 1970.

Hinkle, Ch.: The Strategy of Price Deals, Harvard Business Review 43 (July–August 1965), 75–85.

Hirsch, W.Z.: Firm Progress Ratios, Econometrica 24 (April 1956), 136–143.

Hirschmann, W.B.: Profit from the Learning Curve, Harvard Business Review 42 (January–February 1964), 125–139.

Hirschleifer, J.: Price Theory and Applications, London 1980.

Hodock, L.W.: Scanner Data Will Professionalize Promotion Research, Marketing News, (January 9, 1981), 1.

Holdren, B.R.: The Structure of a Retail Market and the Behavior of Retail Units, Englewood Cliffs: Prentice Hall 1960.

Holton, R.H.: Price Discrimination at Retail: The Supermarket Case, Journal of Industrial Economics 6 (October 1957), 13–32.

Hoffmann, K.: Der Produktlebenszyklus – eine kritische Analyse, Freiburg: Herder 1972.

Hotelling, H.: Stability in Competition, Economic Journal 41 (March 1929), 41.

Houston, F.S. and D.L. Weiss: An Analysis of Competitive Market Behavior, Journal of Marketing Research 11 (May 1974), 151–155.

Howard, J.A. and J.N. Sheth: The Theory of Buyer Behavior, New York: Wiley 1969.

Humbel, P.: Preispolitische Gewinndifferenzierung im Einzelhandel, Zürich: Schultess 1958.

Huppert, E.: Das Marktexperiment als Entscheidungshilfe, Der Marktforscher 6 (1974), 3–17.

Huppert, E.: Neue Produkte vor Einführung erst testen, aber wie?, Nielsen Beobachter (1977), 3–15.

Huppert, E.: Produkt-Lebenszyklus: eine Entscheidungshilfe, Marketing Journal (May 1978), 416–423.

Hutton, B.R. and W.W. Wilkie: Life Cycle Cost: A New Form of Consumer Information, Journal of Consumer Research 6 (March 1980), 349–360.

International Business Machines Corp. vs. United States, 298 V.S. 131 (Sup.Cr. 1936).

Irons, K.W., J.D.C. Little and R.L. Klein: Determinants of Coupon Effectiveness, in: Zufryden, F. (ed.): Proceedings of the Marketing Science Conference, University of Southern California 1983, 157–164.

Isermann, H.: Strukturierung von Entscheidungsprozessen bei mehrfacher Zielsetzung, OR-Spektrum 1 (Juli 1979), 3–26.

Jackson, B.B.: Manage Risk in Industrial Pricing, Harvard Business Review 58 (July–August 1980), 121–134.

Jacob, H.: Preispolitik, 2nd ed., Wiesbaden: Gabler 1971.

Jacob, H.: Preispolitik bei der Einführung neuer Erzeugnisse unter besonderer Beachtung dynamischer Aspekte, in: Koch, H. (ed.): Zur Theorie des Absatzes, Wiesbaden: Gabler 1973.

Jacob, H:: Preisbildung und Preiswettbewerb in der Industriewirtschaft, Köln: Carl Heymanns 1985.

Jacoby, J. and R.W. Chestnut: Brand Loyalty, Measurement and Management, New York: Wiley 1978.

Jacoby, J., J.C. Olsen and R.A. Haddock: Price, Brand, Name and Product Composition Characteristics as Determinants of Perceived Quality, Journal of Applied Psychology 55 (December 1971), 470–479.

Jain, A.K., F. Acito, N.K. Malhotra and V. Mahajan: A Comparison of the Internal Validity of Alternative Parameter Estimation Methods in Decompositional Multiattribute Preference Models, Journal of Marketing Research 16 (August 1979), 313–322.

James, B.: A Contemporary Approach to New Product Pricing, in: Taylor-Wills (eds.), Pricing Strategy, Princeton: Brandon 1969.

Jeuland, A.P: Brand Preference over Time: A Partially Deterministic Operationalization of the Notion of Variety Seeking, Educators' Proceedings, Chicago: American Marketing Association 1978.

Jeuland, A.P: Pricing over the Brand Life Cycle, Paper presented at the ORSA/TIMS-Meeting, Milwaukee, October 1979.

Jeuland, A.P.: Parsimonious Models of Diffusion of Innovation, Part A: Derivations and Comparisons, Working Paper, University of Chicago, Graduate School of Business 1981 (1981a).

Jeuland, A.P.: Parsimonious Models of Diffusion of Innovation, Part B: Incorporating the Variable of Price, Working Paper, University of Chicago, Graduate School of Business 1981 (1981b).

Jeuland, A.P and R.J. Dolan: An Aspect of New Product Planning: Dynamic Pricing, Working Paper, Graduate School of Business, University of Chicago, September 1980.

Jeuland, A.P. and R.J. Dolan: An Aspect of New Product Planning: Dynamic Pricing, TIMS Studies in the Management Sciences, Special Issue on Marketing Planning Models, A. Zoltners (ed.) 1982.

Johnson, G.: The Pricing of Consumer Goods, in: Taylor-Wills (eds.): Pricing Strategy, Princeton: Brandon 1969.

Johnson, R.M.: Trade-Off Analysis of Consumer Values, Journal of Marketing Research 11 (May 1974), 121–127.

Jones, J.M.: Will Individual Choice Models Replace Macro-Models?, Paper presented at the International Marketing Science Workshop, Cergy 27.6.1980.

Jones, J.M. and F.S. Zufryden: Implementing a Decision Relevant Multivariate Model of Consumer Purchase Behavior, Discussion Paper, University of Southern California, March 1979.

Jones, J.M. and F.S. Zufryden: An Approach for Assessing Demographic and Price Influences on Brand Purchase Behavior, Journal of Marketing 46 (Winter 1982), 36–46.

Kaas, K.P.: Diffusion und Marketing, Stuttgart: Poeschel 1973.

Kaas, K.P.: Empirische Preisabsatzfunktionen bei Konsumgütern, Berlin-Heidelberg-New York: Springer 1977.

Kaas, K.P.: Preiseinfluss und Markenwahl, in: Meffert, H., H. Steffenhagen and H. Freter (eds.): Konsumentenverhalten und Information, Wiesbaden: Gabler 1979.

Kaas, K.P.: Preisschwellen bei Konsumgütern (-gibt's die?-), Vortragsmanuskript Marketing-Workshop, Schotten 10.5.1980.

Kaas, K.P. and Ch. Hay: Preisschwellen bei Konsumgütern – eine theoretische und empirische Analyse, Zeitschrift für betriebswirtschaftliche Forschung 36 (Mai 1984), 333–346.

Kalish, S.: Models of the Diffusion of Innovations and Their Implications for Government Policies, Master Thesis, MIT (June 1980).

Kalish, S.: Monopolist Pricing with Dynamic Demand and Production Cost, Marketing Science 2 (Spring 1983), 135–160.

Kalish, S.: A New Product Adoption Model with Price, Advertising, and Uncertainty, Management Science 31 (December 1985), 1569–1585.

Kalish, S.: Pricing New Products from Birth to Decline: An Expository Review, in: Devinney, T.M. (ed.), Issues in Pricing – Theory and Research, Lexington (Mass): Lexington Books 1988.

Kamen, J.M. and R.J. Toman: Psychophysics of Prices, Journal of Marketing Research 7 (February 1970), 27–31.

Kamen, J.M. and R.J. Toman: Psychophysics of Prices: A Reaffirmation, Journal of Marketing Research 8 (May 1971), 252–257.

Kamien, M.J. and N.L. Schwartz: Limit Pricing and Uncertain Entry, Econometrica 39 (May 1971), 441–454.

Katona, G.: The Role of Price Expectations, in: Taylor-Wills (eds.), Pricing Strategy, Princeton: Brandon 1969.

Kaufer, E.: Industrieökonomik, München: Vahlen 1980.

Kempken, J.: Optimale Preisstrategien bei Ausschreibungen, Düsseldorf: Mannhold 1980.

Kilger, W.: Die quantitative Ableitung polypolistischer Preisabsatzfunktionen aus den Heterogenitätsbedingungen atomistischer Märkte, in: Koch, H. (ed.), Zur Theorie der Unternehmung, Wiesbaden: Gabler 1962.

Kilger, W.: Flexible Grenzplankostenrechnung und Deckungsbeitragsrechnung, 8th ed., Wiesbaden: Gabler 1981.

Kinberg, Y., A. Rao and M.F. Shakun: A Mathematical Model for Price Promotions, Management Science 20 (February 1974), 948–959.

Kistner, K.P.: Produktions- und Kostentheorie, Würzburg-Wien: Physica 1980.

Klein, R.L.: Scanner Data Can Measure Long-Run Promotion Response, Marketing News (January 11, 1980), 3.

Kluyver, C.A. de: Innovation and Industrial Life Cycles, California Management Review 20 (Fall 1977), 21–33.

Knödel, W.: Artikel-Nummern-Systeme, Wirtschaftswissenschaftliches Studium 8 (Juni 1979), 283–285.

Koch, H. (ed.): Zur Theorie des Absatzes, Festschrift zum 75. Geburtstag von Prof. Dr. Dr. h.c. mult. Erich Gutenberg, Wiesbaden: Gabler 1973.

Köhler, R.: Das Problem "richtiger" preispolitischer Entscheidungen bei unvollkommener Voraussicht, Zeitschrift für betriebswirtschaftliche Forschung 20 (April 1968), 249–274.

Köhler, R.: Das Informationsverhalten im Entscheidungsprozess vor der Markteinführung eines neuen Artikels, Wiesbaden: Gabler 1973.

Koll, W.: Inflation und Rentabilität, Wiesbaden: Gabler 1979.

Kotler, P.: Competitive Strategies for New Product Marketing over the Life Cycle, Management Science 12 (December 1965), 104–119.

Kotler, P.: Marketing Decision Making: A Model Building Approach, New York-Chicago: Holt, Rinehart & Winston 1971.

Kotler, P.: Marketing Management: Analysis, Planning and Control, 4th edition, Englewood Cliffs (N.J.): Prentice Hall 1980

Kotler, P.: Marketing Management: Analysis, Planning and Control, 6th. ed., Englewood Cliffs, (N.J.): Prentice Hall 1988.

Kraushar, P.M.: New Products and Diversification, London: Business Books 1970.

Krautter, J.: Zum Problem der optimalen Marktsegmentierung, Zeitschrift für Betriebswirtschaft 45 (Februar 1975), 109–128.

Krelle, W.: Produktionstheorie, Tübingen: Mohr-Siebeck 1969.

Krelle, W.: Preistheorie, 2nd ed., Tübingen: Mohr-Siebeck 1976.

Kretschmer, H.J. and A. Kretschmer: Perspektiven inflationsbedingter Preispolitik, Der Betrieb 27 (1974), 1585–1590.

Kroeber-Riel, W.: Absatzpreisänderung und Unternehmenserhaltung, Zeitschrift für betriebswirtschaftliche Forschung 22 (1970), 359–371.

Kroeber-Riel, W.: Konsumentenverhalten, 3rd ed., München: Vahlen 1984.

Kucher, E.: Scannerdaten und Preissensitivität bei Konsumgütern, Wiesbaden: Gabler-Verlag 1985.

Kucher, E.: Absatzdynamik nach Preisänderung, Marketing – Zeitschrift für Forschung und Praxis 9 (August 1977) 177–186.

Lal, R.: Delegating Pricing Responsibility to the Salesforce, Marketing Science 5 (Spring 1986), 159–168.

Lambert, Z.V.: Price and Choice Behavior, Journal of Marketing Research 9 (February 1972), 35–40.

Lambin, J.J.: Measuring The Profitability of Advertising: An Empirical Study, Journal of Industrial Economics 17 (April 1969), 86–103.

Lambin, J.J.: Modèles et Programmes de Marketing, Paris: Presses Universitaires de France 1970.

Lambin, J.J.: A Computer On-Line Marketing Mix Model, Journal of Marketing Research 9 (May 1972), 119–126.

Lambin, J.J.: Advertising, Competition and Market Conduct in Oligopoly Over Time, Amsterdam: North-Holland Publ. Co. 1976.

Lambin, J.J. and A. Peeters: La gestion marketing des entreprises, Paris: Presses Universitaires de France 1977.

Lambin, J.J., Ph.A. Naert and A. Bultez: Optimal Marketing Behavior in Oligopoly, European Economic Review 6 (1975), 105–128.

Landau, H.: Pricing in a Dynamic Model with Saturation, Econometrica 44 (November 1976), 1153–1155.

Lange, M.: Preisbildung bei neuen Produkten, Berlin: Duncker & Humblot 1972.

Langen, H.: Dynamische Preisuntergrenzen, Zeitschrift für betriebswirtschaftliche Forschung 18 (1966), 649–659.

Lanzilotti, R.: Pricing Objectives in Large Companies, American Economic Review 48 (December 1958), 921–940.

Larréché, J.C. and D.B. Montgomery: A Framework for the Comparison of Marketing Models: A Delphi Study, Journal of Marketing Research 14 (November 1977), 487–498.

Lattin, J.M. and R.E. Bucklin: The Dynamics of Consumer Response to Price Discounts, Working Paper, Graduate School of Business, Stanford University 1987.

Laufner, W.: Preisstarrheit und Preisbewegungen im unvollkommenen Duopol, Dissertation, Universität Bonn 1979.

Launhardt, W.: Mathematische Begründung der Volkswirtschaftslehre, Aalen: Scientia 1885.

Leavitt, H.J.: A Note on Some Experimental Findings About the Meaning of Price, Journal of Business 27 (July 1954), 205–210.

Leeflang, P.S.H. and J.C. Reuyl: On the Predictive Power of Market Share Attraction Models, Journal of Marketing Research 21 (May 1984), 211–215.

Leitherer, E.: Absatzlehre, Stuttgart: Poeschel 1969.

Lekvall, P. and C. Wahlbin: A Study of Some Assumptions Underlying Innovation Diffusion Functions, Swedish Journal of Economics 75 (1973), 362–377.

Lenzen, W.: Preisgünstigkeit als hypothetisches Konstrukt – Ergebnisse einer empirischen Untersuchung, Zeitschrift für betriebswirtschaftliche Forschung 35 (November–Dezember 1983), 952–962.

Lenzen, W.: Die Verarbeitung von Preisen durch Konsumenten, Frankfurt: Deutsch 1984.

Levinson: Guerilla-Marketing, Boston: Houghton & Mifflin 1984.

Levitt, T.: Exploit the Product Life Cycle, Harvard Business Review 43 (November–December 1965), 81–94.

Levitt, T.: Putting the Product Life Cycle to Work, Management Review 55 (1966), 19–25.

Lieberman, M.B.: The Learning Curve, Diffusion, and Competitive Strategy, Strategic Management Journal 8 (1987), 441–452.

Lilien, G.L. and P. Kottler: Marketing Decision Making: A Model Building Approach, New York: Harper & Row 1983.

Little, J.D.C.: A Model of Adaptive Control of Promotional Spending, Operations Research 14 (November 1966), 1075–1097.

Little, J.D.C.: Models and Managers: The Concept of a Decision Calculus, Management Science 16 (April 1970), B. 466–485.

Little, J.D.C.: Entscheidungsunterstützung für Marketingmanager, Zeitschrift für Betriebswirtschaft 49 (November 1979), 982–1007.

Lynn, R.A.: Price Policies and Marketing Management, Homewood: Irwin 1967.

Mahajan, V. and E. Muller: Innovation Diffusion and New Product Growth Models in Marketing, Journal of Marketing 43 (Fall 1979), 55–68.

Mahajan, V. and R.A. Peterson: Innovation Diffusion in a Dynamic Potential Adopter Population, Management Science 24 (November 1978), 1589–1598.

Majer, W.: Lebenszyklusanalysen als Grundlage unternehmenspolitischer Entscheidungen, Absatzwirtschaft 10 (Oktober 1967), 1147.

Malhotra, N.K.: The Use of Linear Logit Models in Marketing Research, Journal of Marketing Research 21 (February 1984), 20–31.

Mallen, B.: Introducing the Marketing Channel to Price Theory, Journal of Marketing 28 (July 1964), 29–33.

Mansfield, E.: Technical Change and the Rate of Imitation, Econometrica 29 (October 1971).

Marting, E. (ed.): Creative Pricing, New York: American Management Association 1968.

Massaro, D.W.: Experimental Psychology and Information Processing, Chicago: Rand McNally 1975.

Massy, W.F. and R.E. Frank: Short Term Price and Dealing Effects in Selected Market Segments, Journal of Marketing Research 2 (May 1965), 171–185.

May, Ch.K.: Planning the Marketing Program Throughout the Product Life Cycle, Ph.D. Dissertation, Columbia University 1961.

McClelland, W.G.: Costs and Competition in Retailing, London: Macmillan 1966.

McConnell, J.D.: Effect of Pricing on Perception of Product Quality, Journal of Applied Psychology 52 (1968), 331–334.

McCurry, D.R.: Marketing-Informationen aus Scannerkassen, Nielsen-Beobachter 2 (1980).

McFadden, D.: Conditional Logit Analysis of Qualitative Choice Behavior, in: P. Zarembka (ed.), Frontiers in Econometrics, New York: Academic Press 1973.

Meffert, H.: Interpretation und Aussagekraft des Produktlebenszyklus-Konzeptes, Arbeitspapier Nr. 5, Institut für Marketing, Universität Münster 1974.

Meffert, H. (und Mitarbeiter): Marketing-Entscheidungen bei der Einführung des VW-Golf, Fallstudie, Institut für Marketing, Universität Münster 1977.

Meffert, H.: Die Einführung des Kundengruppenmanagements als Problem des geplanten organisatorischen Wandels, Arbeitspapier Nr. 16, Institut für Marketing, Universität Münster 1979.

Meffert, H. and H. Steffenhagen: Konflikte zwischen Industrie und Handel, Wiesbaden: Gabler 1976.

Meffert, H. and Bruhn M.: Marktstrategien im Wettbewerb, Wiesbaden: Gabler 1984.

Mertens, P. and G. Rackelmann: Konzept eines Frühwarnsystems auf der Basis von Produktlebenszyklen, Zeitschrift für Betriebswirtschaft 49 (Ergänzungsheft 2, 1979), 70–88.

Mesak, H.I. and R.C. Clelland: A Competitive Pricing Model, Management Science 25 (November 1979), 1057–1068.

Michael, G.C.: Product Petrification: A New Stage in the Life Cycle Theory, California Management Review 14 (Fall 1971), 88.

Mickwitz, G.: Marketing and Competition, Helsingfors (Finland): Centraltryckeriet 1959.

Missner, P.: Marketing-Mix: Theorie und empirische Ergebnisse, Diplomarbeit, Universität Bielefeld 1981.

Mittelbach, R.: Auswirkungen der steuerlichen Belastung des Ertrages auf die Preiskalkulation, Betriebs-Berater (1974), 781–784.

Mock, A.: Die zukünftige Rolle der deutschen Industrie in der Weltwirtschaft, Zeitschrift für Betriebswirtschaft 49 (Februar 1979), 118–125.

Möller, H.: Kalkulation, Absatzpolitik und Preisbildung, Tübingen: Mohr-Siebeck 1962.

Monroe, K.B.: Psychophysics of Prices: A Reappraisal, Journal of Marketing Research 8 (May 1971), 248–251, (1971a).

Monroe, K.B.: Measuring Price Thresholds by Psychophysics and Latitudes of Acceptance, Journal of Marketing Research 8 (November 1971), 460–461, (1971b).

Monroe, K.B.: The Information Content of Prices: A Preliminary Model for Estimating Buyer Response, Management Science 17 (1971), 519–532, (1971c).

Monroe, K.B.: Pricing, Englewood Cliffs: Prentice Hall 1979.

Monroe, K.B. and M. Venkatesan: The Concept of Price Limits and Psychophysical Measurement: A Laboratory Experiment, in: Proceedings Fall Conference, American Marketing Association, Chicago 1969.

Monroe, K.B. and A.J.D. Bitta: Models for Pricing Decisions, Journal of Marketing Research 15 (August 1978), 413–428.

Monroe, K.B. and T. Mazumdar: Pricing Decision Models: Recent Developments and Research Opportunities, in Devinney, T.M. (ed.), Issues in Pricing – Theory and Research, Lexington (Mass.): Lexington Books 1988.

Montgomery, D.B.: Conjoint Calibrations of the Customer/Competitor Interface in Industrial Markets, in: Backhaus, K. and D.T. Wilson (eds.): Industrial Marketing, Berlin: Springer Verlag 1986.

Moore, W.L.: Levels of Aggregations in Conjoint Analysis: An Empirical Comparison, Journal of Marketing Research 17 (November 1980), 516–523.

Moorthy, K.S.: Consumer Expectations and the Pricing of Durables, in: Devinney, T.M. (ed.), Issues in Pricing – Theory and Research, Lexington Books 1988.

Moran, W.T.: Insights from Pricing Research, in: Bailey, E.L. (ed.): Pricing Practices and Strategies, New York: The Conference Board 1978.

Morgenroth, W.M.: A Method for Understanding Price Determinants, Journal of Marketing Research 4 (August 1967), 17–26.

Morgenroth, W.M. and T.J. Sims: Simulation: Methods and Applications, in: Ferber, R. (ed.), Handbook of Marketing Research, New York: McGraw Hill 1974.

Moriarty, M.: Cross Sectional, Time Series Issues in the Analysis of Marketing Decision Variables, Journal of Marketing Research 12 (May 1975), 142–150.

Moskal, B.S.: Pricing: New Forces Prompt New Philosophies, Industry Week, (December 11, 1978), 48–56.

Müller, S. and J. Hoenig: Die Preisbeachtung in einer realen Kaufsituation, Jahrbuch der Absatz- und Verbrauchsforschung 29, Heft 4 (1983), 321–343.

Müller-Hagedorn, L.: Zeige mir Deine Preise, Lebensmittel-Zeitung (October 28, 1983), 38.

Mulvihill, D.F. and St. Paranka (eds.): Price Policies and Practices, New York: Wiley & Sons, Inc. 1967.

Murphy, M.E.: Price Discrimination, Market Separation, and the Multi-Part Tariff, Economic Inquiry 15 (October 1977), 587–599.

Myers, J.G., St.A. Greyser and W.F. Massy: The Effectiveness of Marketing's "R&D" for Marketing Management: An Assessment, Journal of Marketing 43 (January 1979), 17–27.

Naert, Ph.A.: Should Marketing Models Be Robust?, Working Paper 74–43. European Institute for Advanced Studies in Management, Brussels 1974.

Naert, Ph.A. and A. Bultez: Logically Consistent Market Share Models, Journal of Marketing Research 10 (November 1973), 334–340.

Naert, Ph.A. and P.S.H. Leeflang: Building Implementable Marketing Models, Leiden-Boston: Nijhoff 1978.

Nagle, Th.: Economic Foundations for Pricing, Journal of Business 57 (January 1984), 3–26.

Nagle. Th.: The Strategy and Tactics of Pricing, Englewood Cliffs (N.J.): Prentice-Hall 1987.

Nagtetaal, H.: Der Verkaufspreis in der Industrie, Wiesbaden: Gabler 1974.

Narasimhan, Ch.: A Price Discrimination Theory of Coupons, Marketing Science 3 (Spring 1984), 128–147.

Nash, J.F.: Two-Person Cooperative Games, Econometrica 21 (1953), 124–140.

Nason, R.W. and A.J.D. Bitta: The Incidence and Consumer Perceptions of Quantity Surcharges, Journal of Retailing 59 (Summer 1983), 40.

Nakanishi, M.: Measurement of Sales Promotion Effect at the Retail Level – An New Approach, Proceedings, Spring and Fall Conferences, American Marketing Association, Chicago 1972.

Neale, R.: The Sales Effects of Newspaper Supermarket Advertising, Working Paper, Newspaper Advertising Bureau, New York 1980.

Neslin, S.A.: A Market Response Model for Coupon Promotions, Working Paper, Amos Tuck School of Business Administration, Dartmouth College, December 1985.

Nevin, J.R.: Laboratory Experiments for Estimating Consumer Demand: A Validation Study, Journal of Marketing Research 11 (August 1974), 261–268.

Newport, J.P.: Frequent-Flier Clones, Fortune, (April 29, 1985), 113.

Nicholls, W.H.: Price Leadership: The Case of the Cigarette Industry, in: Samuelson, P.A. (ed.): Readings in Economics, 6th. ed., New York: McGraw Hill 1970.

Niehans, J.: Preistheoretischer Leitfaden für Verkehrswissenschaftler, Schweizerisches Archiv für Verkehrswissenschaft und Verkehrspolitk 11 (1956), 293–320.

Niehans, H.: Monopolpreis, vertikale Integration und Mengenrabatt, Schweizerische Zeitschrift für Volkswirtschaft und Statistik 95 (1959), 328–335.

Nielsen, A.C.Co. (ed.): How to Strenghten Your Product Plan, London 1966.

Nielsen Clearing House Report: Coupon Distribution and Redemption Patterns by Product Group, Number 2, Chicago: A.C. Nielsen Company 1984.

Nimer, D.: Nimer on Pricing, Industrial Marketing (March 1971), 48–55.

Novich, N.St.: Price and Promotion Analysis Using Scanner Data: An Example, Master's Thesis, Sloan School of Management, Massachusetts Institute of Technology 1981.

Nwokoye, N.G.: Subjective Judgements of Price: The Effects of Price Parameters on Adaptation Levels, Combined Proceedings, American Marketing Association 1975.

Nyström, H.: Retail Pricing – An Integrated Economic and Psychological Approach, Stockholm: Economic Research Institute at the Stockholm School of Economics 1970.

Oberender, P. (ed.): Marktstruktur und Wettbewerb in der Bundesrepublik Deutschland, München: Vahlen 1984.

Ohmae, K.I.: The Mind of the Strategist, New York: McGraw Hill 1982.

Opitz, O. and K. Spremann: Optimale Steuerung von Kaufverhaltensprozessen, in: Topritzhofer, E. (ed.): Marketing, Neue Ergebnisse aus Forschung und Praxis, Wiesbaden: Gabler 1978.

Oren, S.S., S.A. Smith and R.B. Wilson: Linear Tariffs with Quality Discrimination, Bell Journal of Economics 13 (Autumn 1982).

Ott, A.E.: Ein statisches Modell der Preisbildung im Einzelhandel, Jahrbücher für Nationalökonomie und Statistik 172 (1958), 1–31.

Ott, A.E.: Gewinnmaximierung, Reaktionshypothese und Gleichgewichtsgebiet beim unvollkommenen Duopol, Jahrbuch für Nationalökonomie und Statistik 175 (1963), 428–440.

Ott, A.E. (ed.): Preistheorie, Köln: Kiepenheuer & Witsch 1965.

Ott, A.E.: Vertikale Preisbildung und Preisbindung, Göttingen: Vandenhoeck & Ruprecht 1966.

Ott, A.E.: Grundzüge der Preistheorie, Grundriss der Sozialwissenschaft, Band 25, Göttingen: Vandenhoeck & Ruprecht 1968.

Ott, A.E.: Grundzüge der Preistheorie, 3rd ed., Göttingen: Vandenhoeck & Ruprecht 1979.

O.V.: How Much Do Customers Know About Retail Prices?, Progressive Grocer 43 (February 1964), 104–106.

O.V.: Tastsinn, Capital (October 1980), 194.

O.V.: Scanning as a Productivity Booster – The Most Important Research Tool Ever, Progressive Grocer 46 (December 1977), 60–61.

Oxenfeldt, A.R.: Multi-Stage Approach to Pricing, Harvard Business Review 38 (July–August 1960), 124–133.

Oxenfeldt, A.R.: Pricing for Marketing Executives, San Francisco: Wodsworth Publ. Co. 1961.

Oxenfeldt, A.R.: Product Line Pricing, Harvard Business Review 44 (July–August 1966), 137–145.

Oxenfeldt, A.R.: An Analysis of Present Product Pricing, in: Mulvihill-Paranka (1967).

Oxenfeldt, A.R.: How Housewives Form Price Impressions, Journal of Advertising Research 8 (September 1968), 9–17.

Oxenfeldt, A.R.: A Decision Making Structure for Price Decisions, Journal of Marketing 37 (January 1973), 48–49.

Oxenfeldt, A.R.: Developing a Favorable Quality-Price Image, Journal of Retailing (Winter 1974–75).

Oxenfeldt, A.R.: Pricing Strategies, New York: Amacom 1975.

Pack, L.: Zum Problem statischer und dynamischer Preisuntergrenzen, in: Koch, H. (ed.), Zur Theorie des Absatzes, Wiesbaden: Gabler 1973.

Palda, K.S.: Pricing Decisions and Marketing Policy, Englewood Cliffs (N.J.): Prentice Hall 1971.

Parfitt, J.H. and B.J.K. Collins: Use of Consumer Panels for Brand Share Prediction, Journal of Marketing Research 5 (May 1968), 131–145.

Parsons, L.J. and R.L. Schultz: Marketing Models and Econometric Research, New York-Amsterdam: American Elsevier, North-Holland 1976.

Patton, A.: Stretch Your Product's Earning Years – Top Management's Stake in the Product Life Cycle, Management Review (June 1959), 9–14.

Peckham, J.O.: The Wheel of Marketing, Nielsen Co., 1973.

Peles, Y.: Economies of Scale in Advertising Beer and Cigarettes, Journal of Business 44 (January 1971), 32–37.

Pessemier, E.A.: A New Way to Determine Buying Decisions, Journal of Marketing 24 (October 1959), 41–46.

Pessemier, E.A.: An Experimental Method for Estimating Demand, Journal of Business 33 (October 1960), 373–383.

Pessemier, E.A.: Experimental Methods of Analyzing Demand for Branded Consumer Goods with Applications to Problems in Marketing Strategy, Washington: Washington State University Press, Pullmann 1963.

Pessemier, E.A.: New Product Decisions – An Analytical Approach, New York: McGraw Hill 1966.

Peterson, R.A.: The Price-Perceived Quality Relationship: Experimental Evidence, Journal of Marketing Research 7 (November 1970), 525–528.

Phlips, L.: The Economics of Price Discrimination, Cambridge: Cambridge University Press 1983.

Picconi, M.J. and Ch.L. Olson: Advertising Decision Rules in a Multi-Brand Environment: Optimal Control Theory and Evidence, Journal of Marketing Research 15 (February 1978), 82–92.

Plenge, F.-W.: Analysepotential von Scanner-Haushaltspanel-Daten – Eine empirische Studie, Unpublished Master's Thesis, Universität Bielefeld 1984.

Polli, R. and V. Cook: Validity of the Product Life Cycle, Journal of Business 42 (October 1969), 385–400.

Porter, M.: Competitive Strategy, New York: The Free Press 1980.

Porter, M.: Competitive Advantage, New York: The Free Press 1985.

Prasad, K. and W.L. Ring: Measuring Sales Effects of Some Marketing Mix Variables and their Interactions, Journal of Marketing Research 13 (November 1976), 391–396.

Preston, L.E.: Profits, Competition and Rules of Thumb in Retail Food Pricing, Berkeley: University of California 1963.

Preston, L.E. and E.C. Keachie: Cost Functions and Progress Functions: An Integration, American Economic Review 54 (March 1964), 100–106.

Rao, V.R.: The Salience of Price in the Perception and Evaluation of Product Quality: A Multidimensional Measurement Model and Experimental Test, Unpublished Dissertation, University of Pennsylvania 1970.

Rao, V.R.: Pricing Research in Marketing: The State of the Art, Journal of Business 57 (January 1984), 39–60.

Rao, R. and F.M. Bass: Competition, Strategy, and Price Dynamics: A Theoretical and Empirical Investigation, Journal of Marketing Research 22 (August 1985).

Rehder, H.K.: Mehrdimensionale Produktmarktstrukturierung, Meisenheim am Glan: Hain 1975.

Reichmann, T.: Kosten und Preisgrenzen. Die Bestimmung von Preisuntergrenzen und Preisobergrenzen im Industriebetrieb, Wiesbaden: Gabler 1973.

Richter, R.: Preistheorie, Wiesbaden: Gabler 1963.

Riebel, P.: Die Preiskalkulation auf der Grundlage von Selbstkosten oder von relativen Einzelkosten und Deckungsbeiträgen, Zeitschrift für betriebswirtschaftliche Forschung 16 (1964), 549–612.

Riebel, P.: Deckungsbeitragsrechnung, in: Kosiol, E. (ed.), Handwörterbuch des Rechnungswesens, Stuttgart: Poeschel 1970.

Riebel, P.: Kosten und Preise bei verbundener Produktion, Substitutionskonkurrenz und verbundener Nachfrage, Opladen: Westdeutscher Verlag 1971.

Riesz, P.C.: A Major Price-Perceived Quality Study Reexamined, Journal of Marketing Research 17 (May 1980), 259–262.

Rink, D.R. and J.E. Swan: Product Life Cycle Research: A Literature Review, Journal of Business Research 7 (September 1979), 219–242.

Rinne, H.: An Empirical Investigation of the Effects of Reference Prices on Sales, Thesis, Purdue University 1981.

Robertson, T.S.: The Process of Innovation and the Diffusion of Innovation, Journal of Marketing 31 (January 1967), 14–19.

Robertson, T.S.: Innovative Behavior and Communication, New York: Holt, Rinehart & Winston 1971.

Robinson, J.: The Economics of Imperfect Competition, London: Macmillan 1933.

Robinson, P.J.: Applications of Conjoint Analysis to Pricing Problems, in: Montgomery, D.B. and D.R. Wittink (eds.): Marketing Measurement and Analysis, Proceedings of the 1979 ORSA/TIMS Conference on Marketing.

Robinson, B. and C. Lakhani: Dynamic Price Models for New Product Planning, Management Science 21 (June 1975), 1113–1122.

Röske, W. and H. Gansera: Strategisches Marketing – Ein Vorschlag für ein computergestütztes Marketing-Support-System in den 80er Jahren, in: Thome, R. (ed.), Datenverarbeitung im Marketing, Berlin-Heidelberg-New York: Springer 1981.

Rogers, E.M.: Diffusion of Innovations, 6th ed., New York: The Free Press 1983.

Rogers, E.M. and F.E. Shoemaker: Communication of Innovations: A Cross-Cultural Approach, New York: The Free Press 1971.

Rose, G.: Absatz und Besteuerung, in: Koch, H. (ed.), Zur Theorie des Absatzes, Wiesbaden: Gabler 1973.

Roselius, T.: Consumer Rankings of Risk Reduction Methods, Journal of Marketing Research 35 (January 1971), 56–61.

Ross, E.B.: Making Money with Proactive Pricing, Harvard Business Review (November–December 1984), 145–155.

Ruppe, H. and E. Bochtler: Nielsen-Modell PAKOM, ein neuer Weg zum optimalen Preis für Verbrauchsgüter, in: Haedrich, G. (ed.), Operationale Entscheidungshilfen für die Marketingplanung, Berlin-New York: de Gruyter 1977.

Saaty, T.L.: The Analytic Hierarchy Process, New York: McGraw Hill 1980.

Saaty, T.L.: Axiomatic Foundation of the Analytic Hierarchy Process, Management Science 32 (July 1986), 841–855.

Sabel, H.: Produktpolitik in absatzwirtschaftlicher Sicht, Wiesbaden: Gabler 1971.

Sabel, H.: Zur Preispolitik bei neuen Produkten, in: Koch, H. (ed.), Zur Theorie des Absatzes, Wiesbaden: Gabler 1973.

Sabel, H.: Zur Diskussion des Gutenbergoligopols, Zeitschrift für Betriebswirtschaft 46 (March 1976), 205–224.

Sachs, L.: Angewandte Statistik, 5th ed., Berlin-Heidelberg-New York: Springer 1974.

Salcher, E.F.: Marktpsychologische Probleme der Preisgestaltung, in: Haedrich, G. (ed.), Operationale Entscheidungshilfen für die Marketingplanung, Berlin-New York: de Gruyter 1977.

Samuelson, P.A.: Readings in Economics, 6th ed., New York: McGraw Hill 1970.

Sandler, G.: Account-Management in der Praxis, Marketing-Zeitschrift für Forschung und Praxis 2 (December 1980), 225–228.

Sandler, G.: Zum Verhältnis zwischen Industrie und Handel, Markenartikel 43 (August 1981), 463–464.

Scherer, F.M.: Market Structure and Economic Performance, Chicago: Rand McNally 1970.

Scherer, F.M.: The Welfare Economics of Product Variety: An Application to the Ready-to-Eat Cereals Industry, Discussion Paper, Department of Economics, Northwestern University 1978.

Scherer, F.M.: Industrial Market Structure and Economic Performance, Chicago: Rand McNally 1980.

Scheuing, E.E.: Das Marketing neuer Produkte, Wiesbaden: Gabler 1970.

Schildbach, Th. and R. Schweigert: Die Auswirkungen der Besteuerung des nominellen Gewinns auf die Preispolitik in Inflationszeiten, Der Betrieb 27 (1974), 541–544.

Schlüter, M.: Der Verlauf von Preisabsatzfunktionen bei polypolistischer Konkurrenz, Dissertation, Universität Köln 1965.

Schmalen, H.: Ein Diffusionsmodell zur Planung des Marketing-Mix bei der Einführung langlebiger Konsumgüter auf einem Konkurrenzmarkt, Zeitschrift für Betriebswirtschaft 47 (November 1977), 697–714.

Schmalen, H.: Marketing-Mix-Entscheidungen im dynamischen Oligopol, Zeitschrift für Betriebswirtschaft 48 (December 1978), 1038–1060.

Schmalen, H.: Marketing-Mix für neuartige Gebrauchsgüter, Wiesbaden: Gabler 1979.

Schmalensee, R.: On the Use of Economic Models in Antitrust: The Realemon Case, Working Paper, Sloan School of Management, Massachusetts Institute of Technology 1978.

Schmitz, G.: Zwischenbetrieblicher Vergleich der Einzelhandelspreise sortengleicher Konsumwaren, Köln-Opladen: Westdeutscher Verlag 1964.

Schneider, E.: Einführung in die Wirtschaftstheorie, II. Teil, 13th ed., Tübingen: Mohr-Siebeck 1972.

Schreiber, K.: Beurteilt der Verbraucher die Qualität nach dem Preis?, Markenartikel 3 (1960), 636–639.

Schuchard-Ficher, Ch., K. Backhaus, U. Humme, W. Lohrberg, W. Plinke and W. Schreiner: Multivariate Analysemethoden, Berlin-Heidelberg-New York: Springer 1980.

Schultz, R.L. and W. Vanhonacker: A Study of Promotion and Price Elasticity, Working Paper 657, Krannert School of Management, Purdue University 1978.

Scitovsky, T.: Some Consequences of the Habit of Judging Quality by Price, The Review of Economic Studies 12 (1944–45), 100–105.

Selten, R.: Spieltheoretische Behandlung eines Oligopols mit Nachfrageträgheit, Zeitschrift für die gesamte Staatswissenschaft 121 (1965), 301–324 and 667–689.

Selten, R.: Preispolitik der Mehrproduktunternehmen in der statischen Theorie, Berlin-Heidelberg-New York: Springer 1970.

Sen, S.: Issues in Optimal Product Design, in: Srivastava, R.K. and A.D. Shocker (eds.), Analytic Approaches to Product and Marketing Planning: The Second Conference, Cambridge, Mass: Marketing Science Institute 1982, 265–274.

Sexton, D.: A Cluster Analytic Approach to Market Response Functions, Journal of Marketing Research 11 (February 1974), 109–114.

Shapiro, B.P.: The Psychology of Pricing, Harvard Business Review 46 (July–August 1968), 14–25.

Shapiro, B.P.: The Pricing of Consumer Goods: Theory and Practice, Working Paper, Cambridge (Mass): Marketing Science Institute 1972.

Shapiro, B.P.: Price Reliance: Existence and Sources, Journal of Marketing Research 10 (August 1973), 286–294.

Shapiro, B.P.: Deere & Co, Industrial Equipment Operations, Harvard Business School, Case 9-577-112, 1977.

Shapiro, B.P.: Common Fallacies (in Industrial Pricing), in: Bailey, E.L. (ed.), Pricing Practices and Strategies, New York: The Conference Board 1978.

Shapiro, B.P. and B.B. Jackson: Industrial Pricing to Meet Consumer Needs, Harvard Business Review 56 (November–December 1978), 119–127.

Shoemaker, R. and L.G. Pringle: Possible Biases in Parameter Estimation with Store Audit Data, Journal of Marketing Research 18 (February 1980), 91–96.

Silk, A.J. and G.L. Urban: Pre-Test-Market Evaluation of New Packaged Goods: A Model and Measurement Methodology, Journal of Marketing Research 15 (May 1978), 171–191.

Simon, H.A.: How Big is a Chunk, Science 183 (1974), 482–488.

Simon, H.: Preisstrategien für neue Produkte, Opladen: Westdeutscher Verlag 1976.

Simon, H.: Strategische Preispolitik bei neuen Produkten, Zeitschrift für die gesamte Staatswissenschaft 133 (1977), 257–275, (1977a).

Simon, H.: Preisabhängige Qualitätsbeurteilung – Grundlagen, Operationalisierung, Preispolitik, Jahrbuch der Absatz- und Verbrauchsforschung 22 (January 1977), 86–104, (1977b).

Simon, H.: Preispolitik bei erwartetem Konkurrenzeintritt: Ein dynamisches Oligopolmodell, Zeitschrift für Betriebswirtschaft 47 (December 1977), 745–766, (1977c).

Simon, H.: An Analytical Investigation of Kotler's Competitive Simulation Model, Management Science 24 (October 1978), 1462–1473.

Simon, H.: Marketing Multiplier and Marketing Strategy, Working Paper 1050–79, Sloan School of Management, Massachusetts Institute of Technology 1979, (1979a).

Simon, H.: Dynamics of Price Elasticity and Brand Life Cycles: An Empirical Study, Journal of Marketing Research 16 (November 1979), 439–452, (1979b).

Simon, H.: Dynamisches Produktlinienmarketing, Habilitationsschrift, Universität Bonn 1980.

Simon, H.: ADPULS-An Advertising Model with Wear Out and Pulsation, Journal of Marketing Research 19 (August 1982), (1982a).

Simon, H.: PRICESTRAT – An Applied Strategic Pricing Model for Non-Durables, in: TIMS-Studies in the Management Sciences, Vol. 17, Amsterdam: North-Holland Publ. Co. 1982 (1982b).

Simon, H.: Preismanagement, Wiesbaden: Gabler 1982 (1982c).

Simon, H.: Goodwill und Marketingstrategie, Wiesbaden: Gabler 1985.

Simon, H.: Politique du Prix, in: Hersent, E. (ed.), Encyclopédie de Gestion, Paris: Economica 1987.

Simon, H.: Management Strategischer Wettbewerbsvorteile, Zeitschrift für Betriebswirtschaft 4 (April 1988), 461–480.

Simon, H.: Preisstrategie zur Erschliessung von Ertragsreserven, in: Henzler, H.A. (ed.), Handbuch Strategischer Unternehmensführung, Wiesbaden: Gabler 1988, 559–579.

Simon, H. and E. Kucher: Conjoint Measurement – Durchbruch bei der Preisentscheidung, Harvard Manager 3 (1987), 28–36.

Simon, H., E. Kucher and K.H. Sebastian: Scanner-Daten in Marktforschung und Marketingentscheidung, Zeitschrift für Betriebswirtschaft 52 (Juni 1982), 555–579.

Simon, H. and K.H. Sebastian: Diffusion and Advertising: The German Telephone Campaign, Management Science 33 (April 1987), 451–466.

Simon, H. and M. Thiel: Hits and Flops among German Media Models, Journal of Advertising Research 20 (December 1980). 25–29.

Simon, J.S.: The Price Elasticity of Liquor in the U.S. and a Simple Method of Determination, Econometrica 34 (January 1966), 193–205.

Smallwood, J.E.: The Product Life Cycle: A Key to Strategic Marketing Planning, MSU Business Topics 21 (Winter 1973), 32.

Sowter, A.P.: Pricing Models, Paper presented at the Symposium on Mathematics in Marketing, London, May 1973.

Sowter, A.P., A. Gabor and C.W.J. Granger: The Effect of Price on Choice: A Theoretical and Empirical Investigation, Applied Economics 3 (March 1971), 167–181.

Spiegel-Verlag (ed.): Spiegel-Dokumentation: Männer & Märkte, Hamburg.

Spremann, K.: Optimale Preispolitik bei dynamischen deterministischen Absatzmodellen, Zeitschrift für Nationalökonomie 35 (Heft 1–2, 1975), 63–76.

Spremann, K.: The Nerlove-Arrow Theorem and Dynamic Marginal Costs, Working Paper No. 74, Institut für Wirtschaftstheorie und Operations Research, Universität Karlsruhe 1976.

Stackelberg, H.v.: Marktform und Gleichgewicht, Berlin: Springer 1934.

Stackelberg, H.v.: Preisdiskrimination bei willkürlicher Teilung des Marktes, Archiv für mathematische Wirtschafts- und Sozialforschung 5 (1939), 1–11.

Stafford, J.E. and B.M. Enis: The Price-Quality Relationship: An Extension, Journal of Marketing Research 6 (November 1969), 456–458.

Stapel, J.: "Fair" or "Psychological" Pricing, Journal of Marketing Research 9 (February 1972), 109–110.

Stephenson, P.R., W.L. Cron and G.L. Frazier: Delegating Pricing Authority to the Sales Force: The Effects on Sales and Profit Performance, Journal of Marketing 43 (Spring 1979), 21–28.

Stern, H.: Lebenszyklus neu eingeführter Marken, Nielsen Beobachter (March 1967), 17–18.

Stigler, G.J.: The Kinky Oligopoly Demand Curve and Rigid Prices, The Journal of Political Economy 55 (August 1947), 432.

Stigler, G.: The Theory of Price, 3rd. ed., New York: Macmillan 1967.

Stigler, G.: The Organization of Industry, Homewood: Irwin Inc. 1968.

Stoetzel, J.: Psychological/Sociological Aspects of Price, in: Taylor-Wills (eds.), Pricing Strategy, Princeton: Brandon 1969.

Stout, R.G.: Developing Data to Estimate Price-Quantity Relationships, Journal of Marketing 33 (April 1969), 34–36.

Strang, R.A.: Sales Promotion – Fast Growth, Faulty Management, Harvard Business Review 54 (July–August 1976), 115–124.

Sultan, R.G.M.: Pricing in the Electrical Oligopoly, Cambridge (Mass): Harvard University Press 1974.

Super Value Study, Progressive Grocer 1958, in: Preston (1963).

Suzuki, R.: Worldwide Expansion of U.S. Exports – A Japanese View, Sloan Management Review 20 (Spring 1979), 1–6.

Swan, J.E. and D.R. Rink: Effective Use of Industry Product Life Cycle Trends, Educators' Proceedings, Chicago: American Marketing Association 1980.

Sweeny, D.J.: Improving the Profitability of Retail Merchandising Decisions, Journal of Marketing 37 (January 1973), 60–68.

Sweezy, P.M.: Demand under Conditions of Oligopoly, The Journal of Political Economy 47 (1939), 568.

Swoboda, P.: Die Kostenbewertung in Kostenrechnungen, die der betrieblichen Preispolitik oder staatlichen Preisfestsetzung dienen, in: Coenenberg, A.G. (ed.): Unternehmensrechnung, München: Vahlen 1976.

Tacke, G.: Nichtlineare Preisbildung: Theorie, Messung und Anwendung, Wiesbaden: Gabler 1988.

Taylor, B. and G. Wills (eds.): Pricing Strategy, Princeton: Brandon 1969.

Taylor, W.J. and R.T. Shaw: Marketing, 2nd ed., Cincinnati: Southwestern Publ. Co 1969.

Tellis, G.J.: Beyond the Many Faces of Price: An Integration of Pricing Strategies, Journal of Marketing 50 (October 1986), 146–160.

Telser, L.G.: The Demand for Branded Goods as Estimated from Consumer Panel Data, The Review of Economics and Statistics 44 (1962), 300–324.

Teng, J.T. and G.L. Thompson: Optimal Pricing and Advertising Policies for New Product Oligopoly Models, Management Science Report No. 461, Carnegie Mellon University 1980.

Theil, H.: Principles of Econometrics, New York: Wiley 1971.

Theisen, P.: Die betriebliche Preispolitik im Einzelhandel, Köln-Opladen: Westdeutscher Verlag 1960.

Thomas, L.: Conjoint Measurement als Instrument der Absatzforschung, Marketing-Zeitschrift für Forschung und Praxis 1 (September 1979), 199–211.

Thompson, G.L. and I. Teng: Optimal Pricing and Advertising Policies for New Product Oligopoly Models, Marketing Science 3 (Spring 1984), 148–168.

Thummel, D.: Die Entwicklung einer Konzeption zur Bestimmung des langfristigen Marketing-Mix, Dissertation, Universität Freiburg 1972.

Tollefson, J.O. and P.V. Lessig: Aggregation Criteria in Normative Market Segmentation Theory, Journal of Marketing Research 15 (August 1978), 346–355.

Topritzhofer, E.: Grundzüge einer behavioristischen Theorie des Produktlebenszyklus, in: Behrens, K.Ch. and J. Bidlingmaier (eds.), Modernes Marketing – Moderner Handel, Wiesbaden: Gabler 1972.

Topritzhofer, E. (ed.): Marketing, Neue Ergebnisse aus Forschung und Praxis, Wiesbaden: Gabler 1978.

Topritzhofer, E., M. Nenning and U. Wagner: Zur Kompatibilität alternativer kommerziell verfügbarer Datenquellen für die Marktreaktionsmodellierung: Die Verwendung von Prewhitening-Filtern und Kreuzspektralanalyse sowie ihre Konsequenzen für die Analyse betriebswirtschaftlicher Daten, Zeitschrift für Betriebswirtschaft 49 (April 1979), 281–297.

TRIM (Tele Research Item Movement): Scan Data User's Guide, Los Angeles 1981.

Tsurumi, H. and Y. Tsurumi: Simultaneous Determination of Market Share and Advertising Expenditure under Dynamic Conditions: The Case of a Firm Within the Japanese Pharmaceutical Industry, The Economics Studies Quarterly 22 (1971), 1–23.

Tull, D.S., R.A. Boring and M.H. Gonsior: A Note on the Relationship of Price and Imputed Quality, The Journal of Business 38 (April 1964), 186–191.

Tully, J.P.: Field Information for Competitive Bidding, in: Bailey, E.A. (ed.): Pricing Practices and Strategies, New York: The Conference Board 1978.

Twedt, D.W.: Does the "9 Fixation" in Retail Pricing Really Promote Sales?, Journal of Marketing 29 (October 1965), 54–55.

Udell, J.G.: How Important is Pricing in Competitive Strategy?, Journal of Marketing 28 (January 1964), 44–48.

Urban, G.L.: A Mathematical Modeling Approach to Product Line Decisions, Journal of Marketing Research 6 (February 1969), 40–47.

Urban, G.L. and J.R. Hauser: Design and Marketing of New Products, Englewood Cliffs (N.J.): Prentice Hall 1980.

Vernon, R.: International Investment and International Trade in the Product Cycle, Quarterly Review of Economics 80 (1966), 40–47.

Vogel, E.F.: Japan as Number One, Lessons for America, Cambridge (Mass): Harvard University Press 1979.

Wacker, G.F.: Die Steuerwirkungen im Industriebetrieb, Dissertation, Wirtschaftshochschule Mannheim 1962.

Wacker, P.A.: Die Erfahrungskurve in der Unternehmensplanung, München: Florentz 1980.

Wagner, U.: Reaktionsfunktionen mit zeitvariablen Koeffizienten und dynamische Interaktionsmessung zwischen absatzpolitischen Instrumenten, Zeitschrift für Betriebswirtschaft 50 (April 1980), 416–426.

Walker, O.C., G.A. Churchill and N.M. Ford: Motivation and Performance in Industrial Selling: Present Knowledge and Needed Research, Journal of Marketing Research 14 (May 1977), 156–168.

Weinberg, Ch.B.: An Optimal Commission Plan for Salesmen's Control over Price, Management Science 21 (April 1975), 937–943.

Weinberg, Ch.B.: Jointly Optimal Commissions for Nonincome Maximizing Sales Forces, Management Science 24 (August 1978), 1252–1278.

Weiss, D.L.: Determinants of Market Share, Journal of Marketing Research 5 (August 1968), 290–295.

Weiss, D.L.: An Analysis of the Demand Structure for Branded Consumers Products, Applied Economics 1 (1969), 37–49.

Weizsäcker, C.-.C.v.: Barriers to Entry, A Theoretical Treatment, Berlin-Heidelberg-New York: Springer 1980.

Wells, L.G.: The Product Life Cycle and International Trade, Cambridge (Mass): Harvard University Press 1972.

Welzel, K.: Marketing im Einzelhandel, dargestellt am Beispiel des Einsatzes von Sonderangeboten, Wiesbaden: Gabler 1975.

Wentz, Th.: Realism in Pricing Analyses, Journal of Marketing 30 (April 1966), 19–26.

Weston, J.F.: Pricing Behavior of Large Firms, Western Economic Journal 10 (March 1972), 1–18.

White, R.N.: How to Use "Product Life Cycle" in Marketing Decisions, in: Berg, Th.L. and A. Shuchman (eds.): Product Strategy and Management, New York-Chicago: Holt, Rinehardt & Winston, Inc. 1963.

Wiechmann, U.E. and L.G. Pringle: Problems that Plague Multinational Marketers, Harvard Business Review 57 (July–August 1979), 118–124.

Wied-Nebbeling, S.: Industrielle Preissetzung, Tübingen: Mohr-Siebeck 1975.

Wied-Nebbeling, S.: Das Preisverhalten in der Industrie, Tübingen: Mohr-Siebeck 1985.

Wildt, A.R.: Multifirm Analysis of Competitive Decision Variables, Journal of Marketing Research 11 (January 1974), 50–62.

Willeke, F.U.: Autonome Preisintervalle im heterogenen Duopol, Jahrbücher für Nationalökonomie und Statistik 180 (1967), 373–396.

Willenbrock, J.H.: Utility Function Determination for Bidding Models, Journal of Construction 99 (July 1973), 133–153.

Wind, Y.: Issues and Advances in Segmentation Research, Journal of Marketing Research 15 (August 1978), 317–337.

Wind, Y. and R.N. Cardozo: Industrial Market Segmentation, Industrial Marketing Management 3 (March 1974), 153–165.

Winer, R.S.: A Price Vector Model of Demand for Consumer Durables: Preliminary Developments, Marketing Science 4 (Winter 1985), 74–90.

Winer, R.S.: A Reference Price Model of Brand Choice for Frequently Purchased Products, Journal of Consumer Research 13 (September 1986), 250–256.

Wisniewski, K.J. and R.C. Blattberg: Response Function Estimation Using UPC Scanner Data: An Analytical Approach to Demand Estimation under Dealing, Working Paper, University of Chicago 1983.

Wittink, D.R.: Exploring Territorial Differences in the Relationship between Marketing Variables, Journal of Marketing Research 14 (May 1977), 145–155.

Wittink, D.R. and D.B. Montgomery: Predictive Validity of Trade Off Analysis for Alternative Segmentation Schemes, in: Beckwith et al. (eds.), 1979, 69–73.

Wöhe, G.: Betriebswirtschaftliche Steuerlehre, Band II, 2. Halbband, 2nd ed., München: Vahlen 1985.

Womer, N.K.: Estimating Learning Curves from Aggregate Monthly Data, Management Science 30 (August 1984), 982–992.

Woodside, A.G. and G.L. Waddle: Sales Effects of In-Store Advertising, Journal of Advertising Research 15 (June 1975), 29–33.

Wright, J.: On a Clear Day You Can See General Motors, New York: Avon Books 1980.

Wright, J: Factors Affecting the Cost of Airplanes, Journal of Aeronautical Sciences 3 (1936), 122–128.

Yelle, L.E.: The Learning Curve: Historical Review and Comprehensive Survey, Decision Sciences 10 (1979), 302–327.

Yelle, L.E.: Industrial Life Cycles and Learning Curves: Interaction of Marketing and Production, Industrial Marketing Management 9 (1980), 311–318.

Yon, B. and T.D. Mount: The Response of Sales to Advertising: Estimation of a Polynomial Lag Structure, in: Topritzhofer, E. (ed.): Marketing – Neue Ergebnisse aus Forschung und Praxis, Wiesbaden: Gabler 1978.

Yoo, P.H., R.J. Dolan and V.K. Rangan: Dynamic Pricing Strategy for New Consumer Durables, Zeitschrift für Betriebswirtschaft 57 (Oktober 1987), 1024–1043.

Yoon, E.: New Product Introduction Timing Models: R&D and Marketing Decisions Considering Diffusion Dynamics, Unpublished Ph.D. Thesis, Pennsylvania State University 1984.

Young, S., L. Ott and B. Feigin: Some Practical Considerations in Market Segmentation, Journal of Marketing Research 15 (August 1978), 405–412.

Zarth, H.R.: Effizienter verkaufen durch die richtige Strategie für das Preisgespräch, Markenartikel 43 (Februar 1981), 111–113.

Zeithaml, V.A.: Consumer Perceptions of Price, Quality and Value: A Means-End Model and Synthesis of Evidence, Journal of Marketing 52 (July 1988), 2–22.

# *Index*

315